DIVINE JUSTICE

This book considers the ways in which religious beliefs and practices have contributed to the formation of Chinese legal culture. It does so by describing two forms of overlap between religion and the law: the ideology of justice and the performance of judicial rituals.

One of the most important conceptual underpinnings of the Chinese ideology of justice is the belief in the inevitability of retribution. Similar values permeate Chinese religious traditions, all of which contend that justice will prevail despite corruption and incompetence among judicial officials in this world and even the underworld, with all wrongdoers eventually suffering some form of punishment. The second form of overlap between religion and the law may be found in the realm of practice, and involves instances when men and women perform judicial rituals like oaths, chicken-beheadings, and underworld indictments in order to enhance the legitimacy of their positions, deal with cases of perceived injustice, and resolve disputes. These rites coexist with other forms of legal practice, including private mediation and the courts, comprising a wide-ranging spectrum of practices.

Divine Justice will be of enormous interest to scholars of the Chinese legal system and the development of Chinese culture and society more generally.

Paul R. Katz is Research Fellow at the Institute of Modern History, Academia Sinica in Taiwan.

DIVINE JUSTICE

Religion and the development of Chinese legal culture

Paul R. Katz

Routledge
Taylor & Francis Group
LONDON AND NEW YORK

First published 2009
by Routledge
2 Park Square, Milton Park, Abingdon, Oxon OX14 4RN

Simultaneously published in the USA and Canada
by Routledge
270 Madison Ave, New York, NY 10016

Routledge is an imprint of the Taylor & Francis Group, an informa business

Typeset in Times by
RefineCatch Limited, Bungay, Suffolk
Printed and bound in Great Britain by
TJ International, Padstow, Cornwall

British Library Cataloguing in Publication Data
A catalogue record for this book is available from the British Library

Library of Congress Cataloging-in-Publication Data
Katz, Paul R., 1961–
Divine justice : religion and the development of Chinese legal culture / Paul R. Katz.
p. cm.
1. Customary law—China—History. 2. Religion and law.—China—History. 3. Justice, Administration of—China—History. 4. Rites and ceremonies—China—History. 5. China—Religious life and customs—History. I. Title.
KNN469.K38 2009
340.5′251—dc22
2008030173

ISBN10: 0–415–44345–8 (hbk)
ISBN10: 0–203–88368–3 (ebk)

ISBN13: 978–0–415–44345–6 (hbk)
ISBN13: 978–0–203–88368–6 (ebk)

TO JUSTICE, FOR ALL . . .

CONTENTS

Figures ix
Tables x
Preface xi
Notes on citation and transliteration xiii

Introduction 1

1 The development of the judicial underworld 24

2 The judicial continuum 47

3 Oaths and chicken-beheading rituals 61

4 Indictment rituals 82

5 Trials of the insane and dressing as a criminal 105

6 Judicial rituals in Asian colonial and immigrant history 116

7 Judicial rituals in modern Taiwan 142

8 Case study 160

Conclusion 179
Bibliography 185
Index 219

FIGURES

1	Underworld court	57
2	Blood covenant	65
3	Indictment ritual	87
4	Trial of the insane	108
5	Taiwanese penitents wearing cangues	112
6	Statue of Judge Bao in Singapore City God temple	124
7	James Soong beheads a chicken	148
8	Filing an underworld petition	157
9	Giant abacus	158
10	Scribe preparing a plaint	163
11	Certificate of gratitude	175

TABLES

1	Ages of people who wore cangues during Xinzhu City God temple procession, 2004–2007	113
2	Petitions filed at the Dizang Abbey, March–September 2006	164
3	Worshippers' requests made at the altar of the Dizang Abbey's spirit-medium, 1st–3rd lunar months, 2006	171
4	Certificates of gratitude, January 1996–August 2001	173
5	Certificates of gratitude, February–September 2006	173

PREFACE

This book represents the culmination of over two decades of research on the judicial aspects of Chinese religious traditions. My interest in this topic began with the study of plague expulsion festivals in late imperial China and modern Taiwan, and has expanded over time to beliefs and practices related to the cults of underworld deities. My primary goal in undertaking this research has been to elucidate the ways in which a wide range of religion has contributed to the formation of Chinese legal culture. In particular, I have relied on the concept of the "judicial continuum" to stress the reverberation between different forms of Chinese legal practice, including private mediation, the courts, and rituals like oaths and underworld indictments. I have also explored the differences between judicial rituals and formal legal procedures, particularly the lack of torture in the former and the rejection of oath-making rites by the latter.

In the course of studying these topics, I have benefited from unstinting support provided by numerous organizations and individuals. My research was initially supported by a two-year grant from Taiwan's National Science Council (NSC-88–2412-H-008–001-L5; NSC-89–2412-H-008–001-L5), which allowed me to undertake research at Xinzhuang's Dizang Abbey from 1999 to 2001. It was subsequently funded by a three-year grant (NSC 93–2411-H-001–054), which was used for interdisciplinary research in China, Singapore, and Taiwan from 2004 to 2007. I am deeply grateful to my research assistants, Huang Ping-ying 黃萍瑛, Kang Shih-yu 康詩瑀, and Wang Ho-an 王和安, whose dedication proved invaluable in collecting and sorting substantial amounts of historical and ethnographic data. Thanks also to Ping-ying and Shih-yu for allowing me to use some of their photographs in this book.

I have been privileged to enjoy the assistance of friends and colleagues at the Institute of Modern History, Academia Sinica, especially Chang Jui-te 張瑞德, Chang Li 張力, Chang Ning 張寧, Chen Yung-fa 陳永發, Lai Hui-min 賴惠敏, Sun Huei-min 孫慧敏, and Peter Zarrow. I would also like to express my gratitude to other members of Taiwan's scholarly community, including Chang Hsun 張珣, Kevin Chang (Chang Ku-ming 張谷銘), Chen

Wei-hua 陳緯華, Chiou Wentsong 邱文聰, Chiu Peng-sheng 邱澎生, Jung Shaw-wu 容邵武, Ku Kun-hui 顧坤惠, Lai Tse-han 賴澤涵, Lin Fu-shih 林富士, Lin Mei-rong 林美容, Lin Tuan 林端, Liu Tseng-kuei 劉增貴, Liu Ts'ui-jung 劉翠溶, Wang Chien-chuan 王見川, Wang Chiu-kuei 王秋桂, and James Wilkerson. My research also benefited immensely from insights offered by numerous friends and colleagues throughout the world, including Chu Hung-lam, Philip Clart, Paul Cohen, John Comaroff, Kenneth Dean, Thomas DuBois, David Faure, Gordon Grimwade, James Hayes, Paul Jones, David Jordan, Kang Xiaofei, Jon Kehrer, John Lagerwey, Lai Chi-tim, Liu Xun, Marc Moskowitz, Matsumoto Koichi, Susan Naquin, Daniel Overmyer, David Ownby, David Palmer, Michael Puett, Jothie Rajah, Meir Shahar, Donald Sutton, Michael Szonyi, Tam Wai Lun, Barend ter Haar, Timothy Tsu, Ian Welch, Robert Weller, and Yung Sai-shing. A special note of thanks to Vincent Goossaert for his dedication in reading through numerous chapters, and providing both perceptive and at times humorous comments.

Many thanks to Abigail Humphries, Leong Li Ming, Christina Low, Sonja van Leeuwen, and the rest of the staff at Routledge/Taylor & Francis. Thanks also to Donna White and the production staff at RefineCatch.

Some of my initial results were published as chapters in the following books: John Lagerwey, ed., *Religion and Chinese Society*; David K. Jordan, Andrew D. Morris, and Marc L. Moskowitz, eds., *The Minor Arts of Daily Life: Popular Culture in Taiwan*; Robert E. Hegel and Katherine Carlitz, eds., *Writing and Law in Late Imperial China. Crime, Conflict, and Judgment*. I am deeply grateful to The Chinese University Press, University of Hawai'i Press, and University of Washington Press for allowing me to reuse parts of these chapters in this book.

Above all, I have been blessed with the love and support of my family, including my parents, my sisters, and especially my wife, Liu Shufen 劉淑芬, and our two children, Emily and Philip.

Finally, I wish to convey my heartfelt gratitude to the staff of the Dizang Abbey, the Tainan and Xinzhu City God temples, and the Tainan Temple of the Eastern Peak. My ability to conduct research at these sacred sites helped me better understand the importance of judicial rituals in Taiwanese legal practice, as well as ponder the larger question of the role of religion in furthering legal reform in China. While the discerning historian would be well-advised not to spend too much time speculating about the future, it is my sincere hope that this book can inspire others to better appreciate the fundamental importance of religious beliefs and practices in Chinese legal culture, particularly when it comes to helping people attain some measure of justice.

Paul R. Katz
June 21, 2008

NOTES ON CITATION AND TRANSLITERATION

Primary sources in the bibliography are listed by title; modern writings, however, are listed by author.

The bibliography includes only items actually mentioned in the book. Not included are many standard and essential research tools, unless they are cited in the text or the notes. Chinese and Japanese characters for all authors and texts cited are provided in the bibliography.

The following standard systems have been adopted for the transliteration of Asian names and terms: Pinyin for Chinese, except for personal names and place names in Taiwan; and Hepburn for Japanese Kanji.

INTRODUCTION

As China ascends to its place as a leading nation on the world stage, one of the many pressing issues facing its leaders involves the role of the legal system. Will China become more open to some forms of Western legal practice, especially as it examines the experiences of neighbors like Japan and Taiwan, where the development of the legal system has played a role in furthering democratization and the evolvement of civil society? Or will it follow the other Asian model, that of a "benevolent" authoritarian state, with the law often serving as a tool for the state to silence dissenters?[1] As the Chinese Communist Party strives to enhance its legitimacy by creating a viable legal system, it continues to grapple with the thorny issue of whether its leadership should be subject to the rule of law, or whether the law will continue to function as a tool for sustaining power and privilege. As Joseph Kahn noted in a feature article entitled "Deep Flaws, and Little Justice, in China's Court System" (published in *The New York Times* on September 21, 2005),[2] "Justice in China is swift but not sure". Many protests in China today center on the issue of justice (Cai 2006; Diamant, Lubman, and O'Brien 2005; O'Brien and Li 2006; Perry and Goldman 2007), with one blogger responding to the January 2008 fatal beating by parapolice officials of a man trying to videotape a protest by lamenting "Where is justice? Where is the law? Aren't there any rules in China?"[3]

A related issue involves the extent to which the future course of China's legal system may impact its economic development. Despite the fact that numerous experts insist that mature market economies are predicated on the proper functioning of the legal system, China seems able to sustain its pace of rapid growth despite a weak judicial sphere and widespread corruption. One reason for this seems to be that while increasing numbers of Chinese do turn to the courts to seek justice, many prefer to dodge the legal system

1 For more on these issues, see Alford 2007; Chen 2004; Hope, Yang, and Li 2003; Potter 2001.
2 http://www.nytimes.com/2005/09/21/international/asia/21confess.html
3 http://www.nytimes.com/2008/01/18/world/asia/18china.html

altogether, relying instead on private mediation or networks of personal relationships (*guanxi* 關係), or seeking out the support of sympathetic officials (in some cases following a bribe).[4] All of this suggests that despite the persistent advice China currently gets about the need to reform its judicial system, Western legal norms and practices may not be the only possible prerequisite for economic progress, with a recent article by Elizabeth Perry observing that Western observers who fault China's leaders for their failure to expand political rights overlook the leadership's concern for attaining socioeconomic objectives to ensure the welfare of the people (Perry 2008: 41). China's development also problematizes the conventional wisdom that cultures in which entrepreneurs rely on informal, personal relationships (especially family ties) for the conduct of business will inevitably turn out to be less successful than those where business transactions are consummated by means of formal, legally-binding documents.[5]

Meanwhile, across the Taiwan Strait, both economic growth and legal reform continue to proceed apace, but with one big difference: the continuing importance of religion and ritual in the pursuit of justice. When accused of vote-buying or other forms of wrongdoing, politicians ranging from city councilors to presidential candidates do not hesitate to make oaths of innocence, and until recently even beheaded live chickens as a means of stressing the rightness of their causes (the implication being that their fate would be equally gruesome should they commit perjury). Ordinary citizens embroiled in various financial and commercial disputes not only perform oath-making rites, but also file underworld indictments against their enemies. And, when it comes to family feuds, parents petition the bureaucratic deities of the underworld to help locate runaway teenagers, while wives implore these deities to use their numinous powers to steer adulterous husbands back to the straight and narrow and punish the hussies who led them astray. All of these rituals coexist with other forms of legal practice and dispute resolution, including private mediation and the courts, comprising a wide-ranging spectrum of practices that I refer to as the "judicial continuum" (see below and Chapter 2). The presence of this continuum can also be seen in the fact that policemen or prosecutors regularly make offerings at temples to underworld deities in order to crack tough cases, and there have even been cases of judges allowing disputants to make oaths inside their courtrooms. Such practices are not limited in geographic scope to Taiwan, but also exist in Hong Kong and among overseas Chinese communities.

4 For more on the importance of personal mediation in Chinese culture, see Huang 1996, 2005, 2006; Tay 1997, as well as Chapter 2 below.

5 Examples of this revisionist thinking may be found in Berger 1995; Clegg and Redding 1990; Redding 1990. See also Sarah Schafer's essay "China: Rich and Lawless", which was published in the February 19, 2007 issue of *Newsweek* (Schafer 2007). I am greatly indebted to Paul A. Cohen, Michael Szonyi, and Robert P. Weller for helping me clarify these issues.

The remarkable variety of judicial and dispute resolution practices that still flourish in Chinese communities indicates a pressing need for scholars to adopt broad-minded and culturally sensitive approaches to the study of Chinese legal theory and judicial practices. To begin with, what do terms like "law" (*falü* 法律 in Chinese; literally "laws and codes") and "legal system" (*fazhi* 法制; "laws and institutions"), which were transmitted from the West to China via Japan during the late nineteenth century, mean in the context of Chinese culture? What sorts of mechanisms have the Chinese people relied on in order to obtain justice? What roles do religion and ritual play in the sweeping spectrum of Chinese law and judicial practice? All of these questions center on a particularly thorny conundrum, namely the extent to which it may be reasonable to expect that Chinese legal practice should develop according to Western models of jurisprudence, which are hardly monolithic themselves (see below). Inasmuch as legal practice in Chinese culture has featured the amalgamation of the Chinese and Western systems for dispensing justice, it would seem essential to examine these practices in their own terms, not according to preconceptions based on Western models, especially those that emphasize the supposedly "rational" nature of the law or rank societies according to evolutionary schemes of legal development. As Jerome A. Cohen, distinguished scholar of Chinese jurisprudence at Columbia University, pointed out during a recent lecture: "The worst kind of comparative law is that which compares our theory to their practice" (Cohen 2008).[6]

Accordingly, this book will attempt to shed new light on two quintessentially Chinese forms of overlap between religion and the law: the ideology of justice and the performance of judicial rituals. In doing so, I acknowledge the differences between theory and practice,[7] while also attempting to delineate the ways in which they overlap. The Chinese ideology of justice extends to the ways in which the gods control all human affairs in this life and the next, including health, wealth, punishment in the underworld after death, and reincarnation.[8] This involves a wide range of deities who play many different roles. Some observe and record the good and evil deeds of the living, others respond to prayers for divine intervention, while others administer justice in the underworld, which is largely punitive or "legal", as opposed to the predominantly "moral" hell (purgatory) of the West (see Chapter 1). Such ideas are expressed in sayings like "the gods hover three feet above one's head" (*jutou sanchi you shenming* 舉頭三尺有神明) or "people do deeds under heaven's [watchful] eye" (*lang teh tso, thi teh khoa*

6 Many thanks to Michael Szonyi for this reference.

7 As Vincent Goossaert points out, "In theory, there is no difference between theory and practice. In practice, there is" (personal communication, February 14, 2008).

8 By ideology I mean a systematic body of concepts or beliefs (usually political) about human life or culture that are held by an individual or group.

人(郎)在做，天在看 in Southern Min). One example of such beliefs may be found in a northern Chinese opera in which the actor portraying the Jade Emperor sings:

> The Record of Good and Bad is open on the desk. I observe the record to find the causes . . . I lift up my head and observe the Shansi (Shanxi) region. There is a bad man . . . who does no good. He beats his parents and scolds his neighbours. White Tiger, you are sent to Shansi. At noon he will be killed . . . Feeling uneasy, I lift up my head again and see the people in Lo-yang (Luoyang 洛陽), Honan (Henan). There is a man . . . who repairs bridges and roads and builds temples for the gods. This good man should have nine sons but he has none. From my Dragon Hall I send out a magical air to call Sung-tzu Niang-niang (Songzi niangniang 送子娘娘; a goddess of childbirth). A golden boy and a jade girl will be given to you and you will send them to [his] house . . .
>
> (Chao 1944: 27–29)[9]

One of the most important conceptual underpinnings of the Chinese ideology of justice is the belief in the inevitability of retribution (*baoying* 報應). The English term derives from the Late Latin *retribtiōn* (or *retribūtiō*; punishment or reward resulting from a judgment), which is the equivalent of the Latin *retribūt*(*us*) (past participle of *retribuere*), literally to restore or give back. Thus, punishment for wrongdoing can be viewed as a form of "payback" or "just deserts". Similar values permeate Chinese religious traditions, all of which contend that justice will prevail despite corruption and incompetence among judicial officials in this world and even in the underworld, with all wrongdoers eventually suffering some form of punishment, perhaps as soon as during their own lifetimes (*xianshibao* 現世報) (Brokaw 1991; Eberhard 1967). As Timothy Brook, Jérôme Bourgon, and Gregory Blue note in their stimulating new book entitled *Death by a Thousand Cuts*, "The world of the dead does not so much recapitulate the world of the living as propose what the world of the living could be if it had the rationality, order, and systematic moral logic that are imagined to govern the world of the dead" (Brook, Bourgon, and Blue 2007: 126). In addition, it seems that one element common to many of the world's religions is the belief in postmortem punishment, which has the potential to rectify injustices in this world and ensure that even if the guilty may be able to elude punishment while alive, they cannot escape it after death. The Chinese ideology of justice differs from that of many other religious traditions, however, in its

9 I discovered this passage while reading the manuscript of Daniel Overmyer's forthcoming book on local religion in north China.

formulation of a complex underworld judicial system charged with keeping track of the words and deeds of the living, as well as duly administering the requisite forms of retribution after death. Such ideas also shaped formal legal procedures, with Charlotte Furth's research revealing that one key jurisprudential issue in traditional Chinese law was deciding the appropriate level of punishment for a given crime, which resembles the emphasis on retribution in the Chinese ideology of justice (Furth 2007: 12; see also Chang 2000).

The second form of overlap between religion and the law may be found in the realm of practice, and involves instances when men and women call upon the gods to help them deal with cases of perceived injustice or to resolve disputes. Chinese people have long performed judicial rituals featuring the leading deities of the underworld, especially the City God (Chenghuangshen 城隍神), the Emperor of the Eastern Peak (Dongyue dadi 東嶽大帝), and the Bodhisattva Dizang (Dizangwang pusa 地藏王菩薩). Such rites have generally been held in temples dedicated to these deities, or at least in front of their statues. Chinese judicial rituals are many and varied, but the most common appear to be making oaths (*lishi* 立誓) and filing underworld indictments (*gao yinzhuang* 告陰狀; also known as *fanggao* 放告). The category of oaths is an expansive one, encompassing blood covenants (variously referred to as *xuemeng* 血盟 or *shaxue* 歃血), covenant and malediction rituals (*mengzu* 盟詛), and oaths accompanied by the beheading of a chicken (*zhan jitou* 斬雞頭). Underworld indictment rituals also exhibit considerable variation. Apart from ritually indicting other members of the living, people could also initiate countersuits against plaints filed by the dead, or even lodge complaints against malevolent sprites. It is also necessary to distinguish between judicial rituals performed to reconcile parties (including disagreements between family members and friends), as opposed to judicial rituals performed to invoke retribution on wrongdoers (particularly in the case of crimes or financial disputes among business associates). This book also treats penitential rituals designed to counter the perceived effects of being charged with wrongdoing in this life or a previous existence, including trials of the insane (*shen fengzi* 審瘋子) and dressing up as a criminal (*ban fanren/zuiren* 扮犯人/罪人). All of these judicial rituals, while highly diverse, do share some features, especially a profound concern with attaining justice and the tendency for worshippers to invoke precisely those divinities who officiate in the underworld.[10]

The primary goal of this book is to consider what the ideology of justice and judicial rituals reveal about the larger context of Chinese legal culture.

10 For an introduction to the long and complex history of these rites, see Ch'ü 1961: 210; Huang 1986; Lewis 1990; Liu 1998; Niida 1964: 676–702; ter Haar 1998: 151–203; Xia 1990, 1993; Zhang 2000; and Zheng 1991.

For example, the public nature of many judicial rituals, combined with the fact that officials often oversee or even participate in such rites, suggests that the search for a Chinese civil society or public sphere (see for example Rowe 1990, 1993; Brook and Frolic 1997) may need to reach beyond tea houses, theaters, guild halls, and yamens to include temples and their rituals, especially since temples constitute an important public space where people attempt to resolve disputes outside of the framework of the official judicial system. In addition, judicial rituals have been performed by people from all levels of Chinese society (including the officialdom) since ancient times, a fact which points to the problematic nature of analytical frameworks centering on dynasties, not to mention bifurcations such as "traditional" vs. "modern" or "elite" vs. "popular". Such rites also call into question the very nature of the adjective "Chinese", inasmuch as they were performed in both Han and non-Han communities. Finally, when one considers that Western legal history also featured its share of mediation, as well as judicial rites like oaths and ordeals, the very distinction between "China" and "the West" seems somewhat less relevant. Indeed, the idea of a single "Western" legal system with which the Chinese one can be contrasted is itself an oversimplification. This is because Western legal practice resembles its Chinese counterpart in encompassing other forms of jurisprudence. Apart from statutory (positive) law, these include natural law, i.e. the idea that the legal system is just one aspect of God's will or divine providence, thereby constituting an approximation of fundamental and universal principles (Haakonssen 1995), as well as common law, namely unwritten customs and usages based largely on precedents not all that dissimilar from so-called "customary law" (*xiguan fa* 習慣法) in China,[11] and which are often enacted into statutory law with modern variations (Arnheim 1994; Edlin 2007). In addition, ritual has long been an integral component of many Western legal systems, including the use of robes and wigs as well as the cry of "All rise!" when a judge enters the courtroom.[12] One particularly noteworthy facet of the overlap between religion and the law in Western culture is the belief in "immanent justice", which maintains that divine intervention in human affairs such as the administration of justice is a regular and predictable occurrence (Lea 1974 (1866)). This belief does not seem all that different from the Chinese ideology of justice. Nonetheless, one striking contrast between China and the West is that judicial rituals have never been formally incorporated into

11 An interesting comparative perspective from modern Korean history may be found in Kim 2007. See also G.C.J.J. van den Bergh's analysis of the highly contradictory and distinct ideological overtones of the German term "Volksrecht", which he argues reflect "a binary way of thinking which has haunted the social sciences from their beginning" (van den Bergh 1994: 22). For more on this issue, see Renteln and Dundes 1994.

12 Paul A. Cohen, Michael Szonyi, and Robert P. Weller provided valuable guidance for the above discussion.

Chinese court procedures, with high-ranking officials responsible for drafting China's modern civil and penal codes during the late nineteenth and early twentieth centuries considering but eventually rejecting the adoption of the Western practice of swearing in witnesses (for more on this issue, see Chapter 3).

This book views the pursuit of justice in Chinese culture as a cogent cultural system covering a wide range of options for achieving legitimation and dispute resolution, something that I would tentatively term the "Chinese judicial continuum". These options, which include mediation (with judgments being made by elders and other elites), going to court (judgments made by officials), and performing rituals (judgments made by the gods), can be done in succession, or in some cases even in tandem. Moreover, while the satisfaction of successfully staging a judicial ritual certainly differs from that provided by winning one's case in court, both processes can contribute to the resolution of disputes, thereby constituting integral components of the Chinese ideology of justice. The presence of the judicial continuum also challenges dichotomies like "rational" vs. "irrational" by demonstrating that Chinese legal culture is characterized by the concurrent use of both formal and informal judicial mechanisms, with rituals constituting acceptable and even integral measures for attaining justice. Accordingly, I follow Lawrence Rosen in underscoring "the coherence of the entire system – of prayers and rituals, beliefs and practices, judicial inquiry and subjective assessment, oral witnessing and divine oaths – that contributes to the acceptability of any one element within the cultural scheme" (Rosen 1989: 36). I should also note the important work of Wendy Davies and Paul Fouracre, which stresses the importance of judicial rituals as part of a comprehensive battery of legal procedures not unlike the Chinese judicial continuum described in this book (Davies and Fouracre 1986: 223, 228, 232, 233).[13]

The overlap between theory and practice mentioned above may be seen in the importance of *li* 禮 (generally translated as "ritual", "ceremony", or "etiquette", depending on its usage) in undergirding the Chinese judicial continuum. Along with laws (*fa* 法), *li* lies at the heart of state and elite efforts to regulate human behavior.[14] *Li* is understood to be cosmic in origin, with classics like the *Book of Rites* (*Liji* 禮記) viewing adherence to prescribed forms of behavior as expressions of universal order. Each

13 For more on these issues, see Chanock 1985: 83, 86; Renteln and Dundes 1994: 13; van Hoecke and Warrington 1998: 498. Further inspiration may be found in the work of Jonathan Ocko, who uses Stanley Fish's concept of "interpretive communities" to analyze the parties involved in a legal case, while also acknowledging the interrelation of temporal and spiritual worlds in processes of dispute resolution (Ocko 2007: 261–265; Fish 1980).

14 The importance of both *li* and *fa* was recognized early on by intellectuals like Max Weber (1864–1920), who was interested in the role of religion and the law in the state's quest to achieve social control (Weber 1951; see also Lin 2003; Yang 1961).

individual's actions are to be regulated by *li*, as promulgated by the state, lineages and families; adherence to *li* defined what was properly human (Overmyer 1989–1990: 192–193, 221). Accordingly, *li* serves as a benchmark for all aspects of the judicial continuum, including (but not limited to) the realm of ritual. A related ideal is the quest for harmonious equilibrium, referred to in the *Doctrine of the Mean* (*Zhongyong* 中庸) as "equilibrium and harmony existing in perfection" (*zhi zhonghe* 致中和). According to Li Yih-yuan, the attainment of this ideal state is believed to depend on the achievement of harmony in the following three systems: the natural order, the individual, and the community (Li 1995). The third system, with its emphasis on harmony in communal life (especially family relations and the relationship between the living and the dead) is also a key element of Chinese legal culture, which stresses the importance of both *li* and *fa* in judicial practice as means of achieving social harmony (Qian 1998).

I first observed the relationship between religion and justice in Chinese legal culture during the 1980s, while undertaking fieldwork on plague expulsion festivals in southern Taiwan and historical research on the origins of these festivals in China. The results of this early research indicated that, despite local variations, such festivals have long shared some features, including a profound concern with the problem of divine justice. Many of the rituals described in this book, including filing underworld indictments and dressing as a criminal, have been staged during plague expulsion festivals in order to cope with both physical misfortune in the form of disease and the sociocultural problems seen as prompting the wrath of the gods. Accordingly, some people file underworld indictments as a means of correcting instances of injustice that disrupt communal harmony, while others dress as criminals as an act of penance to atone for previous misdeeds. My field research in Taiwan also reveals that such practices are still widespread today.[15]

Previous scholarship

The prevalence of judicial practices centering on underworld deities suggests that our understanding of Chinese law cannot possibly be regarded as complete until we consider such phenomena to be worthy of our attention. Unfortunately, however, despite the fact that an impressive body of research has been undertaken on the ethical and judicial aspects of the Chinese underworld,[16] few scholars have paid attention to the ways in which China's

15 The initial results of my research on this topic include Katz 1995a: 143–174, 1998, 2000, 2001, 2003a, 2004b, 2004c, 2007b.

16 Prominent works include Brokaw 1991; Eberhard 1967; Goodrich 1964, 1981; Hayden 1978; Johnson 1989; Lin 1995; Ma 1998; Nickerson 2007; Sawada 1968; Teiser 1988, 1993, 1994; Wang-Toutain 1998; Zhiru 2007.

underworld deities also administer justice for the living in their temples. Moreover, while a growing number of scholars have begun to consider the political and social aspects of Chinese law,[17] relatively little work has been done on the religious aspects of Chinese legal culture. This may be due to the fact that scholarship on Chinese jurisprudence has largely been dominated by two starkly contrasting viewpoints: the first, embraced by neo-conservative scholars who celebrated the importance of traditional Chinese culture, insisted that Chinese jurisprudence has always been secular (or secular humanist); the second, propagated by intellectuals who sympathized with or even supported May 4th calls for thoroughgoing Westernization and modernization combined with the rejection of Chinese traditions, scorned China's legal heritage as having been marginal. As we will see below, both of these approaches are anachronistic, and ignore the on-going reverberation between religion and the law in Chinese legal culture.[18]

One example may be found in Philip C.C. Huang's conceptualization of the so-called "third realm", a form of public space situated between state and society in which the two interacted. Despite the fact that the theoretical facets of Huang's arguments are convincing, his attempt to locate the third realm pays too little attention to the importance of popular religion and judicial rites (Huang 1996, 2001, 2006). Such neglect also detracts from Perry's analysis of the importance of distributive or socioeconomic justice in Chinese culture. While her claim that "workers who demand that as 'citizens' they have a 'right' to eat would seem to be following more in the moral economy footsteps of Mencius and Mao than in the liberal tradition of Locke or Jefferson" (Perry 2008: 45) has merit, it is grounded almost exclusively on the analysis of Chinese political philosophy, including the well-known concept of the Mandate of Heaven (*tianming* 天命). This not only downplays the importance of China's religious traditions (which also feature their share of ethical discourse, including the Mandate of Heaven), but even more importantly overlooks the ways in which the ideology of justice could both express Chinese conceptions of rights and also serve as a basis for popular protest against the state.[19]

A similar problem occurs in Jérôme Bourgon's recent critiques of the attempts by Philip Huang and Liang Zhiping (Liang 1996) to posit the existence of civil law in pre-modern China, particularly in terms of customary law (Bourgon 2002, 2004). Bourgon's points are well taken, yet he tends to neglect the extent to which legal practice was not simply fashioned from the top down but also from the bottom up, including officials

17 See for example Allee 1994a; Bernhardt and Huang 1994; Brook, Bourgon, and Blue 2007; Goh 2002; Huang 1996, 2001; Macauley 1998; Reed 2000.

18 I am most grateful to David Ownby for sharing his thoughts on these issues.

19 Many thanks to Donald Sutton for bringing this article to my attention.

performing oath-making rituals or filing underworld indictments in the presence of the City God, as well as oaths being absorbed into the *lijia* 里甲 and *xiangyue* 鄉約 systems. In yet another instance, Goh Bee Chen's book-length study of Chinese mediation, promisingly entitled *Law without Lawyers, Justice without Courts*, consists mainly of truisms about "Confucianism" in Chinese social life, while completely ignoring the importance of judicial rituals (Goh 2002). Finally, while the Society for the Study of Chinese Legal History (Zhongguo fazhishi xuehui 中國法制史學會) in Taiwan has produced nearly a decade of solid results (including publishing a journal since December 2000), its scholarship has centered largely on the institutional, philosophical, and socioeconomic facets of Chinese legal history.[20]

One probable cause for the oversight of religion and ritual may be that, when it comes to the study of Chinese law, scholarship continues to be trapped by post-Enlightenment hermeneutical frameworks that highlight secularization and the advent of "rational" systems of law. Secularization is a thorny concept because of its various uses in disciplines such as philosophy, social sciences, theology, etc. (Dobbelaere 2002 (1981)). Moreover, I have no intention of following in the footsteps of renowned intellectuals such as Karl Marx, Sigmund Freud, Max Weber, and Emile Durkheim, all of whom predicted that the modernization of society would spark a decline in religiosity (Bruce 1992: 3; Stark 1999; Wilson 1992). For the study of Chinese legal culture, the concept of secularization proves relevant because of the idea that secularized societies become differentiated or atomized into autonomous sub-systems (economy, polity, law, education, etc.) that are highly discrete in relation to each other, with religion being restricted in influence to its own integral sub-system. This in turn seems closely linked to the concept of the secular state, one that distinguishes between governmental and religious institutions, and derives its legitimacy not from divine law but from man-made legal codes (Luckmann 1967; Tschannen 1992; Wallis and Bruce 1992). At the same time, however, there is considerable disagreement over the degree of secularization possible, with Talal Asad arguing that the interdependence of the political and religious spheres inhibits total dif-

20 One of the few exceptions to this pattern is an on-going inquiry by some of the Society's members into the question of whether monastic crime increased during the Song dynasty. However, even if Song sources contain more accounts of monastic crime than works from earlier dynasties, the real question is whether such incidents actually did increase, or instead whether this perceived rise in the monastic crime rate is due to the better quality of the source base after the Song or the state's growing emphasis on regulating monastic communities. A related possibility is that descriptions of monastic crimes were actually stereotypical accounts that represented part of a labeling process used by the state in the process of suppressing groups that it felt were a threat to imperial authority (for more on this key point, see ter Haar 1992: 1–15).

ferentiation (Asad 2003: 201), as opposed to José Casanova, who steadfastly adheres to the idea of the secular sphere being differentiated (and even emancipated) from the world of religious institutions and ethics (Casanova 1994: 65–66; see also Casanova 2006).

There are legitimate reasons for caution about applying this concept to the cultural history of China, especially because many definitions of secularization treat it as an historical process of the modern West by which the religious system loses its dominance over communal life (Wallis and Bruce 1992: 12, 14). In the case of Chinese history, however, religion has continuously co-existed with a range of other sub-systems from ancient times to the present day, including legal ones. Nevertheless, the concept of secularization appears to have had a profound impact on many Chinese intellectuals during the modern era, particularly when those who viewed their religious traditions according to Western criteria decided that religion represented a form of backwardness and decline (Duara 1995; Goossaert 2006). This concept also influenced the esteemed Chinese legal historian Derk Bodde (1909–2003), who noted that, "A striking feature of the early written law of several major civilizations of antiquity has been its close association with religion . . . A notable feature of Chinese historical and philosophical thinking, apparent already in early times, is its *strongly secular tone . . . When we turn to the legal sphere, therefore, it should not surprise us that here too the atmosphere is secular*" (Bodde and Morris 1967: 8, 12–13, emphasis added; see also Bodde 1963: 380, as well as the discussion of this issue in Dutton 1992: 111–114).[21] Such analyses distort the complex overlap between the judicial and religious traditions in Chinese culture, a process of reverberation that even shaped the etymology of the Chinese word for law (*fa* 法), as the upper right half of the original and far more complex form of this character (*fa* 灋) contains the character *zhi* 廌, which refers to a mythical one-horned creature known as the *xiezhi* (variously written as 解廌 or 獬豸) said to be able to identify guilty parties by butting them after they had performed an oath-making ritual in its presence (Ch'ü 1961; MacCormack 1995: 74–77; Zhu 2001: 76–79).

The on-going neglect of the role of judicial rituals in Chinese culture may also result from the influence of scholars like the legal historian Harold Joseph Berman. While noting the "sanctity of custom" and the fact that the words "crime" and "sin" can be used interchangeably (Berman 1983: 70, 82), Berman tends to view rites like oaths and ordeals as "primitive", in contrast to "mature" legal systems, which feature "professionalization and systematization", as well as an "increased emphasis upon *rationality* in the law"

21 The continuing emphasis of such views even extends to the entry on Chinese law in Wikipedia, part of which reads, "Unlike many other major civilizations where written law was held in honor and often attributed to divine origin, law in China was viewed in purely secular terms"; http://en.wikipedia.org/wiki/Chinese_law#_note-3.

(*ibid.*: 57, 76–77, 253, 479; emphasis added). Despite the fact that Berman's views in this regard have been largely discredited by historians of European legal history, with Rebecca Colman pointing out that the use of terms like "rational" constitutes a form of value judgment reflecting a reluctance to recognize cultural phenomena when they manifest themselves in unfamiliar forms (Colman 1974: 572–573, 577; see also Bourdieu 1987; Davies and Fouracre 1986), many researchers in China today continue to cite Berman's work as a basis for treating so-called "divine judgments" (*shenpan* 神判) as "primitive" and "unscientific", while so-called "human judgments" (*renpan* 人判) are labeled with the more favorable term "modern" (see for example Du 2002; Xu and Wu 2000). A related example may be found in the following claim advanced by Geoffrey MacCormack in his 1996 book ironically entitled *The Spirit of Traditional Chinese Law*: "At all stages of its development the law appears to have been characterized by a spirit of *rationality* and fairness. . . . Methods of proof were *rational*, based on the investigation of the circumstances of the case by the officiating magistrate and the interrogation of the parties and the witnesses. *At no time, even in cases involving allegations of sorcery or witchcraft, was there resort to ordeals or oracles*" (MacCormack 1996: 15; emphasis added).[22]

The prevalence of such ideas has led some to maintain that since judicial rituals can be differentiated from official legal procedures, it might be better to refer to them using the term "quasi-judicial". Such arguments are not without merit, especially since the practices described below are undoubtedly religious events, and, like all other rituals in China, accentuate burning incense and making offerings to the gods. However, judicial rituals possess unmistakable legal characteristics in the sense of being held by people who identify themselves as plaintiffs, defendants, or witnesses, as well as being staged in temples to bureaucratic deities that are often arranged to resemble a magistrate's yamen, and highlighting written texts often referred to using the official term "petitions" (*cheng* 呈). Legal metaphors are especially obvious for judicial rituals performed when a dispute has entered the court system (especially financial and land disputes), as opposed to judicial rituals performed to resolve issues that the courts generally do not deal with (such as family and marital tensions).

Part of the problem may be one of semantics. Few would disagree about the essential meaning of the term justice, namely the achievement of fairness, equitableness, and rightness. The adjective judicial, however, can be subject to a wider range of interpretations, from narrow ones centering on procedures sanctioned by judges in courts of law to broader ones subsuming the

22 I am grateful to Terry F. Kleeman for calling this issue to my attention in the introduction to his unpublished paper entitled "Traditional Chinese Jurisprudence and the Supernatural" (Kleeman 2005).

administration of justice and mediation of disputes by means of legal or other proceedings. A similar gamut of exegesis surrounds the noun law, from the circumscribed (regulations prescribed by the nation-state, as well as the specialized knowledge thereof) to the capacious (principles and rules established and administered by communal authority), while the term legal is largely used in a restrictive sense to describe state-sanctioned practices or the profession of lawyers. My research has stressed expansive understandings of these concepts, but such a view does not always find ready acceptance among scholars (especially legal historians) who view legal practice as being almost exclusively linked to laws and regulations promulgated by the state.

I should also admit that Western conceptualizations of the law and legal practice have inevitably impacted my own discourse. Perhaps the most pertinent example involves the term "divine justice" in the book's title, which can be highly problematic when applied to Chinese legal culture. This is because in the West divine justice (or divine law) is generally viewed as constituting a complex system of jurisprudence designed by God for the salvation of souls, thereby being superior in status and value to human law and unable to be changed by government authority (Ferrari 2002: 50–51). As Randall Peerenboom has shown, the uncritical adoption of this concept structured the views of eminent sinologists like Joseph Needham (1900–1995) and Derk Bodde, both of whom argued that the lack of a transcendent religious source for laws (especially an autochthonous supreme being) inhibited the development of law and science in China (Peerenboom 2002: 84–85). Nonetheless, while law in China may not have a strictly "divine" origin, religion and ritual have consistently played a key role in Chinese legal culture, and continue to do so today. A slightly different problem surrounds my use of the term judicial rituals, which are generally referred to in Chinese as *shenpan yishi* 神判儀式 (literally "rites of divine judgment"). This term is a modern academic exonym used by scholars whose work has been influenced by the paradigms of Western legal history (see for example Xia 1990; Zhang 2000). While there are numerous terms for individual judicial rites (see above), there has never been a single emic category for all the rituals described in this book prior to the modern era.

In the long run, however, nit-picking over definitions obscures an essential fact, namely that Chinese legal culture has consistently featured both state-sanctioned procedures as well as less formal practices at the communal level, including ritual ones. On the surface, referring to such practices using the term "judicial" may not seem highly appropriate, as no legal codes and specific laws appear to be involved (or at least they are hard to name). On the other hand, I would argue that the question of whether the religious phenomena studied in this book should be labeled quasi-judicial is of less significance than the problem of determining their function in the broad spectrum of the Chinese judicial continuum. Such an understanding is based on the idea that Chinese legal culture consists of three equally important and interactive components: structural (legal institutions), substantive (laws), and cultural (values, ideas, and practices, including religion and rituals) (Tan 1997a: 6–9; see also Friedman 1975). As William P. Alford points out in his analysis of the field of Chinese legal history, it is necessary to pay closer attention to the disjunction between law and practice, as well as the need for conceptualizing law as a "contested dynamic" intimately intertwined with the functioning of communal life (Alford 1997). Thus, I concur with Randall Peerenboom's assertion that "law and religion are on the whole complementary and interdependent", and that religion can be a source of law while also providing a normative foundation for legal institutions (Peerenboom 2002: 89–91).[23] All of this is patently related to the fact that Chinese culture did not "secularize" in the same way as the West (even if some of China's twentieth-century elites wished for this to happen), with religion continuing to have potential legal and political importance in ways that are rarely seen in the West.

Methodology

My research on the cultural significance of Chinese judicial rituals has benefited considerably from reading some of the leading works in legal anthropology.[24] In its formative years, some founders of this field, including Sir Henry Sumner Maine (1822–1888) and E. Adamson Hoebel (1906–1993), promoted the use of evolutionary models that arrayed human societies according to their level of development, and postulated a dichotomous distinction between those societies in which legal rights and responsibilities rested on social status, as opposed to those in which they rested on contractual agreements (Hoebel 1954; Maine 1917). Other anthropologists, including Bronislaw Malinowski (1884–1942), argued for the necessity of long-term field research in order to observe the complex nature of legal practice in everyday life (Malinowski 1926: 56, 126). The past decades have witnessed a paradigmatic shift, however, with some legal anthropologists now placing greater emphasis on legal behavior as opposed to legal institutions. This shift appears to have commenced during the 1950s and 1960s, when two leading figures in the field – Max Gluckman and Paul Bohannan –

23 This problem might also be considered in light of Chang Wejen 張偉仁's discussion of the terms *fazhi* 法治 and *renzhi* 人治, as well as his arguments in favor of considering the term *fa* 法 (law) as only one of many norms considered essential to the preservation of social and cosmic harmony, including *dao* 道 (the Way), *de* 德 (virtue), *li* 禮 (rites), and *xisu* 習俗 (custom) (Chang 2000: vii). Similar ideas may also be found in the writings of Qian Mu 錢穆 (1895–1990); see Qian 1998.

24 I am grateful to Adam Chau for his help in guiding me to this field. Much useful information may also be found in the following website (now restricted access): http://www.indiana.edu/~wanthro/legal.htm.

engaged in a lengthy debate over the issue of whether and how legal anthropologists should apply Anglo-American legal categories to the study of non-Western societies.[25] By the 1970s, legal anthropologists had begun to focus on dispute-processing models of law, critiquing earlier emphasis on rules of adjudication and pushing instead for more research on the processes by which disputes are resolved and norms are elaborated (Comaroff and Roberts 1981; Merry 1992: 359–360). The influence of postmodernist discourse and practice theory during the 1980s prompted new challenges to traditional categories, with legal anthropologists turning their attention to the production and transmission of legal systems, as well as their links to networks of power (Starr and Collier 1989; see also Merry 1992: 360; Vanderlinden 2002: 169–179).

In reading the works of legal anthropologists, I have been struck by their vivid descriptions of judicial practice and conflict management, as well as their ability to link these practices to the political, social, and cultural contexts in which they take place. For example, Peter Just's *Dou Donggo Justice* reveals that disputes tell us about what is important in a given community, and how communal values can interact and change (Just 2001: 17). Similarly, in her influential book entitled *Harmony Ideology*, Laura Nader argues that one key aspect of informal justice involves its emphasis on solving conflicts rather than deciding legal merits of a case (Nader 1990: 295). This is certainly the case for Chinese dispute resolution, as I will show below. The importance of legal anthropological analysis may also be seen in the distinction between the court model (adjudication based on the establishment of past facts by legal efforts in order to achieve a conclusive verdict) and the bargain model (mediation by elders or elites aimed at the attainment of a compromise acceptable to both parties) (Ergene 2004: 52–53). Both models exist in Chinese legal practice (and in the West as well, with many cases being settled out of court), and one of this book's main goals is to delineate the relationship between these two models in the context of Chinese culture.

I also draw on the following two concepts in order to elucidate the importance of Chinese judicial rituals: legitimacy and speech acts. The fact that people in China, Taiwan, and overseas communities have long attempted to attain credibility and resolve disputes by performing judicial rituals indicates that such practices can constitute a process of legitimation, whereby people attempt to ensure that their ideas, values, or actions gain sanction in the context of culturally-accepted norms. Convincing other people about the validity of one's own concerns, especially during a dispute, is a challenge in any society. In Chinese communities, judicial rituals have long provided individuals and communities the opportunity to prescribe exactly which forms of behavior could be considered legitimate, and continue

25 The results of this debate were published in Nader 1969; see esp. pp. 349 and 401.

to do so today.[26] Of critical importance is the fact that the gods worshipped during these rituals are judicial deities (divine bureaucrats generally associated with judgment and punishment in the underworld), meaning that willingness to invoke them in an oath or indictment rite serves to reinforce the legitimacy of one's position. Thus, people making an oath would usually hesitate to invoke a deity like Guanyin 觀音, the Bodhisattva of Compassion. Other instances can be more complicated. Gods of loyalty and integrity like Guangong 關公 (Guandi 關帝) are usually not invoked during disputes, yet some secret society initiation rituals feature the making of an oath of loyalty in the presence of this deity (ter Haar 1998: 192), and he is often worshipped by police forces in Hong Kong and Taiwan (Li Huiyun 2003). When it comes to disputes between two individuals, however, the imagery of punishing courts seems central.

It is also essential to consider that while the term legitimation literally means "to make lawful", the actual processes by which ideas or actions become recognized as legitimate far exceed the scope of any court system. Lawrence Rosen, for example, maintains that the term "legal proceedings" should be applied to both court cases and rituals, all of which are designed to present the views of parties embroiled in a dispute in ways considered culturally legitimate (Rosen 1989: 20). In addition, scholars like Peter Just and Laura Nader demonstrate that disputes frequently center on competing views of legitimacy, with the parties involved attempting to persuade the mediators of the legitimacy of their arguments (Just 2001: 21; Nader 1990: 295). Even modern legal systems, with their emphasis on impartial and scientific justice that is based not on religion or personal connections but rather on forensic evidence, lie detectors, DNA testing, etc., still find it a struggle to enhance their own legitimacy when it comes to ensuring reliable testimony or fair verdicts by local juries in racially-charged cases. In many Asian communities today, the legitimacy of the state continues to be partially based on its relationship with a wide range of religious groups, while legal practice continues to incorporate judicial rituals as a means of attaining or enhancing legitimacy.[27] As we will see in the book's last two chapters, this is particularly the case in Taiwan, which boasts one of the most dynamic religious environments in East Asia.

26 Adam Yuet Chau has published a book-length study of the post-Mao revival of communal religious traditions in Northern Shaanxi (Shaanbei 陝北), which contains vivid descriptions of how elites use oaths and curses to attack their rivals and legitimize their interests (Chau 2006: 203–210). For more on legitimacy in Chinese legal cultures, see below and Chau 2005; Katz 2004a; Smith 1998; Yu 2005.

27 The above analysis was partially inspired by comments made by Karel Dobbelaere and Joël Thoraval during the International Conference on Religion and Social Integration in Chinese Societies: Exploring Sociological Approaches to the Study of Religion in the Chinese World. The Chinese University of Hong Kong, June 28–30, 2007.

Research in legal anthropology also points to the importance of speech acts as performative texts featuring reflexive processes of negotiation that actors utilize to claim legitimacy and authority, including (but not limited to) legal authority. Greg Beckett and Peter Just have demonstrated the importance of rituals (including oaths and indictments) as speech acts that announce the presence of conflict, and in some cases help play a role in its mediation (Beckett 2004: 2, 12; Just 2001: 97, 98, 106, 123–124). Corinne A. Kratz's research on judicial rites performed by the Okiek (an ethnolinguistic group based in northern Tanzania and southern Kenya) focuses on the links between ritual ways of speaking and hierarchies of social power, especially how such rites can not only reinforce but also challenge and even transcend power structures, with their effectiveness depending in part on the relative age and relation between those who perform them (Kratz 1989: 636–646).[28] In the case of Chinese judicial rituals, the data presented below indicate that oaths and indictment rites can serve as speech acts designed to enhance the performer's innocence or legitimacy, as well as emphasize the guilt of the opposing party, while trials of the insane and even dressing as a criminal serve to emphasize penance and reconciliation. At the same time, however, any analysis relying on the concept of speech acts must take into account the shift from oral to written that occurs when a disputant hires a temple scribe or other religious specialist to prepare a written version of the ritual to be performed. As Yasuhiko Karasawa notes in his study of Qing-dynasty legal plaints, which makes expert use of the work of Jack Goody and Walter Ong (Goody 1987; Ong 1982), the transition from oral account to written text involves considerable changes on the part of the scribe, particularly in terms of packaging events and use of rhetorical skill as a means of shaping reality (Karasawa 2007a: 68–69). One particularly striking aspect of the indictment rituals that I have observed at temples in Taiwan is how highly emotive oral narratives of injustice are tamed and standardized as they are transformed into written plaints to be submitted to the judicial deities of the underworld, a process which may help explain the importance of such rites in terms of allowing for the expression of tensions while also defusing them.[29]

Another anthropological concept that is relevant for this study but does not directly derive from the field of legal anthropology is that of rites of affliction, which Victor Turner (1920–1983) developed while doing fieldwork among the Ndembu tribe of central Africa. According to Turner, rites of affliction are redressive rituals performed during the third stage of social dramas. Turner also emphasized that while rites of affliction appear to be

28 For more on speech acts and their links to power structures, see Bauman and Briggs 1990; Mertz 1994; Starr and Collier 1989.

29 For more on the rhetorical significance of the shift from oral to written, see Hegel 2007b; Idema 1990; Katz 1999b: 90–91; West 2003.

addressing so-called "mystical causes" of calamities, they also reflect and in many cases even bring to light various social and familial conflicts (Turner 1968). Turner's most concise analysis of such rituals (including their performance in non-tribal societies) may be found in his later works, particularly a posthumous collection of essays entitled *On the Edge of the Bush* (Turner 1985). Two stimulating essays in this book clearly demonstrate that rites of affliction involve a strong element of reflexivity, in the sense that communities examine their moral condition through ritual actions which allow expressions of anger, resentment, or guilt. Rites of affliction thus represent an attempt to confront and deal with the wounds created by social conflict and competition through a process of seeking reconciliation between both the living and the spiritual world, as well as among the living (Turner 1985: 124, 132, 232–235; see also Beckett 2004: 1, 11). While it would be ill-advised to apply Turner's theories uncritically, some medieval European historians have also noted the importance of oaths and ordeals in terms of coping with social tensions (Bartlett 1986: 35, 37; Davies and Fouracre 1986: 222, 233, 236–237; Lea 1974 (1866)). Moreover, the data presented below, as well as research by Edward Davis, Peter Nickerson, and Michel Strickmann, suggest that some judicial rituals resemble rites of affliction in terms of their therapeutic nature, providing a cathartic opportunity for built-up tensions and resentments to be expressed in ritually-controlled settings (Davis 2001: 101–106; Nickerson 2007; Strickmann 2001).

Apart from utilizing the conceptual frameworks discussed above, I have made every effort to follow in the footsteps of scholars such as Kenneth Dean, David Faure, John Lagerwey, Michael Szonyi, and Yang Yanjie by drawing on historical and ethnographic data to delineate the complex relationship between ritual practice and social life.[30] As Peter Just pointed out in a review article about the field of legal anthropology in the 1990s, "In the scramble to see 'law as discourse' or 'law as power' or even 'law as culture' . . . [we] seem to be losing touch with law as something that happens in the real world, with law as event, as experience, as ethnography" (Just 1992: 383). Therefore, my analysis is based on the close reading of written sources and extensive field research. This book, like my previous study of the Ta-pa-ni Incident, accentuates the importance of event and experience, as these are essential to both the ethnographic and social historical enterprise (Katz 2005; see also Cohen 1997).

Nonetheless, a number of caveats are in order. Because the data for premodern China are insufficient for undertaking in-depth research on religion and the law at the local or regional levels, the first five chapters of this book will offer wide-reaching surveys of various phenomena related to this

30 See for example Dean 1998a, 1998b; Faure 1986, 2007; Lagerwey 1994, 1998; Szonyi 2000, 2002; Yang 1996.

topic, with the overall time frame centering on the late imperial era but also including data from ancient times as well as the early twentieth century. There will inevitably be lacunae in the discussion and sketchiness in the analysis, as well as the risk of conveying an ahistorical impression of unchanging cultural unity. I have proceeded despite these risks, inspired by the skilled research of pioneering European sinologists like Vincent Goossaert, Rolf Stein, and Barend ter Haar, who have undertaken broad-based surveys of key cultural phenomena (Goossaert 2005; Stein 1990 (1987); ter Haar 2006a). I have also been heartened by the presence of some striking examples of historical continuity, such as the similarities between the tomb ordinances and sepulchral plaints described in Chapter 1 and the underworld petitions currently filed at Taiwanese temples described in Chapters 7 and 8. This book is not intended to provide detailed answers to all the questions raised by my research; if it succeeds in sparking further investigations into these issues, it will have largely succeeded in its purpose.

In terms of sources, precious few firsthand accounts of judicial rituals survive, particularly since oaths and plaints filed to the gods were supposed to be burned. My main sources for this study range from more conventional historiographical sources written by local officials and other commentators on legal administration, to eyewitness reports by foreign officials and travelers in the nineteenth century, to field research in more recent times. Other important texts include historical accounts of oath-making rituals in ancient China, archival descriptions of blood oaths performed by martial groups that supported or opposed the state, gazetteers on local customs (*fengsu zhi* 風俗志) compiled during the late imperial and modern eras, as well as works of fiction (especially anecdote collections known as *biji* 筆記). The pursuit of justice is also a common theme in courtroom dramas, Mulian目連 operas, and crime novels (*gong'an* 公案) from the late Ming and late Qing.[31] The last two chapters feature newspaper articles as well as extensive ethnographic data, including the results of field research at the Xinzhu 新竹 (Hsin-chu) City God temple (Chenghuang miao 城隍廟), the Tainan 台南 Temple of the Eastern Peak (Dongyue miao 東嶽廟), and the Dizang Abbey (Dizang An 地藏庵), a popular temple in Xinzhuang 新莊 (Hsin-chuang; a city just south of Taipei) jointly dedicated to the Bodhisattva Dizang and another chthonic deity known as the Lord of the Hordes (Dazhong ye 大眾爺).

Attempting to make any generalizations based on such a widely scattered body of texts is admittedly highly risky, particularly since their textuality involved diverse processes of production, a wide range of intended audiences, and varied forms of transmission and reception. I also do not assume that all the descriptions of judicial rituals to be described below are of equal

31 For more on these texts, see Hansen 1995; Johnson 1989; Ma 1975; Waltner 1990.

validity in terms of their ability to reflect actual legal practice, as these range from more "factual" accounts of oaths and indictments in gazetteers and ethnographies to more fanciful (and sometimes satirical) stories of plaints filed by living human beings, ghosts, foxes, and even pythons. In particular, works of fiction might best be used to try and corroborate findings in historical and ethnographic sources, as well as to demonstrate that literati did believe in the unseen world and the inevitability of divine retribution, and were familiar enough with judicial rituals to elaborate on and/or parody them. Such stories served a range of purposes, from ostensibly didactic to obviously entertainment reading. Some were written in terse classical style; others are in vernacular language. The former, collected and circulated for the amusement of the highly educated elite, range between reportage of perceived reality through embroidered anecdotes about real people to self-conscious fictional creation. The latter could be more self-consciously fictional, but were also produced by highly educated writers, even if their readership was somewhat more widespread. However, while such texts could certainly be manipulated to serve artistic, political, and entertainment ends, it might not be wise to simply assume their pure "fictionality", as many literati not only believed in the unseen world and the inevitability of divine retribution, but also proved willing to perform judicial rituals in order to legitimate their causes or resolve questions of innocence or guilt.[32] The diversity of all these texts should also not prevent us from acknowledging one seemingly indisputable fact, which is that Chinese men and women from all social classes have consistently viewed the official judicial system as having a parallel in the religious realm, with the two systems being interwoven and interacting.

Chapter outlines

Chapter 1, which draws on my cooperative research with Alan Bernstein, considers the growth of the Chinese ideology of justice by conducting a comparative study of the history of the underworld in China and the West from ancient times up to approximately the ninth century of the common era. There are numerous similarities, including the belief in retribution, journeys/visions, the importance of confession, the need to provide aid for the dead who are suffering in the afterlife, etc. In terms of variance, the Chinese idea of the underworld appears to place greater emphasis on judicial

32 I am grateful to Robert Hegel for his guidance in considering these methodological issues. See also Davis 2001: 1–4, 19–20, 43. Jeffrey C. Kinkley's study of justice in modern Chinese fiction makes the important point that fiction and legal codes appear to have mutually influenced each other, and that novels which portray officials righting wrongs (including by means of judicial rituals) have enjoyed widespread popularity during both the late imperial and modern eras (Kinkley 2000: 101–169).

process and less on final judgment, in contrast to Judeo-Christian ideas of the underworld, which seem to be more moral and less legalistic. One key factor that appears to underlie the largely legalistic view of the underworld in China involves the growth of the imperial state's legal authority, as well as its ability to exact brutal punishments on its enemies. It is also essential not to overlook the importance of Taoism, including legalistic spirit codes governing the behavior of demons and deities, as well as many striking similarities between exorcisms and actual trials, including processes of detection, accusation, investigation, interrogation, imprisonment, and even the use of cangues. Thus, contrary to conventional wisdom, the Chinese underworld was conceived of as a prison prior to Buddhism's arrival, although Buddhist rituals featuring monks and nuns appealing to underworld authorities in order to save the souls of one's ancestors or hungry ghosts made a profound impact on Chinese religious life by at least the sixth century of the common era.

Chapter 2 presents an holistic view of three forms of dispute resolution that helped mold the Chinese judicial continuum during the late imperial and modern eras: mediation, formal legal procedures, and judicial rituals. Depending on the nature of the dispute and the status of those parties involved, people could choose one or a combination of these options. Moreover, a wealth of evidence indicates that officials would not hesitate to rely on dreams and other forms of divine intervention to solve difficult legal cases, right instances of injustice, capture bandits/thieves, and even fight spirits that haunted their offices or homes. All this suggests that China's judicial continuum covered both the official and religious realms, with considerable interaction occurring between the two. This continuum could even extend to the underworld, where the aggrieved dead were believed to have the right to file suits against the living.

The next three chapters describe different forms of judicial rituals. Chapter 3 considers the cultural significance of one rite that has been performed by Chinese since ancient times: the making of an oath, including oaths of allegiance/loyalty, oaths/vows of commitment, and oaths of innocence. I provide a survey of all three forms of oath-making, but focus on the third, especially its role in increasing one's credibility and providing an opportunity for parties involved in a dispute to release pent-up tensions. This chapter also discusses oaths accompanied by chicken-beheading rituals, and explores the extent to which oath-making rites might also be considered ordeals. I conclude by showing that the use of oaths of innocence contrasts sharply with traditional and modern Chinese court practices, which have not included the swearing in of witnesses.

In Chapter 4, I describe an extensive range of indictment rituals that have flourished throughout China since ancient times, including plaints filed against other members of the living, countersuits and other ritual measures taken in response to being accused by the dead, and indictments against haunting spirits. Some indictment rites could be used to counter imperial authority, with people using state-supported sacred sites like City God temples as settings to ritually accuse officials of wrongdoing. Others vividly reflected and expressed family tensions, particularly countersuits against the deceased who had filed plaints against living relatives or acquaintances in the courts of the underworld. Still others centered on gender issues, especially cases of female ghosts (*nügui* 女鬼) accusing men of rape, attempted rape, adultery, etc. However, men could also rely on indictment rituals to accuse their wives of being disobedient.

Chapter 5 examines two forms of judicial rites that attempt to deal with the consequences of divine retribution for wrongdoing in this lifetime or a previous existence: trials of the insane and dressing as a criminal. The former ritual features admissions of guilt, statements of penance, pleas for any aggrieved spirits to leave, and threats of punishment by underworld deities should they fail to do so. Another judicial rite that involves people attempting to atone for their misdeeds is that of dressing up as criminals during the processions that accompanied festivals to underworld deities. Both of these rites generally involve acknowledgement of guilt on the part of individuals suffering from disease, as well as acts of confession (*chanhui* 懺悔) and penance (*shuzui* 贖罪), yet their performance also features actions based on actual judicial practice, be it putting a suspect on trial or placing a convicted criminal in a cangue. This chapter also marks a shift to descriptions of current practices, concluding with a description of how hundreds of people still dress up as criminals during processions organized by Xinzhu's City God temple.

In the book's final three chapters, we shift our attention to the role of judicial rituals in the modern era, beginning with Chapter 6, which treats the encounter between Chinese and Western judicial practice. This chapter describes how Western police officers and judicial officials attempted to make sense of and at times utilize Chinese judicial rituals in the context of two different settings: (1) colonial courts in Asia, and (2) courts in Australia and the United States that tried cases involving Chinese immigrants. Such interaction involved extensive experimentation, and often messy attempts to find solutions acceptable to Westerners and Chinese alike. In an even broader sense, then, the willingness of Western authorities to tolerate Chinese judicial rituals can be seen as one aspect of the problem of how modern nation-states could choose to deal with traditional legal practices, as well as the limits of accommodating cultural diversity and customary authority.

Chapters 7 and 8 examine the ongoing popularity of judicial rituals in modern Taiwan. Data presented in Chapter 7 reveal that actual performances of chicken-beheading rites have experienced a marked decline during the past two decades, in large part due to pressure from animal rights groups and unwillingness on the part of temple managers to have their sacred sites serve as stages for such bloody spectacles. However, the threat to perform such a ritual has become a frequent ploy that politicians use in order to assert their innocence, put pressure on their opponents, or simply attract voter and media attention. Other politicians continue to make oaths at temples, while dropping the practice of beheading live chickens or using surrogates such as a vegetarian substitute for chicken or even boiled eggs. There are also numerous examples of loyalty oaths (including blood covenants) still being performed by more marginalized individuals in today's modern society, including gang members and prostitutes. Oaths and indictment rituals remain common in cases of family and financial disputes, while people accused of crimes or wishing to enhance their legitimacy continue to make oaths of innocence.

Chapter 8 features a detailed case study of Dizang Abbey (Dizang An), based largely on three types of data that I collected during a year's worth of field research there: (1) Underworld petitions, including indictments (referred to as *suzhuang* 訴狀 or *diewen* 牒文) prepared by the temple's scribe (*bisheng* 筆生), Lai Ming-hsien 賴明賢; (2) records of worshippers consulting the temple's spirit-medium (*jitong* 乩童; *tang-ki* 童乩 in Southern Min), Yang Wen-li 楊文禮, who is possessed by the Lord of the Hordes; and (3) certificates of gratitude (*ganxie zhuang* 感謝狀) that worshippers post in the temple if they feel its deities have been efficacious. This chapter also discusses instances of police and prosecutors performing judicial rituals at the temple.

From ancient times to the present, the ideology of justice and judicial rituals have played integral roles in the formation and even perpetuation of Chinese legal culture. In Taiwan, a high-tech democracy with a vibrant civil society, the reform of the legal system has done little to disrupt the continuity represented by the ideology of justice, while judicial rituals remain an accepted means of legitimizing causes and resolving disputes. On the other side of the Taiwan Strait, legal reform is only starting to gain some momentum, and while the ideology of justice may persist, judicial rituals remain essentially underground practices. All this suggests that the effective functioning of Chinese jurisprudence, or for that matter any legal system, requires a certain degree of wholeness. How this can be achieved in today's age of globalization remains to be seen, but the data presented below may at least provide some clues as to the integrality of Chinese legal culture.

1

THE DEVELOPMENT OF THE JUDICIAL UNDERWORLD

A comparative perspective

One of the most important aspects of the history of religious traditions throughout the world has involved the reverberation between images of the neutral underworld and the punitive underworld. This chapter, which is based on the fruits of a joint scholarly effort with Alan Bernstein,[1] traces this interaction in China, the Middle East, and Europe during the ancient and early medieval eras, while also exploring the ways in which it may have been a result of the growth of organized religions (Christianity, Buddhism, and Taoism) and the state.

Let us begin with Bernstein's tripartite distinction between porous death, neutral death, and moral death. Porous death, which stresses the on-going interrelationships of the living and the dead, seems to have been a relative constant in most religious traditions, and is especially relevant for discussing both ancestor worship and hauntings by the aggrieved dead, which could include the filing of indictments against the living. Neutral death centers on the attempt to prevent such hauntings by segregating the living from the dead, whose souls are confined to a dark land of no return that is under the control of various underworld spirits. The neutral underworld is thus conceived of as being home to all of the dead, regardless of what good or evil deeds they may have committed. In contrast, moral death is based on the belief in postmortem judgment that determines the fate of the deceased soul in the afterlife. As a result, the punitive underworld is both a court where all the souls of the dead are judged and a prison where the guilty are subjected to horrific torments as punishment for their wrongdoings while alive. As Bernstein points out, these visions of death and the afterlife should not be

1 I am deeply grateful to Alan Bernstein for his guidance in helping me understand this topic. Apart from his path-breaking scholarship (Bernstein 1993, 2006), other histories of the Western underworld include Brandon 1967; Himmelfarb 1983; Kohler 1923; Le Goff 1984; Segal 2004.

considered as ideal types that developed according to an evolutionary model; instead, they co-existed, competed, and influenced each other (Bernstein 1993).

Such patterns of cogeneration and reverberation are apparent in the religious traditions of the ancient Middle East and Europe. In ancient Mesopotamian religion, for example, the underworld appears to have been mainly a distant land where the dead were banished to in order to segregate them from the living (Dalley 1989). However, the nearly contemporary Egyptian *Book of the Dead* describes trials by underworld judges and the use of scales to weigh the sins of the deceased (Kohler 1923: 18–23; Hornung 1999).[2] The ancient Greek underworld of Hades could be neutral, with the idea of drinking Lethe water and forgetting one's previous existence appearing similar to that of drinking a potion provided by the old woman Mengpo 孟婆 in the Chinese underworld. Greek mythology also depicted Tartarus as an eternal prison far beneath the realm of Hades, but such a punishment was reserved solely for the Titans, not for wicked mortals (in contrast, heroes were allowed to enter the realm of Elysium) (Kohler 1923: 44–46, 49). However, by at least the age of Plato (429–347 BCE) some people believed that the souls of sinful men and women would be judged in the underworld, made to suffer the consequences of their misdeeds, and even returned to this world in a form of reincarnation to put into practice the lessons they had learned while dead (Kohler 1923: 46–51; Turner 1993: 28–33). Representations of the underworld in ancient Greece, which may have been influenced by Egyptian models, also emphasized the importance of retribution to be suffered under the administration of judges of the dead like King Minos (Guthrie 1962: 217–220; Nilsson 1925: 141; Stilwell 2005). Roman religion continued to stress the inevitability of underworld torments for the wicked. In Vergil (70–19 BCE)'s *Aeneid*, for example, Anchises explains the fate of souls in the underworld to his son Aeneas, concluding: "And so the souls are drilled in punishments, they must pay for their old offenses" (*Aeneid*, pp. 206–207, Book 6, lines 853–854). Another characteristic of ancient Roman culture was the use of religion to enhance the authority of laws (referred to as sacred or *leges sacrae*), and the idea that criminals could be viewed as offerings whose execution would restore divine favor to the community (King 1998; Robinson 2007; Rüpke 1992).[3]

Ancient Judaism also experienced the interaction of neutral and punitive death. The oldest texts, especially the Book of Psalms, refer to a neutral

2 Scales are also mentioned in some Buddhist scriptures (Ch'en Teng-wu 2005: 362), but the more common instrument of measurement in Chinese temples (particularly those to the City God) appears to have been the abacus (Duara 1988: 12; Lü 1992: 23).

3 Such views were also common in Chinese culture, see Lewis 1990: 46–48, 67–96, 195–205; Rowe 2007: 5–8; Sutton 2003a; ter Haar 2006a: 91, 118, 174–175, 332–340.

underworld called Sheol, the abode of the dead, where all souls must journey to regardless of how righteous or wicked they may have been. However, other works in the Hebrew Bible, such as 2 Chronicles and 2 Kings, refer to a punitive underworld known as Ge-Hinnom (later transliterated as "Gehenna" in Greek and Latin), a ravine outside of Jerusalem said to have served as a garbage dump and a site for sacrifices of children to the god Moloch. The souls of evildoers were sent there to suffer torments vividly depicted in Jeremiah 7:33–8:2: ". . . the dead bodies of this people will be food for the birds of the air, and for the beasts of the earth . . . They shall be as dung on the surface of the ground."

Christianity drew profoundly from the Greek, Roman, and Hebrew traditions. Thus, from its inception, its concept of death was moral (see for example Matthew 25: 31–46; Mark 9: 43). Moreover, visions of the early Christian afterlife featured many punishments based on Roman law, primarily mutilation, devouring by wild animals, stoning, and of course burning. In one example, the Book of Revelation 14:11 (cf. 20:10) refers to a lake of fire and sulfur into which all evildoers will be cast, "and the smoke of their torment goes up forever and ever". Other contemporary writings, such as the Apocalypse of Peter and the Apocalypse of Paul, further expanded and combined these torments (Kohler 1923: 95–108; Trumbower 2001).[4] Medieval European visions of the underworld continued to be inspired by judicial practices associated with the world of the living, particularly the use of fire as instrument of both underworld torment and judicial torture (or capital punishment) on earth (Bernstein 2006; Le Goff 1984: 8, 210–213).

The history of the Christian underworld was also influenced by debates among Rabbinic scholars from the School of Hillel and the School of Shammai, who wrestled with the issue of whether the damned were condemned to suffer forever or whether, after a maximum of 12 months, they would either ascend to paradise or be annihilated. In terms of practice, as early as the time of St. Augustine (354–430) and St. Gregory (ca. 540–604), the belief in an interim period between death and the Resurrection, during which the souls of the dead could be saved from torment, prompted descendants to strive to alleviate the conditions of parents and ancestors by prayer and other pious actions (almsgiving and masses), which were collectively called "suffrages". By the twelfth century, this facet of the Christian hellscape contributed to the rise of beliefs in a distinct place known as "Purgatory", where venial (minor/pardonable) sins could be expurgated, but not mortal sins (Bynum and Freedman 2000; Le Goff 1984: 5, 220–221).

The data presented above suggest the existence of many similarities between representations of the underworld in China and the West,

4 In addition, the *Koran* (*Qur'ān*) is full of references to "the fire" and "the burning" (Kohler 1923: 129, 132–133; Smith and Haddad 1981).

particularly: (1) concurrent ideas of the underworld as both a neutral place where all souls reside yet also a penal world organized on ethical principles and dedicated to imposing retribution upon wrongdoers; (2) the need for the living to make offerings and/or perform penitential rituals in order to improve the postmortem condition of their parents and ancestors by alleviating their punishments in the underworld; (3) visions or dreams that narrate underworld journeys; and, (4) the tendency to quantify good and evil deeds. These similarities should not, however, obscure important differences. Chinese conceptions of the underworld feature chthonic deities who serve as officials in the afterlife while also functioning like earthly bureaucrats in using legal procedures to judge the deceased (and in some cases the living), as opposed to the Western conceptions that stress the role of fallen angels tormenting the souls of the damned who have already been judged. This is not to deny that Western beliefs in the underworld also had legalistic features, including infernal punishments similar to those in this world and the belief that on the Day of Judgment God (or Christ) would preside over a court. Nonetheless, while both cultures are profoundly concerned with the problem of justice in the afterlife, the Chinese underworld separates the dead into the criminal and the law abiding, while the Western underworld is occupied by the souls of the damned, namely those alienated from God. Another key difference involves eschatology and related temporal concepts. Religions like Judaism and Christianity, which are based on linear conceptions of time, warn of eternal torment for all sinners. This differs from religions featuring cyclical concepts of time (including Taoism and Buddhism; see Bokenkamp 1994; Huang and Zürcher 1995), where postmortem punishments can be harsh but not eternal. Accordingly, when compared to medieval Christianity, the Chinese underworld appears to have emphasized judicial procedure over final judgment. Similarly, in contrast to Christian sources, which appear to be more concerned with an individual's faith, Chinese texts emphasize the importance of ethical conduct, particularly pertaining to ideals of ritual propriety (*li* 禮).[5]

This chapter treats the following four hypotheses:

1. The Chinese conceived of the underworld as a prison prior to Buddhism's arrival, in large part due to a combination of indigenous religious traditions and judicial practices that arose during the Spring and Autumn (ca. 722–481 BCE) and Warring States (ca. 475–221 BCE) eras, and became systematized during the Qin (221–206 BCE) and Han (206 BCE–220 CE) dynasties.
2. There was a form of reverberation between the imperial legal system and Taoist ritual, with the state providing a model for the underworld

5 For more on this point, see Watson 1985, 1988, 1993; see also Katz 2007a.

bureaucracy and Taoism formulating new legalistic rites for dealing with its officials.

3 By the Eastern Han dynasty (25–220 CE), as the pious increasingly invited Taoist priests to help perform legalistic rituals on behalf of the tormented souls of the deceased, Taoism ended the monopoly over the ancestral cult previously enjoyed by "Confucianism" (i.e., the scriptural and ritual tradition claiming Confucius as its core codifier) (Bokenkamp 2007; Poo 1998: 2, 36, 67);

4 Buddhism arrived in China during the Han dynasty, but did not make a significant impact on the Chinese cult of the dead until the sixth-eighth centuries. While Buddhism did make contributions to the Chinese underworld, it did so mainly in terms of new deities and rituals. In contrast to Taoist rituals of the underworld, which often involved "lawsuits" between the living and the dead, Buddhist rites featured monks and nuns appealing out of compassion to underworld authorities to aid one's ancestors or hungry ghosts suffering torment.

Early visions of the Chinese underworld

The earliest records of the Chinese underworld, which date from the Shang-Zhou era, portray it as a bureaucracy controlled by deceased members of the royal family, complete with written documents, record-keeping, and the use of official titles (Keightley 1978). Subsequent accounts refer to a grim and unpleasant place generally referred to as the Yellow Springs, Nine Springs, or Dark City.[6] The terrors awaiting the dead are graphically recounted in the song "Summoning the Soul", which dates to the Warring States period:

> O soul, come back! Go not down to the Dark City,
> Where the Earl of the Soil lies, nine-coiled, with dreadful horns on his forehead,
> And a great humped back and bloody thumbs, pursuing men, swift-footed;
> Three eyes he has in his tiger's head, and his body is like a bull's.
> O soul, come back! Lest you bring on yourself disaster.
> (*The Songs of the South*, pp. 225–226)

Poo Mu-chou considers this passage to be as an example of a neutral underworld, where all souls suffer torment regardless of their deeds while alive (Poo 1998: 64). The monstrous Earl of the Soil has an official title, and because commentaries to this text use the verb "to rule/govern" (*zhi* 治) to

6 The watery nature of the underworld expressed in the term "Springs" may have links to the problem of digging up actual springs while preparing tombs (Poo 1998: 65).

describe the Earl's responsibilities, it seems safe to conclude that this deity was charged with administering the underworld, even if not part of a systematized bureaucracy.

Another brief passage alluding to the underworld deities may be found in the renowned philosophical text known as the *Zhuangzi* 莊子 (*Chuang Tzu*), which dates from the fourth century BCE. This work describes an official known as the Director of Fate (Siming 司命), who is tasked with calculating all mortal life-spans. Additional evidence concerning the Director of Fate may be found in a 297 BCE resurrection account that has been studied by Donald Harper. This text provides clear bureaucratic imagery of the underworld, which could process lawsuits filed by the living on behalf of the recently deceased in the courts of judicial officials (Harper 1994: 6, 13, 16–19; see also von Falkenhausen 1994). Again, however, the overall view of the underworld seems largely neutral, with no obvious punitive aspects. Resurrection may be possible, but only after submitting an application through the proper channels. The moral standing of the deceased does not appear to be an issue.

A wealth of data on ancient Chinese beliefs and practices relating to the underworld may be found in tomb ordinances (*zhenmu wen* 鎮墓文) from the Han dynasty. Such documents were composed by ritual specialists (some of whom may have been Taoist priests) and were buried with the deceased in order to ease his/her passage through the chthonian bureaucracy, which was populated by officials with titles like the Magistrate of the Grave Mounds, the Neighborhood Head of the Gate of Souls, the Police of the Mounds, the Count of the Graves, the Official of Underneath, etc. Han tomb ordinances are highly significant because of their transitional nature. On the one hand, they preserve older aspects pertaining to neutral death, including the correct disposition of the deceased and his or her possessions beneath the earth. On the other hand, some ordinances also move towards beliefs that would become more common later, portraying the underworld bureaucracy as possessing aspects relating to moral death, with concomitant judgment and consequent punishments. The bureaucratic nature of the underworld may be seen in the fact that the oldest and most common ordinances are known as "lists of [items] dispatched" (*qiance* 遣冊), a term also used in Han dynasty official documents. Such items often included offerings designed to appease the officials of the underworld. Here is one example: "Respectfully we offer lead figurines, gold and jade, in order to gain release from culpability for the dead and elimination of misdeeds for the living" (Seidel 1987: 43; see also Poo 1998: 173). This and other works present an image of a judicial underworld with the power to punish the living and the dead, yet which is also susceptible to offerings that one might argue are thinly-disguised bribes. As Poo Mu-chou has noted, this also reflects clear similarities between the worlds of the living and the dead, especially in terms of social class. The wealthy could have a pleasant and comfortable existence; the poor, however, had to bear burdens such as taxes, corvée, and official harassment (Poo 1998: 65, 170, 171).

Other texts (like the following ordinance from 147) express an all-too-well-known fear of bureaucratic bungling:

> When the recently deceased woman Jia 加 died, she was just twenty-four. [Re-]calculate [the lifespans] in your name records![7] Perhaps it is an overlapping due to the year and month [of birth] being the same [as someone else due to die]. Collate the dates of death! Perhaps it is an overlapping due to the day and time being the same. Collate the dates of death!
>
> (Nickerson 1996a: 83–84)

A similar picture emerges in an ordinance about a recently-deceased member of the Chen 陳 household, which was composed just nine years later:

> His date and time of death have become overlapped with the fate of another; his registers have become stuck to those of another living member of his household.[8] Restore this person's fated span, and erase the overlapping writing. Erase the records binding him to a group of five (for corvée labor), so that the dead and the living have different files . . . Promptly, promptly, in accordance with the statutes and ordinances!
>
> (Nickerson 1996a: 151–152)

One striking aspect of this ordinance is the desire for the strict segregation of the living and the dead, regardless of any issues involving wrongdoing.[9] Apart from this, however, we find the same fear of bureaucratic bungling, which implies that punishments are not due to one's wrongdoing but rather to errors in record-keeping. Note also the persistent fears of taxes and corvée labor, as well as the importance of laws and legal proceedings.

The growing importance of moral death may also be seen in the fact that some of the living had profound worries about having to suffer for misdeeds committed by their forebears, a belief referred to in Taoist texts as "inherited burden" (*chengfu* 承負), which contrasts sharply with Buddhist ideas of karmic retribution (see below, as well as Bokenkamp 1997: 129, 174, 360). As one 173 CE tomb ordinance noted, descendants would prosper if their

7 Seidel has "Check, compare, and recheck" (Seidel 1987: 32).

8 Seidel has "so that living family members have been implicated (imprisoned)" (Seidel 1987: 33).

9 For more on this point, see Seidel 1987: 32, 33.

forebears had been good, but if they had committed evil deeds at least five generations would suffer the malefic consequences (Seidel 1987: 43). One salient example of these beliefs can be found in a tomb ordinance dating from around 170 CE:

> The Celestial Thearch (Celestial Monarch) sealed up the tomb of the deceased Xu Wentai 胥文泰 . . . and dispatched orders to the Tumulus Adjutant, the Lord of the Tomb, the Infernal "Two-Thousand-Bushel" Officers . . . stating:
>
> "The family of Xu Wentai, including his sons, grandsons, and all later generations, no longer have any connection with the deceased. Heaven above is clear and bright; the earth below is dark and obscure. The dead return to the world of *yin*, while the living belong to the world of *yang* . . . When the Lord of Mount Tai (Taishan fujun 泰山府君) reviews the records of conduct of the dead, let the ginseng serve[10]. . . If in the underworld Xu is found guilty of crimes, let a wax figure substitute for him in performing convict labor. Never again, in a thousand autumns, in ten thousand years, shall [Xu] again make any imposition on the living."
>
> [The descendants speak:] "We humbly offer gold and silver . . . in gratitude to the Lord of the Tomb, that he keep the tomb firmly sealed . . . The [ancestors within] three generations and five grades of mourning residing in the Xu family tombs, our august fathers and mothers, must not compel the more recently interred to perform penal servitude in their place . . . Once the door of the tomb is closed, let not the deceased ever again disturb future generations. In all matters the order of the Celestial Thearch shall be followed."
>
> (von Glahn 2004: 55–56)

The overriding concern of this tomb ordinance is the segregation of the living and the dead. One can distinguish levels of generational tensions, and in particular the fear of ancestors who have the ability to both haunt their descendants and force the recent dead to perform penal servitude in their stead. This ordinance asks members of the underworld officialdom to seal up the tomb at the request of, and following payment from, the descendants of the deceased Xu Wentai, who make expenditures of gold, silver, and ginseng to ensure that members of the living would not be punished as a result of their forebears' wrongs.[11] In this sense then, the preparation of a tomb

10 As Richard von Glahn notes, the use of ginseng root may have been due to its resemblance to the human body; see von Glahn 2004: 278 (note 25).

11 One should also recall that not only was filial piety considered a virtue, but unfilial children could be punished by the authorities.

ordinance could constitute a means of addressing family tensions, and seems somewhat similar to the rites of affliction studied by Victor Turner (Turner 1968, 1985).

Tomb ordinances clearly indicate that the chthonic bureaucracy had the authority to judge the conduct of the dead, as well as exact punishment for wrongdoings. Anna Seidel's research shows that the Chinese phrase "gain release from culpability" (*jiezhe* 解謫) so frequently found in tomb ordinances literally means to be found not guilty (Seidel 1987: 42–43). Seidel also notes that the dead who were found guilty by the underworld bureaucracy faced a situation comparable to "that of a parent in prison", and that the Chinese term for prison (*yu* 獄) is part of the term for the underworld, literally the "Earthly Prison" (*diyu* 地獄); hence the frequent appearance in Eastern Han tomb ordinances of terms like "prison scribes who rule the tomb", "police", and "jailors" (literally "prison messengers" or *yushi* 獄使), as well as descriptions of neighborhood work teams devoted to the performance of corvée labor (groups of five under the supervision of chthonic officials) (Seidel 1987: 31, 44, 46; see also Nickerson 1996a: 164; Wu and Jiang 1990: 162–165). Such representations of the underworld are evident already in the *Xiang'er* commentary to the *Laozi* 老子 (Lao Tzu) (*Laozi Xiang'er zhu* 老子想爾注), which states that those who are less virtuous will be "taken away in service of the Earth Offices" (Bokenkamp 1997: 102).

Tomb ordinances are also noteworthy for the development of the sacred site Mount Tai (Taishan 泰山) as a realm for the judgment and punishment of the dead, and frequently refer to the renowned underworld deity known as the Lord of Mount Tai (Taishan fujun 泰山府君; later worshipped under the title Emperor of the Eastern Peak), whose task was to "review the records of conduct of the dead" (Poo 1998: 167–168; Strickmann 2001: 82). However, they have little to say about actual punishment and/or torment in the netherworld, and the Chinese term *yi* 役, which is occasionally translated as "convict labor", actually refers to the forced labor that the Qin and Han dynasties assigned to all citizens, regardless of whether they had been convicted of a crime.[12]

To sum up, tomb ordinances mark a gradual shift in Chinese religions from a neutral to a punitive underworld, a transition that took place in the context of interplay between the three overarching ideas of death outlined at the beginning of this chapter. As a result, these texts ended up combining ancient fears of death pollution with newer legalistic visions of chthonic officials who rely on records of the living's good and evil deeds as a means of passing postmortem judgments. Tomb ordinances also indicate that the underworld became an integral component of the "bureaucratic metaphor" that many previous scholars have stressed in their analyses of Chinese

12 This point is discussed in Poo 1998: 171; Nickerson 2002.

religions.[13] However, while the judicial bureaucracy in the underworld certainly had the potential to be punitive, it is also essential to note that chthonic officials could be placated with offerings that bore a close resemblance to bribes.

Taoism and the punitive underworld

The punitive nature of the Chinese underworld, as well as the idea of moral death, become even clearer with the growth of Taoist religious movements during the Eastern Han dynasty, as well as the appearance of the venerable *Scripture of Great Peace* (*Taiping jing* 太平經).[14] This text stresses that officials of the four judicial departments (*cao* 曹) keep track of evil deeds committed by the living, and will order the souls of the dead determined to be guilty to face interrogation and torment in the underworld. Unlike the tomb ordinances described above, there is no room for negotiation or bribery; the guilty dead are doomed to torment:

> If a man commits evils unceasingly, his name will then be entered into the Register of Death. He will be summoned to the Underworld Government . . . Alas! When can he ever get out? His soul will be imprisoned and his doings in life will be questioned. If his words are found to be inconsistent, he will be subject to further imprisonment and torture (torment). His soul is surely going to suffer a great deal. But who is to blame?
>
> (Yü 1987: 390)

Another passage from this text envisions divine retribution as being similar to earthly punishments:

> Even if Heaven has indicated that it will kill the sinners, they yet pray for long life and put their faith in Heaven, as if nothing was wrong. Even if Heaven has begun to punish them, they yet cry out to Heaven and Earth and loudly wish for forgiveness. This is because they do not understand the importance of their own sins . . . If you want to know what this kind of judgment feels like, just think of the examination of a criminal by an enlightened ruler. If he confesses his crimes and accepts the blame for them, the ruler will not have him killed. It is just the same with Heaven.
>
> (Masaaki 2002: 47)

13 For more on the bureaucratic metaphor, see Wolf 1974. Essays challenging this concept may be found in Shahar and Weller 1996.

14 This text is a philological headache. The earliest surviving version is from the eighth century, but it was in circulation long before then, meaning that its current version might best be viewed as the earliest surviving example of a previously circulating tradition. See Hendrischke 2006; Kaltenmark 1979.

Early Taoist works like the *Scripture of Great Peace* may have been influenced by ideas about Heaven exacting retribution on wrongdoers expressed in Han-dynasty philosophy. One example may be found in the writings of the Han intellectual Wang Chong 王充 (27–97), who tells of a man named Zi Xia 子夏 (Tse Hsia) becoming blind while mourning for his son. As Zi bemoaned his fate, one of his friends explained that Heaven was punishing him for previous wrongs, and that he would only regain his sight after acknowledging his guilt. Wang's commentary on this story reads as follows:

> Heaven inflicts its punishments on man, as a sovereign does on his subjects. If a man, thus chastised, submits to the punishment, the ruler will often pardon him.
>
> (*Lun-heng*, part I, p. 164)

Note that explicit comparison of Heaven and the ruler as punitive forces is strikingly similar to that in the *Scripture of Great Peace*.

Beliefs resembling those expressed in the *Scripture of Great Peace* may be found in a fifth-century Taoist exorcistic text entitled *Demon Statutes of Nüqing* (*Nüqing guilü* 女青鬼律):

> The Ten Thousand Zhang Demon of High Heaven . . . lives on the southern spur of Mount Tai. All people who die on the road or in the water return to him. The demon also ascends to heaven to collate inquisitions and punishments . . . The Thrice Venerable Demon of the Southern Township . . . is in charge of inquisitions and calculations for the registers of the dead; the sins of the living [also] are all directed there. This demon also dwells on . . . Mount Tai, and also has subordinate officials.
>
> (Nickerson 1996a: 554)[15]

Taoism also contributed to the formation of China's most renowned indigenous earthly prison, the subterranean realm of Fengdu 酆都. Accounts of this netherworld dating back to the fourth century CE detail its gigantic and complex judicial administration, which consisted of offices, law courts, and prison cells, with records of the living and the dead being kept and updated on a regular basis (Chenivesse 1998; Mollier 1997; Mollier 2008: 183).

Early medieval Taoist texts added a second new wrinkle to beliefs in the punitive underworld, namely the idea that aggrieved spirits could file suits (known as "sepulchral plaints" or *zhongsong* 塚訟) with the underworld's legal bureaucracy. According to Peter Nickerson, while some sepulchral

15 For more on the history of this text and its links to the underworld bureaucracy, see Lai 2002.

plaints resulted from digging a tomb at a site that disturbed the spirits of the earth, most were "lawsuits initiated by aggrieved spirits in the courts of the underworld, which could also implicate the living (especially the living kin of the accused) and punish them with illness" (Nickerson 1997: 231, 242; see also Bokenkamp 2007: 56–58, 111–118, 130–138). As we saw in the preceding discussion of Han dynasty tomb ordinances, the belief in inherited burden meant that people feared being punished for the misdeeds of their forebears. By the early medieval era, the increasing prevalence of beliefs in the bureaucratic nature of the underworld meant that wronged souls (*yuanhun* 冤魂) did not necessarily have to return to the world of the living in order to wreak vengeance on their tormentors.[16] Instead, they could file a sepulchral plaint and then allow the legal institutions of the underworld to exact their terrible judgment. Some could even be granted permission to legitimately haunt their foes if their prosecutions were successful. As we will see in subsequent chapters, such beliefs have persisted throughout Chinese history and up to the present.

Here is one example of these beliefs from a 366 vision preserved in a revealed Taoist text entitled *Declarations of the Perfected* (*Zhengao* 真誥):

> Xu Chao 許朝 violently murdered Zhang Huanzhi 張煥之 . . . He also unjustly killed Qiu Longma 求龍馬. These men have both been waiting for an opportunity and recently placed an accusation before the Water Official (Shuiguan 水官, the feared chthonic judge who served in one of the Three Offices). The Water Official has compelled Xu Dou 許斗 (Tao Kedou 陶科斗; a deceased wife of the Xu 許 family) to return to her tomb, there to keep watch for a child in her household who is due to weaken.
>
> (Nickerson 1997: 236)

This text presents a clear link between misdeeds and sepulchral plaints, although it is essential to note that the living are not being punished for wrongs they committed in previous lifetimes, but rather for the evil actions of their parents or ancestors. Thus, we are not witnessing Buddhist karma, but Taoist inherited burden. The *Zhengao* also notes that this vision occurred shortly after Tao's death, and coincided with her living relatives suffering illnesses and nightmares. These relatives viewed their suffering as being a form of retribution for Xu Chao's misdeeds. Punishment was to be exacted through the deceased wife, who, forced to return to her tomb, was to select a child whose illness and death might requite the two plaintiffs.

In order to counter these plaints, the living resorted to hiring Taoist priests to access the underworld bureaucracy and file petitions on their behalf. The

16 Stories of vengeful ghosts may be found in Cohen 1982.

following paragraphs are from the Great Petition for Sepulchral Plaints, compiled prior to the sixth century CE:

> Now (so-and-so), of (such-and-such) region, district, township, and village, has provided a full statement in which he has said that the auspices of his house are in disastrous decline, and the members of his household have been burdened with successive illnesses. Their activities are unprofitable; their dwelling is unquiet. Thus he has pleaded for a petition for the dispersal and elimination of a sepulchral plaint.
>
> Now, judging by the appearance of the situation, one might seek out the [plaint's] roots in a rough fashion. One must suspect that, among his ancestors to the seventh generation, or his forebears to the ninth, among his close relatives or near kin [there was someone whose trespasses, when alive, were excessive, and who], after death, became subject to all manner of inquisitions and punishments. His descendants having yet to redeem him, in the darkness, he is crying out bitterly.
>
> Perhaps it is a plaint [*from someone who suffered*] drowning in water, or being burned by fire, or wounding with vermin, or poisoning with drugs. Perhaps it is a plaint over weapons and imprisonment, or plague and ulcers. Perhaps there are paternal uncles or brothers, or paternal aunts, nieces, nephews, or sisters, infecting each other in succession and causing calamities and harm . . . (Note: Italicized words indicate my modifications to the original translation)
>
> Your servant . . . respectfully invites his superiors:
>
> The Lord of Celestial Glory and his hundred thousand troops dressed in yellow to apprehend these demons in [so-and-so's] household . . . and annihilate them all . . .
>
> (Nickerson 1997: 261–263)

This fascinating text preserves ancient themes of segregating the living and the dead, albeit with rawer expressions of family tensions than those seen in some of the tomb ordinances discussed above. As Nickerson has observed, "That ancestors could be innocent victims, guilty sinners, or malicious aggressors no doubt reflected ambiguous attitudes – products of medieval family life – toward one's senior kin, dead and living" (Nickerson 1997: 252). Despite these continuities, however, what seems particularly striking about this petition is its reliance on seemingly *legal* methods to deal with family tensions. According to the above text, Party A (a living person) would go to Taoist priests to launch a countersuit against Party B, a deceased person who was suing (or had already successfully sued) one of Party A's forebears in the courts of the underworld (see especially the passage beginning "Perhaps it is a plaint . . ."). The motivation for filing a petition was that Party A had been suffering in real life and attributed his misfortunes to lawsuits launched from the underworld by someone (Party B) who was victimized or otherwise wronged/offended by misdeeds committed by Party A's ancestors. One particularly noteworthy feature is that members of the living were entitled to file countersuits, as this suggests that the judgments of the underworld bureaucracy were not irrevocable, and that men and women being sued by the dead could attempt to litigate themselves out of being punished. Another is the emphasis on military power, with Taoist deities envisioned as leading celestial soldiers to utterly annihilate any malevolent spiritual forces. A third key aspect of this text is the lack of any suffrages. This is not to deny that Taoism did have a salvationist aspect, but this was largely a result of Taoist adaptations of Buddhism, especially in the Lingbao 靈寶 scriptures composed during the fourth and fifth centuries, which provided suffrages for one's own parents/ancestors or the pitiful dead (hungry ghosts), not for wronged souls who haunted the living after successfully filing lawsuits in the underworld.[17] Finally, such texts exhibit rhetorical overlap with actual plaints filed in a magistrate's court (You 2007), a phenomenon that persisted into the late imperial and modern eras (see Chapters 4, 7, and 8).

The Great Petition for Sepulchral Plaints also helps show how moral death in ancient and early medieval China developed important legal overtones; the interaction between the living and the dead and the search for hidden wrongdoing take place as a series of suits and countersuits, which are distinctly legal procedures. This text reveals that the dead do not rest in peace, and must suffer the penalties for their misdeeds.[18] However, while the Great Petition is clearly concerned with the moral shortcomings of the deceased, it also treats them as legal transgressions (moral death in legal dress). Inasmuch as underworld gods are officials who judge the deceased and administer punishments to those found guilty of wrongdoing, the legitimacy of one's suit before the underworld authorities, whether initiated by the deceased (as in a sepulchral plaint) or by the living (in a countersuit), depends on correct adherence to certain legal norms. Nonetheless, the need for these legal procedures only arises because of perceived moral shortcomings either in the survivors' devotion to forebears or in the actual transgressions of the deceased, which must be expiated either by the dead themselves or with the help of the living. The living can either pay off offended parties (on earth or in the underworld) or propitiate the complaining predecessors with sacrifices that presumably the ancestor or parent will

17 See Bokenkamp 1997: 374–375, 385–389; Nickerson 2002: 61. The only possible exception was that the living could be forced to perform suffrages to appease wronged souls if an exorcism failed.

18 For more on medieval Taoist ideas of retribution, see Kohn 1998; Mollier 2008: 101–107; Yoshioka 1970: 167–227, 290–339.

use to pay off some god portrayed as an official of the underworld. Thus, the Taoist underworld can be punitive, but not in the sense of moral death as usually depicted in Western sources.

Taoist priests continued to perform legalistic rituals to exorcise the unruly dead and other malevolent spirits into the late imperial and modern eras, a time that also witnessed the increasing integration of local deities into Taoism, with many serving in the judicial bureaucracies of the City God and the Emperor of the Eastern Peak.[19] Edward Davis has convincingly demonstrated that Song-dynasty Taoist rituals for "investigating and summoning" (*kaozhao* 考召) occasionally paralleled the legal system in terms of including rites for accusation (*he* 劾), investigation (*kao* 考), and interrogation (*xun* 訊; *wen* 問), as well as shackling offending spirits by using cangues (*jia* 枷) or confining them to underworld prisons (*yu* 獄) (Davis 2001: 23, 61, 93–106; see also Hymes 2002: 33; Liu 2002: 378–382). This was also the case for thunder rituals (*leifa* 雷法), a repertoire of administrative, meditative, and judicial techniques that became an integral component of many Song-dynasty ritual systems (Skar 1996–1997: 2000). All of these rites also resemble the Great Petition in terms of their martial language and deployment of sanctioned violence. Judith Boltz's path-breaking research clearly shows that the Taoist exorcistic rituals of that era were "fundamentally framed as acts of violence", including the use of the term *sha* 殺 ("to kill") and punishments for offending demons that included beheading, dismemberment, or being disemboweled. In addition, such rites featured copious imagery from actual warfare, including references to fire-birds (crows, pheasants, sparrows), fire-beasts (rhinoceros), and flaming chariots, not to mention possible links between thunder rites and the use of gunpowder (Boltz 1993: 272–286). Taoist exorcistic rituals proved especially appealing to Song-dynasty officials (including military officers), who learned how to perform them in order to assert their authority over local cults in southern China, especially those of its non-Han ethnic groups and their shamans (*wu* 巫) (*ibid.*: 242–250, 253, 264, 268, 271–272). At the same time, however, all of this weaponry cannot be deployed at will. Only after the proper rituals have been performed and demonic forces have been tried and convicted can the power of those martial deities in the Taoist's arsenal be unleashed.[20]

Inasmuch as the specialists who performed Taoist judicial rites not only exercised spiritual powers but also assumed the roles of judicial officials,

19 These trends are discussed in Cedzich 1995; Davis 1985; Hansen 1990; Katz 1995a; Matsumoto 2006; von Glahn 2004: 122–129, 169–173.

20 This important point, as well as the links between martial deities and so-called "vernacular" forms of Taoist ritual (Schipper 1985), is discussed in Meulenbeld 2008. See also Katz 2008; Rowe 2007: 2–3.

they were also subject to the rigorous restrictions of Taoist codes (*ke* 科) that attempted to regulate the practices of specialists and their followers.[21] Members of the spirit world were also subject to legalistic constraints on their behavior, which were promulgated in so-called "demonic codes" (*guilü* 鬼律) and "celestial codes" (*tianlü* 天律).[22] For example, spirit codes preserved in chapters (*juan* 卷) 251–252 of the fourteenth-century Taoist ritual compendium *A Corpus of Taoist Ritual* (*Daofa huiyuan* 道法會元; *TT* 884–941; *CT* 1220) contain a lengthy series of rules and regulations entitled "The Supreme Celestial Code as Proclaimed in Vermillion by Nüqing from the Cave of Primordial Chaos" (*Taishang hundong chiwen Nüqing zhaoshu tianlu* 太上混洞赤文女青召書天律).[23] This text reveals that the chthonic judges of the underworld faced even more regulations than the dead whose fate lay in their hands. In addition to rules concerning the correct use of bureaucratic forms, other regulations threaten judges with demotion, forced labor, and even death for offenses such as holding the accused beyond a specified time period without trial, accepting bribes, deciding excessive punishments, willfully adding or deducting from people's lifespan, etc. Qing-period works of fiction preserve these beliefs, containing numerous accounts of corrupt or incompetent judicial deities being punished for their wrongdoings.[24]

Whether or not the above-mentioned codes were common knowledge is not clear, but their presence in the *Taoist Canon* testifies to the hope of receiving fair and impartial justice when dealing with the chthonic bureaucracy. Valerie Hansen notes that some of the above regulations are quite idealistic (the rule against holding a suspect without trial seems strikingly similar to some notions of Western jurisprudence), a fact which may reflect a longing for the earthly court system to function as effectively as its chthonic counterpart (Hansen 1995: 219–221). As we have seen above, one key facet of medieval Taoism was its role as a religion promulgated and enforced by a hierarchy of ritual specialists who would file petitions with celestial and chthonic officials on behalf of their patrons. The perceived ability of Taoist legalistic rituals to manipulate the chthonic bureaucracy contributed to the social standing and income of these specialists, and it seems highly significant that one traditional term for a Taoist priest (*faguan* 法官, which literally means "legal official" or "official of ritual techniques") is the same as the modern term for a judge.

21 Bokenkamp 1997: 149–185; Nickerson 1996a, 1996b. See also Dudbridge 1995: 51–53, 109–113, 186, 208, 209–210; Gjertson 1989: 136, 251–255.

22 See for example Kleeman 1994: 164–166, 173–175; Strickmann 2002: 80, 85–87.

23 For more on the *Daofa huiyuan*, see Boltz 1987: 47–49 and van der Loon 1979. While the latest works in this collection date from the fourteenth century, most appear to have been composed by Song-dynasty religious specialists.

24 Some examples may be found in *Zibuyu*, 9.170–171, 22.434–435; *Xu Zibuyu*, 1.6, 2.19–20.

The advent of beliefs and practices centering on a vast underworld bureaucracy that supervised, judged, and punished the dead coincided with a change in visionary literature about journeys to and from the realm of the dead. Early medieval texts centered on the experiences of the living in the world of the dead following an official summons to assume a post in the underworld bureaucracy. One on-going theme in many of these accounts is that people could be summoned due to clerical error (this belief can be traced back to the tomb ordinances discussed above), although stories of underworld officials being inefficient or corrupt have also been viewed as commentaries on the problems of the actual judicial system.[25] While there are descriptions of the chthonic bureaucracy (which could even include monks serving as officials), little detail is provided as to legal process or the administration of punishments (Campany 1995; Campany 1996: 58–59, 257–258, 377–384). In contrast, tales from the Tang dynasty (618–907) provide much more detail on judicial procedures and punishments in the underworld (Dudbridge 1995: 51–61, 109–113).

Buddhism's impact on the Chinese underworld

Although many scholars have observed the ways in which Buddhism reshaped the Chinese cult of the dead, particularly in terms of the belief in karmic retribution for one's own misdeeds,[26] they have tended to downplay the persistence of the indigenous Chinese belief that the underworld remained the abode of all the dead, who were subjected to judgment and legalistic punishment for wrongdoing. Some aspects of these beliefs were absorbed into Buddhism, with early translations of Buddhist scriptures using "Mount Tai Earthly Prison" (Taishan diyu 泰山地獄) for the Buddhist term *niraya* (hell). One example may be found in a collection of *avadāna* (tales of past lives of Buddha's disciples) that was translated in China between 290 and 306, and stated that wrongdoers would "fall into the Mount Tai Earthly Prison" (Gjertson 1989: 120–121, 136–137).

The fact that the Chinese Buddhist underworld remained largely a bureaucratic realm of penal servitude, thus reproducing fundamental aspects of ancient Chinese religious traditions while also adapting Buddhist beliefs and practices from India and Central Asia, is also demonstrated in an indigenous Chinese Buddhist scripture entitled the *Consecration Sutra* (*Guanding jing* 灌頂經), which dates to the fifth century:

25 The use of the underworld as a means of alluding to official corruption persisted up to the Qing dynasty; see Carlitz 2007; Chan 1998: 149–185; Waley-Cohen 1993; Youd 2007; Zeitlin 1993: 43–48, 93–95.

26 See for example Teiser 1988; Mollier 2008: 174–208; Zürcher 1959.

> King Yama has charge of the entries in the registers of those living in the world. If people are evil and commit various acts that are against the Law, if they are not filial and obedient[,] . . . then the spirits-beneath-the-earth and the watchers will submit a memorandum about them to the Five Officers. It is the Five Officers who arrange the slips in the registers, removing names from the books of death and certifying them in the books of life . . . King Yama investigates each case and prescribes punishments in accordance with the gravity of the crime.
>
> (Strickmann 2001: 118)[27]

Apart from the mention of King Yama (a Buddhist import from Hindu mythology) in place of the Lord of Mount Tai, the vision of the punitive underworld in this Buddhist text is almost identical to Taoist representations, including its systems of surveillance, officials who rely on registers to keep track of the words and deeds of the living, and mechanisms of judicial investigation and punishment. In both Buddhist and Taoist visions of the underworld, the dead are not simply imprisoned but must also suffer for their wrongdoings, with underworld officials adding physical pain to the terror of confinement.

What Buddhism *did* add to Chinese beliefs in the punitive underworld was the hope for salvation through Buddhist mortuary rituals and reincarnation. This may be seen in the following passage from the *Scripture on the Ten Kings* (*Shiwang jing* 十王經), a tenth-century Buddhist text that has been studied by Stephen F. Teiser:

> At one hundred days (after death) people are subject to more annoyances;
> Their bodies are cangued and shackled and they are wounded by whips.
> If sons and daughters exert themselves in cultivating merit,
> Then [the dead] will be spared from dropping into underground prisons, those places of eternal suffering.
>
> (Teiser 1993: 122; see also Teiser 1994)

The above passage seems related to the Western idea of suffrages, by which the living can dedicate good deeds to benefit specific dead persons. It clearly points out that parents/ancestors can be released from underworld torment by their descendants' performance of meritorious acts, especially hiring Buddhist specialists to perform suffrages for the dead. These rituals featured fasting, the recitation of Buddhist scriptures, and offerings of spirit money in order to propitiate the recently deceased, hungry ghosts, or ancestors,

27 For more on the importance of indigenous Buddhist scriptures, see Buswell 1990.

depending on the ritual being performed. One implication was that it would no longer be necessary for descendants to hire Taoist priests to perform rites of filing petitions on behalf of the dead.

Works like the *Scripture on the Ten Kings* constituted the final component of the vision of the underworld now common among the Chinese people today: a synthesis of Indian, Central Asian, and Chinese beliefs about a punitive underworld realm where the dead get their just deserts for evils committed in previous lifetimes. Of special importance is the fact that the dead have some hope of salvation, but only if members of the living sponsor memorial services on their behalf every seven days after death for a period of up to 49 days. Such rituals were originally performed by members of the *sangha* (Buddhist monks and nuns), but later absorbed into Taoist and sectarian traditions as well (Teiser 1993: 115–119, 123–124).

Religion, the state, and the Chinese underworld

The above presentation has traced the interaction between the neutral underworld and the punitive underworld in China, as well as the roles that the state and organized religions like Taoism and Buddhism played in this process. We have seen that the Chinese underworld was conceived of as a prison prior to Buddhism's arrival, which had important implications for members of the living who wished to intercede on behalf of souls in the afterlife. Peter Nickerson argues that the ancient Chinese underworld possessed a moral aspect before Buddhism arrived in China, but that Buddhism enhanced these aspects. He also notes that, "The judicial metaphor mediates . . . between archaic anxieties over [death] pollution and emerging medieval worries about sin" (Nickerson 1996a: 158).[28] Prior to Buddhism's arrival, therefore, Taoism had already developed a *legalistic* system of intercession and exchange between this world and the afterlife as seen in the ordinances and sepulchral plaints discussed above. Buddhism proved unable to alter this aspect of the Chinese underworld, but did provide a means of escaping its torments *without having to resort to legalistic rituals*. All one had to do was hire Buddhist monks and/or nuns to perform rituals on behalf of the dead. Taoist rituals are legalistic because they involved actual lawsuits, with plaintiffs (the Party A mentioned above) hiring Taoist priests to file petitions (including countersuits) after being sued in an underworld court by the dead. In the Buddhist *Scripture on the Ten Kings*, the intercession is made by the descendants through the Buddhist priests on behalf of suffering forebears. In other words, the act of a Taoist priest filing a petition has some overlap with legal practice, while the act of a Buddhist

28 While his analysis is largely on the mark, the use of the term "sin" here risks reading Western values onto non-Western beliefs.

specialist chanting scriptures or performing a penitential ritual avoids legal procedures but effectively provides salvation for the condemned soul. This would seem to be an essential difference between the ways in which Buddhists and Taoists deal with the dead. From early medieval times Taoists also chanted scriptures and performed penitential rites for the dead (especially at the moment of death and during funerals), but it seems they learned many of these rituals from the Buddhists. Conversely, the durability of Taoist rituals even in the face of spreading Buddhist influence may be seen in the fact that many worshippers continued to file petitions, a practice that persists to this day.[29]

One factor underlying the advent of the punitive underworld in China appears to have been the development of a standardized legal system during the Qin-Han era (Idema and Zürcher 1990; Loewe 2002 (1967); Scogin 1990), when a highly centralized bureaucratic state superseded the decaying feudal system of the Zhou dynasty (ca. 1100–256 BCE) and written legal texts began to be used in place of oaths in order to command assent and obedience (Lewis 1999). Chinese legal traditions developed during the Spring and Autumn and Warring States periods, incorporating the two rival schools of Confucianism and Legalism. The first law codes (literally "books of punishment" or *xingshu* 刑書) were promulgated by individual states during the sixth century BCE, while a unified code was instituted throughout the realm during the reign of the First Emperor of China (Qin Shihuang 秦始皇; r. 221–210 BCE) (Bodde 1981 (1963)). This era also witnessed an increasing prevalence of state-sanctioned violence, which can be seen in the frequent mention of punishments in legal texts (Lewis 1990; ter Haar 2000). The Chinese term for punishment (*xing* 刑) clearly indicates the administration of physical agony, as the right half of this character includes the pictogram for a knife. In addition to execution, ancient punishments encompassed various forms of mutilation, including nose-cutting and castration, and it is striking that the term *xing* appears more often in ancient legal texts than the term *fa* discussed above (Bodde 1981: 174–175). As Du Wenzhong notes, there may also be links between ideas of punishment and the belief that the execution of criminals could resemble a sacrificial offering (Du 2004: 48, 50; see also ter Haar 2006a: 91, 118, 174–175, 332–340).

The rise of the imperial state's legal authority, as well as its ability to exact brutal punishments on its enemies, clearly shaped the development of the Chinese underworld. As Donald Harper points out, "by no later than the end of the fourth century B.C. the underworld already resembled a bureaucratic state, and dealings with the underworld bureaucracy conformed to the norms of Warring States bureaucracies" (Harper 1994: 17). Moreover, the

29 A highly stimulating analysis of the mutual influence between these two religions may be found in Christine Mollier's new book (Mollier 2008).

Han dynasty witnessed a profound shift in beliefs about ancestors, who were transformed from powerful figures to abject ghosts (or pitiful sinners) in the underworld (von Glahn 2004: 31–33, 45–48, 52–57). It seems highly significant that the decline in ancestors' status coincided with the underworld becoming more prison-like, which also occurred at a time when the Chinese state was becoming increasingly powerful, as this may reflect the state's increasing hegemony over family affairs, including in the realm of legal practice.

During the period of time covered by this chapter, China, the Middle East, and Europe witnessed extensive significant overlap between governmental and religious ideas of judicial practice. For example, Polybius in antiquity and Alcuin in the early Middle Ages stressed the importance of beliefs in postmortem punishment as a deterrent force (Bernstein 1993, 2006). In China, officials frequently cited the writings of ancient philosophers such as Mozi (Mo-tzu) 墨子 (ca. 470–390 BCE), due to their emphasis on the inevitability of divine retribution (*Mo Tzu*, pp. 94–95). Moreover, the ancient and medieval Chinese state proved independent enough to produce a legal code that was separated from the religious sphere, and at times was able to assert its hegemony over it. For example, Ch'en Teng-wu hypothesizes that Buddhism attempted to make itself more appealing ("orthodox") to the imperial state by emphasizing its ability to restrain people from doing wrong (Ch'en Teng-wu 2005: 285–286). This seems to contrast with early medieval Western law codes, which were written with the advice of clerics and included provisions enforcing clerical morality (Bernstein 2006).

It would be advisable not to overemphasize the parallels between worldly and postmortem justice, however, and to remember that any overlap between these two systems was not unidirectional but reciprocal. On the one hand, numerous scholars have demonstrated the profound impact of the Chinese bureaucracy on Buddhist beliefs in the underworld, including the presence of judges, clerks, and runners, as well as judicial torments similar to those in use at that time, including beatings, being placed in cangues, and various forms of mutilation (Ch'en Teng-wu 2005: 296–306, 320–324; Eberhard 1967; Goodrich 1981; Nickerson 1996a; Teiser 1993). On the other hand, the work of Brook, Bourgon, and Blue points to the "distorting mimesis" of the homology between worldly legal institutions and their representations in Chinese religious traditions, as the underworld judicial system not only reflects actual legal practice but also refashions it, with depictions of underworld torments serving to remind viewers of earthly punishments, even if such punishments were not identical. In other words, representations of the underworld imagine the power of the state without having to accurately depict it (Brook, Bourgon, and Blue 2007: 145–149; see also Dutton 1992: 3–4).

Nevertheless, while the Chinese imperial state may have provided a *model* for the underworld bureaucracy by the Qin-Han era, it was Taoism that worked out a new *system* of legalistic rituals for dealing with chthonic officials during the Eastern Han and early medieval period, one that became highly attractive to the Chinese people. In addition, Taoism's development as an institutionalized religion during the second century CE meant that the interaction between Buddhism and Chinese indigenous religious traditions differed from the interaction between Catholicism and so-called "pagan" religious traditions in early medieval Europe, which do not seem to have been nearly as institutionalized as Taoism. While Buddhism resembles contemporary Latin Christianity in the sense of promoting the salvation of the dead through suffrages, and both of these religious traditions stand in sharp contrast to Taoism in their rejection of legalistic rituals, Buddhism did not take root in China as a totally new belief system. Instead, it grafted some of its own key elements onto Taoist beliefs and practices already considered fundamental to the Chinese underworld. Perhaps the best-known example is the belief in karmic retribution, which supplanted that of inherited burden, thereby transforming the relationship between the living and their forebears. Belief in karma meant that people were less likely to attribute their suffering to the wrongdoings of their ancestors than to their own misdeeds in this life or a previous existence. In addition, while filial descendants still worried about whether their parents or ancestors were being punished in the underworld, they did not have to fear being indicted by ghosts who had suffered for wrongs committed by their forebears. Buddhism also introduced deities and rituals believed to be effective in saving the souls of the dead while bypassing its chthonic bureaucracy. Thus Buddhism did not create the punitive underworld in Chinese culture, but it significantly altered the ways in which the living could aid its inmates. Moral death continues to exist, but Buddhist rituals, much like the suffrages of medieval Europe, can help some people escape its worst consequences.[30] Part of what accounts for the widespread patronage of Buddhist rites was the ongoing reverberation of legal practices and notions of postmortem retribution, which provided mutual reinforcement and legitimation.

Concluding remarks

The data presented above contain important implications for the history of distinctions between hell and purgatory. In particular, the belief in the Earthly Prison cannot be exaggerated, since it clearly designates a punitive underworld, with those who fall under the jurisdiction of the Lord of Mount Tai and other chthonic deities doomed to undergo gruesome forms of torment. Given the nature of karma, however, these sentences are limited, not eternal, thus tempting Western scholars to read back into them the

30 This point is eloquently argued in Teiser 1993; Wang-Toutain 1998; Zürcher 1980.

specifically Catholic notion of Purgatory. Whatever the similarities of the Earthly Prison to Purgatory (particularly temporary and purifying torments in the underworld), Purgatory emerged from a specific background: as a protest against and a contrast to an eternal, unchanging hell (Bernstein 1993; Le Goff 1984). Absent these oppositions, it may be advisable to retain "Earthly Prison" for China and whatever term is most appropriate for the West prior to the standardization of beliefs in Purgatory during the twelfth century.

The above comparison also suggests a striking feature of the nature of moral death in China, where it seems to combine more features from legal practice than in the West. Ancient and early medieval Chinese sources contain vivid descriptions of judicial procedures in the courts of underworld deities conceived of as bureaucrats, with the guilty being forced to suffer torments that resemble punitive measures of earthly justice. Even the parallel between the term *yu* (prison) and *diyu* (earthly prison) implies antecedent sentencing, a judicial procedure. This conception seems different from moral death in the Middle East and Europe, which also features the punishment of deviation from right belief and proper behavior (including the judicial procedures of the Last Judgment), but with a less bureaucratic representation of judicial process. These concepts of death may differ depending on shifting historical and cultural conditions, but what seems especially striking is the roughly contemporaneous appearance, across great distances and cultural divisions, of reverberating representations of neutral and moral death, which, because of their punitive nature, encouraged concern on the part of the living for the dead, with consequent actions (suffrages) to aid them through their postmortem trials.

2

THE JUDICIAL CONTINUUM

This chapter provides an overview of the Chinese judicial continuum from the Ming dynasty to the Republican era. As noted in the Introduction, the judicial continuum was made up of a coherent cultural system consisting of mediation, formal legal procedures, and rituals like the making of an oath. Such practices could coexist, and at times even be performed concurrently, playing an integral role in processes of legitimation and dispute resolution while also contributing to the vitality of the Chinese ideology of justice. Because extensive research has already been done on mediation and the courts (see the works cited in the notes to the Introduction), I will focus here on the ritual remedies for disputes. I also provide examples of officials relying on judicial rituals to deal with various administrative and legal matters.

Mediation

With the exception of elites who had the wealth and connections necessary to adjudicate their cases according to the procedures of the formal legal system, most people embroiled in disputes tended to first resolve their cases by means of private mediation. Such mediation featured a wide range of subtle and not-so-subtle pressures, the use of moralistic language, and in some cases even material inducements. The goal of the mediation process was the achievement of some form of compromise, with the need to establish peace and harmony based on customary ethical values proving more important than adjudicating right and wrong according to the law. In the best of all possible worlds, the mediated conclusion to a dispute should provide some degree of legitimation for all parties who successfully complete this process, meaning vindication for the victors and a face-saving solution for losers. One well-known form of mediation in late Qing and Republican China was the ceremony of "drinking mediation tea" (*chijiangcha* 吃講茶), in which teahouses could serve as a sort of public court where disputes could be resolved (Wang 2000, 2006).

Because conflict resolution involved knowledge of the intricacies of local knowledge and customs, the delicate role of mediating disputes was generally entrusted to community leaders.[1] These included middlemen (*zhongren* 中人) for contracts and transactions, as well as elders (*qilao* 耆老; including family/lineage heads) and other local elites ranging from the heads of community policing units (*baojia* 保甲) to the leaders of ritual associations (*huishou* 會首) (Allee 1994b; Huang 2005: 51–75; Huang 2006: 156; Jung 2007a, 2007b; Qiang 2001; Su 2000). Other organizations led by local elites that could mediate disputes included community compacts (*xiangyue* 鄉約) and associations for communal welfare (known as "public offices" or *gongju* 公局), as well as more modern organizations like chambers of commerce (*shanghui* 商會) and formal mediation committees (*tiaojie weiyuanhui* 調解員會) (Chiu 2008; Goodman 1995; Huang 2005: 68–75; Qiu 2005; Zhao 2006: 221–231).

The Chinese state had a vested interest in supporting local mediation, as this could save officials the time and hassle of having to adjudicate all manner of seemingly petty disputes. In one example, the founding emperor of the Ming dynasty (Ming Taizu 明太祖; Zhu Yuanzhang 朱元璋; r. 1368–1398) decreed the establishment of Pavilions for Explicating Clarity (Shenming Ting 申明亭) where village elders could adjudicate disputes (Han 2000; Tatsuo 1952). The names of criminals and wrongdoers were posted in these pavilions, which also served as sites for the performance of judicial rituals (see Chapter 4). I should note, however, that most late imperial sources merely describe how mediation systems were supposed to operate. The extent to which justice was fairly and effectively administered is far less clear, and in some cases these institutions could be abused by local elites for their own personal gain.

Examples of how mediation was actually undertaken at the local level may be found in Philip Huang's analysis of the Mantetsu 滿鐵 surveys of north China, which were undertaken during the 1930s and 1940s. In one instance, landlord Liu 劉 and tenant Ma 馬 were engaged in a dispute over switching rent from cash to kind during a period of rapid inflation. The middleman for their original contract mediated a compromise, according to which the tenant would pay in cash during the second year of contract and in kind during the third. A second case concerned two parties laying claim to the wood from a tree planted on one side of a boundary, the branches of which crossed to the other side. This time the mediators were from the village "well-to-do", who decided that the wood from the upper branches would go to one party, and the wood from the lower branches to the other (a decision that was noteworthy for showing no regard for law of the state; *guofa* 國法). In the third dispute, a widow and son disagreed as to the disposition of family lands, with the allegedly spendthrift widow wishing to sell the land

1 See especially the discussion of local knowledge in Geertz 1983.

and the son refusing to grant his approval. The enraged widow first sued her son, but after losing her case in court went to the family and village heads, who arranged for the estranged widow and son to live separately (Huang 1996: 54–55, 61–63). This final case seems particularly noteworthy for its unhappy conclusion, as well as the fact that the widow chose the legal system over mediation as her avenue of first recourse.

Despite the prevalence of mediation, both state and society faced the constant threat of disputes degenerating into vigilante justice (referred to euphemistically in Chinese as *sixing* 私刑 or "private punishments"), namely extralegal and violent coercion that could also be used to maintain the status quo and/or reinforce existing power structures (Ingalls 1988: xv–xvi). In late imperial Fujian and Taiwan, for example, people accused of stealing who never had their cases heard by human magistrates could have their tendons cut, be hung by ropes and beaten, or be force-fed excrement, while accused rapists were often buried up to the neck and left to die. Such practices were commonly prescribed in lineage regulations, which further indicate the role of such punishments in supporting established hierarchies (Kataoka 1981 (1921): 61–68; Macgowan 1912: 167–168). Philip Kuhn's research on soul-stealing panics during the eighteenth century also cites numerous examples of wrongly accused sorcerers being brutally lynched by angry mobs before officials had a chance to try their cases (Kuhn 1991; see also ter Haar 1992: 173–195, 263–281; ter Haar 2006a: 99, 118–150; Wang and Wang 1997: 426–427).

The practice of private punishments persists to this day. In Taiwan, for example, people deemed guilty of having caused shame to others may be forced to publicly present gifts (including cigarettes or betel nuts) or red envelopes filled with money (*hongbao* 紅包) to members of their community, and can even be ordered to sponsor grand feasts or dramatic performances. Such punitive measures, generally referred to as "cleansing a family's reputation" (*xi menfeng* 洗門風), emphasize the need for the guilty party to suffer public humiliation. In traditional times, such measures were especially common in cases when a new bride was determined to have lost her virginity prior to marriage (Huang 1994, 1995). As recently as September 2007, considerable consternation and at times heated debate followed the decision by a local mediation committee in Baojhong (Baozhong 褒忠) Township, Yunlin 雲林 County to instruct an adulterer to kneel in a local market for four straight hours. Court officials complained that such a decision ran against Taiwan's established legal principles, but the chairman of the mediation committee, a former township chief, emphasized that while the courts might not agree with such a course of action, it had proven the sole means of satisfying all parties involved in the dispute.[2] This argument is clearly related

2 See the September 12, 2007 issue of the *United Daily News*, p. C2.

to the ideology of justice, particularly the idea that attaining the ideal of harmonious equilibrium outweighs the need for strict adherence to legal codes (see below).

Vigilante justice appears to be alive and well in China as well. A Google search using the characters *sixing* will reveal numerous news stories, including some of dubious veracity and others published by respected news organizations and accompanied by photographs of the victims. The most common cases involve various punishments against thieves, ranging from tooth pulling to beatings, sometimes even to death.[3] In one widely publicized case, the Shenzhen 深圳 police ordered 100 convicted prostitutes to parade the streets dressed in yellow with large name cards hanging from their necks,[4] a practice similar to that of dressing as a criminal (see Chapter 5) that also brings back memories of what could happen to people purged during various struggle campaigns, including the Cultural Revolution. As Barend ter Haar has observed, the presence of vigilante justice in Chinese society raises questions as to how local communities choose to define crime and punishment, as well as the very idea of justice (ter Haar 2006a: 97–99). However, more research will need to be undertaken in order for us to better understand the circumstances that prompted communities to resort to extralegal measures.

Formal legal procedures

Formal legal procedures are characterized by a standardized and well-organized system of judicial practices, as well as obligatory reviews of more serious cases (Karasawa 2007b: 102–103). The state also distinguished between different types of legal cases, although the extent to which they conform to the modern Western dichotomy of "civil" and "criminal" is the subject of considerable debate (see for example Bourgon 2002, 2004). Six or nine days of each month were devoted to hearing what we might call "civil" cases (referred to as *minshi* 民事 in Qing archival sources), particularly family, marital, and land disputes, while criminal cases (*xingshi* 刑事) could be tried at any time. District magistrates heard cases and issued verdicts, while also conducting investigations and inquests, combining the roles of detective, prosecutor, judge, and coroner (Ch'ü 1962: 116–127; Hegel 2007a: 15–17). There was also a third type of legal case that concerned administrative matters (*xingzheng* 行政), the existence of which can be explained by the

3 One example may be found at http://www.gx.xinhuanet.com/newscenter/2007–07/19/content_10625005.htm.

4 See http://www.eastlaw.net/chinanews/legal/shenzhen-saohuang.htm. Additional information on such practices may be found at http://news.sina.com.cn/z/shizhongts/index.shtml.

fact that in traditional China there was no division between judicial and administrative powers, meaning that local magistrates accepted petitions for administrative assistance as well as lawsuits. Mark Allee's study of the Dan-Xin Archives (Dan-Xin dang'an 淡新檔案) from nineteenth-century northern Taiwan shows that of a total of 1,161 cases nearly half (574 or 49.4 percent) dealt with administrative matters; of the remaining 587, 365 (62.2 percent) were criminal and 222 (37.8 percent) civil (Allee 1994a: 10–13; see also Buxbaum 1971).

The act of filing a lawsuit generally involved the following three-stage process, beginning with the filing of a formal plaint written using standardized language (for more on such plaints, as well as their overlap with ritual indictments, see Chapter 4). The composition of these texts required the mastery of specialized knowledge and rhetorical skills, which were the intellectual property of specialists like litigation masters (*songshi* 訟師) and scribes (*daishu* 代書, *bisheng* 筆生). Once he had received the plaint, the magistrate could delegate the matter to a member of the local elite for further mediation, request more documentation, or search for more evidence. If the case continued, the parties were eventually summoned for the second stage of the lawsuit, the court inquiry (*chuanxun* 傳訊). These sessions, which were held in the magistrate's yamen, allowed the parties in a dispute to confront each other in the magistrate's presence. They could file counterplaints, present additional information, or call witnesses. Mediation efforts were not abandoned during this stage, with some disputes being resolved before matters progressed any further. The third and final stage was the formal court case, following which the magistrate could make a decision or instruct the parties to submit to further mediation (Huang 1996: 111–124, 163–164; Ocko 2007: 268–276). Even if one lost one's case in court, there was always the chance that the verdict might be overturned on appeal (Buoye 2007), although this often proved too late for innocent subjects who died in prison (Kuhn 1991).

One fascinating aspect of the three-stage process described above is that the act of filing a plaint or the resultant threat of a court session could induce disputants to reach a settlement and intensify community and kin efforts to get involved in the mediation process, although at times mediation did not succeed until the later stages of a lawsuit. This can be seen in the account of a land boundary dispute between the Jin-Liu-He 金六和 land development partnership (*gonghao* 公號) and four villages located near Xinpu 新埔 (today's Xinzhu County in northern Taiwan), which raged from the fall of 1887 to the summer of 1888. Both sides accused each other of crop destruction, which resulted in a flurry of prompting petitions (*cuicheng* 催呈; discussed further in Chapter 4). The case went to court, but the magistrate proved unable to take any decisive action, so the mutual destruction of property continued and gradually escalated to beatings and a murder, with suspects being jailed and even dying in prison. The dispute was not resolved until mediation efforts by members of the Xinzhu City gentry (including the prestigious Zheng 鄭 and Lin 林 families), as well as a Plains Aborigine government student (*fan shengyuan* 番生員) surnamed Liao 廖, all of which points to what Mark Allee describes as the "importance of the court in prompting, maintaining, and validating a mediation process that technically took place outside the court system" (Allee 1994b: 102–117). The above account also confirms what Jiang Yonglin and Wu Yanhong point out in their recent study of Chinese legal reasoning, namely that the magistrate often played a role somewhat similar to that of a mediator in terms of attempting to achieve harmony and fairness by balancing both legal rules and sentiment (*qing-fa liangpan* 情法兩判) (Jiang and Wu 2007: 47, 51–52).[5] This in turn suggests the artificial nature of the distinction between the "mediatory" and "adjudicatory" activities of magistrates, which has been proposed by scholars like Shiga Shūzō (Shiga 1984).

Three other points need to be made about traditional Chinese legal procedures. The first involves the importance of judicial torture, for, as has long been observed, "An important aspect of Chinese justice is that there can't be conviction without confession (hence torture)" (Brook, Bourgon, and Blue 2007: 41–50; see also Conner 2000). The use of judicial torture, while often condemned for being excessive, was nonetheless considered a legitimate means of obtaining admissions of guilt, especially in criminal matters (Allee 1994a: 226–229; Ch'ü 1962: 125). At the same time, however, there were numerous instances of corrupt magistrates using torture to pursue illicit profits or personal vendettas (Macauley 1994: 97–103), and the fear of venal and brutal magistrates was a common theme in many works of literature (St. André 2007: 198–204; Xu 1995). The second point, which is related to the first, is that witnesses were not required to swear oaths, as rigorous interrogation, torture, or the threat thereof were deemed sufficient for convincing people to tell the truth (this problem will be discussed in greater detail in Chapter 3). Finally, many people were reasonably familiar with the law and judicial procedures, including as portrayed in works of fiction (Hegel 2007a: 10–15; see also Carlitz 2007). This was especially the case for literati, many of whom were current or former officials, who used fictional writings to describe, caricature, or criticize the legal system that they knew better than most others.[6]

5 See also Charlotte Furth's discussion of morality in judicial thought, as well as the need to balance competing claims of "reason/principle" (*li* 理), "sentiment" (*qing* 情), and "law" (*fa* 法) (Furth 2007: 12).

6 Ghost stories that are also critical of actual judicial practice may be found in *Xu Zibuyu*, 2.19–20; *Yuewei caotang biji*, 15.3584; *Zibuyu*, 20.382; see also Yuan 1995.

Judicial Rituals

Judicial rituals such as making oaths and filing underworld indictments also served as integral components of dispute resolution processes. I present data on actual performances of these rites in Chapters 3 and 4. Here, I would like to emphasize that, while the Chinese state never chose to incorporate judicial rituals into its formal legal procedures, it did encourage their performance at the communal level as a means of ensuring the maintenance of social order (Wang and Wang 1997: 496–497; see also Huang 2005). In one well-known example, Ming Taizu incorporated oaths into the local taxation and surveillance (*lijia* 里甲) system. According to official regulations preserved in the *DaMing huidian* 大明會典, the people of each village (*li* 里) were required to sacrifice to the gods of the soil (*sheji* 社稷) twice a year, during the spring and autumn. After the ritual, a member of the community recited an oath committing all men of the village to preserve local harmony, protect the weak, and punish trouble-makers (Overmyer 1989–1990: 207; Taylor 1990: 145–146; Zheng 1997: 183). Judicial oaths were also an integral component of late imperial community compact (*xiangyue* 鄉約) dispute resolution, with elites making oaths to judge the case fairly or suffer disasters inflicted on themselves and their families (*chushi bugong, shenjia bei huo* 處事不公、身家被禍) (*Lügong shizhenglu*, *juan* 5; *Taiquan xiangli*, *juan* 5). Plaintiffs, defendants, and even those individuals charged with recording the details of each case, had to make similar oaths.[7] Michael Szonyi's research on late imperial Fuzhou reveals that villagers occasionally staged trials in the presence of the Earth God or other deities (particularly chthonic ones), and that members of the elite who managed these temples (*dongshi* 董事) often served as judges (Szonyi 2000: 115).[8] Szonyi also cites a highly important story preserved in a late-Qing gazetteer from Houguan 侯官 County (near Fuzhou 福州, which clearly indicates how elites employed judicial rituals in dispute resolution. This account states that a member of the local elite once urged the mother of an unfilial son not to go to the officials. Instead, he ordered local villagers to seize the lad and take him to the temple of the local tutelary deity (*shegong miao* 社公廟), where in the presence of the god he interrogated both mother and son and attempted to facilitate their reconciliation (Szonyi 2002: 190; *Houguan xian xiangtu zhi* (1906), 1:29b–30a). In addition, Zheng Zhenman's essay on law and local society in Putian 莆田 (northern Fujian) contains numerous examples of judicial rituals performed at the local temple of the Eastern Peak during the late nineteenth and early twentieth centuries, including temple managers requiring disputants to make oaths (*duzhou fashi* 賭咒發誓) (Zheng 1997: 178–183). In all these

7 I am very grateful to Chu Hung-lam 朱鴻林 for helping me locate relevant data.

8 For similar data from north China, see Duara 1988: 138.

cases, performing a judicial ritual not only contributed to the maintenance of local order, but also helped enhance the legitimacy of the elites who were in charge of such events.

However, as has been noted in the above discussion of mediation, while many elites tended to adhere to state-approved practices (including rituals), they could also use such actions to advance their own interests. The division of labor between officials and elites in attempting to shape judicial rituals performed at the local level was far from clear, particularly since representatives of these two groups had very different views of communal religious traditions.[9] This is not to deny that in some cases elites and the state could cooperate in promoting specific judicial rites, but elite support could be also motivated by a wide range of pragmatic local factors. When it came to judicial rituals, elites performed such rites not only to support the social order but also to further their own interests, including in ways that could challenge state authority. Tanaka Issei's work on Qing local dramas preserves a 1766 account from the *Hunan shengli cheng'an* 湖南省例成案 complaining that those who won court cases would stage dramatic performances out of gratitude, while those who lost filed plaints to the gods written on banners, signboards, or yellow paper, in which they attempted to assert their own legitimacy while also accusing local officials of wrongdoing (Tanaka 1968, Volume 2, p. 49).[10] While this text does not specifically mention elites, it seems reasonable to assume that individuals with sufficient means to sponsor dramatic performances or perform numerous rituals possessed some degree of status or influence in local society.

It was not just elites who performed judicial rituals, however. Such rites could play an important role in legitimizing the state, its representatives, and the legal system as a whole. There are numerous sources that describe late imperial officials combining the judicial practices of the official and religious realms, with some performing judicial rituals and others holding formal trials in temples to judicial deities.[11] For example, during the Yuan dynasty, the high official Tian Zi 田滋 (*fl.* 1290s) worshipped the City God in order to help clear a lower official of false corruption charges (*Yuanshi*, 191.4359), while late Ming officials attempting to suppress a major uprising in Shengze 盛澤, Shuanglin 雙林, and Wu 吳 counties of Jiangsu province chose to hold trials and execute rebels at the City God temple (*Chongzhen jiwenlu*, pp. 76–86). By the Qing dynasty, renowned magistrates such as Wang Huizu

9 For more on these issues, see Duara 1988: 138–146; Hymes 2002; Pomeranz 1997; Szonyi 1997; Watson 1985: 311–315; Wong, Huters, and Yu 1997: 14, 22.

10 Many thanks to Vincent Goossaert for bringing this important account to my attention.

11 For an overview of this phenomenon, see Ch'en Teng-wu 2005; Kleeman 2005; Waley-Cohen 1993. Other scholars have also noted the fact that some officials relied on judicial rituals, but have failed to study this topic in depth; see for example Ch'ü 1961: 212–213; Hao 1997: 139–140; Ling 2003: 22–23, 127–129, 189–193; Zheng and Wang 1994: 175.

汪會祖 (1730–1807), Lan Dingyuan 藍鼎元 (1680–1733) and Huang Liuhong 黃六鴻 (1633–1693) not only made oaths to the City God in order to augment their legitimacy but also relied on this deity's assistance to crack tough cases, and even chose to hold trials in City God temples in order to determine the truth.[12] One account in the 1871 edition of the Shanghai county gazetteer describes how one local official investigating a murder case conducted an exhaustive criminal investigation, which included interviewing suspects and witnesses and examining wounds on the victim's corpse.[13] However, when he proved unable to crack the case, he decided to interrogate the prime suspect in front of the City God. This tactic proved effective, as the man broke down and confessed (*Shanghai xianzhi, juan* 32).

One striking eighteenth-century example of official use of divine assistance recounts the case of an Imperial Academy student (*jiansheng* 監生) from Putian named Wang 王 who forged a land contract in order to acquire an old woman's property and bribed the county magistrate to accept the text as authentic. When the old woman went to the student's home to protest, he had her killed and then sent for her son to retrieve the corpse. He then tied up the son, dragged him to the county yamen, and accused him of committing the murder. Wang convinced some of his friends to bear false witness, and as the young man could not stand up to torture he confessed to the murder, the magistrate recommending death by slicing. However, the Governor-General (*zongdu* 總督) was not convinced, and ordered the prefects of Fuzhou and Quanzhou 泉州 to try the case in the provincial City God temple.[14] The two prefects also recommended the death penalty, whereupon the son cried out: "City God, City God, our family has been wronged and you have completely failed to be efficacious! How do you still have the face to accept people's offerings!" When they prepared to lead the son away, two statues of the City God's lictors suddenly leaned forward and barred the way with their staffs. The two terrified prefects hastily retried the case, acquitted the son, and found Wang guilty of murder (*Zibuyu*, 9.168–169; see also Hao 1997: 148–149).[15]

Additional information may be found in a collection of 300 late Ming legal judgments (*pandu* 判牘) entitled *Hu-Xiang yan lue* 湖湘讞略. The author of this text, Qian Chun 錢春, who served as a censorial official from 1612 to 1614 in the Huguang 湖廣 region (which included Hubei and Hunan), did not hesitate to state his conviction that gods and ghosts could

12 The case Huang Liuhong invoked the City God to help solve was none other than the "Death of Woman Wang" made famous in Jonathan Spence's book of that name; see *Fu-hui ch'üan-shu* 福惠全書, pp. 28, 343–351, esp. p. 347; Spence 1978.

13 For more on forensic knowledge during the Qing, see Will 2007.

14 Why the prefect of Quanzhou became involved in a case from Fuzhou is unclear.

15 For a story of how an official in Amoy resolved a difficult inheritance case by staging a trial at the City God temple, see Macgowan 1912: 140–142.

become involved in legal cases, apparently accepting as a matter of course the integral role of religion in administering earthly justice (Chien 2001). In another example of such sentiments, the Qing-dynasty *biji* 筆記 text *Xu Zibuyu* by Yuan Mei 袁枚 (1716–1797) contains the story of a shop assistant who, while offering incense in a temple to the deity Marshal Wen (Wen Yuanshuai 溫元帥; Wen Qiong 溫瓊),[16] screamed that he was being beaten and then confessed to having stolen money from his master. The Renhe 仁和 County magistrate who witnessed these events is reported to have said: "This is the law of the netherworld (*mingfa* 冥法), not official law (*guanfa* 官法). Wait until he calms down and then take him to the yamen."[17] Another story, this time from Yuan Mei's *Zibuyu*, describes an official trusting in dreams sent by judicial deities to help fulfill his legal duties (*Zibuyu*, 12.233), while yet another in Ji Yun 紀昀 (1724–1805)'s *Yuewei caotang biji* reveals that some officials would take the initiative to pray for a dream from the City God when dealing with complicated cases (*Yuewei caotang biji*, 4.3252).

The overlap between religion and the formal judicial system was so profound that it helped shape popular ideas of the relationship between officials and judicial deities. Numerous late imperial *biji* contain stories of officials interacting with the City God, one of the most striking (contained in the late Qing *Zhiwen lu* 咫文錄; 1843 preface) being entitled "The Prefects of the Underworld and Earthly (Bureaucracies)" (Yinyang taishou 陰陽太守). According to this account, a new prefect met the City God from his jurisdiction while traveling there by boat, and relied on the god's help in solving a number of difficult crimes.[18] The *Gengsi bian* by Lu Can 陸粲 (1494–1551) describes an official from Suzhou 蘇州 who served as prefect for Gunzhou 袞州 (Shandong). One night after taking up his post he went to worship in the local temple to the Emperor of the Eastern Peak. There he saw five deities from the temple's underworld bureaucracy, who came out to welcome him (*Gengsi bian*, 1.7). A third story, preserved in the *Zibuyu*, tells of an official who judged human cases by day and underworld cases by night, taking an iron pill (*tiewan* 鐵丸) before each chthonic session in order to fortify his heart. After witnessing the numerous torments of the underworld, he exhorted his subjects to observe good conduct, and especially proscriptions against the consumption of bovines (the so-called "beef taboo" or *niujie* 牛戒) (*Zibuyu*, 16.311–312).[19] Even literati who hoped to become

16 While Marshal Wen was renowned as a plague-quelling deity, he also served in the chthonic bureaucracy headed by the Emperor of the Eastern Peak. For more on his cult, see Katz 1995a.

17 *Xu Zibuyu*, 4.59–60. Other accounts that portray the parallels between the earthly and underworld bureaucracies include *Zibuyu*, 3.47–48, 6.109–110, 9.176–177; *Xu Zibuyu*, 1.5–6.

18 See *Qingdai biji xiaoshuo leibian: Anyu juan*, pp. 216–220. Similar stories may be found in *ibid.*, pp. 105–109, 192–196, 270–272, 290–292.

19 For more on the beef taboo, see Goossaert 2005.

officials could be called upon to serve in the underworld's legal bureaucracy. One story from the late Qing pictorial *Dianshizhai huabao* describes a student from a Hangzhou 杭州 prefectural or county school (*xiangxu* 庠序) working as an underworld judge. The illustration's depiction of the torments the dead would suffer includes a starvation cage (*julong* 踞籠; *dianlong* 踮籠) similar to that used in actual judicial practice, with the added feature of hot coals beneath it. The latter two torments, roasting and tongue-pulling, would have been unique to the underworld (see Figure 1). This further confirms the homology between images of the underworld and real world institutions in Chinese legal culture, a topic also discussed in Chapter 1.

The ideology of justice also had a profound impact on the bureaucratic metaphor. It is a well-known fact that the temples of many underworld deities were built to the same specifications as a magistrate's yamen, including furniture, brushes, and ink slabs (Guo 2003: 42–46). However, such temples featured a bureaucratic system that was far more complex than the worldly one, including the Office of Speedy Retribution (Subao si 速報司), one of 72 (or sometimes 76) departments run by the chthonic bureaucracy (Chen 1999; Goodrich 1964: 242–243; Goodrich 1981: 27). These deities not only judged the dead, but also had the power to become involved in

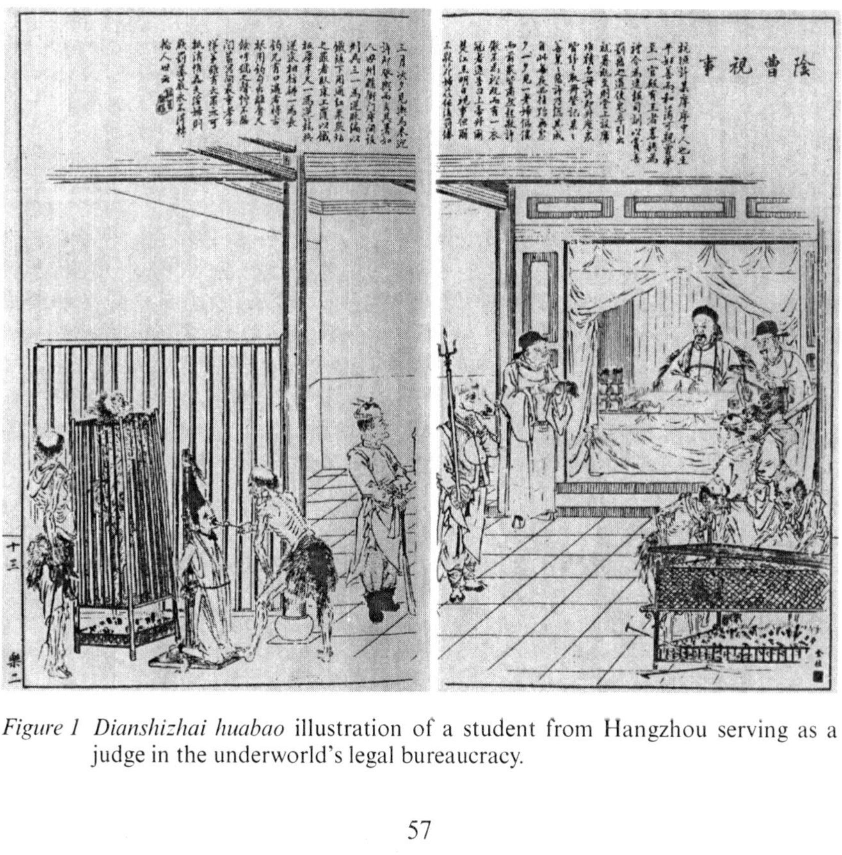

Figure 1 *Dianshizhai huabao* illustration of a student from Hangzhou serving as a judge in the underworld's legal bureaucracy.

worldly affairs, including helping to identify the guilty party in a dispute and ensuring the people did not file false plaints (Goodrich 1964: 135–138, 224), functions still performed by underworld deities in Taiwan today (see Chapters 7 and 8). The underworld judicial system could also punish corrupt earthly officials. Thus, it is probably no coincidence that many temples to the Emperor of the Eastern Peak contain statues of a deity known as the Censor (Ducha si 督察司), who is tasked with keeping a close eye on officials as they administer earthly justice (*ibid.*: 138–139). One story in the early nineteenth-century *biji* collection *Lüyuan conghua* describes the City God punishing officials indicted by members of the Miao 苗 ethnic group whom they had wrongfully put to death (*Lüyuan conghua*, 22.594–595; see also Sutton 2003a).[20]

Other Qing period writers recorded instances of spirits who would appear in a magistrate's court of their own volition in order to correct miscarriages of justice. One moving story in the eighteenth-century *xiaoshuo* 小說 collection *Liaozhai zhiyi* tells of a young man named Zhu 朱 from Yanggu 陽穀 County (Shandong) who confessed to a murder that he had not committed in order to save the woman he loved. On the day of Zhu's execution, a man who appeared possessed stormed into the yamen, glared at the magistrate, and scolded him for being a dull-witted fool. The magistrate ordered his runners to arrest the man, but he easily resisted their efforts. Terrified, the magistrate prepared to flee, whereupon the man bellowed: "I am General Zhou (Zhou Cang 周倉), who serves under the Emperor Guan (Guandi 關帝). If you, foolish official (*hunguan* 昏官), dare move, you will be punished immediately!" He then went on to reveal that the actual murderer was named Gong Biao 宮標, following which he collapsed. Upon awakening and returning to normal, the man stated that he was none other than Gong Biao. Zhu was acquitted, Gong punished, and the official dismissed and forced to pay restitution (*Liaozhai zhiyi*, 7.975–979). In considering the implications of this account, one must not forget the existence of tales about incompetent or corrupt officials being punished by the underworld bureaucracy (see above and Chapter 1). This is not to deny that such accounts had entertainment and didactic value, but one might also consider the possibility that literati composed so many stories about their peers because they believed in the underworld bureaucracy and feared retribution for errors performed on the job.

Other accounts focus on the grim fate awaiting those elites who abuse the earthly legal system, including one about the son of a *jinshi* 進士 from Pinghu 平湖 (Zhejiang) who in 1691 encouraged his neighbors to sue each other over an alleged case of adultery, thereby taking advantage of his father's gentry

20 Examples of the judicial role of the deity Wenchang 文昌 may be found in Kleeman 1994: 164–166, 173–175.

status to make a handsome profit by playing the role of mediator. On the first day of the seventh lunar month (the date when ghosts are released from the underworld), the son went to offer up incense at the local City God temple. While he was worshipping the god, he suddenly keeled over, and it seemed to onlookers that he was suffering a beating. He then started spitting blood, and promptly proceeded to confess his misdeeds, but it was too late; he died a few days later (*Xinzheng lu*, 22a–22b). There are also a number of stories describing unscrupulous litigation masters getting their just deserts as a result of divine retribution or graphically portraying the torments they could expect to suffer in the underworld,[21] while the Qing novel *Qilu deng* 歧路燈 by Li Lüyuan 李綠園 (1707–1790) contains the story of a litigation master making an oath never to get involved in legal cases in the future.[22]

Concluding remarks

Taken as a whole, the evidence presented above indicates that one fundamental aspect of Chinese legal culture is the belief that the judicial mechanisms of this world can interact and even overlap with those of the underworld. While judicial rituals have not found a place in the state-sponsored legal system, with its standardized procedures and reviews, both forms of practice have combined with mediation to help mold the formation of the judicial continuum, and feature significant overlap in terms of rhetoric and legitimation processes. Moreover, despite the fact that most legal cases are usually adjudicated on the basis of testimony and physical evidence, oaths and other judicial rituals have consistently been considered an appropriate means of resolving disputes and attaining justice. The reverberation of these different forms of judicial practice has been so extensive that police and court officials have long been represented as parallel to the City God and other chthonic deities, and have often sought divine assistance when the need arises. This acceptance of the overlap of religious and legal authority worked both ways, with late imperial patrons recognizing the importance of legal decisions by the state in settling disputes over temple properties (Brook 1993: 170, 174; Goossaert 2001: 13–15; Katz 1999b: 111–116). During the Republican era, however, some elites and specialists chose to go to court and file lawsuits that challenged state policies towards religion (Nedostup forthcoming).

The extent to which the judicial continuum will continue to shape legal practice in Chinese communities today remains to be seen. As noted in the Introduction, many people in China currently bypass the courts in favor of

21 See for example the accounts in the *Qingdai biji xiaoshuo leibian: Anyu juan*, pp. 53–58, 151–152.

22 For more on this work, see Epstein 2007: 28; Youd 2007: 227–230.

private mediation based on personal connections and/or material inducements. Data to be presented below will show that judicial rituals have survived the trials of China's modernization, but their role in dispute resolution seems less prominent than in the past, particularly in urban areas. In contrast, Taiwanese legal culture continues to encompass all three aspects of the judicial continuum, despite the fact that Taiwan has developed into a modern high-tech society. This suggests that in the case of China one phenomenon that merits further observation is the state's attitude towards "customary law" (*xiguan fa* 習慣法), which was respected under KMT and early PRC rule but suffered reversals during the Cultural Revolution (Tay 1997: 60–65; see also Wang and Wang 1997: 415–607). The extent to which informal judicial practices (including rituals) are able to regain legitimacy in the eyes of both the people and the state may well help determine the future course of China's legal culture.

3

OATHS AND CHICKEN-BEHEADING RITUALS

Oath-making rituals have been an integral part of judicial practice worldwide, persisting in many cultures up to the present day. Oaths in ancient Greece were similar to those being performed in China during the same era in featuring the summoning of chthonic deities as witnesses and judges, as well as the recitation of a curse stating one's willingness to suffer the same fate as the victim if one committed perjury (Burkert 1985: 199–203, 221–222; Harrison 1991 (1903): 64–67; Nilsson 1925: 89; Zaidman and Pantel 1992 (1989): 94).[1] The rise of Christianity did nothing to diminish the importance of these rites, and in some cases they were even incorporated into Christian liturgy, being held during masses, featuring the use of crosses or relics, and including the now standard phrase "so help me God". The swearing in of witnesses remains standard court procedure, and our own term for jurors derives from the practice of allowing defendants to choose their own "con-jurors"/compurgators (Kadri 2006: 37, 71–72; Lea 1974 (1866): 26–32, 58–59).

One main reason underlying the prevalence of oath-making rites throughout the world is their role in enhancing the legitimacy of those men and women who perform them. Declaring one's innocence, especially in the presence of incriminating circumstantial evidence or widespread disbelief, is a challenge in any society. Oaths serve as speech acts designed to legitimize one's claims, and, if successful, can help to create or reinforce facts in ways that are considered culturally sanctioned (Rosen 1989: 20–25, 32–36; see also Ja'affar 2007). Accordingly, oaths can be a vital means of establishing innocence or simply confirming promises, particularly when they are made at a sacred site, in the presence of a deity, or accompanied by the holding of a sacred object (Westermarck 1926: 492–496, 515–517). Oaths also possess

1 In Euripedes' (ca. 480 BCE–406 BCE), *Electra*, an old man describes one such offering that had just been made at the tomb of Agamemnon's son Orestes: "And there I saw on the burning-altar a black-fleeced sheep, throat cut and blood still warm in its dark stream" (*Electra*, p. 29, lines 513–514).

tactical value, especially in terms of putting pressure on recalcitrant suspects. As one Ohio Supreme Court justice observed in his remarks on the 1877 case *Clinton v. State*, "The purpose of the oath is not to call the attention of God to the witness, but attention of the witness to God; not to call upon [the Almighty] to punish the false-swearer, but on the witness to remember that God will surely do so." (Rosen 1989: 33).[2] In disputes that occur outside the courtroom, willingness to make an oath is viewed as a sign of confidence in the legitimacy of one's cause, while those who back out at the last minute are often viewed as guilty and forced to pay restitution (Davies and Fouracre 1986: 236; Kadri 2006: 19–21; Kratz 1989: 639, 643–644; Westermarck 1926: 505–506, 509–510). While some people still prove willing to perjure themselves by crossing their fingers, holding their penises, or other similar tricks (Westermarck 1926: 508), the main belief undergirding oath-making rituals is that the gods will punish the guilty party, particularly if he/she has violated communal norms (Bohannan 1989: 47).

Oaths are also noteworthy for their frequent inclusion of contingent curses in which the oath-maker voices a self-imprecation that includes future retribution to befall if perjury is committed. Such speech acts appear to be an interesting generic sub-category of cursing, with potentially provocative contrasts to other forms. For example, contingent curses differ from categorical ones ("Damn you!", "Drop dead!", etc.) in that they are frequently used to wish misfortune on oneself, not one's opponent, while also avoiding the goal of immediate harm. Contingent curses can also be attached to a wide range of circumstances, only some of which need be in the control of the person who will be the recipient of the curse. Finally, it appears that people are not always literalistic about cursing: the retribution suffered by the guilty party does not necessarily have to match the contents of the curse, and perjurers who in theory are supposed to die only suffer illness (especially insanity) or other forms of misfortune.

Perhaps most importantly, however, many of the rites to be described in this chapter (as well as some of the indictment rituals in Chapter 4) are clearly marked by a window of opportunity for the parties embroiled in a dispute. While the gods invoked during such rites are not necessarily obliged to pass and execute their grim judgments immediately following the ritual's conclusion, people scrutinize what happens to the participants in the hours and days thereafter. In some instances people suffer divine retribution shortly after a rite has been performed, but in others the results remain unclear. As a result, the performance of a judicial ritual accompanied by a contingent curse, and especially the period of waiting for divine judgment that follows, may allow for tempers to cool and the entire matter to be brought to a peaceful resolution before a dispute degenerates into vigilante

2 The original quotation may be found in *Ohio State Reports*, vol. 33 (1877), p. 33.

justice (Bohannan 1989: 36, 41–42, 44, 47; Kratz 1989: 639–640; Westermarck 1926: 479–492, 497, 502).[3]

Throughout the history of Chinese legal culture, oath-making rituals have consistently played a vital role in legitimation processes, including the formation of alliances, the declaration of commitment, and the proclamation of innocence. This chapter examines all of these oaths, but places greatest emphasis on the third type and its links to dispute resolution. I also consider the importance of chicken-beheading rituals performed to accompany oaths, and explore the extent to which oaths resemble ordeals.

Types of Chinese oath-making rituals

Type 1: Allegiance/loyalty

The oldest forms of Chinese oath-making appear to have been oaths of allegiance, specifically the blood covenants of ancient times. Such rites, which are discussed in detail by Mark Edward Lewis in his seminal work *Sanctioned Violence in Early China*, could be performed in a number of circumstances, including forming alliances, resolving conflicts, or determining guilt, with the gods serving not only as witnesses to these rituals, but also as potential punitive agents should the participants fail to keep their word (Lewis 1990; see also Liu 1998; ter Haar 1998: 163, 178, 181). The *Zuozhuan* 左傳 contains numerous examples of blood covenants performed before battles during which the gods or even ancestors were summoned to act as both witnesses and judges with the power to punish wrongdoers. The participants in such rites first purified themselves through fasting. After the composition of a written agreement (*zaishu* 載書), the killing of an animal victim (referred to as *sheng* 牲) took place at an altar, following which its left ear was placed in one vessel and its blood in another. Blood was then sprinkled on the altar as a means of summoning the gods or ancestors, following which the text of the covenant was read. Each of the participants in the covenant then drank some of the victim's blood, or in other cases smeared the blood on his lips (*shaxue* 歃血). One copy of the covenant was buried in a pit (*keng* 坑) containing the corpse of the animal victim, while the parties to the ritual also ratified their alliance (*limeng* 涖盟). Another copy of the covenant was stored in an archive (*mengfu* 盟府) (Dobson 1968: 271–272). Dobson also cites the use of human blood, including in oaths between lovers to take care of illegitimate children (*ibid.*: 272–273, 278). As we will see below, human blood could also be used in oaths that accompanied banner worship rituals.

3 I am deeply grateful to David K. Jordan for his guidance in formulating the above analysis.

Blood covenants invariably included a contingent curse on those who violated their terms in the form of a "malediction" (*zu* 詛). The texts of these maledictions do not seem all that different from the imprecations performed during the chicken-beheading rituals to be described below. One passage in the *Zuozhuan* describing a covenant rite performed in 562 BCE contains the following malediction:

> If anyone violates these commands, may the guardians of reverence and covenants, the spirits of the great mountains and rivers, the collected heavenly spirits and spirits who receive sacrifice, the former kings and lords, and the ancestors of the seven surnames and twelve states destroy him so that his people desert him, he loses rank and clan, and his state and family are extinguished.
>
> (Lewis 1990: 47–48)

According to the text of an even earlier (631 BCE) curse,

> "Should anyone abrogate this agreement, may the gods and spirits strike him dead, bring about the downfall of his peoples so that (his heirs) might not enjoy the government of the state. Down to the fourth generation, may none, old or young, survive"
>
> (Dobson 1968: 274).

People continued to perform blood covenants in medieval China, including some women warriors of the Tang dynasty who did so before launching an attack on a rebel camp (*Xin Tangshu*, 205.5826). A waterway in today's Yunnan province was even named Gambling on an Oath River (Duzhou He 賭咒河) due to the fact that it had been the site of one such rite performed by two non-Han ethnic groups (*Quan Tangwen*, 237.2392–2393).[4] During the late imperial era, members of militias and other self-defense organizations also performed blood covenants as oaths of allegiance. In one example from fifteenth-century Foshan 佛山 (Guangdong), a force of local braves formed to ward off the depredations of pirates was divided into 25 *pu* 鋪 units, each of which made a blood covenant by sacrificing an animal victim before the martial deity Zhenwu 真武 and smearing its blood (Faure 1990; ter Haar 1995: 31).[5] Niida Noboru's work on Chinese legal history contains "covenants of prohibition" (*jinyue* 禁約) prepared by local citizens who banded together to prevent the misuse of their lands. Such texts stipulate that all participants in the covenant had to smear their lips with the blood of a slaughtered pig. The gods were called upon as witnesses to the rites, and those mortals who violated the terms of the covenant were to be

4 For more on non-Han peoples performing blood covenants while forming mutual aid and self-defense alliances, see Zhang 2000: 100–121, 396–513; see also Yang 1989.

5 Detailed information on *pu* 鋪 and their importance in state and local versions of the *pujing* 鋪境 defense system may be found in Wang 1995.

Figure 2 *Shibaokan wushen quannian huabao* illustration of elites from Taizhou (Zhejiang) performing a blood covenant.

punished by loss of life and family (Niida 1964: 684–687). One such rite was performed by Taizhou 台州 (Zhejiang) local elites in 1908 in the course of forming a local militia to resist the depredations of bandits and thieves (see Figure 2). Blood covenants even played a role in the history of the Chinese Communist Party. One report dated May 1944 from Tai 泰 County in northern Jiangsu describes how local cadres led members of the gentry as well as commoners to make oaths in front of deities such as the Bodhisattva Guanyin 觀音. Some of these rites were accompanied by the beheading of a cockerel (Chen 1986; see also Tai 1985: 41–45).[6]

6 I am extremely grateful to Professor Chen Yung-fa 陳永發 for taking the time to photocopy the relevant documents, which are stored in the Bureau of Investigation (Diaocha ju 調查局) in Taipei.

Blood covenants have consistently been a key practice of sworn brotherhoods, including gambling associations (Jordan 1985: 233–234, 247–252; Ye 2003: 203),[7] while those who took up arms against the state performed such rites to enhance a sense of group identity. For example, the *Hanshu* 漢書 describes how prisoners set free by Wang Mang 王莽 (45 BCE–24 CE) to fight on his side drank the blood of a pig in the course of undertaking one such covenant (*Hanshu*, 99.4190). Late imperial rebel leaders, including Liu Futong 劉福通 (1321–1365) and Deng Maoqi 鄧茂七 (d. 1449), made blood covenants that featured the sacrifice of white horses (representing Heaven) and black oxen (representing Earth) as a means of claiming imperial legitimacy (Aubin 1978; Goossaert 2005: 26, 110, 131, 272).[8] Another example of the links between blood covenants and resistance movements took place in Fuzhou in 1518. When a group of soldiers felt that they had been cheated out of a percentage of their wages, they filed a complaint with the local censor (*yushi* 御史), but to no avail. Outraged, they gathered in the City God temple and performed a blood covenant ritual (*jiudang meng Chenghuang* 鳩黨盟城隍), following which they launched a mutiny (Wu 2000: 28). Blood covenants were also an integral part of the initiation rituals of so-called "secret societies" usually referred to as Triads (Sanhe hui 三合會) or Heaven and Earth Associations (Tiandi hui 天地會), with recent research by David Ownby and Barend ter Haar clearly demonstrating that such rites could transform initiates into legitimate members (Ownby 1996: 38–42; ter Haar 1998: 152–164; see also Chin 1996). One interesting aspect of Triad oaths is that they tended to involve the deity Guandi, and did not invoke the City God (ter Haar 1998: 192). This may have been due to the latter deity's place in the imperial state cult, but it should also be noted that the City God could be worshipped by other groups that resisted the state, such as bondservants and the leaders of urban riots (ter Haar 1995: 31; Wu 2000: 33, 35).

Certain military rituals (*junli* 軍禮) also featured the use of blood covenants, including a variety of banner worship rites (usually referred to as *jiqi* 祭旗, *maya* 禡牙, or *jianya* 建牙) that have been performed by both Han and non-Han peoples since at least the Han dynasty.[9] One of the most detailed accounts of such rites may be found in the *Suishu* 隋書. According

7 Chapter 10 of the Qing novel *Flowers in the Mirror* (*Jinghua yuan* 鏡花緣) by Li Ruzhen 李汝珍 (ca. 1763–1820) describes a blood covenant made at the creation of a sisterhood.

8 The Ming dynasty founding emperor Zhu Yuanzhang is also said to have performed a blood covenant when he launched his rebellion against the Yuan dynasty.

9 The banners worshipped during these rituals were known as *junqi* 軍旗, *bingqi* 兵旗, or *qidao* 旗纛, and included the White Banner (*baiqi* 白旗), Numinous Banner (*lingqi* 靈旗), and Tooth Banner (*yaqi* 牙旗). In some cases, the blood of animal or human victims could also be smeared on drums (*xingu* 釁鼓). For an overview of these rites, see Katz 2006a; Wang 2002; Yang 2002.

to this text, the rites began with a blood covenant, with the blood and hair of the victim (usually an ox) being smeared on the army's drums. In some cases, the victim's ear would be cut off; in others, the participants (including, occasionally, the emperor himself) would daub their lips with its blood (*shaxue* 歃血) (*Suishu*, 8.159; see also Graff 2000: 99–101). Banner worship, blood covenants, and smearing animal blood continued into the Song-Yuan era, which was also a time when military banners known as *qidao* 旗纛 became the objects of imperial sacrifices (Skrynnikova 1992/1993). In 1368, the founding emperor of the Ming dynasty incorporated worship of the *qidao* banner into the state cult. Four types of rites could be performed, one of which featured offerings to a large number of banner gods and other martial deities, including Marshal Zhao (Zhao Yuanshuai 趙元帥; Zhao Gongming 趙公明) and his renowned subordinates, the Five Furies (Wuchang 五昌/五猖).[10] This rite was also noteworthy for including a sacrifice of six cockerels, whose blood was smeared on the banner (Guo 2003: 38–41). The Qing dynasty followed the Ming system of *qidao* banner worship, but also incorporated such rites into the Eight Banners (Baqi 八旗) system (*Qingchao wenxian tongkao*, 194.6584–6586). As late as the Republican era, soldiers performed banner-worshipping rituals (Liu 1993), while oaths and banners played roles in the military history of the Chinese Communist Party, particularly during the Long March of 1934–1935, as well as the civil war period of 1945–1949 (Zeng 1999).

While the victims of banner worship rituals were mainly oxen, horses, pigs, sheep, or cockerels, in some cases human beings could be offered to banners as well, often after trials to determine their guilt. Such practices were particularly common among rebel forces. In 1452, for example, a group of Yishan 宜山 County (Guangxi) villagers led by one Xie Bao 謝包 reported that rebels had attacked four villages and killed Xie's uncle. The same group of rebels later killed 36 villagers and took 69 male and female prisoners, including Xie's father. They then chose four victims – Xie's father was among them – and dragged them back to their camp, where they cut their flesh open to draw blood in order to sacrifice the blood to a banner (*cixue jiqi* 刺血祭旗). The rebels then composed a plaint protesting against alleged abuses by Xie's father and other members of the Yishan elite (whether the filing of this plaint included a judicial ritual is unclear). The next day, the rebels sacrificed three more victims to their banner, including a man named Xie Nuan 謝暖, who may have been related to the other people named Xie mentioned above (*Zhongsu ji*, *juan* 3).

10 While previous research on Zhao has focused on his popularity as a money god (von Glahn 2004), he was also worshipped as a spirit general (*shenjiang* 神將) who served in the underworld bureaucracy and could be summoned during blood covenant rituals (*Erke pai'an jingqi*, 10.189; Guo 2003: 26–27, 137–138; Nickerson 2008: 66; *Zhongguo minjian zhushen*, volume 2, pp. 727–733).

Rebel groups and secret societies in Taiwan also performed banner worship rituals involving both blood covenants and human sacrifices, including during the Zhu Yigui 朱一貴 (1690–1722), Lin Shuangwen 林爽文 (1756–1788), and Dai Chaochun 戴潮春 (*fl.* 1862–1865) uprisings.[11] The sacrifice of human victims to banners following indictments and trials was also a key ritual during one of the most dramatic acts of armed resistance in Taiwan during the colonial era, the Ta-pa-ni 噍吧哖 Incident (also known as the Xilai An 西來庵 Incident or the Yu Qingfang 余清芳 Incident) of 1915. According to one account, soon after Yu Qingfang (1879–1915) and his forces arrived in one village on August 3, 1915, they set up an encampment outside the home of a local landowner who recruited many others to join the rebellion. Yu's followers from other parts of southern Taiwan, as well as local villagers who had chosen to join their cause, then worshipped a banner and held a trial for two villagers suspected of being informants, with Yu serving as judge. The two were found guilty, whereupon Yu passed a "beheading official's red banner" (*zhanguan hongqi* 斬官紅旗) to a member of the landowner's family and ordered him to execute them. The two suspected informants were then summarily beheaded on the outskirts of the village (Ch'en 1979: 101, 104; Ch'eng 1978: 51–52; Katz 2005: 112–116). The above accounts illustrate that banner sacrifice performed by rebel groups could serve as a judicial ritual that involved a manifold combination of symbolism. On the one hand, such rites represented a means of legitimizing resistance, as well as visiting justice on people the community detested. At the same time, however, the brutal execution of victims, as well as the mutilation of their corpses, suggests that such rites contributed to a process of dehumanizing the victims of communal justice.[12]

Human sacrifice in the context of banner worship was not unique to rebel groups, however. State military forces also made offerings of human victims, including both criminals and captured enemies, to banners and drums. For example, officials suppressing a Guangxi uprising beheaded 100 rebels outside the gates of the army camp and offered the heads as a sacrifice to a banner and to the soldiers and officials who had died during the fighting.[13] Another important example comes from Qing-dynasty Taiwan, where armed forces involved in suppressing the Lin Shuangwen rebellion sacrificed seven rebels to a banner in 1787 (*Qinding pingTai jilue*, p. 152). The rebels had also performed human sacrifices to banners at the start of their uprising (see above), so in this case the state might have been imitating rebel practices, perhaps even as a form of revenge. However, the ways in which such rites

11 For more on such rites, see Lo 2002; Ownby 1996; *Taiwan tongzhi*, pp. 544–545, 595, 612–614, 799, 806, 814, 831–832; *Zhanghua xianzhi*, 11.377.

12 For more on these issues, see Cohen 1997; Weller 1994.

13 These events are described in detail in Sutton 2003a.

were performed differed significantly depending on whether the actors supported or opposed the state. Bandits and other rebel groups usually performed human sacrifices to banners *before* going into battle, and their victims tended to be officials or other people who represented state authority. Sacrificing such a person to a banner represented more than an act of revenge or outpouring of pent-up frustrations; it also demonstrated that those performing the ritual were formally challenging state authority and claiming legitimacy for their cause by assuming the judicial right of punishing those whom they considered to be wrongdoers. In contrast, representatives of the state generally sacrificed captured rebel leaders or other individuals deemed to have opposed state authority *after* a military campaign had been successfully completed. While a few sources state that such rites constituted a blood sacrifice to the fallen, in most cases they seem to have been designed to display the inevitability of the state's victory and the futility of resistance.

Despite the conventional wisdom that the Chinese state and elites gradually came to shun many forms of violence, some scholars have begun to emphasize the cultural significance of state-imposed violent punishments. Virgil Kit-yiu Ho's research on executions convincingly demonstrates that such acts of violence may be viewed as sacrificial dramas portraying archetypal meanings, particularly the inevitability of retribution for those who engaged in acts of non-sanctioned violence that challenged ethical norms or the established political order (Ho 2000). Indeed, it hardly seems a coincidence that state performances of human sacrifices to banners could resemble executions, with many prisoners being publicly beheaded in front of banners, following which their severed heads were displayed for all to gaze upon. As Donald Sutton has shown, the horrific execution of rebels, as well as the dismemberment of their corpses, not only dehumanized the victims of state violence, but also served to reestablish the emperor's absolute authority and even restore a sense of imperial dignity (Sutton 2003b; see also Brook, Bourgon, and Blue 2007). Barend ter Haar has also advanced the highly important observation that violent punishments like executions can be viewed as public exorcisms in their own right, with victims being stigmatized and redefined as demons (ter Haar 2006a: 91, 174–175, 332–340).[14]

Type 2: Commitment

Oath-making rituals were also important for Chinese men and women who faced momentous personal decisions that did not necessarily involve the

14 A fascinating variant of such stigmatization involved the exhumation and desecration of corpses of old women blamed for causing droughts (ter Haar 2006a: 282–295). Corpses could also be tried and desecrated in the West (Kadri 2006: 160, 174).

establishment of alliances or dispute resolution. For example, such rites played an integral role in the late imperial Chinese cult of chastity, particularly chaste widows (literally "virtuous women" or *jiefu* 節婦). While considerable research has been done on this topic,[15] few scholars have stressed the importance of the fact that many newly widowed woman would make oaths to preserve their chastity (*shi buzai shi/jia* 誓不再適/嫁; *shisi bujia* 誓死不嫁; *shoujie zishi* 守節自誓), which served to further legitimize their adherence to this ideal. The "Widows who Refuse to Remarry" (*guijie* 閨節) chapter of the "Beautiful Women of the Inner Chambers" (*guiyuan* 閨媛) section of the imperially-sponsored Qing encyclopedia *Qinding Gujin tushu jicheng* contains numerous examples of these practices, but fails to indicate whether such rites were performed in temples or featured judicial deities. This is also the case for accounts preserved in Qing-dynasty *biji*, including one from the *Huizui bian* by Yu Yue 俞樾 (1821–1906) that describes a young widow with two children from Xiangyang 襄陽 (Hebei) making an oath of chastity and never again setting foot outside her house. When this chaste widow died heroically defending herself from an attempted gang rape, the county magistrate in charge of the case attempted to protect her murderers by claiming that she was a lascivious woman who had committed suicide, despite evidence to the contrary provided by the coroner and witness testimony. Disgusted by his corruption, local elites gathered at the City God temple to make an oath that the widow in question had indeed been chaste. In the end, the corrupt official was impeached, and his replacement succeeded in apprehending the criminals, who were eventually executed.[16] A similar account describes the City God punishing a corrupt county magistrate from Jiangdu 江都 (Jiangsu) who accepted a bribe and subsequently refused to investigate the case of a chaste widow who died resisting attempted rape (*Yongxianzhai biji*, 2.20).

Oaths were also an integral part of acts of filial piety such as cutting off a piece of one's own flesh in order to heal a family member (*gegu liaoqin* 割骨療親). The "Surnames" (*shizu* 氏族) section of the *Qinding Gujin tushu jicheng* contains the story of a young man named Dou Gui 竇桂, who, distraught by his mother's illness, decided to fast, burn incense, and make an oath to Heaven that he was willing to sacrifice himself to achieve a cure. He then cut a piece of flesh from his arm to be used in the making of a healing potion.[17]

In addition, I have uncovered evidence that oaths were important legitimation rituals in Chinese Buddhism, and could be performed when

15 See for example Mann 1997: 32–31; Ko 1994: 185–187; Sommer 1996, 2000; Theiss 2004.

16 *Huizui bian, juan* 18. For more on Yu and his writings, see Huntington 2007.

17 See Chiu 1995 for a detailed study of these practices. See also Buoye 2007 for a fascinating discussion of how concerns for filial piety influenced late imperial legal reasoning.

undertaking ascetic practices.[18] For example, the Yuan-dynasty monk Pudu 普度 (1255–1330) composed a disapproving account of what he considered unwarranted conditional curses to keep Buddhist precepts, including ". . . when I break the precepts I will willingly accept that evil illnesses envelop my body and that I fall in the underworld forever" and ". . . [when I break the precepts,] my left eye shall start to bleed and pus shall come out of my right eye" (ter Haar 1998: 163–164). Oaths appear to have been highly prevalent among Buddhist women, including both lay believers and nuns, many of whom were inspired by the legend of Miaoshan 妙善 (Dudbridge 2004 (1978); Idema 2008). Such rites were also an essential part of the transmission of oral spells in some sectarian groups.[19]

Some late imperial officials made oaths to the City God in order to demonstrate their commitment to resolving crises, especially drought, often threatening to have themselves (and sometimes statues of the City God) put to the torch should the deity fail to provide the needed rainfall (*Beiyou lu, jiwen, xia*, 135.402).[20] As Donald Sutton noted in a recent article, emphasizing the official's relationship with the City God could serve as an important means of legitimation. Late imperial officials were expected to cope with natural disasters like drought by a variety of means, including ritual. When making oaths in the presence of the City God, they found the deity to be "a valuable ally or at least a useful foil" (Sutton 2004: 15). Moreover, by addressing the City God as a fellow official (see Chapter 2) they invoked a relationship that provided a degree of flexibility when coping with the pressures of dealing with calamities.

Other officials relied on oaths involving the City God as a means of eliciting the commitment of recalcitrant local elites, as well as asserting their authority. One Qing-dynasty account tells of an official named Jiang Zhonglie 江忠烈 (Jiang Zhongyuan 江忠源; 1818–1854), who, upon returning to his native province of Hunan during a famine, first exposed a local bully in a cage as a warning to others. He then invited members of the local gentry to the City God temple, and asked them to sign an oath invoking fearsome punishments for those who did not contribute to the relief effort. None of those present dared refuse. Another tactic he used to "persuade" local elites to contribute was to prepare two different placards (*bian* 匾), one reading "Ready and willing to be charitable and make donations" (*leshan haoshi* 樂善好施) and one reading "So-and-so is wealthy but lacking humanity" (*weifu buren moumou* 為富不仁某某), which were then hung over the appropriate doorways (*Shuichuang chunyi*, pp. 8–9).

18 See for example Benn 1998, 2007; Georgieva 2000; Kieschnick 1997; Tsai 1994.

19 Some information may be found in ter Haar 2006b.

20 The high official Zhang Ying 張英 (1637–1708) wrote a necrology for his son which stresses the importance of such rituals (*Wenduan ji, juan* 43).

Type 3: Innocence

People involved in disputes who wished to demonstrate their innocence could make an oath simply by facing the heavens (*duitian lishi* 對天立誓). In more serious cases, when a simple oral expression of innocence was unable to provide the sense of legitimacy necessary for resolving a dispute, the parties involved would make an oath in the presence of the City God or other judicial deities. The Chinese term for oath-making (*duzhou* 賭咒, literally "to gamble on an oath") clearly expresses the elements of risk and danger involved in submitting to the rigors of this ritual process. As noted in this book's Introduction, such oaths served as dramatic speech acts, especially in terms of the willingness of the party who spoke falsely to accept any punishment the gods might choose to inflict, including premature death or the death of his/her entire family.

Although the blood covenants of ancient China are best known for their links to alliances, scattered evidence also indicates that such rites could be performed to resolve legal disputes. One frequently cited passage from the *Rites of Zhou* (*Zhouli* 周禮) states that if legal disputes occurred the parties were to publicly perform covenant and malediction rituals (*mengzu* 盟詛) using victims supplied by their neighbors. The *Zuozhuan* also records an incident that took place in 712 BCE when the state of Zheng 鄭 attacked the state of Xu 許. Two officers quarreled over a chariot, with one taking advantage of the chaos of battle to kill his rival. Nobody actually witnessed the murder, but in order to find the guilty party the Zheng ruler ordered his troops to sacrifice pigs, dogs, and chickens in a malediction rite aimed at destroying the killer (Shirakawa 1983: 76–93; Zhao 1995: 23–24).[21] Liu Yongping has used Western Zhou bronze inscriptions to show that oaths could play an important role in resolving tensions in ancient China, especially cases involving the settling of land disputes. In one example Liu cites, 25 officials attended an oath ritual that accompanied a boundary agreement, swearing that those who broke the agreement would be liable for heavy fines (Liu 1998: 151–152).

Oaths of innocence were frequently performed in late imperial and modern times. One Ming-dynasty account describes what happened following the disappearance of a silver goblet at a lavish wedding banquet for a member of the local elite. This member suspected some servants of being guilty of theft, so in order to demonstrate their innocence they decided to jointly prepare a written oath, which they then signed and presented at a City God shrine (*xiangshuai lieming shuzhuang wei shi, tou zhi Chenghuang shenci* 相率列名書狀為誓, 投之城隍神祠). The member of the elite was later

21 The *Book of Odes* (*Shijing* 詩經) also contains a poem describing the use of these three animals in malediction rites.

reprimanded by the City God for having doubted his servants, who had disturbed his bureaucratic routines by submitting a needless oath (*Gengsi bian*, 4.43). Such practices persisted in supposed bastions of modernity like Shanghai, where the newspaper *Shenbao* contains accounts dated 1874 and 1875 of citizens making oaths of innocence when accused of theft.[22] Niida Noboru and others who have researched the commercial history of late imperial China have also found numerous cases of members of guilds and other commercial organizations making oaths in front of statues of their patron deities and asking the gods to judge their cases when disputes occurred (Goodman 1995: 87; Niida 1950, 1964).

Yao Hanqiu 姚漢秋's study of popular customs in modern Fujian and Taiwan notes that in parts of southern Fujian individuals suspected of theft were often brought before images of judges (*panguan* 判官) and instructed to make oaths proclaiming their innocence. Then, someone hiding behind the image would move its right arm to point at the defendant, who if guilty would supposedly break down and confess (Yao 1981: 120). Overseas Chinese also made oaths to resolve disputes, and examples of some texts have been preserved in the Dutch colonial archives of Batavia (see also Chapter 6). One instance concerns a man named Guo Naijin 郭乃進 (b. 1717), a Hakka from Jiayingzhou 嘉應州 (Guangdong) who was engaged in a dispute with three other members of the same surname group concerning a loan that had been made in 1768. In the fourth lunar month of the year 1775, in the presence of a Chinese elite with the title "captain" (Jiabidan 甲必丹), Guo made the following oath:

> . . . If I have lied or deceived, claiming that people who already repaid the loan still owed me money, or stating that completed transactions remained unfinished, may the gods conduct hidden investigations and the officials examine (*sheming ancha, shiguan jiange* 神明暗察, 時官鑑格). [If I lie], may my family fall apart; may blood pour from my bodily orifices and I die in the presence of onlookers; and may I have no heirs. What I swear is the truth (*suoshi nai shi* 所誓乃實) . . .
>
> (Bao and Wu 2002: 26)

Qing-dynasty texts of varying degrees of self-consciousness in their fictionality also describe similar practices. In just one example, Chapter 74 of the renowned Qing novel *The Story of the Stone* (*Shitou ji* 石頭記; also known as *The Dream of the Red Chamber* or *Honglou meng* 紅樓夢) describes a maid who had been accused of leaking information about the

22 See the October 10, 1874 and January 10, 1875 issues. Many thanks to Vincent Goossaert for sharing these sources with me.

pawning of household items. In order to demonstrate their innocence, they "knelt down in terror and swore by the most sacred oaths that they had said nothing" (*xiao yatou huangle, dou guixia duzhou fashi* 小丫頭慌了, 都跪下賭咒發誓) (*The Story of the Stone*, Volume 3, pp. 456–457).

Chicken-beheading rituals

The most dreaded form of oath-making featured the beheading of a chicken in the presence of judicial deities while making contingent curses that expressed one's willingness to suffer the fate of the unfortunate fowl in the event of perjury. Chicken-beheading rituals consist of two main components: the making of an oath and the slaughter of the cockerel. A white cockerel was usually the bird of choice, perhaps because it has long symbolized the sun and *yang* 陽 forces of life and vitality, but on a more practical level, cockerels were cheaper to purchase than other animals (de Groot 1892–1910, Volume 1, pp. 200–218; Volume 6, pp. 965–970; ter Haar 1998: 157, 183; Xiang 2003). One scholar has even suggested that cockerels were never eaten because of their potential use in oaths (Williams 1941: 199–200), but further research will be necessary to clarify this point.[23] Blood also symbolized life, while providing added force to the oath. The use of chicken blood and the performance of chicken-beheading rites is also an important part of some Chinese ritual dramas (Werle 1973: 80; Cai 1986: 48–49), as well as Hakka mortuary rituals.[24]

While some disputes could be settled by oath-making alone, more complex or potentially explosive cases clearly required the sacrifice of an animal victim (Wu Ying-t'ao 1987: 167–168). This was the case during a money-lending dispute that occurred in Panyu 番禺 (Guangdong) in 1863, when a debtor told his creditor that he had already returned the money. Since the creditor had failed to keep a receipt documenting the transaction, both parties made an oath and beheaded chickens in the presence of unidentified deities. The outcome of the ritual is unclear (*Youtai xianguan biji*, 1.16). Similar rites could also be performed in the course of lineage disputes, including one between the powerful Wang 王 and Zheng 鄭 lineages from the town of Zhuotian 濯田 (in Changting 長汀 County, western Fujian). This dispute, which concerned the rights to an ancestral cemetery (*zufen* 祖墳), dragged on for three years and included the performance of a chicken-beheading rite (Yang 2002: 544–546).[25]

23 Other scholars maintain that the character *yi* 彝 is a pictograph of someone holding a bleeding chicken (Du 2002: 113).

24 Huang Pingying 黄萍瑛, personal communication, December 22, 2006.

25 Additional evidence on judicial rituals and lineages, including the role of ancestors as witnesses, may be found in Liu 2003: 55, 57–58.

Chicken-beheading rituals could also be performed by soldiers, militiamen, gangsters, and members of secret societies as part of their blood covenant rites. For example, Xie Zhi 謝志, a follower of the Taiwanese Triad leader Lin Shuangwen, sacrificed a cockerel and instructed his own pupils to pass through a gate of swords as part of a blood covenant performed in Taiwan in 1790. Triad leaders in Guangdong and Guangxi also used cockerels in blood covenants performed during the 1820s. Such rites continued to be performed in Hong Kong until at least the 1960s (ter Haar 1998: 181–189).

Taoist specialists from south China also beheaded chickens in the course of making blood covenants with the deities that both protected them and aided them during the performance of exorcistic rituals. According to examples of such rites preserved in the *Daofa huiyuan*, a Taoist specialist wishing to form an alliance with guardian deities (usually martial or thunder gods) would first pace the Steps of Yu (*Yubu* 禹步), offer wine to the gods, chant spells, and burn charms. Taking a squawking cockerel in his left hand, he would then chop its head off and allow the blood to drip into a cup of wine, using his sword to mix the two substances together. This was followed by the specialist's making an oath stating his willingness to serve heaven by protecting the people and the nation and calling on the gods to send their armies to help in his cause. Like other Chinese blood covenants described in this chapter, these rites invariably included a curse on those who violated their terms. After completing the oath and curse, the Taoist drank the blood wine (*xuejiu* 血酒). Cockerels were not the only animals used by Taoists; in some cases they also beheaded geese, goats, and eels. A few texts even describe Taoists as cutting their fingers open and drinking their own blood (Katz 2000: 179–180; ter Haar 1998: 154–159, 202). The importance of such rites in Taoist practice, which can be traced back to early medieval works like the *Shangqing Huangting neijing jing* 上清黃庭內景經 and persist in Taoist ritual traditions today (Mozina 2008), may finally lay to rest scholarly misconceptions of Taoism as a religion consisting solely of Pure Codes (*qingyue* 清約) which vehemently opposed or even attempted to control local cults Taoist leaders condemned for their "licentious sacrifices" (*yinsi* 淫祀) and "bloody [=meat] offerings" (*xueshi* 血食).

Detailed accounts of chicken-beheading rituals may be found in the writings of the British Presbyterian missionary John Macgowan. A member of the London Missionary Society, Macgowan journeyed to Amoy (Xiamen 廈門) in 1863 and preached the gospel there while also traveling to other parts of China for over 50 years. In two books published in 1910 and 1912, he provides gripping accounts of oaths and chicken-beheading rites he witnessed at Amoy's City God temple. The data Macgowan presents largely conform to what we know about chicken-beheading rituals in Taiwan, particularly their links to irresolvable social conflicts, the fearful imprecations accompanying the rite, the grim consequences which could be visited upon the guilty, and the potential for local officials to become involved.

Macgowan's first account describes what happened when a shop owner accused one of his two apprentices of stealing 100 dollars. The suspect promptly decided to file an indictment against the other apprentice, whom he suspected of having stolen the money, and so, with a large white cockerel in his left hand and the newly accused in tow, he led a throng of people to the City God temple. There, in the presence of the god, he hurled imprecations against the as yet unknown individual who had actually stolen the money. Macgowan records his words as follows:

> Let his life be one long torture . . . May every enterprise in which he engages end in disaster; may his mother and father die and let him be left desolate . . . may he become a beggar with ulcered legs . . . may he never have a son . . . may madness seize upon him so that his reason shall fly and he shall be a source of terror to his fellow-men; and finally, may a tragic and horrible death bring his life to a sudden end, even as I bring to an end the life of this white cock that I have brought with me [Beheads the cockerel].
>
> (Macgowan 1910: 140)

The young man then took a previously prepared written indictment and burned it. The other apprentice remained silent during the rite, perhaps due to his own guilt feelings, for just two weeks after the conclusion of the rite his sister drowned and his family's fields were washed away in a flood. Eventually, the poor fellow went insane, and aimlessly wandered the streets muttering about ghosts chasing him. His madness soon turned violent, and he had to be restrained with ropes to prevent him from hurting himself or others. Finally, his distraught father somehow located or produced the stolen amount, and the assistant who had performed the chicken-beheading rite submitted a written petition to the City God in which he dropped the charges. The guilty party recovered shortly after the completion of this rite (*ibid.*: 140–145).

The second chicken-beheading rite Macgowan witnessed involved a wealthy man who had a considerable sum of money stolen from his home. When he blamed his assistant, the latter denied all knowledge of the crime and volunteered to bring a white cockerel to the temple of the City God and make an oath in the deity's presence in order to prove his innocence. This ritual differed from the one described above in that while the plaintiff also read aloud and burned a written indictment, this time the defendant solemnly proclaimed his innocence and declared his willingness to submit to any punishment the gods saw fit to inflict should he in fact be lying. After concluding by stating his willingness to suffer sudden death, the defendant beheaded the white cockerel he had brought with him. A few days after the ritual, the real culprit became so terrified at the thought of his impending doom that he found a way to return the wealthy man's money without revealing his identity. At this point, the plaintiff had to take the rather embarrassing action of appearing in public before the City God and withdrawing his indictment of the original defendant (Macgowan 1912: 137–140).

Fujianese who migrated to Taiwan also practiced chicken-beheading rituals (see Chapter 7), as did many overseas Chinese (see Chapter 6). For example, one account of Chinese communities in Singapore states that: "[the beheading of a cockerel] is a procedure which the Chinese only resort to in cases of the greatest importance, for many of them intensely dislike thus killing the cockerel . . . I have seen men turn livid and perspire when they have had to cut off a cock's head on such occasions" (Ward and Stirling 1925 I: 71; ter Haar 1998: 164–165).

The earliest possible antecedents to chicken-beheading rituals include the blood covenants described above, as well as oath-making rites that concluded with a sacred animal butting the guilty party (referred to by scholars today as the "divine judgment by a goat" or *yang shenpan* 羊神判) (Huang 1986; MacCormack 1995: 74–77, 80–81, 86–87). For example, the Han scholar Wang Chong 王充 (27–97?) recorded in his *Lunheng* 論衡 a legend about Gao Yao 皋陶, a minister of the sage-king Shun 舜, who asked a single-horned animal known as a *xie* 獬 or *xiezhi* 獬豸 to butt the guilty party in cases where he proved unable to resolve disputes (Ch'ü 1961: 210; Huang 1986: 16–17).[26] Images of *xiezhi* were frequently sewn or embroidered on the robes of judicial officials from the Han dynasty on (*Lunheng*, p. 321; Xu and Wu 2000: 16).

Another account may be found in the *Mozi* 墨子 (*Mo Tzu*), which describes an incident that occurred in the state of Qi 齊 (which had links to the Qiang people). When two sons of an official became embroiled in a legal dispute which dragged on for three years, the exasperated ruler of Qi ordered them to produce a goat and engage in a covenant ritual at the Qi *she* 社 altar. The goat's neck was then cut open, and the sons ordered to read their oaths of innocence aloud. The goat lay still during the reading of the first son's oath, but before the second son was halfway through his text it jumped up and butted him. The guilty son was executed on the spot (*Mo Tzu: Basic Writings*, pp. 98–99). In late imperial Guangdong, people relied on snakes to determine innocence or guilt. The parties to a dispute would make oaths in front of snakes that were kept in temples to gods known as the Deities of the Three Realms (Sanjie shen 三界神). These snakes were said to turn their

26 Lewis makes the interesting observation that Gao Yao was also the reputed ancestor of the Qiang 羌, a generic exonym applied to peoples of the areas to the west and northwest of the Han Chinese heartland who worshipped the goat as a totemic animal (Lewis 1990: 198).

backs on those who were telling the truth, but lash out at those who had committed perjury (*Guangdong xinyu*, 6.218).

If we cast our nets even wider in search of evidence about such rituals, we soon discover that numerous non-Han peoples of southwest China also practiced such rites well into the twentieth century. The ethnologist Xia Zhiqian documented a wide variety of non-Han judicial rites in a path-breaking study completed over a decade ago entitled *Shenpan* 神判 (*Divine Judgment*). One of the most detailed accounts of a chicken-beheading ritual concerns the Miao 苗 of Rongjiang 容江 County (Guizhou). When disputes over land or stolen property arose and all efforts at mediation had failed, the plaintiff and defendant would seek out the services of a ritual specialist referred to in the text as a "ghost master" or *guishi* 鬼師 (the term is most likely an exonym) and gather at the local Earth God temple. The specialist stood in the center of an open space, with the plaintiff and defendant taking up positions three meters to his right and left. Two stakes linked by a rope marked with string were driven into the ground next to the plaintiff and defendant. When all was ready, the plaintiff would make the oath, stating his or her version of the facts and concluding, "If I have wronged him (the defendant), may I die in less than three months. If he really . . . [is guilty of the crime I accused him of], may he die in less than three months!" The defendant made a similar oath, following which the specialist grabbed a chicken produced by the plaintiff, proclaiming "Chicken! Chicken! Open your eyes! You know who is true and who is false. Find the one who has done wrong!" Then he would fatally cut the chicken in the neck with a knife. As the poor bird writhed on the ground, it would roll towards the plaintiff or the defendant. If it rolled past the string attached to the rope, the person it approached was deemed guilty and forced to pay restitution (Xia 1990: 31–32; see also Lü 2002: 86–86; Sutton 2003a: 54–56). Xia also describes how some non-Han groups cut the forelegs from dogs in the course of oath-making rituals (*ibid.*: 30–31). In terms of relying on an animal's ability to locate the guilty party, such non-Han rites also seem similar to the ancient Chinese goat-butting rituals described above.

The slaughter of animals in the ritual described above appears particularly significant because such victims may have served as scapegoats for the parties involved in disputes, and perhaps even the entire community. In a stimulating treatment of ritual violence, the French scholar René Girard maintains that violent tendencies with the potential to disrupt communal life are frequently redirected onto defenseless surrogate victims during rituals (Girard 1979). Practices such as beheading a chicken or cutting open the neck of a goat all feature the violent deaths of animals as part of an attempt to prevent outbreaks of violence between plaintiffs and defendants, and thus may fit Girard's ideas.

The ordeal in Chinese legal culture[27]

Xia Zhiqian and other scholars have also documented non-Han trials of the flesh remarkably similar to the ordeals of medieval Europe and the Near East (see below), including pulling objects out of pots of boiling oil (*lao youtang* 撈油湯) and holding or walking on objects of red-hot iron (*retie shenpan* 熱鐵神判). Such rites continued to be documented as late as the 1950s (Xia 1990: 1–21, 44–51; see also Du 1999; Xia 1993; Zheng 1991). Ordeals could also be performed by Han Chinese, including two friends from Lin'an 臨安 Prefecture (Hangzhou) named Zhang Shi 張適 and Li Er 李二 who had become embroiled in yet another money-lending dispute, with the latter attempting to prove his innocence by pulling a coin from a pot of boiling oil in the City God temple (*Xu Zibuyu*, 1.12).

A somewhat different form of this practice, namely the rite of "jumping off the theater platform" (*tiao xilou* 跳戲樓), was performed at the City God temple in Zhenping 鎮平 (Henan) during the early Republican period (especially the 1920s) as an established way to resolve commercial disputes. Local business owners and merchants involved in disputes would come to the City God temple, make oaths of innocence, and then leap simultaneously off the high theater platform behind the temple. The injured party, or the party refusing to jump or resorting to climbing down the high platform, was deemed to be guilty. In one unfortunate instance, a merchant-devotee known as Boss Lin (Lin Laoda 林老大) broke his leg in a particularly disastrous leap (his opponent had first slipped away, preferring not to jump), landing him both in some serious debt and in the infamy of suspected fraud. This account does not spell out the exact relationship between the Zhenping City God temple and the local merchants (often silk traders and retailers), but it is quite conceivable that the City God was their patron deity (Wang 1996: 102–105).[28]

While some scholars consider ordeals to be little better than "primitive lie detectors" (Berman 1983: 57, 451), others emphasize their role in reducing communal tensions, which may help to explain their longevity among cultures in both the West and the East (Bohannan 1989: 46; Chanock 1985: 86, 93; Lariviere 1981). Although the term ordeal usually prompts images of men or women walking over burning ploughshares or sticking their hands in boiling oil, research on medieval European ordeals clearly indicates that, as in China, such rites could involve the making of oaths without trials of the flesh.[29] The fact that there was often a three-day gap in judging effects

27 See especially an article by Itō Seiji that documents this practice not only for China, but also for Japan and parts of South and Southeast Asia (Itō 1986: 139, 140–142).

28 I am most grateful to Liu Xun 劉迅 for sharing this account.

29 Leading works on this subject include Bartlett 1986; Fleming 1998; Klinger 1987, Lea 1974 (1866): 26–32, 58–59; Roberts 1965; Sabbatucci 1987.

of an ordeal (Kadri 2006: 26) seems especially important, as this indicates that such rites might be similar to conditional curses in terms of positing eventual and not immediate retribution, thereby providing an opportunity for mediation efforts to have an effect (Katz 2001: 114–115; MacCormack 1995: 72–73).

Concluding remarks

In light of the importance of oaths in Chinese legal culture, it seems especially surprising that such rites never became part of formal legal procedures, including those of either traditional yamens or modern courts. Even when the late Qing and early Republican authorities decided to implement a Western-style legal system, the practice of swearing in witnesses by means of judicial oaths was not deemed worthy of incorporation. This might not be surprising for an era during which Chinese elites attempted to redefine the state as a modern secularist entity,[30] but it is interesting to note that the use of judicial oaths was given serious consideration. During the late Qing, one of the scholars invited to China to explain the workings of Western jurisprudence was the renowned Japanese legal expert Okada Asatarō 岡田朝太郎 (1868–1936), whose lectures contained detailed descriptions of oaths used in Western courtrooms (Wang 1910: 148–151; see also Huang 1999, 2001). As a result, when Wu Tingfang 伍廷芳 (1842–1922) and Shen Jiaben 沈家本 (1840–1913) formulated a draft penal code in 1906, they included a section on oaths to be used in modern Chinese courts. However, such practices were eventually excised from the final version of the code, due to the objections of high officials like Xi Liang 錫良 (1853–1917) and Lin Shaonian 林紹年 (1849–1916), who maintained that oaths would prove ineffective in terms of persuading witnesses to tell the truth (similar arguments were made by Western colonial officials in Singapore and Hong Kong; see Chapter 6).[31] This skepticism did not extend to all aspects of modern Chinese political history, however, with the Chinese Revolutionary Party (Zhonghua gemingdang 中華革命黨; the name of the Kuomintang from 1914–1919) requiring in a 1914 rule that its members swear loyalty oaths (Nedostup 2007: 44–45).

Even today, courts in Taiwan and China do not use oaths to swear in witnesses. In Taiwan, prior to giving testimony in court, the witness merely has to sign a written statement (*jujie* 具結) promising to tell the truth and expressing willingness to suffer the consequences of perjury. Such procedures

30 See the discussions of these trends in Chen 1999; Duara 1995: 85–113; Goossaert 2006; Nedostup forthcoming.

31 For more on these events, see Sun 2006, as well as Lü and Xu 2003. Biographical information on Wu and Shen may be found in Pomerantz-Zhang 1992; Wheeler 1998.

are used in both civil and criminal cases. Moreover, when it comes to oaths of office (*xuanshi jiuzhi* 宣誓就職), such ceremonies are completely secular, being performed facing the Republic of China flag and/or a portrait of Sun Yat-sen, although some members of pro-independence parties have been known to turn their backs on these "sacred" objects. I have yet to determine how witnesses give testimony in Chinese courts, but this does not seem to involve the use of written statements like those described above.[32] In other words, despite the widespread popularity of oath-making as a ritual of legitimation among people ranging in status from high-ranking officials to peasants, such practices have failed to be legitimized by the state. Perhaps this may account for one phenomenon discussed in the Introduction and Chapter 2, namely the inability of the court system to gain full-fledged legitimacy in the eyes of the Chinese people.

32 Many thanks to Kevin Chang (Chang Ku-ming 張谷銘), Chiou Wentsong 邱文聰, and Sun Huei-min 孫慧敏 for helping me to better understand these issues.

4

INDICTMENT RITUALS

Indictment rituals do not seem to have been as widespread as the oath-making rites described in Chapter 3, but have played a role in the development of numerous legal cultures worldwide. For example, research by John G. Gager and others on "curse tablets" (known as *defixiones* or *katadesmoi*) indicates that people from ancient Greece who were entangled in legal disputes would not hesitate to commission or personally inscribe thin sheets of lead with curses against those they felt had wronged them. These sheets were then submitted to underworld deities in their temples. Such rites were strikingly similar to Chinese indictment rituals in involving the invocation of underworld deities who were seen as being able to provide justice (Gager 1992: 116–150, 175–199). Moreover, it seems clear that judicial rites in the ancient world resembled those in China in being designed (in Gager's words) to "deal with the nonlegal side, the emotional dimension, of lawsuits and public trials" (*ibid.*: 116–117). Indictment rituals continued to be performed in medieval Europe,[1] and could also be combined with animals (including pets) being put on trial on charges of having sex with humans and killing innocent people.[2] Such rites have lost much of their popularity in the West today, however, which stands in sharp contrast to the indictment rituals still performed among Chinese communities, particularly in Taiwan, Hong Kong, and parts of Southeast Asia.

This chapter examines three types of indictment rites. The first encompasses an extensive range of underworld indictments filed by people against other members of the living, including indictments filed during festivals and indictments filed at any time by individuals who felt they had been wronged. The second involves ritual measures designed to relieve the effects of being indicted by the dead or even by animal spirits, including

1 See Geary 1994; Little 1993. I am deeply grateful to Patrick J. Geary for referring me to these works, as well as to Gager's book.

2 For more on these practices, see Darnton 1984: 166–167; Kadri 2006: 146–159; see also Cohen 1992. Some animals were even granted court-appointed defense lawyers.

the filing of countersuits. The third features indictments against haunting spirits, usually filed by officials or religious specialists. I conclude by considering the links between indictments and gender issues, which can be seen in accounts of women and in some cases even female ghosts filing accusations of rape, attempted rape, and adultery, or indicting their rivals for men's affections. At the same time, however, men could also rely on indictment rituals to assert their authority over disobedient wives.

Types of Chinese indictment rituals

Type 1: Indictments filed against other members of the living

Indictment rituals whereby people accused each other of wrongdoing (*fanggao* 放告; *gao yinzhuang* 告陰狀) are almost invariably performed before underworld deities, and involve the use of a plaint written on yellow paper. Some people recite their plaints aloud so that all can hear, while others prefer to read them *sotto voce*. We can also distinguish between indictment rituals in terms of whether or not they name the allegedly guilty party. In some cases, people entangled in legal disputes know the alleged wrongdoer's identity and include his or her name in the text of the plaint. In others, people who have been victimized but are unable to identify the alleged criminal (a common occurrence in cases of theft) may ask the gods to both track down and punish the guilty party.

One of the most extensively studied examples of public indictment rites involves those held in Wenzhou 溫州 (Zhejiang) during the annual festival in honor of the plague-quelling deity Marshal Wen. According to an early twentieth-century account, the local rite of filing indictments was held at the military drill grounds (*jiaochang* 校場) in the western suburbs during the annual procession to prevent outbreaks of epidemic. A placard was posted calling on all who were victims of unjust charges or who harbored grievances (*hanyuan yinhen* 含冤飲恨, literally "held wrongs or had drunk resentment") to come forward and file indictments. Members of the temple committee from Marshal Wen's temple, including an individual dressed as Wen's senior runner, would help supervise these rites. When all was ready, a runner would cry out that Marshal Wen was ready to preside over his court (*shengtang* 升堂; the same term used for civil officials when they ascended the bench). This was followed by the summoning of all men and women who were attempting to atone for their misdeeds by dressing as "criminals" (*fanren* 犯人) and "sinners" (*zuiren* 罪人) during the procession (see Chapter 5). Finally, the plaintiffs were allowed to enter. Each individual who chose to file an indictment had to dress in mourning, and leave his/her hair in disarray.[3]

3 As opposed to being tied neatly in a queue. The loose hair, as well as mourning clothes, indicated the plaintiff's liminal status.

Holding sticks of incense and carrying an indictment (*zhuang* 狀) written on yellow paper, he or she would cry out: "Injustice (*yuanwang* 冤枉)! Lord of the Eastern Peak [Marshal Wen], I implore you to right this wrong!" The plaintiff would initially be driven back by men dressed as judges (*panguan* 判官), and was only allowed to approach Wen after three attempts at doing so. Then the plaintiff would kneel down and offer Wen the indictment, crying continuously while presenting his or her grievances. Following this, the senior runner would burn the indictment in an incense burner (in order to transmit it to the gods), and advise the plaintiff to retire (Katz 1995a: 200–201). While some accounts state that those whom Marshal Wen deemed guilty would eventually suffer misfortune, or even death, it appears that the purpose of such rites was not the immediate administration of divine retribution. It might make more sense to consider them as speech acts that featured reflexive processes of negotiation by which context-sensitive and conflicting meanings are brought into the open to be critically examined and interpreted by both the audience and the performers themselves.[4]

Similar rites could be staged throughout other parts of southern Zhejiang, but did not have to correspond to festivals. In early twentieth-century Suichang 遂昌 County, indictments could be filed in the county seat's City God temple on every first and fifth day of each lunar month. As in the case of Wenzhou, such rites closely resembled dramatic performances, with people dressed up as yamen runners and clerks guiding plaintiffs through the different phases of each indictment ritual. Hundreds of people crowded into the temple to witness these rites (Wu 1995: 24). We also have a number of accounts of indictment rites performed during the annual festival to plague deities known as the Five Emperors (Wudi 五帝),[5] which was held in the northern Fujian city of Fuzhou 福州 throughout the late imperial era and into the first decades of the twentieth century (Xu 1993: 86–101). Perhaps the most striking aspect of these rituals is how closely they resembled actual trials in the magistrate's yamen. According to an account in *juan* 卷 55 of the 1871 edition of the *Fujian tongzhi*, which has been translated by Michael Szonyi, "When the officials make decisions, [the people] don't believe and don't obey, but rather must call the Five Emperors as witnesses and only then submit. The documents and ceremonies of their Heavenly Fairy Palace are majestic, and upheld together with those of the officials" (Szonyi 2000: 115). This text is particularly important because it shows that both official and religious legal practices could command considerable legitimacy, and could be integrated by people of all classes into the late imperial judicial continuum described in Chapter 2.

4 For more on these issues, see Bauman and Briggs 1990. I am grateful to James Wilkerson for bringing this and other important theoretical perspectives to my attention.

5 The history and significance of this cult are explored in Szonyi 1997.

Public indictment rites could also be performed during protracted disputes, including those that had entered the courts. One example, which dates from the early eighteenth century, concerns the Chen 陳, Fang 方, and Qian 錢 lineages of Tongcheng 桐城 (Anhui), who had battled for years in order to gain control over the rights to an ancestral cemetery (*zufen* 祖墳). By the 1730s, the Fangs appear to have gained the upper hand, perhaps because of the connections gained when one member of their lineage, Fang Bao 方苞 (1668–1749), rose to a high post in the Grand Secretariat despite having been implicated in the literary inquisition of 1711. In order to protest what they considered to be unfair treatment, between 20 and 30 members of the Chen and Qian lineages marched to the local City God temple and publicly expressed their grievances both en route and in front of the god.[6]

However, the most common form of indictment rituals could be held in temples at any time as a response to real or perceived wrongdoings. Witnesses and written texts might be involved, but were not a required element of the ritual. The earliest example of a private indictment rite that I have located so far may be found in an anecdote from Hong Mai 洪邁's (1123–1201) *Yijian zhi*, which describes how a serving official and his son-in-law embezzled funds during the former's term of office in Zizhou 資州 (Sichuan) and then pinned the blame on an old soldier, who was forced to confess his alleged misdeed after being interrogated and tortured (*xunju* 訊鞠). Overcome with resentment and anger, the soldier filed an indictment at a branch temple (*xinggong* 行宮) of the Emperor of the Eastern Peak, burning the document during tearful worship. He also had a copy prepared,[7] which he tied around his waist before killing himself outside the temple gates. Later, the soldier suddenly appeared to Feng, who exclaimed: "You've been dead for one year. How did you get here?" The soldier replied: "Regarding the money, I have filed a plaint with the Emperor [of the Eastern Peak]. He has ordered you and your son-in-law to appear [in his court]." Feng was terrified, and both he and his son-in-law acted as if possessed (*zhong'e* 中惡). Feng's son-in-law died that very day, while Feng passed away seven days later (*Yijian zhi*, volume 3, pp. 1024–1025).[8]

Late imperial Chinese who felt they had been wronged or victimized could also appeal to the City God. A story from *juan* 4 of Zheng Zhongkui's Ming-dynasty work entitled *Erxin* tells how a thief stole the only ox of a Yiyang 弋陽 (Jiangxi) man named Chen 陳, who in desperation filed an indictment with the City God. Three days later the thief confessed,

6 See *Yongzheng chao Hanwen zhupi zouzhe ziliao huibian*, Volume 29, pp. 87–88. Many thanks to Wu Jen-shu 巫仁恕 for showing me this source.

7 Whether or not the soldier was literate and wrote the indictment on his own is not clear.

8 Similar stories may also be found in *Yijian zhi*, Volume 1, pp. 130, 156–157, 168–169; Volume 2, pp. 655–656.

screaming in agony and claiming that the City God's runners (*chai* 差) were chasing him. He then said that he was being bound and sentenced to a beating, and those who witnessed these events claimed to have heard the sounds of the blows being administered (*Erxin*, 4.21). This story is particularly noteworthy because no written text of the indictment is mentioned, and because the result of the ritual involved the apparent thief losing his mind. As we will see below and in Chapter 5, madness was often considered to be the result of an indictment ritual.

In addition to the historical sources discussed above, there are also ethnographic accounts describing how indictment rituals were performed. Hu Pu'an's gazetteer of Chinese customs during the late Qing and early Republican eras contains the following brief description of indictment rites performed in Jiangsu:

> People who are poor or without recourse will sit on mats on the ground and cover their faces with a cloth. They lay a sheet of paper on the ground, on which is written a resume of their cases or a plaint describing how they have been wronged. This is known as a "chthonic indictment" (*gao dizhuang* 告地狀).
>
> (Hu 1990 [1923]: 27)

According to late imperial gazetteers from this region, some plaintiffs wrote plaints using their own blood in order to emphasize the graveness of their actions and evoke the power of the blood covenants described in Chapter 3. Such texts were referred to as "blood documents" (*xueshu* 血書) or "blood memorials" (*xueshu* 血疏) (*Jiangnan tongzhi, juan* 148, 190).

Numerous other references to indictment rituals, while lacking the detail of the accounts presented above, testify to the popularity of such rites. Consider the case of Peasant Shen 沈 discussed by Philip A. Kuhn in his study of soul-stealing (*jiaohun* 叫魂) panics in eighteenth-century Jiangnan 江南. Archival sources reveal that Shen, a native of Renhe 仁和 County in Zhejiang who fled his home after being tormented and cheated by his relatives, did not go to the authorities but filed an indictment against his relatives by burning a plaint written on yellow paper in a temple dedicated to the Bodhisattva Dizang (Kuhn 1991: 3). The pictorial *Dianshizhai huabao* also contains an illustration of a soldier stationed in Wanyuan 皖垣 (Anhui) accusing a woman of theft in a City God temple. The soldier also swore an oath that his accusation was a true one, while the woman made an oath of innocence (see Figure 3). In his study of Chinese chthonic deities, Ma Shutian reports that during the late imperial era residents of Guangdong would burn indictments in the presence of the City God in a rite popularly known as "Burning Indictments [Filed to] the King" (*shao wang'gao* 燒王告). Zheng Tuyou and Wang Xiansen describe similar rites in their study of the City God, while also noting that *shao wang'gao* could be referred to as

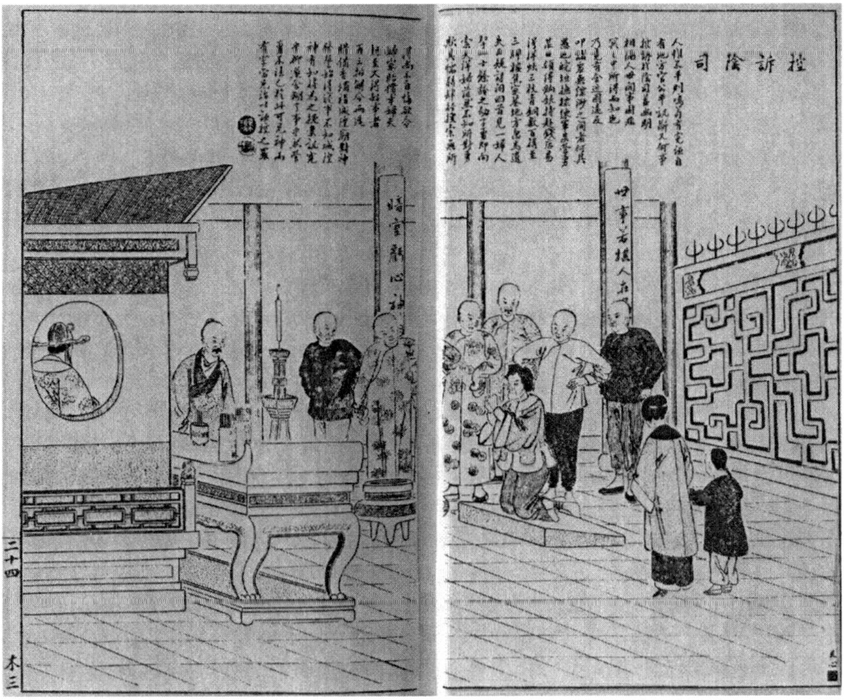

Figure 3 *Dianshizhai huabao* illustration of a soldier filing an underworld indictment (and making an oath) in a City God temple. The accused woman (and her son) are in the foreground.

gao yinzhuang (Ma 1998: 160; Zheng and Wang 1994: 177). Scholars who have researched the commercial history of late imperial China have found numerous cases of members of guilds and other commercial organizations filing indictments in front of statues of their patron deities, and asking the gods to judge their cases when disputes occurred (Goodman 1995: 87; Macgowan 1886–1887: 140; see also Niida 1950). Indictment rituals were also performed in parts of north China (Arkush and Dong 1995: 32–33), as well as Sichuan (*Baxian zhi*, *juan* 23).

A number of valuable accounts may be found in the Qing dynasty classical-language *biji xiaoshuo* 筆記小說 collection *Xinzheng lu* by Xu Qing 徐慶, a work that resembles the well-known Song dynasty collection *Yijian zhi* in being very specific about places and dates, as well as identifying the informant for each account. One story from the *Xinzheng lu* describes a group of counterfeiters from Jiaxing 嘉興 Prefecture (Zhejiang), whose number included a wealthy member of the local elite. In 1692, another member of the elite wanted a piece of the action, but was turned down. He then filed an indictment with the Xiushui County 秀水 magistrate, but the wealthy elite bribed the magistrate into taking no action. When he filed a second indictment, his opponent proceeded to lodge a countersuit. He then filed a suit with the Zhejiang Provincial Governor (*xunfu* 巡撫), but this official also deferred to the wishes of this wealthy (and apparently extremely well-connected) elite. Finally, in a fit of extreme anger and resentment (*huiji* 恚極), he filed an indictment at the Hangzhou City God temple. After a brief respite, all parties were said to have had their cases tried in the god's infernal court, with each and all receiving just punishments for their actions (*Xinzheng lu*, 23a–b).

Another account in the *Xinzheng lu* concerns two residents of Shijiazhuang 石家莊 (Hebei) named Zhong 鍾 and Lao 勞. In 1687, Lao apparently cheated Zhong out of a considerable sum of money. Zhong initially thought of taking his case to the local yamen, but relented when he realized that Lao was close friends with the yamen's clerical staff. Instead, he prepared a "dark indictment" (*yinzhuang* 陰狀) at the local City God temple. After a few days, the Earth God summoned Lao to the underworld while he was on a boat bound for Jiaxing. When Zhong heard of this, he told his wife, "My indictment has been approved, and I am going to die (in order to attend an underworld trial). However, I estimate that my crimes will not result in capital punishment, so do not prepare my body for burial." The trial was held in the Earth God temple, with the Earth God serving as presiding judge. In the end, both men were restored to life, but Lao developed a leg ailment and was lame for the rest of his life (*Xinzheng lu*, 21a-22a).

A second important Qing-dynasty *biji* text, the *Zibuyu*, tells the story a Suzhou man named Wu Sanfu 吳三復, who had failed to prevent his distraught father from hanging himself in 1764. One of Wu's acquaintances named Gu Xinyi 顧心怡 took advantage of Wu's guilt feelings by using a fake spirit-writing cult (*wei she jixian wei* 偽設乩仙位) to summon what he claimed was the ghost of Wu's father, who ordered Wu to use his remaining savings to pay Gu to perform rituals on the Wu family's behalf. When he realized that he had been cheated, Wu tried three times to plead his case at the magistrate's yamen, but his case was turned down each time because he had failed to keep any written records of his financial transactions with Gu. Wu then proceeded to file an indictment with the Suzhou City God. After three days, he passed away, while Gu died three days later. Both were said to have been summoned to the City God's court, but the result of their trial is not clear (*Zibuyu*, 5. 85–86).[9]

We also find the following account of an indictment ritual in the *Yuewei caotang biji*. Set in the late Yongzheng 雍正 reign (1723–1735), this story

9 This story is also discussed in Ling 2003: 37. Another story about an official filing an indictment with the Emperor of the Eastern Peak during an instance of fraud may be found in *Zibuyu*, 14.262

describes two close friends identified only as Jia 甲 (a native of Yunnan) and Yi 乙 (a native of Zhejiang). Jia had asked Yi to help him manage his finances while he successfully pursued a career as an official, but Yi took advantage of his position to cheat Jia out of much of his fortune. When Jia reprimanded Yi, Yi reminded Jia that he knew of certain "concealed [illegal?] affairs" (*yinshi* 陰事). Enraged, Jia filed an indictment against Yi at a City God temple. That night, the City God visited Jia in a dream and scolded him for being so trusting of Yi. He also advised Jia to drop his suit, as Yi was certain to suffer divine retribution sooner or later (*Yuewei caotang biji*, 8.140–141). The above two stories have somewhat less satisfactory conclusions than those previously discussed, because while readers might safely assume that divine justice will be done in due course, they are not treated to witnessing the punishment of the wicked.

Works of fiction from late imperial China written in the vernacular style, including short stories known as *huaben xiaoshuo* 話本小說, also contain depictions of indictment rituals that emphasize the central character or a pivotal event. One account in story 38 of the *Yushi mingyan* tells of a Hangzhou man named Ren Gui 任珪 who was being cuckolded. Enraged, he purchased a knife and a white cockerel, as well as incense, candles, and paper money, and performed an indictment ritual at a temple dedicated to a local water god known as Duke Yan (Yangong 晏公), during which he cursed his wife and her lover while also beheading the cockerel. The account does not depict Ren as having used a written document, suggesting that he preferred to state his case orally. The beheading also had a divinatory element, as Ren stated his intention to kill the same number of people as the number of times the cockerel jumped during its death throes. The bird jumped five times, and Ren ended up killing five people (*Yushi mingyan*, pp. 616–617).[10] Another example of indictment rites described in a work of fiction can be found in Chapter 7 of the court case novel *Shan E Tu* (*The Chart of Good and Evil*), which describes how the novel's villain, a local strongman named Li Lei 李雷 (ironically nicknamed "The Living King of Hell" or Huo Yanluo 活閻羅), attempted to abduct and rape the wife of a Nanjing resident named Lin Kongzhao 林扎昭. Members of Lin's family told him to inform the Stove God, but instead Lin headed to the City God temple. There, in front of the god and his chthonic minions, Lin burned incense and stated his grievances, following which he picked up a sheet of yellow paper and wrote out a formal indictment against Li (*Shan E Tu*, pp. 135–136).[11]

10 For a story of using divination blocks to determine one's guilt or innocence, see *Zibuyu*, 2.33.

11 For more on this work, see Wan 2000. Jeffrey C. Kinkley's study of justice in modern Chinese fiction makes the important point that fiction and legal codes appear to have influenced each other, and that novels which portray officials righting wrongs (including by means of judicial rituals) have enjoyed widespread popularity during both the late imperial and modern eras (Kinkley 2000: 101–169).

Because the texts of plaints used in indictment rituals among the living are supposed to be burned, examples of such documents are hard to come by. Fortunately, Chinese ethnographers have preserved a plaint filed in the course of an indictment ritual in Yining 義寧 County of Guilin 桂林 Prefecture (Guangxi) in 1885. The text of this document reveals that it concerned an on-going land dispute between two brothers of the Liao 廖 family. The younger brother, who apparently lacked the money to file a plaint at the local yamen, chose to express his grievances to the spirits of heaven and earth at the local Earth God temple (dedicated to Great King of Vast Blessings or Guangfu dawang 廣福大王). The younger Liao first prepared a cockerel (whether or not it was beheaded is unclear), a bowl of oil, and a written indictment. In the indictment, the younger Liao asked the gods to send a "numinous official" (*lingguan* 靈官; probably Wang Lingguan 王靈官) to investigate the dispute and arrest his older brother. He also stated that if he were lying he would willingly accept any form of punishment the gods saw fit to inflict, including having his home burned down, being struck by lightning, being attacked by tigers and poisonous snakes, and being infected with contagious diseases (Xia 1990: 26; Zhang 2000: 498–499). Another example of such plaints from southwest China is the "documents of grievance" (*yuanwen* 冤文) that members of the Miao 苗 people file in front of local deities (Zhang 2000: 484–486; see also Sutton 2003a). In addition, Adam Chau's vivid portrayal of religion and society in present-day northern Shaanxi (Shaanbei 陝北) contains accounts of two such texts. The first, a 1998 "Death Notice" (*fugao* 訃告) filed against a local elite known as Boss Wang (Lao Wang 老王) by one of his enemies, ended with the auto-curse "If there were incorrect things in what I have said, I'd let my head be chopped off for everyone to see". The second, a 1989 underworld petition (*yinwen* 陰文) filed by Boss Wang, accused people of trying to block the reconstruction of a temple dedicated to the Great Black Dragon King (Heilong dawang 黑龍大王), and seems similar to the underworld indictments (*yinzhuang* 陰狀) discussed above (Chau 2006: 203–210).[12]

There are also examples of late imperial officials filing underworld indictments in order to capture wrongdoers. In one instance recorded in the *Mingshi* 明史, when Xie Zixiang 謝子襄 (ca. 1409–1428) served in Chuzhou 處州, a group of bandits broke into the yamen and pilfered local funds, to which he responded by filing a petition to the City God (*xi Chenghuang shen* 檄城隍神). Later, when the bandits were counting their ill-gotten gains in a hidden chamber, a sudden gust of wind carried them off and deposited them in the local market place, following which they were promptly rounded up (*Mingshi*, 169.7193).[13] At the same time, however, there are numerous

12 Accounts of plaints filed in the presence of this deity may also be found in Wang and Wang 1997: 425.

13 A similar account may be found in the *Yuanshi*, 192.4374.

instances of indictment rituals being performed as a public means of engaging in symbolic or real acts of resistance against authority, with those accused of wrongdoing including officials, members of the gentry, landlords, etc. In such cases, the exact same judicial rituals normally used to support the established authority could become tools of resistance movements, and in some cases such rites were even staged at sacred sites representing state power like temples to the City God (ter Haar 1995: 35–37; Wu 1988).[14] For example, during an uprising against the gentry that occurred in Wuxi 無錫 County (Jiangsu) in 1640, protestors compiled a list of 17 grievances and presented them to the City God (Wu 2000: 34). Another instance took place in 1740, when weavers in Suzhou 蘇州 who felt that they had been wronged by local officials prepared paper money and a yellow cloth containing a list of grievances (*yuandan* 冤單), which they used to file an indictment at the local City God temple. When the ritual had been completed, they burned the paper money and yellow cloth in front of the official's home (Peng 1984: 94–95; Wu 2000: 33).

In attempting to assess the significance of the indictment rituals described above, it may be fruitful to consider the overlap between such rites and the actual filing of petitions/plaints (usually referred to as *cheng* 呈; counter-plaints were known as *su* 訴). In late imperial China, people could file the following types of petitions: (1) plaints about matters some might compare to Western "civil law", including marriage, divorce, and disputes about commercial transactions or property. Known as "fixed date petitions" (*qicheng* 期呈), these documents could only be submitted on certain days of each lunar month, usually the third, eighth, thirteenth, eighteenth, twenty-third, and twenty-eighth; (2) plaints about criminal cases such as those involving robbery or murder, which were known as "summoning petitions" (*chuancheng* 傳呈). In contrast to fixed date petitions, they could be submitted at any time; (3) plaints submitted directly to local officials in the street, which were known as "stopping the sedan chair" (*lanyu* 攔輿) or "blocking the palanquin to express a grievance" (*lanjiao shenyuan* 攔轎申冤).[15] There were formal prohibitions against this practice, and violators could be punished, but it persisted nevertheless; (4) verbal plaints known as "crying-out petitions" (*hancheng* 喊呈), which could be made at an official's yamen by an individual who had just witnessed a serious crime like homicide; and (5) petitions urging the magistrate's court to act on a particular case. Known as "prompting petitions" (*cuicheng* 催呈), these are the most common form of petition found in local archives. Filing petitions involved the use of standardized forms, including spaces for entering names of parties involved in a case, a grid for writing the petition, a preprinted entry detailing the name and rank of the official who was to review the case, a blank space

14 For more on rituals as forms of resistance, see Weller 1994.

15 For more on this practice, see Allee 1994a: 149, 150, 155.

for the official to write his endorsement of the petition and any additional comments, additional year-month-day entries that could be filled in with dates of earlier or subsequent actions related to the case, and finally a list of procedural rules that had to be followed when submitting a petition (Allee 1994a: 148–161; Ch'ü 1962: 118–119; Huang 1996: 111–122, 190–192, 210–214).

Available evidence reveals important differences between filing an indictment at a yamen and performing an indictment ritual at a temple, many of which indicate that late imperial people may have found it easier to approach and seek justice from the gods than from earthly officials: (1) plaints used in indictment rituals tended to be shorter and less detailed than the petitions scholars have found in local archives, stating only the basic facts of a particular case; (2) plaints filed with the gods did not have to be based on actual law or concur with the letter of the law; (3) ritual plaints could be composed by plaintiffs themselves, although illiterate people had to hire specialists on their behalf. In some cases, no document was required, and the plaint could be an oral one; (4) ritual plaints dealt with a wider range of issues than those dealt with by earthly courts; (5) while some indictment rituals were staged during festivals, most could be held anytime, regardless of the nature of the dispute; (6) plaints were rarely rejected or acted upon immediately, but involved a waiting period to see if divine justice would occur.

At the same time, however, there is no denying the existence of key similarities between performing indictment rituals and filing plaints at an official's yamen. For example, the texts used in both practices were often referred to using the Chinese term *cheng*, while another identical term (*fanggao* 放告) was used to refer to filing a fixed date petition or performing an indictment ritual on a prearranged date, usually during the festival to an underworld deity. Moreover, indictment rites performed just after one had suffered an act of wrongdoing appear somewhat similar to the summoning petitions and crying-out petitions mentioned above. Some accounts describe individuals or lineage groups choosing to perform indictment rituals after a dispute had dragged on for a considerable period of time, a practice that resembles that of filing prompting petitions, while newspaper articles to be discussed in Chapter 7 portray aggrieved Taiwanese blocking the palanquins of deities in order to state their cases, which seems a continuation of the act of obstructing officials' palanquins.

Ritual plaints and legal ones shared one other key feature: the shift from the oral medium to the written one, and its resultant impact on dispute resolution. Karasawa Yasuhiko's research on late imperial plaints indicates the importance of language in composing such texts, which were supposed to be composed by official or private scribes (*guan daishu* 官代書; *bisheng* 筆生) using standardized plaint forms (*zhuangshi* 狀式). On the one hand, legal plaints stressed the importance of consistency in details of dates, action, and motivation of different parties; on the other hand, there was room for textual manipulation (including moralistic rhetoric) based on the scribe's narrative skill (Karasawa 2007a: 65–67; Karasawa 2007b: 107, 116). All of these features appear in the ritual plaints discussed above, with overlap between legal and ritual plaints going back to the medieval era (see Chapter 1). Moreover, legal plaints were meant to be structured along the lines of essays in classical Chinese,[16] which has prompted Robert Hegel to observe that "Legal writers in late imperial China drew from the same rhetorical pool as did writers of fiction and prose in other forms, as self-conscious participants in the larger world of writing" (Hegel 2007b: 81). The same could be said for the temple scribes who compose ritual indictments, and it is surely not a coincidence that such specialists are also referred to using the term *bisheng* 筆生. This suggests that one could expand Hegel's analysis to state that the writers of underworld indictments drew from the same rhetorical pool as did authors of fictional texts and official documents.

While the rhetorical features of a plaint were essential for attempting to convince officials or the gods of the legitimacy of one's case, the composition of such a text could also provide an opportunity for disputes to be resolved before they proceeded any further. As we saw in Chapter 2, filing a plaint could prompt disputants to reach a settlement in order to avoid the hassles of a court session, while data in Chapter 3 demonstrated that the performance of judicial rituals like oaths involved a subsequent waiting period for the gods to pass judgment, during which tensions could be reduced and the dispute brought to a conclusion via mediation. This was also the case for many indictment rituals, with the added feature that the shift from emotive oral expressions of grievance to standardized written texts allowed dispute resolution mechanisms an additional opportunity to take hold. This aspect of filing indictments against the living is especially clear in the case of the underworld petitions filed at the Dizang An, which will be discussed in Chapter 8.

Type 2: Countersuits and other ritual responses to indictments by the dead or animal spirits

As we saw in Chapter 1, by at least the early medieval era Chinese people lived in fear of sepulchral plaints being filed against them by the aggrieved dead. Such beliefs, and the rituals employed to counter these indictments, were widespread throughout medieval China and Central Asia, from the southern economic heartland of what is now Jiangsu and Zhejiang provinces to Silk Road sites like Turfan (Bokenkamp 2007; Lian 1996; Nickerson 1997; You 2007). Apart from hiring Taoist specialists to file countersuits on their behalf (see Chapter 1), people attempted to ward off indictments by the dead by placing crude wooden figurines in tombs, a practice that lasted in parts

16 This is also indicated in the rather humorous tale of a young scholar being reprimanded in the underworld for the poor literary qualities of an underworld indictment he had filed (*Zibuyu*, 9.171–173).

of China (especially Anhui and Jiangxi) to at least the Song dynasty. Such figurines, often carved or painted to resemble officials, were most often made of pine or cypress. The former, referred to as "the pine people" (*songren* 松人), were meant to prevent the deceased being sued in the courts of the underworld. The latter ("the cypress people" or *boren* 柏人) protected the deceased's living relatives from such lawsuits (Zhang and Bai 2005: 101, 118–119; see also Lian 1996). One 1090 text found in the tomb of the eighth daughter of an elite family from Pengze 彭澤 (Jiangxi) contains the following passage:

> If the eighth woman's sons and daughters are summoned [to appear in a chthonic court], the cypress person should block (*dang* 擋) the summons . . . If her family is summoned, the cypress person should block the summons. If the siblings are summoned, the cypress person should block the summons. If the in-laws are summoned, the cypress person should block the summons.
>
> (Hansen 1996: 290; see also Hansen 1995: 196–202)

The belief that the dead could file plaints against the living in the courts of chthonic deities persisted into the Song dynasty and beyond. For example, one story in the *Yijian zhi* recounts how a wealthy Ningbo 寧波 native named Lin 林 incurred a debt of 2,000 strings of cash to Registrar (*zhubu* 主簿) Xia 夏 while jointly managing a government store. When Xia realized that Lin was not going to pay his debts, he sued him in the prefectural court. Lin then bribed local clerks to testify that Xia was the debtor, and then told eight of his underlings to cook the books to prove him right. Xia was then arrested, put in jail, and beaten, following which he soon fell ill. Only one man, named Liu Yuan Balang 劉袁八郎, proclaimed Xia's innocence, and refused to change his mind even after pressure from Lin's underlings. Xia's illness soon took a turn for the worse, and as he lay dying, he told his sons the following: "I die a wronged man. Place in my coffin all the previous leases for wine concessions and contracts specifying each person's share so that I can vigorously sue in the underworld." One month after Xia's death, Lin's underlings died one by one, and after another month Liu suddenly felt dizzy and announced that he was going to be summoned to the underworld as a witness on Xia's behalf. He then passed out, reviving only two days later, after which he related in detail his experiences in the courts of the chthonic kings, including a corrupt clerk asking for a bribe. Hong Mai does not reveal the result of Xia's suit, but it seems safe to surmise that Lin suffered a fate similar to that of his corrupt underlings (*Yijian zhi*, Volume 3, pp. 1086–1088).[17]

17 My summary is based on Valerie Hansen's translation; see Hansen 1996: 290–292. For similar accounts in late imperial sources, see Chan 1998: 297–298; Hao 1997: 146; Zheng and Wang 1994: 46–47.

Qing-dynasty works of fiction are full of stories about the dead indicting the living. According to one story from the *Yuewei caotang biji*, a woman's serious illness was determined to be the result of an indictment filed by her husband's ancestors who were angered by her neglecting ancestral sacrifices (*Yuewei caotang biji*, pp. 3664–3665; see also Chan 1998: 291–293). Another story in the *Zibuyu*, which reveals the thin line that separated drama from reality in late imperial China,[18] recounts the events that occurred during the performance of a drama about the renowned Song-dynasty official Judge Bao (Baogong 包公), later deified as a king of the underworld (Hayden 1978: 20–21; Takahashi 1991: 41). One of the male actors (*jing* 淨) saw the soul of a wounded man with disheveled hair kneeling in front of the stage, in order to present a plaint to Judge Bao about his having been wronged (*shen yuanzhuang* 申冤狀) (*Zibuyu*, 11.219–220; see also *Zibuyu*, 3.47–48, 10.198–199, 10.296). Judge Bao has continued to process complaints from the dead during the modern era as well. In Tingzhou 汀州 (Western Fujian), for example, he was said to hear plaints filed by the dead in the temple of the Emperor of the Eastern Peak (Zhang Hongxiang 1997: 106–107).[19] Other ghosts would present their complaints directly to a living local magistrate (*Zibuyu*, 5.85), while in some cases magistrates would be summoned by the City God to witness the dead filing indictments. Such an event is portrayed in Chapter 35 of the Qing novel *Shan E Tu*, which recounts how a magistrate named Tang 唐 dreams of visiting the City God temple where Lin Kongzhao had filed the indictment mentioned above, and ends up viewing the ghosts of Li Lei's victims filing indictments in the deity's presence (*Shan E Tu*, pp. 716–718, 725–726). Writers also commonly narrated gods filing indictments against the living, including one story that portrays the Earth God successfully filing a plaint with the City God when people misused his temple's lands (*Zibuyu*, 3.50).

The fact that many underworld indictments were believed to be legitimate acts by the wronged dead is confirmed by the following account from the *Zibuyu*. The wife of a man named Shen 沈, who lived near Mount Hua (Huashan 華山) in Shaanxi province, was suddenly possessed by a spirit that spoke with a Shaoxing 紹興 accent (Shaoxing is in northern Zhejiang). The family summoned a Taoist, who prepared a bowl of rice and started to chant spells in order to effect a cure (Shen's wife is described as a "patient" or *bingren/bingzhe* 病人/病者). At this point, the spirit cried out: "Taoist, do not strike me! I have a warrant (*fuming* 符命) to requite injustice (*baoyuan* 報冤)." The spirit then explained that, when but a 4-year-old child, it had broken a bowl while playing at a neighbor's house. One of the women in that

18 The pursuit of justice is a common theme in courtroom dramas and Mulian 目連 operas; see Hansen 1995: 216–218; Hayden 1978; Johnson 1989. This is also the case for *gong'an* 公案 fiction (Carlitz 2007; St André 2007; Youd 2007).

19 In modern Taiwan, the City God is the deity that performs this function (see Chapter 7).

household (who was none other than Shen's wife) had not only scolded the child but also exclaimed that such a naughty brat could only have been the result of an illegitimate union. This was in fact the case, and the child's mother had been so afraid of her secret being revealed that she had beaten it to death. The Taoist realized that the spirit must have been granted its talisman by the Emperor of the Eastern Peak, meaning that it would be necessary for Shen to file a countersuit at Huashan's temple to this deity in order for his wife to be cured. After the required rituals had been completed, the spirit had no choice but to leave (*Zibuyu*, 6.113–114). This account is particularly significant for vividly expressing the belief that illness was a form of divine punishment and that certain hauntings were in fact sanctioned, providing that the spirit in question had first filed a plaint that had been approved by the underworld bureaucracy. In other words, such spirits could not be expelled until the legitimacy of their cases had been overturned in the same chthonic court that had granted them permission to haunt the living.

Chinese who lived during the modern era also performed rituals to remedy the ill effects of being indicted by the dead. Among Hakka communities in southern Jiangxi, for example, this involved performing the rite of "ransoming the soul" (*shuhun* 贖魂), a practice which proved highly popular as late as the nineteenth and twentieth centuries. In Ningdu 寧都, for example, when someone was gravely ill, his or her relatives frequently consulted with a spirit medium or a fortune-teller, and the cause of such an illness was often determined to be the result of a plaint filed by the dead. In such cases, five or six relatives of the afflicted person would prepare large amounts of incense, oil, candles, and spirit money, which they then brought to the local City God temple. They also carried weapons as a show of strength. Upon reaching the temple, they left their weapons outside the gate and went inside, whereupon they proceeded to make offerings to the City God and plead with him to resolve the case in the afflicted person's favor. Then, on the way home, these relatives would perform a "soul-calling" (*zhaohun* 召魂) ritual by continuously calling out the afflicted person's name. (Zeng 1998: 238–239). Other examples of rituals performed in response to indictments by the dead are discussed in Chapters 5, 7, and 8.

There are also stories describing animal spirits indicting humans. One medieval account from Dunhuang 敦煌 tells of a man named Wang Zizhen who made friends with a ghost who served in the chthonic bureaucracy. The ghost warned the man that Wang's father was gravely ill because he was being sued in the underworld, and took him to witness the proceedings. Once they had arrived, the ghost pointed out the plaintiff, who was barefoot but wore white trousers and a purple brocade cap. He then gave Wang a bow and arrow, and told him to shoot the plaintiff dead, but Wang was only able to wound the plaintiff in the left eye. The ghost then took Wang home, and told him to look for his enemy there. After searching his house, Wang noticed that the family's white cock had not crowed for seven days. He searched for it, and found it lying in a coop, blind in the left eye. Realizing that the plaintiff was actually the cock, he killed it and made it into a broth, whereupon his father recovered. The story concludes with the following saying: "Do not keep a white dog; to keep one bars its master's progress. Do not rear a white cock; to rear one brings harm to the head of the family" (Waley 1960: 178–184).[20] An account in the *Xu Zhizhu tan* 續隻麈譚 by the Qing literatus Hu Chengpu 胡承譜 describes a python filing an underworld indictment (*Xu Zhizhu tan, juan xia* 卷下, p. 13), while numerous works of fiction as well as morality books (*shanshu* 善書) contain allusions to bovines filing plaints against the butchers who killed them (Goossaert 2005: 115–121, 183–185, 201–203).

Type 3: Indictments filed against illegitimate haunting spirits

While there are numerous anecdotes about spirits filing plaints against the living, people could occasionally turn the tables and indict gods, ghosts, ancestors, and sprites that were haunting them without having received the permission of the underworld bureaucracy. One story describing this practice preserved in Yuan Mei's *biji* anecdote collection *Zibuyu* recounts how a young woman living in Taizhou 台州 (Zhejiang) was repeatedly haunted by an ugly man dressed in red who tried to force her to marry him. The unfortunate woman moved to her relatives' home to escape, but to no avail. Finally, her parents and relatives filed a plaint with the City God. That night, the god's subordinates summoned the woman to the City God temple to witness the offending ghost's trial. It turned out that he was named Ma 馬, and had been a palanquin-bearer. Ma was sentenced to 40 blows and ordered to wear a cangue. However, the next night Ma's deceased wife attacked the young woman and tried to gouge her eyes out. Once again, her parents and relatives filed a plaint with the City God, and once again the young woman was summoned to the trial that same evening. The City God sentenced Ma to be cut in two at the waist, while his wife was commanded to perform forced labor for demons (*Zibuyu*, 3.61–62).[21]

Another story in the *Zibuyu* tells of a young woman who came down with an incurable illness (including pains all over her body, moaning, and jumping up and down) just three months after marrying the son of a Hangzhou salt merchant. When traditional medicine and Taoist fasts and offerings (*zhaijiao* 齋醮) proved ineffective, her desperate relatives filed a series of indictments at the City God temple. Marshal Wen was subsequently dispatched to capture and interrogate (*qinxun* 擒訊) the demons that had been tormenting

20 I am extremely grateful to Françoise Wang-Toutain for bringing this account to my attention.
21 See also Ma 1998: 155–156; Zheng and Wang 1994: 131.

the newlywed, which turned out to be female monkey, black snake, and white snake sprites (*Zibuyu*, 10.185–186). The use of the terms capture (*qin* 擒) and interrogate (*xun* 訊) is particularly significant, as it indicates that Wen functioned as both a martial and a judicial deity. It is also essential to recall that Marshal Wen was associated with his own set of judicial rituals, the *Dongyue Wen taibao kaozhao bifa* 東嶽溫太保考召祕法, preserved in *juan* 254 of the early fourteenth-century ritual compendium *Daofa huiyuan* (Katz 1995a: 85).

It was essential to be extremely cautious about indicting the gods, however. The Qing-dynasty *biji* collection *Chaolin bitan* by Gong Wei 龔煒 (1704–1769) contains an account of the divine retribution one could suffer for daring to do so in an earthly court. According to Gong's tale, a wealthy man in Fujian murdered a traveling merchant who had taken shelter on his property during a rainstorm. One day, the man's fields were struck by lightning, whereupon he filed a complaint against the Thunder God with the county magistrate. The magistrate did not know what to do, but eventually agreed to send a runner to investigate. While en route to the site, the runner heard a voice from above saying: "Are you under orders to arrest someone? I'm on my way there." The runner then had the rich man brought to the yamen for questioning, during which the runner spoke as if possessed (literally used "ghostly words" or *guiyu* 鬼語), saying: "You murdered the merchant, stole his money, and buried his corpse on your property. Is this true?" Shocked, the rich man confessed to his crime (*Chaolin bitan*, 5.115). In addition, an account in the *Zibuyu* describes a government student (*xiucai* 秀才; also referred to as *shengyuan* 生員) being punished by the City God for filing a false indictment against a local earth god known as the Lord of the Soil (Shegong 社公) (*Zibuyu*, 3.45)

Officials also used indictment rituals to enhance their legitimacy when dealing with malevolent spiritual forces. In one example, a teenage boy was possessed by an evil sprite (*mei* 魅), causing him to moan, mumble and even make lascivious comments while asleep. As this was an illegitimate haunting, his family asked the local official to file a plaint with the Lord of the Soil. That night, the official was visited in a dream by the deity, who confirmed that a sprite was guilty of the haunting but that only the City God had the power to stop it. The official then submitted a plaint to this deity (*Yuewei caotang biji*, 11.3450).

There are also stories of officials indicting animal spirits. One fascinating account describes an official named Zhang Bing 張昺, who earned the *jinshi* 進士 degree in 1472 and was subsequently assigned to serve as district magistrate of Qianshan 鉛山 County (Jiangxi). There, he struggled to maintain social order in the face of challenges to his authority from cults to tree gods and local specialists (including spirit mediums). In the midst of all this, a fierce tiger gobbled up a widow's only son. She appealed to Zhang, who fasted and prayed in the local City God temple. After five days, two tigers turned themselves in for judgment. Zhang ordered the guilty beast to remain still, and then shot it to death with an arrow. The innocent tiger was allowed to leave (*Gengsi bian*, 10.131). Lest we be tempted to consider such accounts to be pure "fiction", I will note that an abbreviated (but no less colorful) version of this story may also be found in the Ming dynastic history (*Mingshi*, 161.4392). Such accounts might best be understood in terms of officials' very real concerns with asserting their legitimacy over local cults and specialists that they considered to be "heterodox" (*xie* 邪) or "illicit/lascivious" (*yin* 淫), thereby posing a very real threat to their authority and the authority of the state as a whole (Boltz 1993; von Glahn 2004).

In addition, Kang Xiaofei's research on the cult of the fox shows that officials would not hesitate to file plaints with the City God in order to stop hauntings by fox spirits. For example, one story in *juan* 卷 8 of Xu Changzuo 徐昌作's (ca. 1602) anecdote collection *Yanshan conglu* 燕山叢錄 describes how a district magistrate in Zhangqiu 章丘 (Shandong) filed a complaint with the City God on behalf of a husband whose wife was being possessed by a fox. In order to avoid being entangled in a lawsuit, the fox ceased its actions (Kang 2006: 168–174; see also Huntington 2003: 135–141). Monkey sprites were also a concern, as can be seen in the account of Fang Bangji 方邦基, who served as magistrate of Fengshan 鳳山 County (southern Taiwan), filing an indictment against one such spirit in the local City God temple. The offending creature was subsequently destroyed by a bolt of lightning (*Dongying shilue*, 7.84). There are even stories of officials filing indictments against pests known as *hou* 鱟 that devoured silkworms (*Zibuyu*, 16.306).

In some instances, different types of indictment rituals could be combined during large-scale festivals. For example, Hakka communities along the border regions of Hunan and Jiangxi performed a "Great Flag" (*dafan* 大幡) offering, which included indictment rituals (referred to as *fanggao*) that were staged on the eighth day of the event. The Taoist masters presiding over the offering would dress up as Lüshan 閭山deities, and set up their altar to look like an official's yamen but referred to as the "Lushan Tribunal" (*Lüshan fayuan* 閭山法院). First, members of the local community were allowed to file plaints and otherwise express their grievances. After these rites had concluded, a Taoist dressed as the Earth God (Tudi gong 土地公) filed a plaint against a local tutelary deity known as the "Officer of the Soil" (Sheguan 社官), accusing him of neglecting his duties. At this point, another Taoist dressed as the Sheguan came forward to plead his side of the story, and the two gods made their cases before the tribunal. The rite ended with the Sheguan being reprimanded and ordered to repent (Liu 2000: 314–315). Later on the same day, straw "substitute" figurines (*tishen* 替身) representing the souls of the wronged or unruly dead were also put on trial before the tribunal. Those with living relatives willing to act as guarantors could be reborn; the rest were beaten and expelled, with some substitutes being burned during a fire-crossing (*guohuo* 過火) rite and the others being burned by the riverside following the sacrifice of a cock (*ibid.*, 315–317).

Indictments and gender issues

The final section of this chapter explores the role of the first two types of indictment rites described above in addressing gender issues in Chinese culture. One example of the first type may be found in a story from the *Lüyuan conghua*, which tells of an aggrieved woman filing a plaint just prior to the hour of her death. According to this account, a young husband from Yangzhou 揚州 named He 何 ran a tofu shop. His wife passed away in 1809, when he was just 25 years old, and he started to have an affair with a newly widowed young woman, whom he promised to marry. Trusting him completely, she gave him over 500 *liang* 兩 of gold for his business (one *liang* is the rough equivalent of 1.3 ounces). However, the young man subsequently took the advice of a matchmaker and married another woman. When the widow heard of this, she began to suffer from what we might now call depression (*youyu chengji* 憂鬱成疾), but dared not tell anyone the true cause of her illness. Wasting away, she finally informed her relatives just before her death that she had filed a plaint with the City God (*kong Chenghuang shen* 控城隍神), and presented her testimony in the god's chthonic court. Convinced by the legitimacy of her arguments, the deity decreed that the young man would suffer death by being cut in two at the waist (*yaozhan* 腰斬). That very winter, he fell into the water while crossing a river, and was sliced in half by a floating piece of ice (*Lüyuan conghua*, 15.414).[22] Another example involves a young woman from Amoy who resisted being gang raped by bandits by throwing herself down a well next to the local temple of the Eastern Peak, one implication of her action being that the chthonic bureaucracy would visit retribution on her persecutors (*Xiamen zhi*, 14.580).

A sizeable number of accounts examine the role of judicial rituals in protecting the interests of chaste widows (*jiefu* 節婦). According to one example dating from Ming-dynasty Wenzhou, when the relatives of a young widow filed a false plaint in order to force her to give up her property, the head of the local Pavilion for Explicating Clarity named Zhou Chou 周紬 instructed her to submit a plaint to the City God. Five days later, the deity descended to the hall (*jiangting* 降庭) to praise Zhou and inform him that a judgment would be rendered in three days.[23] At the appointed time, the heavens

22 Another story in this text that refers to an aggrieved woman's death due to depression (*yiyusi* 抑鬱死) may be found in 17.461–462. Ghosts of depressed women could be subject to exorcism if their plaints were deemed illegitimate; see *Zibuyu*, 9.174–175.

23 This hall may have been located in the temple. Whether a spirit-medium transmitted the deity's words is unclear.

suddenly darkened and the offending relatives were struck by lightning.[24] The practice of women performing indictment rituals is also documented in places like Jianyang 簡陽 County (Sichuan), where women who had been wronged would walk through the streets bearing burning incense and a sheet of yellow paper on which their plaint had been written, crying out to the gods to respond to their grievances (*Jianyang xian xuzhi* (1927), *juan* 24).

The above examples suggest that Chinese women could use judicial rituals as a means of challenging patriarchal authority.[25] At the other extreme are didactic tales extolling the legitimacy of male hegemony. One such account in the *Zibuyu* describes how a shrewish wife made life miserable for her husband's family, particularly her mother-in-law. Desperate to be a filial son and resolve the situation, the husband filed an indictment with the City God, going so far as to ask the deity to kill his wife for his mother's sake. That night, the husband had a dream about being summoned to the City God's court, where he was reprimanded for his inability to control his wife. The City God also told him that he was fated to have only one wife, and that she would bear him two sons. In the end, the City God summoned the wife to the underworld and showed her the torments that awaited her should she persist in her behavior. Cowed, she promptly changed her ways (*Zibuyu*, 5.84–85).[26]

The second type of indictment ritual may be seen in the numerous stories of female ghosts pleading their cases in the underworld in response to instances of rape, attempted rape, adultery, etc., as well as the divine retribution visited on corrupt officials and elites who impinged on their virtue. For example, one story from the Qing-dynasty *biji* entitled *Chibei outan* recounts how the ghosts of chaste widows whose biographies had been omitted from the Zhuozhou 涿州 (Hebei) local gazetteer filed a plaint at the City God temple (*Chibei outan*, 25.613). Female ghosts usually filed indictments with the City God, but would not hesitate to appeal to the Emperor of the Eastern Peak if they were unhappy with the results of the judicial process. One jilted woman proved the old saying that "Hell hath no fury like a woman scorned" by filing 19 plaints with the City God. After failing to persuade the deity of the legitimacy of her cause, she then appealed to a higher court, that of the Emperor of the Eastern Peak, where she finally obtained permission to take revenge on the man in question (*Zibuyu*, 22.440–442; *Zibuyu*, 1.17).

Despite the tongue-in-cheek nature of some of these accounts (which seem to be mocking late imperial red tape), other Qing-dynasty works suggest that

24 See the Introduction (*zonglun* 總論) to the Chapter on Lofty Conduct (*Duxing bu* 篤行部) of the Section on Education and Conduct (*Xuexing dian* 學行典) in the *Qinding Gujin tushu jicheng*.

25 For an analysis of women using judicial practices to resist male hegemony, see Just 1992: 390.

26 Images of shrewish wives in late imperial China, as well as relevant gender issues, are discussed in Sommer 2000 and Wu 1995.

the people of that era were no different from their early medieval forebears in terms of deeply fearing the consequences of being the target of sepulchral plaints filed by female ghosts. According to one story in the *Lüyuan conghua*, a young scholar once came to his teacher in tears, claiming that his deceased mother had visited him in a dream and told him the following: "Something has happened pertaining to your case of three generations ago. Tomorrow, officials from the underworld will arrest and interrogate you." Although his teacher scolded him for believing in such things, that very night the student passed away and was summoned to the court of the Emperor of the Eastern Peak. There, he and a female ghost argued their cases in front of the netherworld officialdom, with the female ghost accusing the student of having had an affair with her after she had been newly widowed. After being restored to life, the student actively engaged in charitable deeds to make up for the effects of his previous wrongdoings (*Lüyuan conghua*, 17.459–460).

Other Qing-dynasty accounts frequently portray female ghosts taking revenge against their persecutors in rape-murder cases, or persuading honest officials to overturn unfair verdicts. For example, one account recalls what happened in Shangqiu 商邱 County (Henan) when the members of a chaste widow's lineage tried to take control of her property. First, they filed a false plaint that she had committed adultery and was pregnant, following which they bribed the magistrate to rule against her countersuit. Realizing that all was lost, the widow disemboweled herself in the magistrate's yamen, and subsequently returned as a female ghost to drive her former persecutors to suicide. The fate of the official is not clear, but the story was told time and time again throughout the area (*Lüyuan conghua*, 17.450–451). There are also stories of honest officials assisting female ghosts, including a prefectural magistrate who cleared the name of a chaste widow who had died resisting attempted rape, only to be falsely accused of adultery. The magistrate ordered the suspects to spend the night in the City God temple until the guilty ones confessed (*Zibuyu*, 22.436)

Scholars working on female suicide have shown that culturally-approved suicides could be linked to ideas of retribution, as well as the social and legal compulsion to find someone to blame.[27] However, less attention has been devoted to the cultural significance of numerous stories about female ghosts who had committed suicide following instances of rape, abuse, and infidelity pleading their cases in the underworld and dealing with its red tape in order to exert retribution on their tormentors. One woman who committed suicide after being cheated out of her fortune by a man who had promised to marry her filed suits in the courts of three different City Gods before finding the one who had proper jurisdiction over her case (*Zibuyu*, 15.280–281). A

27 See especially Huntington 2005; MacCormack 1991; Ropp 2001. See also Theiss 2007 on how the Qing code dealt with instances of domestic violence.

second story tells of a concubine who committed suicide after a jealous senior wife murdered her newborn son by piercing its navel with a needle. It took her over 30 years to complete the process of filing a plaint with the City God and seeking out the offending wife, but in the end she drove the older woman mad before taking her life (*Lüyuan conghua*, 15.409).[28] Some of these accounts may have been poking fun at the glacial pace of the legal system, but the fact that each female ghost was eventually able to take revenge on her persecutor also suggests that their plaints possessed a degree of social and cultural legitimacy.

Another story about the vengeful nature of female ghosts who had committed suicide describes an orphaned Suzhou boy who was adopted by his uncle, but ran away from home after being caught sneaking out of school to watch a dramatic performance. After begging on the streets, he ended up being taken in by a shopkeeper as an apprentice. Because he was a diligent worker, the shopkeeper arranged for him to marry one of his female servants. The newlyweds lived blissfully for nine years until the young man happened to encounter his uncle on the street. The uncle, seeing that his nephew had accumulated some savings, forgave him and allowed him to return home, but on the condition that he divorce his servant wife and remarry. The nephew eventually agreed, and his heartbroken servant wife drowned both herself and their young daughter. After three years, the new couple were blessed with the birth of a daughter, but soon afterwards the young mother began to be haunted by the first wife, who claimed her intention to kill the uncle, the nephew, and the baby girl. The terrified couple hired a Taoist from the Suzhou Temple of the Eastern Peak, who performed a ritual to have the first wife's ghost imprisoned in Fengdu 酆都. This proved to be only a temporary remedy, however, for three years later the first wife's ghost appeared before the nephew. She informed him that, "I have already taken care of your uncle, and now I have come for you. . . The time of my imprisonment has ended, and I have pleaded my wrongs before the City God. The deity approved of my chastity and virtue (*zhenlie* 貞烈), and has allowed me to take revenge. Now where will you flee to?" The nephew then went insane, and all the family's possessions were destroyed. They summoned monks to perform rituals to save the souls of the dead (*chaodu* 超度), but to no avail. The nephew died in ten days, followed by his daughter ten days after that. Only the second wife survived to tell the tale (*Zibuyu*, 15.287–288). Perhaps the most striking aspect of this story is its message that even exorcistic rituals intended to imprison female ghosts would be of no avail if the spirit in question had filed a legitimate plaint, something that we also witnessed in the story of the child ghosts discussed earlier in this chapter.

28 A similar account may also be found in *Zibuyu*, 19.371.

Concluding remarks

The evidence presented above reveals that the three types of indictment rituals described in this chapter functioned as expressions of legitimacy and power, including of the patrons who sponsored them and the specialists who performed them. Indictment rituals filed against other members of the living could legitimate the causes of people involved in disputes, while officials attempted to enhance the legitimacy of the state by filing indictments against rebels, bandits, and even malevolent spiritual forces. At the same time, however, individuals and groups attempting to resist the state's hegemony could file plaints against corrupt officials. A similar pattern of dueling rites of legitimacy could also shape gender and family issues, with husbands indicting disobedient wives and chaste widows or other wronged women filing plaints as "weapons of the weak" against their persecutors.[29] All this suggests that indictment rituals were a multivocal form of judicial practice that could address a wide range of concerns, yet also centered on the core issue of achieving some measure of justice and harmony, be it on the family, communal, or cosmic levels.

This chapter also points to another essential facet of Chinese judicial rituals, namely the need to differentiate between illegitimate hauntings by the unruly dead or malevolent sprites and legitimate retribution by the aggrieved dead. Members of the living who were being persecuted by spirits that had failed to plead their cases before the underworld bureaucracy were generally believed to have not deserved such a fate. Such hauntings were viewed as illegitimate forms of porous death, and the living had every right to expect an exorcism to achieve its stated aim of expelling the offending spirit. In contrast, dead souls with legitimate grievances against the living had the option of indicting them in the courts of the chthonic kings, and if their plaints were approved could be allowed to return to the world of the living in order to wreak vengeance on those who had wronged them. Such actions represented a legitimate form of porous death in the sense that the accused member of the living deserved to be punished. As a result, it could prove nearly impossible to exorcise a spirit that had filed an indictment through proper channels, meaning that people who believed their suffering to be the result of a legitimate indictment by the dead had little recourse but to turn to another form of ritual practice, namely the penitential rites described in the next chapter.

29 For more on the cultural significance of resistance, including its links to ritual practice, see Scott 1985, 1990; Weller 1994.

5

TRIALS OF THE INSANE AND DRESSING AS A CRIMINAL

In this chapter, we shift from judicial rites for resolving disputes to penitential rites that mimic the judicial system, and from legitimation in the form of convincing others of the righteousness of one's cause to legitimation in the form of atoning for one's misdeeds (often in order to merit reincorporation into the family or community). Trials of the insane provide a setting for coping with behavior considered to be both culturally unacceptable and the result of divine retribution, with the friends and relatives of the accused (or patient) attempting to determine the karmic causes of his or her affliction and perform penance in order to achieve a cure. In the case of dressing up as a criminal, while some people do so in order to repay a vow or to petition the deities to help heal family members who are suffering from illness, the main idea underlying these rites is that the participant (or sick person intended to benefit from the ritual) has been suffering as a result of having done something wrong in this life or a previous lifetime. Thus, despite the fact that both rites are broadly penitential in nature, they also have clear links to the Chinese ideology of justice and the dread of divine retribution, including punishments stemming from an underworld indictment. In addition, both rites feature actions that center on judicial practice, namely putting a suspect on trial or placing a convicted criminal in a cangue.

Trials of the insane

While the history of mental illness in China has yet to be fully understood,[1] it does seem clear that from ancient times onwards certain types of behavior culturally defined as "abnormal" were frequently considered to be the result

1 This is not to deny the progress that has been made in our understanding of this problem. See for example Chiu 1981; Kleinman 1980, 1986; Ng 1990; Unschuld 1985. See also the classic studies of the cultural history of madness by Michel Foucault (1926–1984) (Foucault 1971 (1961)) and Roy Porter (1946–2002) (Porter 1987, 2002), as well as Rosen 1968.

of *yin–yang* imbalance (*yinyang shitiao* 陰陽失調), spirit possession, or a form of punishment for wrongful deeds. For example, traditional Chinese medical literature refers to both "epileptic madness" (*dian* 癲) and "frenzy" (*kuang* 狂), the former of which resulted from an excess of *yin*, and the latter from too much *yang*. Mental illness could also be caused by demonic possession, especially sexual congress with sprites (*guimei* 鬼魅), including fox spirits and the Wutong 五通 demons (Strickmann 2001: 238–250; see also Ng 1990:48–59). For most people, however, abnormal behavior could be viewed as retribution for wrongdoing administered by the underworld bureaucracy (Davis 2001; 46, 161, 196; Von Glahn 2004: 99). One account from the *Xinzheng lu* states that in the year 1683 a ruffian named Liu 劉 from Qi 祁 County (Shanxi) rushed to the county magistrate's yamen, claiming that the City God had commanded him to turn himself in. The magistrate refused to hear his case, so Liu ran over to the City God temple, where he clasped his hands behind his back as if they had been bound. He then lay down and screamed that he was being beaten on orders of the City God, following which he marched through the streets like a convicted criminal, claiming that the god had instructed him to do so. After returning home, he collapsed, blood poured from his bodily orifices, and he died (*Xinzheng lu*, 12b-13a; see also Hao 1997: 143). Another story, this time from the eighteenth century, describes a 40-year-old student named Cheng 程 from Changshu 常熟 County (Jiangsu), who suddenly started to scream during the first night of an examination session and "appeared to have gone insane" (*si de fengbing* 似得瘋病). When other students tried to comfort him, he merely hung his head in silence, and packed his bags to leave the next morning. When pressed for an explanation, he simply stated: "My wrongdoing has been discovered" (*Wo you kuixinshi fajue yi* 我有虧心事發覺矣). It turned out that over ten years earlier he had sodomized a younger student after plying him with liquor, which resulted in the distraught lad hanging himself. The younger student's ghost had now shown up at the examination session, and was planning to take him to the underworld to be tried for his misdeeds (*Zibuyu*, 6.116–117; see also *Zibuyu*, 10.173, 20.382).

The latter story confirms the existence of the belief that insanity could well result from being indicted by the soul of the person who had been wronged (see Chapters 1 and 4). To cope with such plaints, as well as to resolve the issues that had prompted their being filed in the first place, people in south China could choose to put the afflicted individual on trial in the presence of underworld deities in a rite known as "trials of the insane" (*shen fengzi* 審瘋子). According to research undertaken by Zheng Tuyou and Wang Xiansen, City God temples in Qing China were frequently the sites for such rites, which involved recitations of scriptures, statements of penance, pleas for the plaintiff spirit to leave, and threats of divine punishment should it fail to do so (Zheng and Wang 1994: 177). Similar rites were also performed at temples to the Emperor of the Eastern Peak. According to the *Zibuyu*, when the son of a Hangzhou peddler was afflicted with madness, his neighbor (who was also a manager at the local temple of the Eastern Peak) arranged for him to file a countersuit against the accusing ghost and hold a trial in the presence of the god. The neighbor even wrote out an indictment on the illiterate peddler's behalf. The trial proved the unfortunate youth's innocence, and he soon recovered his wits (*Zibuyu*, 10.199–200).

A detailed ethnographic account of trials of the insane held during the Ghost Festival (the seventh lunar month) may be found in a 1920s field report about Hangzhou's Temple of the Eastern Peak at Fahua Mountain (Fahua Shan 法華山). According to this text, the man or woman considered insane was sealed in a room known as the "Earthly Prison" (*diyu* 地獄) along with people dressed as judges and lictors of the underworld. These individuals then feasted and got drunk together. At midnight, the afflicted person was abruptly awakened, and, along with a straw image of a substitute (*caoren* 草人; *tishen* 替身), dragged to the temple's main hall. The afflicted person and the substitute were both made to kneel before an image of the Emperor of the Eastern Peak. Individuals standing behind the statue of the Emperor and the afflicted person would then engage in a dialogue describing how the illness was a form of divine retribution for wronging someone during a previous existence (*qianshi yuanjia, jinshi lai baofu* 前世冤家, 今世來報復), and how it would be necessary to sponsor Buddhist rites for the dead in order to cure the affliction (Lin and Zhang 1936: 8–11; see also Fang 2001: 236–238; see Figure 4). Similar rites, known as "Trials of the Deranged" (*shen dutou* 審毒頭; literally "Trials of [People with] Poisoned Heads"), were held in rural areas of northern Zhejiang, but at the homes of those deemed insane. These rituals featured images of spirits known as the Demented Lord and Lady (Chigong 痴公 and Chipo 痴婆), as well as life-size straw figures of substitutes (*tishen*) that were subjected to interrogation (*shenwen* 審問) and torture (*kaoda* 拷打), much like the exorcistic rituals described in Chapters 1 and 4. The trial concluded with the burning of the portraits and the substitute (Xu 1994: 199). In Taiwan, ritual masters (*fashi* 法師) and spirit-mediums (*jitong* 乩童; *tang-ki* 童乩 in Southern Min) also perform judicial rituals for people considered mentally ill, which involve attempts to mediate between the afflicted and the wronged soul of the dead (*tiaojie qianshi yuanchou* 調解前世冤仇) (Huang 1992: 115; see also Hsu 2003; Lin 2005).

Dressing as a criminal

The act of dressing as a criminal provides another opportunity for redressing wrongs, but in an even more public setting than a temple hall or courtyard, the processions that accompany annual festivals to judicial deities like the City God and the Emperor of the Eastern Peak. Records of such rites date

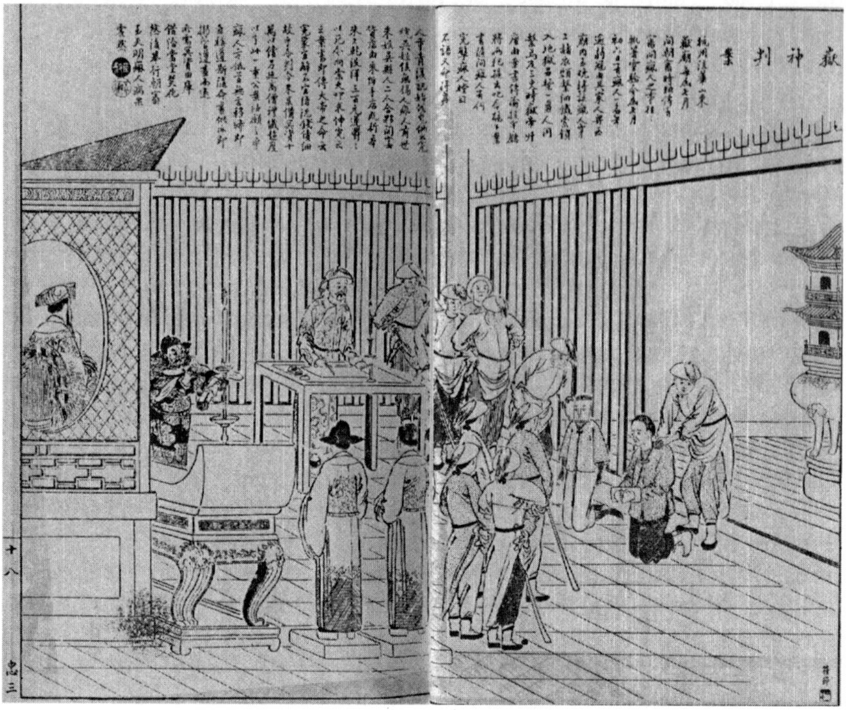

Figure 4 *Dianshizhai huabao* illustration of a trial of the insane at Hangzhou's Temple of the Eastern Peak during the seventh lunar month.

back to at least the Southern Song dynasty,[2] and are extremely common for the late imperial and modern eras.[3] According to Lin Ching-chih's research on these practices (Lin 2007),[4] people dressed as criminals for a number of reasons (which were not necessarily mutually exclusive), including performing penance on behalf of themselves or their family members, fulfilling a vow, and ensuring their own or a family member's good health. Lin also discusses a detailed autobiographical account by the renowned modern writer Mao Dun 矛盾 (Shen Dehong 沈德鴻; 1896–1981), who wore a cangue as a child during the Wuzhen 烏鎮 (Zhejiang) City God festival in an attempt to help cure his father's two-year-long illness. Mao was requested to do so by his grandmother, who had made a vow at the City God temple that one of the family's children would pretend to be a prisoner in the procession.

2 The earliest source I have located to date is the *Mengliang lu*, p. 150.

3 See for example *Qingjia lu*, 3.68–69; *Xihu youlan zhi*, p. 706; see also Yang 1998: 82; Zhang 1995: 114–115.

4 Many thanks to Ching-chih for graciously agreeing to share his paper.

Mao recalled wearing everyday clothes covered by a white skirt and carrying "handcuffs" that were actually golden or jade bracelets. Sadly, Mao's expiation failed to benefit his father, who died the following year (Mao 2001). This account suggests that the act of dressing as a criminal could represent a form of family solidarity that mimicked legal practices while also treating such acts as forms of filial piety (Lin 2007; see also Ch'ü 1961: 74). The role of such rites in stressing family ties can be seen in an account of the "Giving Thanks for a Vow" (*chouyuan* 酬愿) ritual as performed in early twentieth-century Putian. In the course of this ritual, the sponsor would don white clothes and a cangue, behaving like a criminal who has been imprisoned. Family members could provide food and drink only after paying bribes to individuals dressed as jailers, just as would have occurred in many prisons. The ritual ended with the Taoist master removing the cangue, following which the sponsor was presented with celebratory gifts by friends and family members (*Putian xianzhi*, pp. 287–288).[5]

Dressing as a criminal is a rite that also raises a number of fascinating gender issues. Vincent Goossaert has drawn on newspaper articles published in the newspaper *Shenbao* 申報 during the late Qing to analyze how officials and elites in southern Chinese cities attempted to prohibit women from dressing as criminals during City God processions, including doing so in the nude as a form of public humiliation (Goossaert 2008; see also Cao 1996: 36–37; Ye 2003: 192–193).[6] One thing that especially roused official ire was that the role of criminals was often played by prostitutes,[7] who did so as a form of repaying a vow (*changyuan* 償願). The penitential nature of this practice was emphasized in the fact that prostitutes wore red clothes (*zheyi* 赭衣) similar to those of convicted criminals, tied their hair in loose buns or even let it hang disheveled (*zhuiji pengfa* 椎髻蓬髮), and weighed themselves down with heavy chains. Despite their unkempt appearance, crowds of gawking young men were said to follow in their train, which caused officials to label such practices as "lascivious" (*yin* 淫) and strive mightily to ban them (Wang 1969: 43; see also Zhu 2000: 125, 127–128). Such prohibitions could be complicated by the fact that respectable women were fervent practitioners as well, including those who performed self-mortification by hooking heavy bronze lamps to their skin, which was generally referred to as "lighting lamps on one's flesh" (*dian roushen deng* 點肉身燈). Some women were arrested, but this did little to dampen their enthusiasm for taking part in these events.

5 I greatly appreciate the efforts of Zheng Li 鄭莉 and Chuang Shu-chih 莊淑芝 in locating this information.

6 See the following issues of *Shenbao*: July 16, 1872; September 29, 1872; July 17, 1873; October 2, 1875; July 14, 1877; July 18, 1879; July 19, 1889.

7 Prostitutes could also serve as key figures in a number of ritual dramas (Van der Loon 1977).

Goossaert also points out that bans on women participating in public penitential rites were clearly linked to attacks on female religious specialists.[8]

The practice of dressing as a criminal also spread to Taiwan, where it is extensively documented in newspaper articles from the colonial era published in the *Taiwan nichi-nichi shimpō* 臺灣日日新報. This practice seems to have rapidly increased in popularity during the outbreaks of contagious diseases that regularly devastated northern Taiwan cities during the first decades of the colonial era, particularly the bubonic plague and cholera epidemics of the 1900s and 1910s. In 1914, for example, a City God procession held in the city of Yilan 宜蘭 attracted between 500 and 600 worshippers who dressed as criminals and wore cangues. By 1919, the number of worshippers participating in the procession had nearly tripled, to between 1,300 and 1,400.[9] One particularly noteworthy aspect of these rites was that people who decided to dress up as criminals would submit documents known as "petitions of atonement" (*shuzui zhuang* 贖罪狀), which expressed their desire to "follow the gods' palanquin in order to make restitution for wrongdoing" (*suijia peizui* 隨駕賠罪).[10]

Many Taiwanese still dress up as criminals, especially during processions of underworld deities like the City God or plague gods like the Royal Lords (*wangye* 王爺).[11] One of the most spectacular forms of this practice features worshippers who wear cangues (*hangjia* 夯枷) as a means of atonement during the annual procession of the Xinzhu City God on the first day of the seventh lunar month (the inaugural day of the month-long Ghost Festival, which is also the date on which the dead are released from the underworld).[12] According to the late Qing draft of the Xinzhu County gazetteer, these rites were performed in Xinzhu twice a year, the first occasion being the fifteenth day of the seventh lunar month (to accompany the procession of the City God)[13] and the second falling on the fifteenth day of the tenth lunar month (the birthday of the Water Official (Shuiguan 水官), one of the Three Officials or Sanguan 三官), which featured a procession for the Emperor of the Eastern Peak. Regardless of the occasion, people who dressed up as criminals had a common goal, namely to gain release from evil fortune (*jie'e* 解厄) (*Xinzhu xianzhi chugao* (1893), 5.180–181). The *Taiwan nichi-nichi*

8 For more on Chinese anti-clericalism, see Goossaert 2002a.

9 *Taiwan nichi-nichi shimpō* (Chinese edition), March 8, 1914, p. 6; March 12, 1919, p. 6.

10 The historical development of these practices in Taiwan is described in Katz 1998: 144; Ling 2003: 34, 62–63, 73, 90, 102, 128, 177, 182, 195–196.

11 Research on current performances of these rites may be found in Katz 1997: 159–160; Lee et al. 1998: 180–194.

12 Many thanks to Cheng Keng-ya 鄭耕亞, Kuo Ch'ao-ying 郭超瑩, and Chen Shu-ying 陳淑盈 for their invaluable assistance.

13 I have yet to determine how and why the date of the procession was moved from the fifteenth day of the seventh lunar month to the first day of that month.

shimpō contains numerous articles about this practice during the colonial era, by which time it appears to have been held almost exclusively during the seventh lunar month.[14]

The Xinzhu procession of people dressed as criminals has continued to flourish during the postwar era, particularly over the past decade.[15] Today, people are allowed to sign up for this event after the Dragon Boat Festival, which occurs on the fifth day of the fifth lunar month. Those wishing to take part can register at the temple or on-line, with on-site registration also being permitted on the date of the rite. Just over 900 people dressed up as criminals in 2007, the year that my assistant and I studied these rites, including approximately 650 who registered in advance and just over 250 more who signed up on the date of the procession, August 13. Worshippers who had signed up to take part in the procession started to arrive at the temple at around 1:30 p.m., with each one being given a paper cangue and two standardized printed documents: a memorial for requesting a cangue (*qiujia shuwen* 求枷疏文) and a memorial for the removal of the cangue (*tuojia shuwen* 脫枷疏文). Both of these texts refer to the wide range of misfortunes that might have prompted worshippers to dress up as a criminal, including ill health (*shenti weihe* 身體違和), incessant lawsuits (*guansi chanshen* 官司纏身), marital difficulties (*hunyin kanke* 婚姻坎坷), etc., all of which are attributed to karmic retribution for misdeeds in previous lifetimes (*qianshi e'yin, jinsheng yebao* 前世惡因、今生業報). This is followed by an expression of willingness to wear a cangue in the City God's annual procession in order to "gain release from wrongs and misdeeds" (*jietuo yuannie* 解脫冤孽) and "be absolved of all previous and unknown crimes" (*she jiwang wuzhi zhi zui* 赦既往無知之罪).

At approximately 2:30, the City God temple's Taoist priests began reciting each worshipper's memorial for requesting a cangue, following which the paper cangue was placed around his or her neck and the memorial burned. Some worshippers were representing family members who could not be present, while others bore the burden for more than one individual, wearing two or more cangues around their necks. After more than two hours of reciting and torching memorials, the procession finally set out from the temple at around 4:40 p.m., being led by statues of the main deities in charge of the rites, the Officer of Yin and Yang (Yinyang sigong 陰陽司公) and his ghostly attendants Lord Seven (Qiye 七爺) and Lord Eight (Baye 八爺). The gods and the penitents in their wake gradually processed through Xinzhu's

14 *Taiwan nichi-nichi shimpō* (Chinese edition), August 31, 1906, p. 4; August 11, 1908, p. 4; August 27, 1909, p. 4; November 17, 1912, p. 6; December 1, 1924, p. 3; August 24, 1925, p. 4; August 24, 1929, p. 4; May 25, 1933, p. 4.

15 See for example the August 12, 2000 issue of the *United Daily News*, p. 17. See also the August 20, 2001 issue, p. 18; August 10, 2002 issue, p. 17; July 30, 2003 issue, p. B1, August 17, 2004 issue, p. B2; August 6, 2005 issue, p. C2; August 9, 2006 issue, p. C2.

main thoroughfares (see Figure 5) before arriving at their main destination, the Altar of Vengeful Spirits (Litan 厲壇) located near Xinzhu's old Northern Gate, where the Officer of Yin and Yang would receive plaints filed by both the living and the dead for the rest of the seventh lunar month (see also Chapter 7). Once the officer had taken his throne, and all memorials for the removal of the cangue had been recited, the memorials and cangues were burned outside the altar, and the burning marked the conclusion of that year's rites.

The worshippers that we interviewed on that day expressed a range of motives for dressing up as a criminal, but three were most prevalent. Some wore cangues because they had heard that this practice constituted a form of prayers for blessings (*qifu* 祈福) that would enhance their good fortune. These worshippers did not admit to any sense of guilt, but hoped that their penance would prevent ill luck from striking them in the future. Others attempted to make light of their misfortune, jokingly remarking that they must have committed too many misdeeds. Still others admitted that they felt weighed down by wrongdoings from previous lifetimes, and needed to atone for their faults by dressing as criminals. The latter view was also expressed by

Figure 5 Worshippers dressed as criminals processing in front of the Xinzhu City police headquarters; note the smoke from firecrackers and the McDonald's sign in the background, which provide a neat contrast of tradition and modernity; photo by Kang Shih-yu.

Table 1 Ages of people who wore cangues during Xinzhu City God temple procession, 2004–2007

Age	*2004*	*2005*	*2006*	*2007*
0–9	20	22	27	54
10–19	78	45	50	78
20–29	116	95	85	161
30–39	145	109	158	213
40–49	183	121	162	162
50–59	151	103	106	138
60–69	83	30	53	62
70–79	61	32	43	29
80–89	13	14	14	13
90–99	8	3	4	5
Total	858	574	702	915

members of the temple committee, who noted that most worshippers believed that the symbolic act of removing a cangue could also wash away their wrongs from previous existences.

Statistical data that we collected on 3,049 men and women who dressed as criminals from 2004 to 2007 (858 in 2004; 574 in 2005; 702 in 2006; 915 in 2007) reveals a relatively balanced gender ratio: 1,487 men (48.7 percent) and 1,562 women (51.2 percent). More striking, however, was the clear trend of more young people between the ages of 20 and 39 taking part in this ritual, particularly in 2006 and 2007 (see Table 1). The data also reveal that while most participants are from northern Taiwan (Taipei, Taoyuan 桃園, and Xinzhu) an increasing number of people from southern Taiwan (and even from abroad) are beginning to take part in the procession.

Concluding remarks

The evidence presented above indicates that, regardless of the circumstances underlying their performance, the rituals described above are linked by the widespread belief that illness (including abnormal behavior) could result from an indictment filed by the dead against the living. This could prompt the afflicted or their loved ones to respond by performing a wide range of penitential rituals, some of which imitated judicial practices. At the same time, however, the data presented here and in earlier chapters indicate that it is essential for us to distinguish between madness due to unjustifiable demonic haunting (in which case the *offending demon* is put on trial) and madness caused by the aggrieved dead who have sued in the underworld (in which case the *patient* is put on trial). Accordingly, trials of the insane and dressing up as a criminal provide an important opportunity for some afflicted individuals and their loved ones to address concerns about previous wrongdoing, and for others to restore or enhance their legitimacy in the eyes of the community via the successful performance of a ritual trial.

The above rituals also confirm the fact that penance has long been an integral part of Chinese ritual, including Buddhist penitential rites (*chan* 懺) (Kuo 1994) as well as the Dispatching the Writ of Pardon (*fang shema* 放赦馬) in Taoist mortuary rituals (Lagerwey 1987: 202–215). Other Taoist rites, such as the Pacification of Plagues (*hewen* 和瘟), express the links between penance and the ideology of justice. As I noted in an earlier article (Katz 1995b), this plague expulsion ritual features a four-stage ritual process: (1) consecration (marking the Taoist altar as a sacred space for the performance of the ritual); (2) sacrifice (the subsequent invitation of leading deities and patriarchs, as well as plague spirits and those deities who can control them, followed by offerings of incense, tea, wine, and in some cases even meat); (3) expiation (confession of moral impropriety and plea for mercy on the part of the heavenly deities in charge of the plague spirits); and (4) catharsis (purification through the expulsion of the plague deities). The third stage often marks the high point of the Pacification of Plagues ritual, and possesses a judicial aspect in the sense that individuals or the entire community must do penance for misdeeds in order to avoid being punished by the gods. Another rite that expresses the judicial aspects of penance may be found in oaths or blood covenants performed by captured soldiers or rebels as a means of expressing penance (*lishi yi shihui* 立誓以示悔), which appear to have been particularly common during the Song and Ming dynasties.[16]

The practice of dressing as a criminal also indicates a possible link between penance and self-mortification, something that is as old as the ancient Fast of Mud and Soot (*tutan zhai* 塗炭齋) (Maspero 1981 (1950): 381–387) yet continued in the modern example of female penitents performing the act of "lighting lamps with one's flesh". In another example of the occasional overlap between penance, self-mortification, and judicial practice, the starvation enclosures (*guan* 關; *dingguan* 釘關) used by Buddhist and Taoist priests as a form of self-mortification designed to inspire donations actually looked like starvation cages (*julong* 踞籠; *dianlong* 踮籠) that stood outside official yamens (Goossaert 2002b).[17] This is not to suggest that all penitential rites are necessarily judicial, but these two themes seem to be important in both Asia and the West,[18] something that merits further research on this topic in the future.

16 Examples of such rites may be found in the *Xu Zizhi tongjian changbian* 續資治通鑑長編, 87.2005, as well as the *Ming shilu* 明實錄 (Shenzong 神宗), 557.10499.

17 An image of one such cage may be found in Kuhn 1991:8; see also the numerous horrific images on the "Chinese Torture/Supplice Chinois: Iconographic, Historical and Literary Approaches of an Exotic Representation" website (http://turandot.ish-lyon.cnrs.fr/).

18 See Williams 2003 for an interesting comparative study of Japan. For more on penitential rituals in the West, see Tentler 1977.

To conclude, it is essential to recall the importance of confession and remorse as essential components of formal legal procedures. Persuading or forcing a suspect to confess (often with the aid of brutal torture) was vital to securing a conviction, despite the well-known risk of producing unreliable or false testimony, while expressions of remorse (*huiyi* 悔意) have consistently figured in decisions pertaining to the severity of actual sentencing (Bodde and Morris 1967: 97–98, 231–235; Brook, Bourgon, and Blue 2007: 43–50; Dutton 1992: 114–117). Nonetheless, one clear difference between formal legal procedures and judicial rituals is that the latter did not coerce confessions of wrongdoing, instead providing worshippers with an opportunity to publicly atone for past misdeeds and thereby regain legitimacy in the eyes of their peers. This in turn confirms the importance of judicial rituals in not merely mimicking actual legal practice but also reshaping it to better suit the framework of the Chinese ideology of justice.

6

JUDICIAL RITUALS IN ASIAN COLONIAL AND IMMIGRANT HISTORY

This chapter describes the interaction between Chinese and Western legal cultures as seen in colonial courts in Asia, as well as courts in Australia and the United States that conducted trials involving Chinese immigrants. Such interaction first occurred during the late eighteenth and early nineteenth centuries, a time when the hierarchy of state law over customary, canon, and merchant law was only beginning to be fully enacted in European societies. As a result, the Western colonial governments of that era tended to avoid blanket top-down imposition of their legal systems, preferring instead various forms of experimentation in order to establish a legal system that might prove acceptable to both rulers and the ruled. Western states that had to deal with Chinese immigrants may not have been as tolerant or understanding, but also proved willing to exhibit a degree of flexibility. To a certain extent, then, the problem of administering justice in colonial or immigrant settings was less a question of tradition vs. modernity than one of the extent to which the modern nation-state would prove willing and able to tolerate non-Western ideas of judicial authority, with Lauren Benton observing that colonial legal history frequently featured a "contested historical movement from truly plural legal orders to state-dominated legal orders" (Benton 2002: 28; see also DuBois 2006).

The practice of allowing conquered or colonized peoples to retain their judicial practices dates back to at least the Roman Empire (Lariviere 1981: 347), while the coexistence of different legal systems was also a feature of many pre-colonial and Western societies (Tan 1997a: 1–13; see also Chiba 1989; Tie 1999). During the modern era, attempts to introduce Western legal systems played a key role in constructing the nature of colonized subjects (Comaroff 2001: 309). At the same time, however, strategies of legal control involved far more than the imposition of a single system designed to achieve cultural integration by means of social engineering. Instead, the data to be presented below reveal that many colonial powers felt the need to condone indigenous judicial systems, and even infuse their legal systems with other forms of jurisprudence, thereby contributing to the formation of polymorphic judicial cultures.[1] As John L. Comaroff puts it, the challenge facing colonial authorities was as follows: "[Could] a Euromodernist (or, in case of Taiwan, Asiamodernist) nation-state, founded on the sovereignty of one law, actually infuse itself with another [form of] jurisprudence?" (Comaroff 2004: 189). The presence of polycultural judicial practices did not rule out aggressive strategies of legal control and activist attempts to impose legal systems, but generally featured conscious attempts to retain at least some elements of existing legal institutions (Benton 2002: 2, 127, 255–259). Thus, colonial powers were often reluctant to impose their own laws and regulations on colonized peoples, with arguments being made in favor of letting "the natives" manage their own affairs according to local custom, as long as this did not infringe upon the rights and privileges of the colonizers (Mommsen 1992: 10).[2] As a result, the history of colonial law frequently involved a dialogue between colonizers and colonized, a fact that gives credence to Marouf Arif Hasian's claim that, "Legal ideologies are not simply transplanted; they are coproduced by both the colonizer and the colonized" (Hasian 2002: 7). Such interaction involved extensive experimentation, and often messy attempts to find solutions acceptable to colonizers and colonized alike.[3]

My interest in this topic derives from earlier research on religion and society in colonial Taiwan. In contrast to the other examples to be discussed below, Taiwan was colonized by an Asian power, Japan, which had its own long tradition of judicial rituals. As a result, prior to the Kōminka 皇民化 era beginning in the late 1930s, Japanese scholars like Masuda Fukutaro 増田福太郎 (1903–1982) avidly studied and recorded Taiwanese judicial rituals. A graduate of the Law Faculty of Tokyo Imperial University who possessed a profound interest in the relationship between religion and the law, Masuda went to Taiwan in 1929 as chief researcher for religious affairs for the Taiwan Governor-General's Office, and became a professor of law at Taihoku [Taipei] Imperial University (today's National Taiwan University) in 1930 (Tsu 1998: 41–42, 47–50). His writings clearly show that representatives of the colonial government, including police, prosecutors, clerks, and even judges, would not hesitate to observe judicial rituals, and even allow them to be held in the course of adjudicating legal cases that had already

1 M. B. Hooker defines this as "legal pluralism", namely a condition involving extensive interaction between two or more forms of legal practice (Hooker 1975; see also Hooker 2002).

2 A similar reluctance to interfere with indigenous judicial practice, as well as the concurrent use of both formal and informal dispute resolution, also marked the colonial experiences of Malawi and Zambia (Chanock 1985: 71–86). See also David M. Engel's study of Thai law (Engel 1978).

3 For more on these issues, see Comaroff 1997; Comaroff 2001: 310–311; Comaroff and Comaroff 2006; Comaroff and Roberts 1981; Martin 2004.

entered the courts (see for example Masuda 1996 (1942): 58–102; see also Huang 2002: 111–144; Ts'ai 2004; Tsu 1998: 41–42, 47–50; Wu 2003).

Regrettably, however, most previous work on the legal history of colonial Taiwan has centered on the problem of law and colonial governmentality, especially the interaction between modern law and customary law (Wang 2000). One example involves associations for ancestor worship (*jisi gongye* 祭祀公業), which have been discussed using analytical frameworks such as nationalism and modernity to focus on Japanese representations of these associations, as well as debates over whether they should be abolished or accepted as a form of customary law in the course of implementing assimilation (*dōka* 同化) policies (Lin 2000; Liu 2002). As a result, less attention has been paid to the actual practice itself, as well as the ways in which the colonial state attempted to mold its policies in light of the realities of local religious traditions. This contrasts with previous research on colonies like Hong Kong and the Straits Settlements, which paid closer attention to the role of judicial rituals in shaping the interaction between different forms of legal practice (see below).

Finally, a couple of caveats: To begin with, my decision to examine the views of Western officials and elites responsible for dealing with legal issues involving Chinese individuals has inevitably resulted in a neglect of the voices of the Chinese themselves, particularly elites who interacted with Westerners on a regular basis. In addition, many of the works discussed below were written by Westerners who adhered to highly racist views of the Chinese. As a result, the contents of certain texts cited below may seem offensive to some readers. I apologize for this in advance, but have chosen to quote these works in order to provide a full picture of the realities of the Asian colonial experience, including its dark side.

Judicial rituals in colonial settings

In colonial Asia, Western police and judicial officials could choose from the following methods for dealing with legal cases involving Chinese subjects: (1) allowing local elites to manage dispute resolution, including the performance of judicial rituals; (2) tolerating or even encouraging polycultural judicial practices; (3) reform and imposition of Western legal systems. I should also note that there was considerable flexibility in terms of utilizing the second or third methods, something which persists to the present day.

Batavia

One clear example of the first method may be found in the Dutch colony of Batavia, where local elites were given the title of "captain" (Jiabidan 甲必丹) and allowed to take charge of many affairs relating to the lives of Chinese subjects, including mediating most civil disputes. A recent article by Ji

Zong'an 紀宗安 and Yan Lijin 顏麗金 describes how judicial rituals were performed among overseas Chinese communities in Batavia based on a text entitled *Gong'an bu* 公案溥, which contains records of 588 legal cases from October 1787 to February 1791 (Ji and Yan 2004; see also Bao and Wu 2002: 25–28; Kollewijin 1994). These cases included 44 instances of oaths made in the presence of deities (*mengshen fashi* 盟神罰誓) and blood oaths featuring the beheading of a chicken and drinking of its blood (*geji yinxue* 割雞飲血). Such rites were usually held at the Guanyin Pavilion (Guanyin Ting 觀音亭) at 7:00 a.m., one of the busiest times of the day, which ensured a sizeable audience to the proceedings. Based on my own analysis of these cases, I have determined that the majority involved money-lending disputes (18 cases) or disputes over lending objects (seven cases) between friends. A further 15 cases concerned financial disputes between business partners, while four others involved accusations of theft. Not a single case featured violent crime. It is also interesting to note that while plaintiffs initiated oath-making rites in 18 cases, on 11 occasions it was the local captain who instructed that an oath be performed, a fact that indicates the state's recognition of the effectiveness of such rituals (for more on this phenomenon, see below). It goes without saying that disputants also felt such rites were effective: in 13 cases, one party was willing to drop all demands for payment if his/her opponent would make an oath of innocence. These cases also confirm the argument made in Chapter 3 about oaths being a form of pressure, with ten instances of people failing to show up despite the knowledge that such an action might well result in their being judged guilty. The only problem with this collection of data is that in only 13 instances does it record the ultimate outcome of oath-making rituals; in seven cases one party flatly refused to take an oath, while in 24 cases the result of the ritual is unclear.

India

In British colonies, the authorities initially chose a strategy of multiculturalism, and struggled to build an effective legal system that met the needs of colonizers and colonized. Perhaps the most coherent body of research on this problem exists for modern India, and it can be found in the highly influential works of scholars like Dipesh Chakrabarty, Bernard S. Cohn, and Nicholas Dirks.[4] In addition, research by Richard S. Willen reveals the importance of two precedent-setting cases that were frequently cited by officials in the Straits Settlements and Hong Kong as well: *Omichund v. Barker* (1744) and *Ramkissenseat v. Barker* (1786). The former case appears to have been more influential, as it featured a ruling by the renowned jurist Lord Hardwicke (Philip Yorke Hardwicke; 1690–1764) that non-Christians

4 See for example Chakrabarty 2002; Cohn 1996; Dirks 2001; see also Guha 1997.

could be sworn according to the rituals of their own religious traditions. This effectively established the principle that the nature of religious belief determined the validity of an oath, and that the proper form for such oaths depended upon one's own religious beliefs (Willen 1983: 116–117). In justifying his decision, Hardwicke adopted the enlighted position that:

> It is very plain from what I have said that the substance of an oath has nothing to do with Christianity, and that by the Christian religion we are put still under great obligations not to be guilty of perjury: the forms of an oath have been since varied, and have always been different in all countries according to the different laws, religion, and constitution of those countries. But still the substance is the same, which is that God in all of them is called upon as a witness to the truth of what we say.
>
> (Willen 1983: 117)

Similar views were perpetuated in *Ramkissenseat v. Barker*, which noted that "The general rule is that all persons who believe in God are capable of an oath; and what is universally understood by an oath is that the person who takes it imprecates the vengeance of God upon him if the oath is false" (Willen 1983: 117). It was also during this time period (in 1781 to be exact) that the British colonial government directed the Supreme Count at Calcutta to decide inheritance, land, and contract disputes "by the laws and usages of Muhammadans" (Jain 1994: 55; see also van Vollenhoven 1994). Such views were challenged by British administrators during the nineteenth century, with leading officials like Sir Matthew Sausse (d. 1867; Chief Justice of Bombay) attempting to abolish the use of indigenous oaths in their jurisdictions (Norton-Kyshe 1898, Volume 2, pp. 149, 152).

Straits Settlements

Important information on colonial attitudes towards oath-making rituals may be found in research about the history of the Straits Settlements. For example, Maurice Freedman and Roland St. John Braddell emphasize that the British colonial authorities were initially highly tolerant of Chinese and other native forms of judicial practice, especially when it came to civil cases. Thus, Settlement charters of 1807 and 1826 allowed for justice to be administered by "Native Captains" (this was also the case in Batavia; see above), and specifically decreed that witnesses were to be sworn "in the way most binding on their consciences" (Braddell 1915: 77–80; Freedman 1950: 97).[5] Similarly,

5 The following works also contain valuable background information: Hooker 1967, 2002; Purcell 1967; Tan 1997b; Woon 1997.

a minute written in June 1823 by one of Singapore's founding fathers, Sir Thomas Stamford Raffles (1781–1826), argued that it would be impractical for colonial authorities to learn all the laws of their diverse subjects. On the other hand, Raffles stressed that ". . . to apply the law of Europe direct, with all its accumulated processes and penalties, to a people of whom more than nine-tenths will probably be natives of China and the Malay Archipelago, would be as repugnant to universal and natural justice as it would be inconsistent with the benevolence and liberality which has ever marked the British rule in India" (O'Brien 1891: 3). Such tolerance appears to be traceable to eighteenth-century British colonialism in India, particularly the above-mentioned ruling by Lord Hardwicke (*Omichund v. Barker*) that non-Christians could be sworn according to ceremonies of their religion.

These attitudes underwent a drastic change by the 1840s and 1850s, however. For example, in an 1840 case known as *In Re Native Witnesses*, Judge William Norris objected to customary oaths as "antiquated and repulsive", and attempted to institute a system of new Christian oaths that he felt would help attain "one uniform system as to all classes of natives in all the Courts".[6] Norris presented his case for the abolition of such oaths on two different occasions: the opening of the Penang Assizes on June 20, 1840 and at Malacca on August 13, 1840. In both instances, he began by noting the importance of Indian Legislative Act V of 1840, which was passed on February 24, 1840, and extended to Chinese under the Act 9 Geo. IV, c. 74, s. 36. This Act required that all witnesses swear that, "I solemnly affirm, in the presence of Almighty God, that what I shall state shall be the truth, the whole truth, and nothing but the truth". Norris viewed this change in judicial practice as "a just and wise measure, no less due to the honor of Almighty God". While conceding that the Straits Settlements Charter enjoined native witnesses to be administered "such oath in such manner and form, as the Court shall esteem most binding on their consciences respectively" (see above), Norris nonetheless concluded that the new oaths would be acceptable, especially to attain "one uniform system as to all classes of natives in all the Courts". He also decided to adopt the practice from Scottish Courts of asking witnesses to hold up their right hands while being sworn.

In his strong antipathy to indigenous judicial practice, as well as his activist drive for radical judicial reform, Norris seems remarkably similar to some nineteenth-century Hong Kong jurists (see below), yet his efforts to abolish "native oaths" met with limited success. In the case of the Straits Settlements, while judges like Sir Benjamin Heath Malkin (1797–1837) and

6 I am most grateful to to Jothie Rajah for providing me with valuable information about this case, including relevant documents from Singapore's LawNet website (www.lawnet.com.sg); see the section entitled Heritage Law Reports.

Sir Peter Benson Maxwell (1817–1893) attempted to refute earlier tolerance for polycultural judicial practices (Braddell 1915: 81–96; see also Macaskie 1921), the realities on the ground dictated a more nuanced course of development. This can be seen in the writings of Jonas Daniel Vaughan (1825–1891), who served as Superintendent of Police in Penang (1851–1856) and Master Attendant in Singapore (1856–1861). Vaughan claimed that, "The Chinese consider no oath binding on their consciences unless they cut a cock's head off, or burn sacrificial paper, or let a saucer fall on the floor and shiver to pieces", and noted the occurrence of "laughable" scenes when Chinese witnesses were called to testify in court and had no idea of which hand to raise or the meaning of the oaths they uttered (Vaughan 1971: 92–93).[7]

The complexities of trying to impose Western legal practice on the Straits Settlements may also be clearly seen in the writings of Isabella L. Bird (1831–1904), a renowned Victorian-era woman traveler who journeyed throughout Asia in 1877. In Chapter 20 of her book entitled *The Golden Chersonese and the Way Thither*, she described the following conditions:

> THE RESIDENCY, KLANG,[8] February 7: I cannot elicit anything very definite, here or elsewhere, about the legal system under which criminals are tried in these States. Apparently, murder, robbery, forgery, and violent assault come under English criminal law, and must be equally punishable whether committed by a Briton, a Chinaman, or a Malay. But then nobody, except a Christian, can be punished for bigamy. So *criminal law even undergoes modification by local custom* and the four wives of the Mussulman, and the subordinate wives of the Chinaman, have an equal claim to recognition with the one wife of the Englishman.
>
> A Colonial friend tells me that he asked an English magistrate in one of the native States, by what law – English, Colonial, or Malay – he had sentenced some culprits to three years' imprisonment, and that the reply was a shrug, and "The rascals were served right."
>
> The oaths are equally inscrutable, and probably no oath, however terrible in formula, would restrain a Chinese coolie witness from telling a lie, if he thought it would be to his advantage. Sir Benson Maxwell, late Chief Justice of the Straits Settlements, to whose kindness I am much indebted, wrote to me lately thus: "In China I believe an oath is rarely taken; when it is, it is in the form of an imprecation. The witness cuts off a cock's head, and prays that he

7 Vaughan also noted the key role of secret societies in dispute resolution (Vaughan 1971: 110–111), a practice also mentioned in Freedman 1950: 98, Lim 1999, Norton-Kyshe 1898, Volume 2, p. 172, and ter Haar 1998. It is also mentioned in various hearings on Chinese immigration held in the United States during the latter half of the nineteenth century.

8 Port Klang, Malaysia.

> may be so treated if he speaks falsely." "Would you cut off a cock's head to that?" I once asked a Chinese witness who had made a statement which I did not believe. "I would cut off an elephant's head to it," he replied. In the Colonial courts, Chinamen are sworn by burning a piece of paper on which is written some imprecation on themselves if they do not speak the truth.
>
> (Bird 1883; emphasis mine)

This account confirms the assertions in this chapter's introduction pertaining to the relatively chaotic manner in which colonial law actually developed, as well as the tendency by the colonizers to accommodate the customs of the colonized. Thus, the continued use of indigenous judicial oaths and accompanying respect for local judicial traditions is noted for the Straits Settlements as late as the 1880s (Norton-Kyshe 1898, Volume 1, p. 284), and, as I note in the conclusion to this chapter, persists in Singapore today. Judicial rituals also continue to be performed at Singapore's temples to the City God and the Emperor of the Eastern Peak (see Figure 6).[9]

Hong Kong

Similar trends marked British rule over Hong Kong, a territory that truly fits Comaroff's description of having a "messy" experience in colonialism, being initially governed by a diverse collection of well-intentioned but ineffective governors, suspected buccaneers, and corrupt civil servants (Endacott 2005 (1962); see also Sayer 1980; Tsai 1993; Yu and Liu 1994).[10] According to the writings of the colonial official and legal writer James William Norton-Kyshe (1855–1920), as well as subsequent research by Christopher Munn, once the English took control over Hong Kong after the Opium War, one of the first problems they had to confront was how to obtain credible testimony from Chinese witnesses, especially in cases involving charges of perjury (Norton-Kyshe 1898, Volume 1, pp. 275, 282–284, 309). The British had highly negative and stereotypical views of "Chinese characteristics", and felt that their Chinese subjects were morally incapable of being bound by oaths (Munn 2001: 229–231). Nevertheless, during the first decades of British rule over Hong Kong, judicial oaths to Chinese deities (including chicken beheadings, burning sheets of yellow paper, and breaking plates) were

9 I was able to observe such rites being performed in the course of a visiting fellowship at the National University of Singapore in February 2004. For more on the importance of religious beliefs and practices to overseas Chinese communities, see DeBernardi 2004.

10 See also the article by Arthur Hacker entitled "When Eccentrics Ruled the Roost", which was published in the June 20, 1997 issue of *Asiaweek* (http://www.asiaweek.com/asiaweek/97/0620/hkhistory.html).

Figure 6 Oath-making rites are still performed at Singapore's temples to judicial gods, including in front of statues to deities like Judge Bao; photo by the author.

sanctioned by the Hong Kong colonial authorities, with Lord Stanley, Secretary of State for War and the Colonies of the British Government, instructing Sir Henry Pottinger (1789–1856), the second British Administrator of Hong Kong (1841–1843) and also its first governor (Endacott 2005 (1962): 13–22), to honor Chinese traditions and customs. However, many officials expressed unease about the legitimacy and effectiveness of Chinese oaths, which they contemptuously referred to as "eating lettuce" (*shi shengcai* 食生菜), meaning something easy to do (Munn 2001: 231–232; Norton-Kyshe 1898, Volume 1, pp. 296, 310, 315, 410).[11]

11 I am grateful to Elizabeth Sinn and Ho Han-wai 何漢威 for their assistance in locating many of these sources.

The earliest reference to the use of Chinese judicial rituals in colonial courts dates to the year 1842, when a Chinese witness in the case *Regina v. Entrechman* was instructed to smash a saucer in order to ensure that the oath he took would be "binding upon his conscience" (Willen 1983: 118). Two aspects of this case are particularly striking: (1) the fact that colonial officials accepted the legitimacy of performing indigenous oaths, which seems to reflect *Omichund v. Barker*'s emphasis on the "testimonial competency of non-Christian witnesses"; (2) the use of a plate-shattering rite. As we will see below, numerous judicial rituals performed by Chinese in Western courts during the late nineteenth and early twentieth centuries involved shattering plates or blowing out matches or candles. As far as I know, such rituals were not commonly practiced in traditional Chinese dispute resolution,[12] and it is not at all clear why they gained currency in Western courts. One possibility is that Westerners deemed such rites more "civilized" than burning documents or beheading chickens; another is that Chinese elites managed to convince Westerners that these rites represented authentic Chinese religious traditions, thereby making it even easier to lie in court and also resist Western hegemony. I hope to address this issue more systematically in the future.

The prevalence of Chinese judicial rituals in Hong Kong courts, including chicken-beheading rites, is clearly attested to in the following passage from *The Hongkong Almanack* of 1848:

> Philanthropists of every creed look with an eye of pity on that moral degradation – a disregard of truth – which is the peculiar characteristic of the Chinese as a people, . . . men who know not the value and importance of an oath . . . *The first form practiced here was that of cutting off a live cock's or fowl's head; a considerable perquisite was afforded to the court-keepers by this system, who unscrupulously devoured the decapitated bodies.* A cheap form of oath consists in breaking a basin into pieces, intending thereby to symbolize how anxious is the swearer that if he does not tell the truth, his body shall be as unceremoniously smashed into its original dust.
>
> (Norton-Kyshe 1898, Volume 1, p. 313; see also Volume 1, p. 296; emphasis mine)

A similar account, including its description of court-keepers devouring the carcasses of beheaded cocks, may also be found in the writings of Julius Berncastle (1819–1870), another renowned Victorian-era traveler who visited Hong Kong in 1849. Berncastle begins by noting that due to the necessity of meeting the requirements of English law, the colonial authorities had

12 For more on this point, see Norton-Kyshe 1898, Volume 2, p. 147.

struggled to introduce acceptable forms of Chinese oaths into the territory's jurisprudence. His account concludes by stating that other acceptable practices including the burning of "joss paper" containing a written form of the oath as well as imprecations invoking punishments to be administered by the grim deities of the chthonic bureaucracy should the oath be broken (Berncastle 1850).

Even as the colonial authorities tried to figure out which type of oaths should be used in their courts, however, they also held serious doubts as to the effectiveness of such rites. One example may be found in a perjury case tried during the Criminal Sessions of the Supreme Court in June 1850. According to Chief Magistrate Charles B. Hillier, who served in that post from 1846 to 1856 (Endacott 2005 (1962): 84–88), testimony by Chinese witnesses who had been sworn in by burning a written copy of an oath and imprecation might affect his (Hillier's) judgment, but as regards his opinion of the efficacy of such rites in making the Chinese speak the truth, Hillier thought them to be of no use at all (Norton-Kyshe 1898, Volume 1, pp. 282–284, 396).

The practical problem of the effectiveness of Chinese oaths came to a head during a December 15, 1851 forgery case that was being tried in Hillier's court, during which one witness who had taken a Chinese-style oath subsequently admitted perjury and received a prison sentence.[13] Once Hillier had passed sentence, members of the jury complained about "the unsatisfactory manner in which Chinese witnesses were sworn", noting that the procedure "not only appeared to the foreigners absurd, but was laughed at by the Chinese themselves". Hillier responded by stating that "the present mode of swearing Chinese had been practiced since the year he had arrived", while another juryman recalled the initial prevalence of chicken-beheading rituals, which by 1851 had been largely abandoned in favor of burning sheets of yellow paper with oaths written on them.

At that point, the jury recommended consulting a respected member of the Chinese elite named Ching Kum Cheong, who noted that no oaths were used in Chinese courts because magistrates preferred torture. He went on to state that:

> The common way of swearing a man among the people themselves is to make him say his oath standing or kneeling in the open air, to make him write out his oath on a yellow paper and burn it, either in the open air or before some idols. Besides these forms *there are still various other ways, such as to cut off a cock's head, only used by thieves and pirates, and the oath used by the Triad Society, to break a cup or an arrow, to blow out a lamp*, meaning that if his words are

13 A detailed account of this case may be found in Norton-Kyshe 1898, Volume 1, pp. 310–315; see also Munn 2001: 171–173.

> false, his conduct deceiving, or if he will not perform his promises, he shall be like that thing – broken, perished.
>
> (Norton-Kyshe 1898, Volume 1, p. 312; emphasis mine)

Cheong's statement is particularly remarkable for its erroneous assertion that only pirates and thieves would perform chicken-beheading rituals, as well as its emphasis on other judicial rituals such a breaking a cup or an arrow, or blowing out a lamp. Whether such rites were truly prevalent in nineteenth-century Chinese dispute resolution has yet to be determined, but the rite of breaking an arrow as a means of making an oath was prevalent among the Mongols (Serruys 1958).

After hearing from Cheong, the jury expressed a wish to resolve this point of dispute before hearing any more cases, and the court adjourned until January 5, 1852.[14] Once the jury had been reconvened, Registrar Robert Dundas Cay (1807–1888) asked Interpreter Daniel R. Caldwell (1816–1875) about this subject. Caldwell's reply was as follows:

> *I think that the cutting off of a cock's head would be the form of an oath most likely to elicit the greatest amount of truth from a Chinaman*, but . . . this oath, in order to be binding, must be taken before the idol of the swearer; but *Chinese have many different idols, and those idols are feared most which are supposed to be able to punish most; therefore an oath before one idol would not be so much dreaded as an oath before an other idol.* The Chinese have no belief in a God or future state, as we understand them; therefore it would be superstitious, and not a religious fear, which would restrain them . . . Then fear of the oath is more to be attributed to a superstitious dread of some consequences attendant on the act itself in this world, than to any fear of punishment in the world to come . . . I think upon the whole circumstances it would be better to abolish judicial oaths altogether.
>
> (Norton-Kyshe 1898, Volume 1, pp. 314–315; emphasis mine).[15]

Caldwell was an extremely colorful character, and is remembered as a renowned linguist, Freemason, gambler, and even suspected pirate (Endacott 2005 (1962): 95–99). Be that as it may, his remarks, while containing their share of stereotypical language, are relatively accurate to the extent that they grasp the polytheistic nature of the Chinese pantheon and the idea that

14 This adjournment may have been called to allow the collection of additional information, but its length might also be due to its overlap with the Christmas and New Year's holiday season.

15 Many thanks to Elizabeth Sinn for sending me an additional account of Caldwell's response that was published in the *Hong Kong Register* of 1852.

judicial rituals can result in retribution during one's lifetime (*xianshibao* 現世報). Caldwell did err, however, in stating that Chinese religion has no "fear of punishment in the world to come". His call for the abolition of such practices was soon to be heeded by a new group of jurists (see below).

Official frustration at having to rely on seemingly ineffective Chinese judicial rituals finds clear expression in an 1865 article entitled "Chinese Characteristics", which was written by Sir John Bowring (1792–1872), who served as the fourth Governor of Hong Kong from 1854 to 1859 (Endacott 2005 (1962): 36–44). According to Bowring:

> *We tried in Hong Kong different usages which were expected to give some security for obtaining the truth, the whole truth, and nothing but the truth.* Cocks' heads were cut off by or in the presence of the witnesses, and they pronounced denunciations and consented to have their blood shed if there was falsehood in their testimony. Sometimes an earthenware plate was broken, and the parties offered themselves to be shattered and broken to bits as was the plate if they did not tell the truth. Others favoured the writing of an aphorism of the sages on a piece of paper, burning it at a lamp, and requiring the witness to swear that as he hoped not to be burned and tormented he would say all that was true. *But every experiment failed. Oaths, however enforced, with whatever forms invested, were discovered to be utterly worthless*; and it was wisely decided that the penalties of perjury should attach equally to the sworn and unsworn statement.
>
> *It occurred to me to consult a person of some eminence*[16] as to the possibility of administering any form of an oath which would be held binding. He said that there was one temple within the city which was held sacred to truth,[17] and that promises made and contracts entered into within that particular sanctuary were deemed better guaranteed than any other. But he said the place was inaccessible to Europeans; and he thought that nothing but the dread of punishment for falsehood gave any security, and even that security was most insufficient, for the elucidation of truth.
>
> (Bowring 1865; cited in Welch 2006; emphasis mine)

Frustration subsequently developed into attempts at abolition during the tenure of Attorney-General Thomas Chisholm Anstey (1816–1873),[18] a fiery

16 Whether this person was Caldwell or a member of Hong Kong's Chinese elite is unclear.

17 Perhaps a temple to the City God?

18 Anstey gained a reputation for being a hot-headed trouble-maker, and the Anstey Riots are said to have resulted from his uncompromising efforts to crack down on squatters. For more on Anstey, see Endacott 2005 (1962): 89–94, as well as the *Asiaweek* article cited above.

Irish lawyer who in 1856 composed an essay variously entitled "On judicial oaths as administered to heathen witnesses" and "On the administration and value of judicial oaths among the Chinese",[19] which he also presented as a lecture in 1868 after returning to England. James William Norton-Kyshe includes this essay in its entirety in his *History of the Laws and Courts of Hong Kong* (see Volume 2, pp. 144–153), which might indicate his concurrence with Anstey's views. Like Straits Settlement Judge William Norris, Anstey possessed a sense of contempt for Chinese judicial rituals, but proposed an even more radical solution of abolishing all oaths altogether:

> In common with many persons, I entertain the opinion that the abolition of all oaths whatsoever, judicial or promissory, affirmative or compurgatory, would be a very wise and useful measure . . . I have very little doubt that, if the judicial oath shall ever be taken away, in the case of heathen witnesses, the wholesome consequences of that abolition will very soon operate as an encouragement to proceed much further in the same direction. When the heathen is no longer allowed to commit vain and impious blasphemy in our courts of justice, people will begin to consider whether it is worth while to maintain the practice by way of privilege appurtenant to the character of the Christian man.
>
> (Norton-Kyshe 1898, Volume 2, pp. 144–145)

Anstey attempted to buttress his arguments with numerous detailed accounts of the performance of judicial rituals, including shattering saucers, burning papers of oaths and imprecations, and beheading chickens (see for example Norton-Kyshe 1898, Volume 2, pp. 146–149). His efforts appear to have resulted in the issuance of Ordinance No. 15 of 1856, which abolished Chinese judicial oaths, but this was soon disallowed by the Proclamation of May 23, 1857 (Norton-Kyshe 1898, Volume 1, p. 401). The practice of Chinese making oaths in colonial courts according to their customs continued until at least 1860 (Norton-Kyshe 1898, Volume 1, p. 315), but appears to have lost any remaining legitimacy in the eyes of the colonial judicial authorities after that date.[20]

In another contemporary example, the Shanghai Mixed Court, which was founded on May 1, 1864, fully adopted Western legal procedures from the beginning, and did not permit the use of Chinese-style oaths. Nevertheless, the officials who served on this court resembled those described above in their concerns about whether Chinese witnesses would speak the truth, particularly in the absence of torture. From the 1910s on, those Chinese called

19 Anstey's paper is also discussed in Poulter 1986.
20 Some forms of customary law continue to be recognized in Hong Kong (Leung 1997: 76–77).

to testify at the Mixed Court adhered to the Republic of China procedures described in Chapter 3, signing their names to written statements that lacked the slightest concern with religious authority (Kotenev 1925: 46, 54–55, 62–63, 329).

Judicial rites have continued to be performed in some Hong Kong temples, especially the Manmo Temple (Wenwumiao 文武廟), where worshippers would submit indictments written on yellow paper and also behead chickens. One well-known example that also involved colonial judicial officials occurred in 1918, when two famous businessmen were engaged in a financial dispute. Neither could produce enough evidence to win his case in court, and all attempts at mediation failed, so it was decided to hold a chicken-beheading ritual at the Manmo Temple, with the lawyers and scribes acting as witnesses to the proceedings. By the time the ritual was ready to commence, however, neither party was willing to make an oath in the gods' presence, not to mention behead a squawking fowl. They then returned to the court, where the magistrate concluded that since the plaintiff had not been willing to perform a judicial ritual to legitimate his case, his arguments must have lacked merit. The defendant was found not guilty (Lu Jin 2007: 45–46: see also Lu Yan 1979). Twelve years later, when a Guangzhou 廣州 (Canton) boat woman accused a neighbor of killing her husband by a curse, the two women went to the City God temple, beheaded a chicken, and burnt plaints written on yellow paper, believing that the deity would punish the wrongdoer. The account of these events also notes that the carcasses of the chickens were snatched up by "ruffians" (*wulai* 無賴; probably beggars), presumably to be eaten.[21]

The judicial rituals described above also influenced the lives of British colonists and their fellow citizens on the home front. For example, Anstey's essay cites a case from the Old Bailey December Sessions of 1804 for London and Middlesex, which involved two English prisoners (Alsey and Guan) who had been accused of stealing from a Chinese named Er Pinn. As Er Pinn did not speak English, when he chose to take the stand in order to prove his accusations the court sought out the services of an interpreter variously referred to as Anthony or Antonio, who had been born in China and lived there until age 11. He claimed to know about Chinese oaths, and was questioned on this matter by the presiding judge:

> Q: To whom do they make an appeal?
> A: To the god they worship in that country. They break a saucer and then they are told "Your body will be cracked as that saucer is cracked if you do not tell the truth."

21 See the February 12, 1930 edition of the *Yuehua bao* 越華報. I am very grateful to Vincent Goossaert for bringing this account to my attention, and to Poon Shuk-wah 潘淑華 for sharing the original source with me. See also Poon 2008: 259.

Q: What is meant by his body being cracked? Does it mean by the god they worship?
A: Yes. That is the meaning of the oath.
Q: You are quite sure that this is the way of taking an oath in China?
A: Yes.
(Counsel for the prosecution): *Now administer the oath to him* (Er Pinn) *in the usual way in his own country.*

The oath was then administered to him and a saucer delivered to him, which he dashed to pieces.

(Norton-Kyshe 1898, Volume 2, pp. 147–148; emphasis mine)

Another case cited by both Anstey and Norton-Kyshe was Matthysson's Divorce Bill. A British merchant at Macao had gone away on business, during which time his wife had an affair with another merchant. The merchant filed for divorce in November 1845, and the case came before the House of Lords in July 1846. Numerous members of the colonial elite became involved in this case, including Sir Henry Pottinger, who was called as a witness. Things became rather dicey, however, when Lord Brougham (Henry Brougham; 1778–1868) attempted to persuade the wife's maid to take the stand. Lord Brougham first inquired whether it was not required of her to break a saucer before she gave her evidence. The interpreter said that she was very reluctant because "her gods would be very angry with her" The remainder of the account reads as follows:

Lord Brougham: Tell her that her gods with punish us and not her if anything wrong is done.

The interpreter endeavored to induce her to take the oath, but still she declined.

Lord Brougham: Tell her that no calamity can befall her if she will consent to be sworn.

She still persisted in adhering to her religious opinions. After several ineffectual attempts to have her sworn, Lord Brougham said to the interpreter: Tell her that we shall be under the necessity of committing her to prison if she will not be sworn.

She ultimately consented to be sworn.

(Norton-Kyshe 1898, Volume 1, pp. 99–100; see also Volume 2, pp. 149–150)[22]

22 The exact form of the oath is unclear, but it probably involved shattering a saucer.

During the nineteenth century, it was said that the sun did not set on the British Empire. It might also be said that the rites of the colonized could be performed in all regions of that empire, including its very core.

Judicial rituals in immigrant settings

Australia

Similar rituals existed among overseas Chinese in modern Australia during the late nineteenth and early twentieth centuries, particularly those who worked in the gold mining industry in the Croydon and Hill End–Tambaroora districts. According to an unpublished paper by Ian Welch (Welch 2006), when Australian courts had to swear in overseas Chinese witnesses, they allowed them to blow out candles or matches, shatter plates, or even behead chickens. As in the Straits Settlements and Hong Kong, some Australian officials who oversaw such rites possessed highly stereotypical attitudes towards Chinese integrity. Thus, the sources are full of statements like "he would pay as much attention to the chatter of a monkey as to a Chinaman's oath" or "the Chinese will swear themselves black in the face to get revenge". At the same time, however, these officials resembled their colonial predecessors in recognizing that allowing Chinese to make oaths according to their own traditions could be an effective way to persuade them to tell the truth.

The earliest record of such rites that I have located so far survives in the form of a ditty sung by Charles Thatcher, a musical performer on the Victorian goldfields, in about the late 1850s:

> Now blowing out a candle,
> Appears to some a lark,
> It seems to us as if they meant,
> To leave us in the dark . . .
> And the breaking of a saucer
> Appears to me a sell,
> We don't believe in sorcery
> For they break their oaths as well . . .
> As regards the cutting off the head
> Of live cocks, I must say,
> It seems to me as if they wanted
> To introduce fowl play . . .
> Each Chinese witness now is asked
> In every court of law, sir,
> If he'll blow out a candle,
> Or if he'll break a saucer;
> But these, some chicken-hearted ones,

These common modes unheeding,
Prefer to cut a cock's head off,
A very fowl proceeding.[23]

However, most data about Chinese judicial rituals performed in Australia date from between the 1890s and 1910s.[24] According to Ray Poon, court records from the Queensland State Archives relating to the Court of Petty Sessions at Thursday Island stress that each Chinese witness was supposed to be sworn "according to the custom of his country", the preferred method being to blow out a match.[25] In Victoria, oaths featuring the beheading of a chicken continued to be performed during the 1890s as well. This can be seen in the case of one Charlie Fun Chung, who was released from prison on October 26, 1895, after serving 8 months of an 18-month sentence for conspiring to commit perjury. The account of Chung's case mentions notices written in Chinese that were posted during Chung's trial. These notices stated that Chinese witnesses should take an oath by cutting off a rooster's head, and emphasized that the ritual of swearing on the cock's head would ensure the truth was told.[26]

Gordon Grimwade has collected important data on Chinese judicial rituals that were performed in Croydon during the first years of the twentieth century, including two accounts in the *Croydon Mining News*.[27] The first, an article entitled "Broken China", was published on November 1, 1901:

> A very laughable *contretemps* was witnessed in the District Court on Monday. Ah Choe, who was undergoing his trial on a charge of horse stealing, elected to give evidence on his own behalf and proposed to be sworn by breaking a saucer. After some little delay the necessary article was obtained, but it proved rather tough, and at the first attempt it fell on the floor uninjured. The swearer made no mistake the second time. Raising the saucer aloft he dashed it with both hands on to the ledge of the witness box and splinters of broken china flew around in all directions over judge, jury, bar,

23 Many thanks to Paul Anthony Jones for sharing this source during a series of e-mail exchanges that took place in January 2006.

24 Alan Mayne states that use of candles to swear in Chinese witnesses was pretty common in the petty session records for the Hill End-Tambaroora district (especially the New South Wales Turon goldfields) from the 1860s-1900; personal communication, James Hayes, January 12, 2006. According to Jon Kehrer, whose grandfather, Harry Edward Hoyling, was the chief Chinese interpreter for the Victorian police and courts and for the Commonwealth customs and immigration authorities for some five years up until the middle of 1912, "by that time the peculiarities previously accommodated by these authorities had more or less ceased to exist" (personal communication, February 17, 2006).

25 Personal communication, 2002 e-mail from Ray Poon to James Hayes.

26 http://www.prov.vic.gov.au/forgottenfaces/CharlieFunChung.asp.

27 Personal communication, Gordon Grimwade, January 24, 2006.

> police, and public, amidst much laughter. The Johnny completed his oath by declaring that his soul might be broken like that saucer if he did not tell the truth, and His Honour laughingly intimated that if there were any further saucer-breaking to be done it should be performed outside the precincts of the court.

The second reference, an article from the same newspaper, describes an event that occurred nearly 7 years later, on April 10, 1908:

> That a good bit of fun was occasioned in the District Court on Monday last during the hearing of a horse stealing case. That the popular little court bailiff started off by getting a bit excited when swearing the Chinkies by blowing out a match. That after blowing out a half-a-dozen matches he was reminded by the Judge to be careful – otherwise the "consumption of matches will be truly awful". But that the bailiff only smiled – the Government paid for the matches. That it was rumoured that he also had a cock prepared ready for decapitation, but it was not required as that is the Hindoo mode of taking an oath.[28]

Racist overtones aside, these two texts confirm the fact that overseas Chinese in Australia were allowed to make Chinese-style oaths, albeit by means of rites that may not have been widespread in China itself. They also reveal the ignorance of some Australians about Asian religions, as can be seen in the claim that Hindus would take oaths by beheading chickens.

Information on these practices can also be found in a work of community history entitled *The Immigrant Boy: a Townsville Boyhood, 1912–1918*, which was compiled by the oral historian Marion Houldsworth. According to this text, the local Chinese were sworn in by breaking a plate and declaring that if they lie "may their souls be smashed as this plate" or "If I tell lies, may my soul be dashed to pieces as this dish". Apparently there was one instance in which the plate refused to break the first few times, and the frustrated Chinese man ended up jumping up and down on it and shouting "Damn fart!", presumably obscenities taught to him by the local children.[29] Paul Anthony Jones has observed that other oaths from the 1900s refer to the "fires below" and "light above", and speculates that this might reflect the influence of Christianity.[30]

28 A related report of April 6 describes witnesses being sworn in "in the usual Chinese fashion, by blowing out a lighted match".

29 Personal communication, 2002 e-mail from Thomas Harvey to James Hayes.

30 Personal communication, Paul Anthony Jones, January 18, 2006. The importance of Christianity in colonial contexts is discussed in Comaroff and Comaroff 1986; Peterson 2006; Robbins 2004.

The United States

Chinese-style judicial rituals also shaped the experiences of many Chinese-Americans. This is not to deny that numerous Chinese who migrated to the United States during the nineteenth century were excluded from American jurisprudence, while others faced discrimination and derision when they tried to express themselves in court (Doo 1973: 630–633; Wunder 1986: 32–33). In many other instances, Chinese-Americans preferred to rely on various native-place associations (*huiguan* 會館 and *tongxianghui* 同鄉會), to mediate not only disputes among Chinese, but also disputes between Chinese and Westerners (Doo 1973: 638, 640, 649–650; Lammers 1988: 453, 459–460).[31] Nonetheless, nineteenth-century sources clearly show that Chinese could be called on to testify in US courts. If the witness happened to be a Christian, he could swear in the "standard" way, by putting his hand on the Bible. In many other cases, however, the courts had no choice but to accommodate Chinese judicial rituals. In one example discussed by Anstey, the New York Marine Court had to swear in a Chinese witness during proceedings in the year 1840. The state's Revised Statutes clearly specified that "every person, believing in any other than the Christian religion, shall be sworn according to the peculiar ceremonies of his religion", but the court was hard-pressed to comply, and ended up using what the judge determined to be a "Chinese bible", which was none other than Confucius' *Analects* (*Lunyu* 論語) (Norton-Kyshe 1898, Volume 2, pp. 150–151). In commenting on this case, Anstey argued that "a temple and a court of justice in China is one and the same thing", a statement that, although condescending in nature, is also strikingly accurate.

Oaths and chicken-beheading rituals also played a role in the legal history of the American West, including the trial of Le Chow, Ah Hung, Ah Cum, and Chung Lit for the murder of Lum Sow, which took place during the Court of Sessions of Tuolumne County, California, in 1860 (Lammers 1988: 457–459). Another account of such practices is preserved in the records of the Yee Shun murder case (*Territory of New Mexico v. Yee Shun*; Las Vegas, 1882), when a Chinese witness named Joe Chinaman was asked to take an oath considered to be "binding on his conscience" in the presence of Judge Lebaron Bradford Prince of the New Mexico Territory Supreme Court.[32] The sources preserve a dialogue between Yee's attorney (T. A. Green), New Mexico attorney general and prosecutor William Breeden, and Joe Chinaman, who was aided by an interpreter:

31 Important background information may also be found in Barth 1964; Chu 1932; Maurer 2004; McLeod 1947; Ronquillo 1934. See also a racist cartoon in *The San Francisco Wasp*, which mocks the Chinese for their supposed lack of honesty (Dicker 1979: 59).

32 For more on this case, see Wunder 1990.

Q (Mr. Green): I will ask you if you believe in the Chinese Joss house where they worship, where they have their religious services? Do you ever go with the Chinamen in this country where they worship? Do you understand what a God is?
A: I don't know what it is. Yes I believe in the Chinese religion.
Q: Was you ever a witness in Court before?
A: Yes.
Q: Do you know anything about the obligations of an oath under the Christian religion?
A: I don't know it.

Q (Mr. Breeden): Ask him if he knows what he is required to do when he takes an oath here as a witness?
A: He comes here for a witness to prove that a man got killed.
Q: Ask him what he is to do, or what his duty is in telling his story as a witness? If he knows what his duty is as to telling the truth?
A: I can tell the truth in this case.
Q: Do you know that you are sworn here so that you are to tell the truth?
A: Yes.

(Wunder 1986: 29–31)

During the 1870s, Chinese judicial rituals became an important issue when lawmakers were debating anti-Chinese legislation. In the course of holding hearings at the state and national levels, various police officers and judicial officials whose duties encompassed Chinese legal affairs were called to present their views on the subject. Their statements, while disturbing for their bigotry, also indicate the importance of Chinese judicial rituals in that era's jurisprudence. Take, for example, the following testimony by Sacramento police officer George Duffield before the California State Senate in 1876:

> They think no more of taking an oath than they do of eating rice. They have no regard for our oaths at all. Their own oaths they regard as sacred, and the only way you can get them to tell the truth is to cut off a rooster's head and burn China paper. They followed that system here in the early days, but not lately.[33]

33 *Chinese Immigration: The Social, Moral, and Political Effect of Chinese Immigration*, p. 48. This passage is cited in Welch 2006: 13. Testimony by D. J. Murphy and A. Schell on lack of credibility of Chinese oaths may also be found on pp. 83–84.

Similar sentiments, combined with a sense of frustration at the inability to find a suitable way of swearing in Chinese witnesses, may be seen in remarks made by Frank M. Pixley (1825–1895), the founder of a political journal known as *The Argonaut* who also served as the eighth Attorney General of California. During hearings of the Joint Special Committee to Investigate Chinese Immigration, formed during the Second Session of the 44th Congress (1876–1877), Pixley presented the following commentary on Chinese immigrants and their judicial rituals:

> An oath conveys to them no sense of obligation to tell the truth. *We have experimented and exploited in many directions to determine how to enforce the oath and how to perfect it; how to bind their conscience, or how to reach the truth.* We have burnt little paper with characters upon it. We have brought roosters into our court and cut off their heads and sworn these pagans by their blood; we have burned red papers with Chinese characters imprinted thereon; *we have sworn them upon our religious works, the Bible of both kinds*, the Donayan and the St. James' version; *we have placed their hands upon the cross* and we have had them uplifted to heaven where for them there is no God, and still we have been unable to obtain the truth, until the testimony of all our judges and all our professional men is that the Chinese conscience knows no such thing as an obligation to tell the truth.[34]

Despite its disparaging depictions of Chinese integrity, Pixley's statement is of some value for presenting the wide range of ritual techniques that Western judges and lawyers allowed into their courtrooms. As San Francisco Police Court Judge Davis Louderback noted during these same hearings, "We had understood that all that sort of systems had been tried, and absolutely failed; so [here] it was never tried – this cutting the heads off of chickens and burning papers, and things of that kind. We never tried it, for we thought that it amounted to a farce and a disgrace to the court, and did not secure any better results than administering the oath in the usual form".[35] These and other statements[36] reveal that Chinese judicial rituals gradually disappeared from US courts, but more research will be needed to determine the details of how such practices changed over time. Even today, there are still instances where Asian immigrants in the United States have asked to perform chicken-beheading rituals in court. According to an article

34 *Report of the Joint Special Committee to Investigate Chinese Immigration*, p. 13 (emphasis mine).

35 *Ibid.*, p. 188.

36 See for example Seward 1881: 211, 237.

published in the November 22, 1990 edition of the *St. Paul Pioneer Press*, during the trial of a Hmong man accused of rape the defendant's attorney requested that Hmong witnesses be offered the option of drinking "cursed water" (a mixture of water and chicken blood), based on the belief that one who drinks this mixture and then commits perjury will suffer dire consequences, including death. However, the district judge presiding over the case denied the request, stating that such an action constituted "a form of potential intimidation", while the district attorney cited possible health hazards like salmonella. The article also noted that if the witnesses had been allowed to drink the "cursed water", they would have done so at the courthouse following a traditional Hmong ritual, but out of view of the jury. A standard judicial oath would also have been taken. In another case that took place in St. Paul. A Hmong girl accused her stepfather of molestation, but he denied it. When the case went to trial on charges of statutory rape, the stepfather asked to perform a chicken-beheading ritual in court, but the judge refused him permission. In both cases, the expressed willingness to rely on traditional judicial rites appears to have been a legitimation tactic aimed at salvaging the defendant's reputation, rather than addressing specific legal concerns.[37]

Concluding remarks

The data presented above reveal that the encounter between Chinese and Western judicial practice was, among other things, an intense contest over the nature of cultural and religious traditions and their representations in law, which in turn had implications pertaining to the very nature and structure of political authority for both colonizers and colonized (Benton 2002: 2). Much work remains to be done, however, especially in terms of using Chinese sources to better understand the roles of Chinese elites. Previous research has indicated that leading individuals on good terms with Western colonizers – like Ching Kum Cheong, who was asked to explain Chinese judicial rituals in Charles B. Hillier's court – might best be viewed as "cultural intermediaries" who could both support and challenge the legal order that the colonizers were trying so hard to establish. Such elites are especially interesting because they possessed multiple identities and proved able to manipulate both Chinese and Western judicial practices to meet their own agendas, including accommodation, advocacy, and even resistance (Benton 2002: 2–16, 165; Hasian 2002: 3–6, 10; Mommsen 1992: 2, 11). Non-elites also strove to manipulate diverse judicial practices to their advantage, as can be seen in the case of one Chinese prisoner who pleaded that a witness testifying against him should first be forced to perform a chicken-beheading

37 Personal communication, Ann Walter, June 10, 2008.

ritual in Hillier's court, presumably as a means of using colonial authority and traditional Chinese judicial rituals as combined forms of pressure (Norton-Kyshe 1898, Volume 1, pp. 282–284).

Finally, lest we consider the phenomena described above to be fossils of a "messy" and "backward" era, it is essential to be aware of the fact that many legal systems continue to show a high degree of tolerance for the diversity of judicial rituals. One example comes from the former colony of Singapore, where the "Oaths and Declarations Act" of 2000 clearly specifies that members of religions "to which oaths are not of binding force", as well as individuals having a conscientious objection to taking an oath, will be allowed to make an affirmation in place of an oath by substituting the words "solemnly, sincerely and truly declare and affirm" for the word "swear" and omitting the words "So help me God".[38]

In Australia as well, the *Australian Law Reform Commission Report* for 1985 contains a lengthy section entitled "Sworn and Unsworn Evidence – The Oath", which provides detailed instructions on how to avoid asking members of different religious groups to take oaths deemed offensive to their creed, and allows for the following form of oath to be used:

> I swear, *according to the custom of my country*, and the religion I profess that the evidence I shall give in this case shall be the truth, the whole truth and nothing but the truth (emphasis mine).

This text also notes the problematic nature of allowing witnesses to swear oaths that are "binding on their consciences" (note the continued use of this phrase for over two centuries!), inasmuch as the witness has the power to dictate what form of oath should be used. Nevertheless, it concludes that such a paradox was probably unavoidable. The authors of this report were clearly aware of the numerous practical issues that could arise, including the presence of traditional practices like shattering plates and beheading chickens:

> In a number of instances it is necessary to have specific religious texts available and also other materials. It is not unusual for a court to have available a copy of the Bible containing the Old and New Testaments but no other text. *While in most instances evidence can be given by witnesses using the Bible or affirming, from time to time occasions have occurred, and will occur, where the person to be sworn has a religious belief but the appropriate text is not available.* This is unsatisfactory if an oath is to be preferred to an affirmation and could result in courts in some jurisdictions being unable to receive

38 http://statutes.agc.gov.sg/. Many thanks to Jothie Rajah for providing this information.

> the evidence. The alternative of ensuring that all courts should have available to them copies of all the religious texts of the wide range of religions which exist in this country (*not to mention crockery and roosters*) may be thought inappropriate, costly and burdensome. Having a religious form of oath also has the result that the court will on occasions feel compelled to enquire into the witness' knowledge and understanding of the nature and consequences of the oath – for example, when children or mentally ill persons are called to give evidence. The Commission has also been advised of problems experienced in interpreting the form of oath where the witness must repeat "So help me God".[39]

Finally, in Great Britain itself, a handbook compiled just two years after the 9/11 terror attacks entitled "Race and the Court: A Short Practical Guide for Judges" reveals that the authorities were acutely aware of the need for cultural and ethnic tolerance in this highly diverse nation. One section of this work, entitled "Oath-taking – Some Practical Points", reads as follows:

> *The Oaths Act 1978 accords statutory precedence to Christianity, but it is essential that proper respect is paid to the religious beliefs of all litigants . . . The holy book of people from any community who often come to a court should be available*: it is likely that most demand will be for the Gita, the Qur'an and the Sunder Gutka . . . Religious practices in relation to oath taking should be handled sensitively – not as though they are a nuisance . . . Holy books should be covered at all times when not in use in cloth or velvet bags. When uncovered, they should only be touched by the person taking the oath, not by an usher or other court staff. They should not be marked inside or out.[40]

In light of such open attitudes, the uproar surrounding the Archbishop of Canterbury's remarks about Sharia law seems particularly surprising. In early February 2008, Dr. Rowan Williams told Radio 4's *World at One* program that people in the United Kingdom needed to recognize that some citizens do not relate to the British legal system, and that the adoption of some portions of Sharia law in the UK seemed "unavoidable", based on the argument that "There's a place for finding what would be a constructive accommodation with some aspects of Muslim law, as we already do with

39 *Australian Law Reform Commission Report*, Volume 26 (Evidence, Interim), 1985 (emphasis mine); see also the following website: http://www.austlii.edu.au/au/other/alrc/publications/reports/26/Ch_09.html.

40 "Race and the Court: A Short Practical Guide for Judges" (http://www.csren.gov.uk/COURTS.PDF) (emphasis mine).

some other aspects of religious law". Leading politicians, like Conservative leader David Cameron, rejected any expansion of Sharia law as potentially dangerous, while then Culture Secretary Andy Burnham predicted that such a move would create "social chaos".[41] All this indicates that the struggle over multiculturalism in legal practice is far from over, with the advocates of tolerance (like Raffles and Caldwell) continuing to grapple with zealous reformers (like Norris and Anstey). In the end, the ability of modern states to respect and tolerate the beliefs and practices of all their subjects may well determine the degree to which we and our descendants will be able to live in peace and harmony.

41 For more on this controversy, see the following websites: http://news.bbc.co.uk/2/hi/uk_news/7232661.stm; http://news.bbc.co.uk/2/hi/uk_news/7234422.stm; http://news.bbc.co.uk/2/hi/uk_news/politics/7264740.stm. See also http://news.bbc.co.uk/2/hi/in_depth/7235357.stm for information on how Sharia has been incorporated into other legal systems throughout the world.

7

JUDICIAL RITUALS IN MODERN TAIWAN

As I noted in the Introduction and the previous chapter, judicial rituals constitute a legitimate form of legal practice that is largely tolerated by the modern nation-state. This is particularly the case in Taiwan. In contrast with China, where religion is only now gradually emerging from the shadow of long-term oppression by a totalitarian regime, Taiwanese religions are thriving and even expanding. Freedom of religion has always been guaranteed under the Republic of China Constitution, Article 13 of which clearly states, "the people shall have freedom of religious beliefs". However, now that Taiwan has developed into a democracy, people can practice the religious tradition of their choice without fear of state suppression. Temples continue to play an integral role in individual, family, and community life, and temple cults have retained their importance as sites for daily worship, community service, and massive festivals (Katz 2003b; Madsen 2007; Weller 1999).

The past decade has witnessed the publication of a sizeable corpus of scholarship on Taiwanese religions.[1] However, one aspect of Taiwan's cultural legacy has been largely overlooked: judicial rituals performed in the presence of gods of the underworld, especially the City God, the Emperor of the Eastern Peak, and the Bodhisattva Dizang. As we saw in previous chapters, judicial rituals have flourished in Chinese communities for centuries. This chapter considers the development of such rites in Taiwan, but is mainly devoted to addressing the issue of why they continue to enjoy widespread popularity and how they have changed over time. I pay special attention to oath-making rituals performed as a means of demonstrating one's innocence and/or mediating disputes. The Southern Min term for such rites is "oaths and imprecations" (*chiu-chhoa* 咒咀), which, like the Chinese term *duzhou* 賭咒 ("to gamble on an oath") discussed in Chapter 3, indicates the risky nature of submitting to the rigors of this ritual process. The most serious

1 Good introductions to this subject may be found in Chang and Jiang 2001; Chang and Jiang 2003; Clart and Jones 2003; Katz and Rubinstein 2003.

form of these rituals was to make an oath and slaughter a chicken in the presence of the gods, referred to in Southern Min as "killing a chicken while making oaths and imprecations" (*thai-ke chiu-chhoa* 刣雞咒咀) (Kataoka 1981 (1921): 7; Wu 1987: 167–168).

Judicial rituals during the colonial era

Detailed studies of judicial rituals in colonial Taiwan may be found in the work of Masuda Fukutaro 增田福太郎, whose many essays and books contain summaries of newspaper accounts and lengthier field studies of judicial rites performed in Taiwan during the 1930s, particularly chicken-beheading rituals. One such rite took place in the town of Douliu 斗六 (then in Tainan Prefecture; now in Yunlin County) during May of 1934. Some chickens and a pig belonging to one of the town's leading families were poisoned, and suspicions soon focused on 32 households which had been entangled in a land dispute with this family. In order to put an end to these suspicions, the heads of these 32 households gathered together in a local hall, knelt down, proclaimed their innocence, and beheaded chickens in front of an image of the City God from a nearby temple. A Japanese policeman from the local precinct office was also invited to serve as a witness to the proceedings, which were open to the public. The dispute seems to have been resolved shortly thereafter (Masuda 1996 (1942): 97).

The second example of a chicken-beheading ritual took place in Taizhong's City God temple at 2:00 p.m. on September 30, 1933. The events preceding this ritual had to do with a tangled web of connections and interests surrounding an inheritance dispute. Following the deaths of the head of the city's wealthy Lin 林 family and his wife, their adopted and natural descendants as well as other relatives engaged in a bitter struggle for control of their assets, which ended up in the local courts. When the father of one of the parties suddenly died of "pneumonia" on September 3 and was promptly buried the next day, suspicions of foul play arose. Eventually, the relatives gathered in the City God temple, and beheaded three squawking chickens, again in the presence of a crowd of curious onlookers and representatives of the colonial government (this time a prosecutor, a clerk, a native interpreter, and numerous policemen) (Masuda 1996 (1942): 97–100).

The third case, which occurred in Dongshan 冬山 Township (Yilan 宜蘭 County), was witnessed by Masuda and his colleagues, who transcribed a running dialogue in Southern Min purporting to be the actual remarks of the people involved. According to this account, Wang Buren 王不仁 borrowed 50 yen from his friend Chen Youyi 陳有義 (the names appear to be fictitious), but refused to return the money to Chen's widow after his untimely death, claiming that he had already repaid it. The distraught woman and her only son immediately sought assistance from the ward chief, but he stated that he was powerless to do anything because Chen had failed to keep a receipt proving he had lent Wang the money. At that point, Chen's widow suggested going to Dongshan's City God temple and performing a chicken-beheading ritual to determine who was telling the truth. The next morning, Wang, Chen's widow, and the ward chief went to the temple. After kneeling down and worshipping the City God, Wang proceeded to make his oath:

> Lord City God, I live at number 20 in Dongshan and my name is Wang Buren. I'm currently 53 years old. Last year I borrowed 50 yen from my elder brother Chen Youyi,[2] which I returned to him last month. If [in fact] I didn't return the money, may I fail to live out the year, and not even regret the deaths of all my children and grandchildren, just like this chicken [beheads the chicken].

Chen's widow went next:

> Lord City God, I live at number 15 in Dongshan and I am Chen Youyi's wife. I am 51 years old. If my husband had indeed received 50 yen from Buren may I have no descendents and die this year, just like this chicken [beheads the chicken].

Just twenty days later the ward chief spotted Wang running madly through the streets, babbling that he had lied and would now be willing to give 100 yen to Chen's widow to put the matter to rest (Masuda 1996 (1942): 58–83). Regardless of the overall veracity of this story, which in its emphasis on madness as a form of divine punishment resembles Macgowan's account described in Chapter 3, we can again see the tendency for people to rely on judicial rituals when all other means of dispute resolution had failed or were perceived as ineffective. This story also reveals that people did not take cursing literally. Therefore, despite the fact that neither Chen nor Wang actually perished within a year, the entire custom of making curses in the presence of judicial deities did not suffer a loss of credibility. Moreover, Wang's confession of guilt, albeit in madness, solves the problem of the reliability of the ritual being at risk; it does not solve the problem of what would have happened if Wang had *not* confessed.

One of the best-known cases that Masuda recorded involved a protracted inheritance dispute between the head of Xinzhuang's leading Zhang 張 family and the head of the powerful Ye 葉 family of Taipei. After watching their suit languish in court for years, the disputants agreed to participate in two chicken-beheading rituals to be held on the morning of May 10, 1933:

2 The use of the term "elder brother" suggests that Chen and Wang may have been sworn brothers.

the first near the Zhang's original home at Xinzhuang's Dizang Abbey (for more on this site, see Chapter 8); the second near the Ye's home at Taipei's famous City God temple, the Xiahai Chenghuang miao 霞海城隍廟.[3] The impact such rituals had on actual legal proceedings is as yet unknown, but in August of 1934 the Zhang family won their case in court (Masuda 1996 (1942): 88–97). One of the most remarkable aspects of this and many similar accounts from the colonial era is that Japanese policemen and court officials did not attempt to hinder the performance of such rites, but instead witnessed them with keen interest (Kubo 1972: 323; Kubo 1975: 173–175; Masuda 1996 (1942): 46–50, 56–58, 74, 83–85).[4]

Judicial rituals in postwar politics

Data contained in newspaper databases,[5] as well as articles from Taiwanese news websites, provide fascinating examples of how judicial rituals have changed over time, particularly in terms of their role in Taiwan's electoral politics. The rite of making an oath before a god is a key component of many election campaigns, and in some cases candidates accused of lying or vote-buying will behead live chickens in temples dedicated to the gods of the underworld as a way of demonstrating their innocence. Little scholarly research has been done on this topic, but brief articles by Hsu Chia-ming and Li Yih-yuan (Hsu 1978; Li 1983) clearly show that politicians or candidates accused of wrongdoing have not hesitated to publicly behead live chickens in order to demonstrate their innocence, attract sympathy for their cause, and create enough excitement to get out the voters. Such rites were particularly important during the local elections of November 1977, the largest scale experiment in democracy that Taiwan had conducted at that time. For example, Hsu's paper and contemporary newspaper accounts contain detailed descriptions of chicken-beheading rituals performed during Wang Yu-yun 王玉雲's Gaoxiong (Kaohsiung 高雄) mayoral campaign of 1977 as a means of proclaiming his innocence in the face of charges of vote-buying.

A total of 72 articles on chicken-beheading rituals are contained in the *China Times* database, although some of these articles cover the same incident. Because this database covers a relatively recent time period (May 1991–December 1999), the vast majority of articles (67, or 93 percent) describe politicians from all of Taiwan's political parties, including well-

3 For more on City God cults in colonial Taiwan, see Ling 2003; Sung 1995.

4 The history of Taiwan's legal development during the colonial era has been researched by Wang Tay-sheng (Wang 2000).

5 See especially the databases for the *China Times* (*Zhongguo shibao "Quanwen baozhi yingxiang ziliaoku"* 中國時報「全文報紙影像資料庫」; May 1991–December 1999) and *United Daily News* (*Lianhe zhishiku* 聯合資料庫 (http://udndata.com/library/; September 1953–present).

known figures such as Ho Chih-hui 何智輝, James Soong (Song Ch'u-yu 宋楚瑜), and Su Chen-ch'ang 蘇貞昌. Even some members of the now defunct New Party, which was generally unsympathetic towards Taiwanese indigenous culture, claimed that they were willing to perform such rites to prove their innocence in the face of charges of corruption or vote-buying. In only 11 instances (15 percent), however, did the unfortunate fowl actually lose their heads, which indicates that the speech act of claiming willingness to perform a chicken-beheading rite may be more important for ensuring a politician's legitimacy than actually lopping off its head.

The *United Daily News* database, which covers over 50 years (September 1953–present), contains more articles (95), while a smaller percentage is about politicians (71, or 75 percent). Moreover, there were more cases of chickens actually being beheaded (28, or 29 percent), including both during political campaigns and to resolve disputes. Leading political figures mentioned in these stories included Hung Yu-ch'in 洪玉欽, Liu Sung-fan 劉松藩, Lo Fu-chu 羅福助, and Su Nan-ch'eng 蘇南成. In one instance, a cockerel died of suffocation in its box while a Pingdong county representative (*xian yiyuan* 縣議員) kept pressuring the county magistrate to ritually behead the bird as a means of demonstrating the he was not guilty of favoritism in a farmers' association (*nonghui* 農會) election. Whether the politician in question actually intended to perform such a bloody ritual is unclear, but his persistence eventually prompted the speaker to intervene and attempt to mediate a solution to the controversy. This suggests that, like the oaths discussed in Chapter 3, the threat of a chicken-beheading ritual could serve as a tactic to coerce others into pressing for the achievement of a speedy resolution.[6]

The frequent beheading of chickens during the 1970s and 1980s prompted leading temples (such as the Beigang Chaotian Gong 北港朝天宮) and religious figures (such as Dharma Master Hsing-yun 星雲法師) to strongly oppose the performance of such rites, while newspaper reporters also lambasted them as rank "superstition" (*mixin* 迷信). In the face of such criticism, some politicians have resorted to substitute rituals, such as sprinkling red-colored medicine over a dead fowl, beheading a vegetarian chicken (*suji* 素雞), slicing a piece off a cock's crown in order to draw blood, or inflicting ritual violence on substitutes such as an apple or a boiled egg.[7] In one recent example, four Nationalist Party (KMT) candidates competing in a 2007 party primary went to the Xinzhu City God temple and made

6 See the February 8, 1985 issue of the *United Daily News* (*Lianhe bao* 聯合報), p. 2.

7 Accounts of the use of substitutes may be found in the November 16, 2000 issue of the *United Daily News*, p. 20; see also the November 9, 2001 issue, p. 18. Other accounts may be found in the May 18, 1993 issue of the *China Times* (*Zhongguo shibao* 中國時報), p. 13, as well as the July 12, 1994 issue, p. 14, and the January 24, 1998 issue, p. 16.

oaths to obey party rules and support the eventual winner. The text of their oath specifically stated that this rite was intended to replace traditional chicken-beheading rituals.[8] The next year, a candidate running in the 2008 Legislative Yuan elections invited his opponent to a local temple in order to make oaths promising not to engage in vote-buying. He also brought a chicken to the temple as a means of adding further legitimacy to the oath, but refrained from beheading it for fear of causing a public outcry.[9]

Politicians also realize that oaths, while less spectacular than chicken-beheading rituals, can still prove valuable on the campaign trail. During the 1989 Gaoxiong county magistrate election, for example, three candidates participating in a sparsely-attended debate agreed to stop their verbal sparring and engage in a joint oath not to engage in vote-buying as a means of sparking interest in their respective campaigns.[10] In another example that took place in the spring of 2001, Yen Ch'ing-piao 顏清標 (former Taizhong (Taichung) County Council Speaker and current member of the Legislative Yuan), who had been accused of extortion and attempted murder, had his son make an oath in one of Taiwan's most renowned temples (the Zhenlan Gong 鎮瀾宮, dedicated to the goddess Mazu 媽祖) proclaiming his innocence.[11] Whether such an oath augmented Yen's legitimacy is another matter, however, as some critics caustically remarked that if he had really been innocent he would have dared to make his oath in person before a statue of an underworld deity.

Chicken-beheading rituals can also serve as metaphors for political figures who are struggling to prove their innocence in the court of public opinion. For example, during the 2000 presidential campaign, when James Soong was accused of having embezzled funds from the KMT, a local cartoonist published a picture of him performing a chicken-beheading ritual in order to emphasize his innocence, exclaiming: "I am honest! I am honest!" In the background, then President Lee Teng-hui 李登輝 is shown asking KMT Presidential candidate Lien Chan 連戰: "Is this his last trick?" The placard in the lower right corner reads: "Oath-making; chicken-beheading" (see Figure 7).[12] This cartoon was particularly amusing because Soong, a thoroughly Westernized member of the elite, would probably not have even contemplated performing such a rite, and because many people assumed he was in fact guilty as charged.

Indictment rituals have also become politicized, the most notable example being the filing of an underworld indictment against President Chen

8 See http://news.yam.com/cna/life/200704/20070409111376.html

9 See http://news.yam.com/view/mkvideopage.php/20080111226980.

10 See the November 28, 1989 issue of the *United Daily News*, p. 4.

11 See the April 30, 2001 issue of the *China Times*, p. 6.

12 See the December 18, 1999 issue of the *Liberty Times* (*Ziyou shibao* 自由時報), p. 15.

Figure 7 Presidential candidate James Soong (Song Chuyu), wearing a butcher's apron emblazoned with his surname, beheads a squawking fowl in an unidentified temple; used with the permission of the cartoonist Yu-fu 魚夫.

Shui-bian 陳水扁 at the Jiayi (Chia-yi) 嘉義 City God temple on August 19, 2006 by Huang Kuang-kuo 黃光國 and other members of the Democracy Alliance (Minmeng 民盟) as part of the Depose Bian (DaoBian 倒扁) movement. These rites, which were termed "Deposing Bian (Chen Shuibian) and Filing an Indictment with the City God" (DaoBian zhugao Chenghuang 倒扁祝告城隍), included the reading of a written text imploring the City God to display his numinous powers by helping the Depose Bian movement succeed. Chen was able to complete his second term.[13]

Judicial rituals in modern life

Despite the above instances of change, however, Taiwanese judicial rituals also exhibit remarkable continuity. For example, blood covenants continue to be performed by criminals and gang members, who, like the secret society members of late imperial times, generally worship the deity Guanggong 關公

13 See http://www.singtaonet.com:82/hk_taiwan/t20060819_304470.html.

and make oaths promising to help each other in times of need.[14] A more nefarious form of oath-making involves the use of these rites to compel young girls into becoming prostitutes. In one example, a young victim who was being forced into this profession had to kneel in an unidentified temple and swear the following: "I am willing to work (as a prostitute) for Mr. L for a period of two years. Should I resist or tell the authorities, may I die a bad death, and my corpse be dumped by the roadside to be dragged off and eaten by the dogs."[15] However, prostitutes can also use judicial rituals to protect themselves from customers and the police. In one instance, when a prostitute and her client were quarreling over whether they had actually had sex and how much to pay for it, the madam first recommended going to an obstetrics and gynecology clinic for an examination. When they refused, she then suggested an oath-making ritual, whereupon the two disputants went to a nearby temple and did just that. Another case involved a madam who believed that her brothel had been unfairly investigated and searched by the authorities. In order to prove her innocence, she offered to accompany the police to a nearby temple and perform a chicken-beheading ritual. Whether the police took her up on her offer is unclear.[16] I have yet to find any evidence of prostitutes performing (or being forced to perform) similar rites in China, but one suspects that such practices are not unique to modern Taiwan.

Oaths of innocence also remain an important part of legitimation practices among the general populace. In one instance, a woman who was suspected of being involved in the untimely death of a member of the Gaoxiong County elite went to the Fengshan City God temple, where she cried in grief and swore that she had nothing to do with the unfortunate affair. Being illiterate, she was unable to fully recite the text of the oath that was subsequently burned at the temple; someone else had to do this for her.[17] Another example of such a rite occurred when a monk was accused of raping his disciple, prompting the disputants and their relatives to go to the Xinzhu City God temple and make oaths of innocence. Following the completion of this rite, all parties decided to call a halt to the dispute in order to wait for the gods to pass judgment, a fact that confirms the importance of judicial rituals as providing a waiting period during which tensions can be defused.[18] Reducing tensions was also a key factor underlying the performance of an oath-making ritual at the Jiayi City God temple in June

14 See the April 1, 1993 issue of the *United Daily News*, p. 15; see also the May 14, 1962 issue, p. 3.

15 See the September 25, 1958 issue of the *United Daily News*, p. 4; see also the April 30, 1967 issue, p. 3. For more on prostitution in Taiwan, see Hsieh 1972; Shen 1990.

16 See the April 20, 2005 issue of the *United Daily News*, p. C4; see also the June 11, 1962 issue, p. 3.

17 See the September 20, 1989 issue of the *United Daily News*, p. 3.

18 See the September 8, 1953 issue of the *United Daily News*, p. 3.

2008. In January 2006, a trucker had died from a collision involving two trucks. His family accused the driver of the other vehicle of manslaughter, but the authorities ruled that the deceased had been driving while intoxicated, and the accused driver was able to locate two witnesses who supported his claim of innocence. The deceased driver's family continued to press charges until he appeared to his brothers in a dream and told them that all charges should be dropped if the other driver and witnesses proved willing to make oaths of innocence at the above-mentioned temple. They agreed to do so, and, as soon as the rite had been performed, the deceased's relatives not only dropped all charges, but also declined to ask for compensation, all of which suggests that this particular ritual might have provided them with a face-saving solution to a dispute that they realized they had no chance of winning.[19] However, in some cases the authorities will prevent oath-making rituals for fear that they might spark further tensions, which is what occurred when the widow of a murder victim attempted to force the wife of one of the suspects to make an oath of innocence at the Xinzhu City God temple.[20]

People regularly perform oaths of innocence during financial disputes, often as a means of putting pressure on their rivals.[21] One such dispute proved so complex that over 150 debtors and creditors had to take turns making oaths in the Xinzhu City God temple.[22] Other oaths have clearer links to modern Taiwanese life, such as the management of a baseball team that had been accused of throwing games instructing the players to make an oath of innocence at the Taizhong City God temple. Two copies of the oath were prepared: one was burned at the temple, while the other was kept in the team's offices.[23]

Requesting others to make oaths of innocence also continues to be used as a means of pressuring people suspected of wrongdoing. Back in 1959, a teenage girl was questioned by the police on suspicion of having stolen NT$60,000 (a huge sum at that time), only to repeatedly claim that she knew nothing about it. Exasperated, the victim dragged the girl to the Xinzhu City God temple and instructed her to swear that she had not committed theft. Terrified by the threat of divine retribution, she promptly proceeded to confess.[24] There are cases in which oath-making rites are ineffective, however, including one that occurred in Xinzhuang in late August 1961, when some bus company earnings mysteriously disappeared from one of its stations. A female ticket-taker was suspected of the crime, but she steadfastly

19 See the June 24, 2008 issue of the *Liberty Times*, p. 4.
20 See the March 5, 1965 issue of the *United Daily News*, p. 3.
21 See the January 18, 1997 issue of the *China Times*, p. 13.
22 See the December 8, 1959 issue of the *United Daily News*, p. 4.
23 See the February 26, 2000 issue of the *United Daily News*, p. 15.
24 See the January 14, 1959 issue of the *United Daily News*, p. 4.

maintained her innocence, so the bus company ordered all eight workers from the station to go to the Dizang Abbey and make oaths in front of the Lord of the Hordes. Three weeks later, the criminal still had not been caught, and the unfortunate ticket-taker was forced to pay restitution.[25]

The links between oaths and gender issues have also persisted, especially in instances of men and women performing such rites as a means of legitimizing their positions in marital disputes. One newspaper article describes a woman who had her husband make an oath of marital fidelity, and then placed a written copy on the family altar. Her husband cited this as a reason for filing for a divorce, but the court turned down his request as not constituting sufficient grounds.[26] According to another story, a man who suspected his wife of having an affair not only toured local motels with her photo in order to ask if she had been spotted, but also forced her to make oaths of innocence in front of the family's ancestors and in a local temple. Unable to stand such behavior, the wife filed for a divorce, and won her case in court.[27]

One new factor, which contrasts sharply with data discussed in Chapter 3, is people embroiled in legal cases attempting to perform oath-making rituals in Taiwan's courts as a means of convincing the authorities of the legitimacy of their cases. In most instances, judicial officials take a dim view of such proceedings and do all that they can to stop them. This is what happened when a plaintiff who had just lost her case prepared incense and paper money, and tried to force the defendant to make an oath of innocence. Hearing the commotion, court bailiffs told the two disputants to move the oath-making rite to a nearby temple.[28] Another example involved two men who were litigating a money-lending dispute, with the plaintiff's wife suddenly disrupting courtroom proceedings by insisting that the disputants go a nearby City God temple and make oaths of innocence.[29] There are exceptions, however, such as the Tainan judge who allowed two men to make oaths and contingent curses in his courtroom while hearing a case about a money-lending dispute.[30]

Chicken-beheading rituals, while far less common than in the past, still play a role in some financial disputes. As recently as 1983, a client and bank teller who disagreed over a NT$10,000 discrepancy in the client's account

25 See the September 18, 1961 issue of the *United Daily News*, p. 3. For more on the cultural significance of rituals proving ineffective, see Husken 2007. I am very grateful to Chang Hsun 張珣 for suggesting this important source.

26 See the January 28, 2005 issue of the *United Daily News*, p. C4.

27 See the September 5, 2000 issue of the *United Daily News*, p. 19.

28 See the April 29, 1962 issue of the *United Daily News*, p. 3; see also the November 6, 2002 issue, p. 20.

29 See the January 25, 1972 issue of the *United Daily News*, p. 6.

30 See the June 22, 1960 issue of the *United Daily News*, p. 3.

balance chose to behead chickens at a nearby temple. This act was credited with helping to bring about a reduction in tensions, although the eventual outcome of the dispute is not known.[31] In other instances, the threat of having to perform such a rite could constitute a form of constraint, which occurred when two women who had accused bank employees of misusing their savings asked that all parties involved in the case behead chickens at the Xinzhu City God temple. When the bank refused, the women protested so vehemently that a large crowd soon formed, prompting the police to intervene and persuade the bank to pay restitution.[32] The expressed willingness to behead a chicken can also be used as a delaying tactic by businessmen who wish to convince others that they will not liquidate all of their assets.[33]

Some marital disputes can also escalate to the point where it becomes necessary to perform a chicken-beheading ritual. This happened in Hualien 花蓮 in June 1955, when a husband accused his wife of having an affair. The husband, wife, and suspected paramour nearly came to blows before heading over to a local police station to file charges of adultery (*fanghai jiating* 妨害家庭) and defamation (*pohuai mingyu* 破壞名譽). Despite the fact that the police were unable to find enough evidence for a formal investigation, the husband insisted on filing a suit in court, but the judges proved unable to reach a verdict. At this point, the disputants decided to present their cases to the gods by performing chicken-beheading rites at the Hualien City God Temple. The wife and alleged lover began by making oaths of innocence and conditional curses like those described in Chapter 3, expressing a willingness to die if they had committed adultery. The husband then voiced a similar curse should he have filed a false accusation. Finally, a man who claimed to have witnessed a tryst cursed himself with developing a "crooked mouth" (*waizui* 歪嘴) should he have lied (note that only the witness escaped the threat of death). All four parties beheaded black cockerels to emphasize the gravity of the ritual.[34]

Chicken-beheading rituals have even shaped the lives of Taiwan's media idols. In the year 2004, for example, when a religious specialist named Yeh Yun-hsiao 葉雲堯 claimed that Hsiao Ch'iang 蕭薔 had worshipped a "fox immortal" (*huxian* 狐仙) at his temple, her agent filed a NT$20 million lawsuit against him. Yeh then attempted to emphasize the legitimacy of his claims by performing a chicken-beheading ritual in a local Judge Bao temple. In the end, Yeh agreed to issue a public apology in lieu of being sued, but also took the opportunity to thank Hsiao for attracting large numbers of

31 See the December 9, 1983 issue of the *United Daily News*, p. 5.

32 See the May 5, 1962 issue of the *United Daily News*, p. 3.

33 See the September 27, 1993 issue of the *United Daily News*, p. 18.

34 See the June 15, 1955 issue of the *United Daily News*, p. 3.

worshippers to his sacred site.[35] Just two years later, when the talk-show host Chou Yu-k'ou 周玉蔻 implied that Yen Ch'ing-piao and his allies had been involved in wrong-doing, she attempted to demonstrate her innocence by beheading a vegetarian chicken at the Zhenlan Gong.[36]

Apart from oaths and chicken-beheading rites, the practice of filing underworld indictments continues to flourish in Taiwan (see also Chapter 8). In one example that occurred in May 1953, the managers of nine Jilong 基隆 (Keelung) transport companies that were engaged in a lengthy dispute over wharf loading and unloading rights went to the City God temple and filed an underworld indictment against a tenth manager they felt had betrayed their interests. In order to demonstrate his innocence, as well as reduce tensions, the accused manager filed an appeal to the City God, the text of which was published in the newspaper.[37] Another example involved a family whose graves had been robbed, and who chose to file an indictment with the Xinzhu City God asking that the deity help locate the perpetrators.[38] Other instances reflect problems facing the elderly in modern Taiwan: one featured an old man who visited a number of temples in Zhongli (Chung-li 中壢; Taoyuan County) in order to file ritual plaints accusing his wife and children of neglect, prompting local social workers to intervene.[39]

In addition, indictment rituals still play integral roles in resistance movements, including protests against home demolition and opposition to industrial projects blamed for causing pollution.[40] Groups of people who feel they have been wronged may choose to file indictments during processions by blocking the palanquins of local deities until they are allowed to state their cases (Katz 1998: 147), an action that appears similar to the late imperial practice of blocking an official's palanquin to express a grievance (see Chapter 4).[41] However, public indictment rites like those performed during late imperial plague festivals have disappeared, apparently due to fears that they might provoke or exacerbate disputes. For example, in the southern Taiwan town of Xigang 西港 (Hsi-kang; Tainan County), every

35 This incident was reported in detail on TVBS on September 14 and 23, 2004. This station's reporter made a videotape of Yeh's chicken-beheading rite, and the network agreed to give me a copy.

36 See http://www.ettoday.com/2006/06/09/11338-1951840.htm.

37 See the May 20, 1953 issue of the *United Daily News*, p. 4.

38 See the March 28, 1996 issue of the *China Times*, p. 16.

39 See the March 30, 1998 issue of the *China Times*, p. 16.

40 See the June 29, 1991 issue of the *China Times*, p. 14, as well as the October 6, 1991 issue, p. 14. Another example of an oath-making ritual that almost culminated in a chicken beheading occurred during an environmental protest in Gaoxiong; see the May 13, 1990 issue of the *United Daily News*, p. 6.

41 Taiwanese people also do not hesitate to make impromptu pleas to elected officials during their visits to constituents, and if the complaint is about a loved one who died wrongfully, family members will often dress in mourning and bring the coffin of the deceased with them.

three years during a plague boat expulsion festival known as the Royal Lords' Offering (*wangjiao* 王醮), members of the local temple committee place a placard reading "filing indictments" (*fanggao* 放告) outside the temple's main gate but then immediately remove it so as to prevent anyone from actually taking such action (Liu 1983: 365–366).

Taiwanese police still practice judicial rites as well, with numerous newspaper articles describing officers ordering uncooperative suspects to make oaths before statues of underworld deities or of Guangong, who is often enshrined in local police stations.[42] In one case that occurred in Banqiao 板橋 (Pan-chiao) in March 2005, the family of a mentally retarded female patient who had been molested insisted that the suspect being questioned at the police station make an oath of innocence in front of Guangong, which prompted him to break down and confess.[43] Just one month earlier, in the very same city, a thief ended up vomiting blood after making a false oath, following which he also admitted to his crime.[44] In instances where no deity is worshipped at a police station, the police will take the suspect to a nearby temple, or threaten to do so, a tactic that also appears effective despite its human rights considerations.[45] On other occasions, the police may acquiesce to disputants performing a judicial ritual, which occurred in 1959 during a dispute between the adoptive and natal parents of an adopted daughter.[46] And, like their fellow citizens, policemen will readily express a willingness to perform a chicken-beheading ritual in order to demonstrate the legitimacy of their statements.[47] Such rituals rarely end up being performed, but in 1984 a policeman accused of having stolen another officer's gun went to a local temple and beheaded a cockerel as a means of proving his innocence.[48]

Some prosecutors also perform judicial rituals, especially when confronted with particularly trying cases. In February 2005, for example, police and prosecutors working to solve the murder of a woman from Toufen 頭份 (Miaoli County) whose headless corpse was dumped by the roadside visited the Xinzhu City God temple late one night to ask for divine assistance. After making offerings to the deity, they threw divination blocks in order to ask if the case would be solved, and received a favorable response. A few days later, the murderer was arrested.[49] In another case that made headlines in 1991,

42 This is also the case in Hong Kong (Li 2003).
43 See the March 1, 2005 issue of the *United Daily News*, Section C, p. 5.
44 See the February 2, 2005 issue of the *United Daily News*, p. 8.
45 See the August 30, 2005 issue of the *United Daily News*, p. A9.
46 See the March 9, 1959 issue of the *United Daily News*, p. 3.
47 See the April 18, 1988 issue of the *United Daily News*, p. 10, as well as the May 2, 1991 issue, p. 6.
48 See the April 18, 1984 issue of the *United Daily News*, p. 5.
49 See http://210.58.102.66/2003/05/28/139-1461318.htm.

when a woman accused a tenant of raping her, the local prosecutor doubted her story and had her make an oath in a City God temple as a means of proving the validity of her charges. When she backed down, the case was considered closed.[50] As recently as March 2008, a Pingdong district attorney offered a new dragon crown and dragon robe to a deity known as Lord Xing (Xingfu qiansui 邢府千歲) in gratitude for helping him solve a homicide case involving a local vegetable merchant. The attorney and police detective had performed a ritual for drawing divination sticks (*chouqian* 抽籤) at the temple, which confirmed their suspicions that the culprits were family members (the victim's parents), not outsiders. The authorities then ascertained that the dead merchant had visited his parents before his death, and no neighbors had seen him leaving his parents' home. The district attorney then ordered the parents placed under surveillance, which spooked them into fleeing to Hualien, where they were soon captured. Responding to a reporter's questions, the chief prosecutor noted that local police and prosecutors frequently resorted to performing rituals, but tried to be as low key as possible.[51]

Indictment rites can also be used to challenge the authorities, with individuals and their family members who feel that they have been wronged seeking justice from deities like the City God. On March 19, 2007, for example, when Chen Jung-chi 陳榮吉 was wrongfully arrested on charges of having been involved in a freeway shooting, his mother crawled all the way to the local City God temple to plead his case to the deity; the very next day the police admitted that they had made an error, and Chen was released.[52]

Judicial rituals have long been regularly performed at sacred sites like the City God temple in Xinzhu and Xinzhuang's Dizang Abbey. One elderly man who had worked at the City God temple for many years recalled seeing a chicken-beheading ritual performed at this temple, but it was so gruesome and led to such vehement expressions of hatred that the temple decided to ban the practice. Even today, this temple's Taoist specialists are very reluctant to perform indictment rituals in cases involving disputes among the living, and only do so two to three times a year. One exception occurred in 2004, when a bookseller was convicted and fined for having supposedly sold pornographic materials. Following the trial, he filed a plaint at the temple stating that even if worldly courts had ruled against him, he would surely gain the support of the temple's underworld deities (*yangshi guansi dabuying, yinjian zonghui bangmang zhuchi gongdao* 陽世官司打不贏, 陰間總會幫忙主持公道).[53] The temple's specialists are more willing to

50 See the March 13, 1991 issue of the *China Times*, p. 15.

51 See the March 16, 2008 issue of the *United Daily News*, p. A12. I am very grateful to Liu Xun for informing me of this story.

52 See http://news.yam.com/tvbs/society/200703/20070319043495.html.

53 See the February 24, 2004 issue of the *United Daily News*, p. B2.

perform mediation (*hejie* 和解) rituals for resolving disputes between the living and the dead, which worshippers will request when they feel that they have been suffering the ill-effects of a haunting ghost and/or underworld indictment (see Chapter 4, as well as Chapter 8). In addition, on the first day of the seventh lunar month, the City God will dispatch the judicial deity known as the Officer of Yin and Yang to the Altar of Vengeful Spirits located near Xinzhu's old Northern Gate (see Chapter 5), where both the living and the dead may file plaints to right wrongs that occurred during the previous year. Such plaints can be filed during a two-week period concluding with the City God's annual procession through Xinzhu on the date of the Ghost Festival (Zhongyuan jie 中元節), following which the officer is brought back to the temple to report to the City God and ask him to judge all plaints that have been filed.[54]

Another sacred site where judicial rituals continue to enjoy extensive popularity is Tainan's Temple of the Eastern Peak. The scribes at this temple currently make use of seven different types of petitions and plaints (*shuzhuang* 疏狀), the three most common being: (1) petitions to ensure the transfer of money and material objects to ancestors still inhabiting the underworld, a practice that can be traced back to the tomb ordinances discussed in this book's opening chapter; (2) petitions to release the souls of suicides who are suffering in the underworld (suicide is an increasingly serious concern in present-day Taiwan); (3) plaints to prevent vengeful spirits (literally "wronged relatives and creditors" or *yuanqin zhaizhu* 冤親債主) from haunting the living (see Figure 8), which are similar to the mediation rituals performed at the Xinzhu City God temple. Such plaints preserve the ancient theme of segregating the living and the dead, and also reflect persistent fears of being indicted by the aggrieved dead (all of which were discussed in Chapter 1).

Judicial rituals are also performed at Taiwan's spirit-writing temples (literally "phoenix halls" or *luantang* 鸞堂). Of particular interest is the practice of holding underworld trials (*mingpan* 冥判), the proceedings of which are transcribed by the planchette in order to serve as warnings for the living by showing the condemnation of sinful souls.[55] A morality book (*shanshu* 善書) entitled *Precious Mirror for Awakening the Lost* (*Xingmi baojian* 醒迷寶鑑; published in Tainan in 1965) contains detailed descriptions

54 See the following issues of the *United Daily News*: August 20, 2001, p. 18; August 10, 2002, p. 17; July 30, 2003, p. B1; August 17, 2004, p. B2. The year 2004 also witnessed the revival of the annual nighttime patrol of the City God and his minions (*raojing chaye anfang* 遶境查夜暗訪), which is done in order to capture any demons that might be haunting the area.

55 Such rites are also known as "trials of one's [previous] three generations of ancestors" (*pan sanshi* 判三世) (Seaman 1978: 93–94, 102–105).

Figure 8 Temple staff reading a petition on behalf of worshippers at the Tainan Temple of the Eastern Peak; photo by Huang Pingying.

of such rites. The first (and most detailed) case features one of the judges of the underworld confronting a guilty soul and coercing him to confess to acts of wrongdoing such as reviling the gods, disobeying his parents, and sowing communal discord. The guilty soul is sentenced to one year in a pit of fire and 6 months on a mountain of knives, and before being led away to serve hard time he exhorts readers to practice good. The second case is of a dissolute girl who became a prostitute, while the third case involves a love triangle and the fourth a deceitful fortuneteller (Jordan and Overmyer 1986: 114–116). Another well-known example is the *Court Cases of the Underworld* (*Difu shen'an* 地府審案), produced at the Shengxian Tang 聖賢堂 in Taizhong between 1984 and 1985 (Clart 1996: 337; see also Clart 2003). Spirit-writing rituals have also been instrumental is the production of morality books that depict the torments of the underworld, especially the renowned *Journey to Purgatory* (*Diyu youji* 地獄游記), thousands of copies of which still circulate extensively today, including in comic book form (Shahar 1998: 190–195; Sung 1982).

Concluding remarks

The data presented above clearly show that the ideology of justice constitutes an integral part of Taiwan's cultural legacy, with the combination of fear felt towards chthonic deities combined with faith in their judgments remaining both real and profound. Numerous temples to such deities throughout Taiwan contain murals or sculptures vividly portraying the torments wrong-doers can expect to face in the underworld, as well as large abacuses representing the accuracy with which the gods calculate one's good and evil deeds (see Figure 9).[56] The ideology of justice is also actively propagated by the mass media. A television series entitled *Bao Qingtian* 包青天 enjoyed such widespread immense popularity in Taiwan during the 1980s and 1990s that between 8:00 and 9:00 p.m. the streets were almost empty as people stayed home to watch Judge Bao correct cases of injustice and execute the offenders. And now, following the death of Taiwan's renowned former Minister of Justice Chen Ting-nan 陳定南 (also known as Chen Qingtian 陳青天) on

Figure 9 Giant abacus hanging in the Tainan City God temple, which is said to be used by the god to calculate peoples' good and evil deeds; photo by Huang Pingying.

56 Accounts of abacuses in Chinese temples may be found in Goodrich 1964: 242–243; Goodrich 1981: 27.

November 5, 2006, there are reports that he has started to be worshipped as a god, with plans to construct a temple (the Dingnan Gong 定南宮) where he will be enshrined alongside Judge Bao. There are even calls for an online temple in his honor.[57]

At the same time, however, the significance of judicial rituals has changed somewhat in postwar Taiwan, particularly in terms of politicians embroiled in tight electoral contests attempting to use oaths and chicken-beheading rites to enhance the legitimacy of their campaigns. Judicial rituals may well continue to change as a result of Taiwan's on-going democratization, especially as Taiwan's judiciary attempts to assert its own legitimacy and independence from the executive and legislative branches of government. While prosecutors have proven willing to assert their authority to the extent of indicting leading figures like Chen Shui-bian's wife and Ma Ying-jeou 馬英九, the extent to which growing confidence in the legal system may shape the popularity of judicial rituals remains to be seen. All that seems certain at this point is that any shift toward increased reliance on the courts does not seem to have reduced the legitimacy of temples housing underworld deities as sites representing an alternative legal authority. This suggests that the judicial continuum not only persists in Taiwan, but may even be strengthening, particularly as democratic and institutional reforms continue to enhance the reputation of this nation's legal system.

57 For more data on this issue, see http://news.pchome.com.tw/life/cna/20061126/fpt-20061126183747180175.html; http://www.libertytimes.com.tw/2006/new/nov/8/today-fo11.htm#.

8

CASE STUDY

The Dizang Abbey

The previous chapters of this book have considered judicial rituals from the broad perspective of the historical development of Chinese religions; here we adopt an interdisciplinary approach that explores the significance of these rites by means of a case study of the Dizang Abbey (Dizang An), a temple dedicated to the Bodhisattva Dizang and the Lord of the Hordes located in the former market town of Xinzhuang (now a city in Taibei County). This final chapter also marks our return to where we started: the links between the punitive underworld and the world of the living. The judicial rituals performed at the Dizang Abbey resemble those described in Chapter 7 in terms of addressing numerous problems that are unique to modern Taiwanese society, yet also display remarkable continuity. For example, the underworld petitions filed at this temple resemble the ritual indictments described in Chapter 4 in addressing a wide range of familial and commercial disputes, while the practice of offering items to meet the needs of one's ancestors in the underworld may well derive from "the lists of [items] dispatched" (*qiance* 遣冊) described in Chapter 1. Moreover, like the late imperial and modern officials described in Chapters 2 and 7, police and prosecutors continue to worship the temple's underworld deities in order to solve difficult criminal cases.

In order to understand the current popularity of the Dizang Abbey, it is necessary to consider its development in the context of Xinzhuang's history. The town of Xinzhuang was originally a river port located along the Dahan 大漢 River, which began to thrive during the early and middle decades of the eighteenth century, mainly as a result of the growth in trade throughout the region and an ever-increasing inflow of new immigrants. One of the leading figures in Xinzhuang's development was Yang Daohong 楊道弘, a tribute student (*gongsheng* 貢生) from Guangdong 廣東. Yang and his followers were the first to formally apply to settle what is now the city of Xinzhuang, and were awarded a reclamation permit in the year 1727. Three years later, Yang reached an agreement with a Plains Aborigine (*pingpuzu* 平埔族) tribe known as the Wulaowan 武勝灣 to collect their aboriginal tax (*pushe* 贌社),

with the result that 50 *liang* of silver came to be transferred to the state on an annual basis.[1] Xinzhuang's oldest surviving temple, the Ciyou Gong 慈祐宮 (dedicated to the goddess Mazu 媽祖), was also built on Yang's land sometime between 1729 and 1731, although Yang's role in the construction process is not known.[2]

A massive fire destroyed the Ciyou Gong and many of the shops around it in 1748, but the temple was soon rebuilt on an even larger scale from 1751 to 1753. The Dizang An was founded four years later, in 1757 (see below), which is also when an Imperial Academy student (*jiansheng* 監生) by the name of Guo Zonggu 郭宗嘏 donated some of his own land to found an Earth God shrine in the Zhonggang 中港 district of Xinzhuang (Chen 1996: 120–127; Huang 1943: 46; Yin 1989: 75–76, 328–329). Another member of the local elite, the Tingzhou 汀州 tribute student Hu Zhuoyou 胡卓猷, founded the Wusheng Miao 武聖廟 (dedicated to the god Guangong 關公) in 1760. Other new temples constructed in Xinzhuang during this time included the town's first Royal Lord (*wangye* 王爺) temple, the Baoyuan Gong 保元宮 (dedicated to Chifu qiansui 池府千歲; founded in 1767), as well as the Guangfu Gong 廣福宮 (dedicated to Sanshan guowang 三山國王; founded in 1780) (Hung 1976: 71–72; Yin 1989: 366–372). Barend ter Haar has noted that temples marked trade and population movements, and were often built next to bridges, wharves, markets, etc. (Ter Haar 1990: 380–382, 384, 385, 391). Xinzhuang was no exception. As the town became more commercialized, most businesses tended to congregate on one main street parallel to the waterfront that also ran in front of the town's main temples. Xinzhuang's rice markets were located between the Ciyou Gong and the Wusheng Miao, while other markets sat between the Ciyou Gong and the Guangfu Gong.

In contrast to the temples listed above, the Dizang Abbey began its existence as a humble altar for vengeful ghosts (*litan* 厲壇) and the Bodhisattva Dizang located in the town's public cemetery, and did not develop into a popular sacred site until the early years of the twentieth century. This was a result of the following factors: (1) the impact of frequent outbreaks of epidemics during the 1890s and 1900s, which caused leading worshippers

1 Fifty years later, in 1778, the Wulaowan Plains Aborigines were still wealthy enough to be able to donate large-rent (*dazu* 大租) income to Xinzhuang's Earth God temple in order to endow purchases of incense and oil for lamps (Chen 1996: 147–154; Shepherd 1993: 299–300, 509; Yin 1989: 97–115, 369–371).

2 There has been much dispute over the date the Ciyou Gong was founded, with different sources giving the dates 1686, 1729, 1731, and 1753. Based on the fact that the construction of temples large enough to be recorded on stelae and in local gazetteers generally marks the transition of a cult to an advanced stage of development, I would argue that the *cult* of Mazu may have arrived in Xinzhuang as early as 1686 (perhaps in the form of a statue or packet of incense), while the actual *temple* was not founded until the first decades of the eighteenth century.

associated with the Dizang Abbey to form a ritual association (*shenming hui* 神明會) known as the Junxian Tang 俊賢堂 and organize a nighttime exorcistic procession called the "dark visitation" (*anfang* 暗訪) in 1912;[3] (2) increasing support for the Dizang Abbey by Xinzhuang's local elites and other leading individuals who did not reside in Xinzhuang, such as Gu Xianrong 辜顯榮 (1866–1937);[4] and (3) the popularity of rituals designed to both placate the dead and resolve conflicts among the living. The temple has continued to thrive during the colonial and postwar eras, during which time Xinzhuang developed from a market town surrounded by farming villages into a sprawling industrial city. Xinzhuang's socioeconomic transformation is also reflected in the types of worshippers who perform judicial rituals at the Dizang Abbey, many of whom have working-class backgrounds.[5]

In the remainder of this chapter, I present data on underworld petitions prepared by the temple's scribe (*bisheng* 筆生), Lai Ming-hsien 賴明賢, records of worshippers consulting the temple's spirit-medium (Yang Wen-li 楊文禮), who is possessed by the Lord of the Hordes, and certificates of gratitude (*ganxie zhuang* 感謝狀) that worshippers post in the temple if they feel its deities have been efficacious. None of these practices is exclusively judicial in nature, but all are related to the Chinese ideology of justice.

Underworld petitions

In order to better understand the process of filing an underworld petition, as well as the social and cultural significance of these texts in postwar Taiwan, my assistant and I observed and recorded the interaction between Mr. Lai and his clients for at least one afternoon a week during a six-month period covering March–September 2006. My main interest was the petitions that Mr. Lai writes on blank yellow paper, most of which are intended to resolve disputes among the living or put an end to hauntings by the aggrieved dead. For these texts, Mr. Lai first records the worshipper's name and address, followed by a summary of the problems that caused the worshipper to file the petition. The text concludes with pleas to the temple's underworld deities to intercede on the worshipper's behalf (see Figure 10). My assistant and I also recorded the following types of standardized fill-in-the-blank petitions,

3 Since then, the *anfang* has been staged annually in the city of Xinzhuang at the end of the fourth lunar month, and also precedes a mammoth daytime procession held in honor of the Lord of the Hordes on the first day of the fifth lunar month.

4 Gu became a leading political figure as a result of his efforts in coordinating the peaceful surrender of Taipei in 1895, and went on to make his fortune in sugar, salt, and opium. One of his sons, Gu Zhenfu 辜振甫 (1917–2005), served as chairman of the Straits Exchange Foundation (Haixia jiaoliu jijinhui 海峽交流基金會), while another, Gu Kuanmin 辜寬敏 (b. 1926), is a well-known activist for Taiwan independence.

5 For more on the history of this temple, see Katz 1998, 2001, 2003b.

Figure 10 The Dizang Abbey's scribe, Lai Ming-hsien, helps compose a plaint for a worshipper involved in a financial dispute; photo by the author.

which Mr. Lai has devised in order to reduce waiting time for the large numbers of worshippers who consult him: (1) petitions for wronged kin and creditors from previous lifetimes (*leishi yinyuan zhaizhu* 累世冤親債主); (2) petitions for the souls of aborted or miscarried fetuses (*duhua yingling* 渡化嬰靈);[6] and (3) petitions for replenishing one's treasury in the underworld (*bu caiku* 補財庫). Regardless of which type of text is used, worshippers must make offerings to the temple's deities, following which the Abbey's Taoist master Huang T'ien-p'ing 黃天平 recites the contents of the document. The ritual concludes with the worshipper burning the document outside the temple. The entire rite costs NT$400.

From March to September 2006, we recorded a total of 399 underworld petitions filed at the Dizang Abbey, including 177 written on blank yellow paper and 222 written using standardized fill-in-the-blank forms. The latter included 120 (54 percent) written on behalf of the souls of the previous generations of wronged relatives and creditors, 61 (27 percent) to save the souls of aborted or miscarried fetuses, and 41 (19 percent) to replenish one's

6 For more on beliefs and practices related to fetus ghosts, see Moskowitz 2001.

underworld treasury. Of the 177 underworld petitions written on blank yellow paper, four types of issues were most prominent, the foremost being to ensure the transmission of offerings to immediate or distant ancestors (62 petitions, or 35 percent of the total).[7] This was closely followed by dispute resolution (60; 34 percent), the largest number of which (17; 28 percent) concerned financial matters. There were also numerous cases of family tensions (mainly between parents and their children), marital spats (usually involving the husband's having a mistress), and disputes between friends. The third type attempts to resolve the problem of being haunted by the dead (*yinchan* 陰纏; 13 percent). The fourth type involves cases that have entered the legal system, including incidents of crime and various financial disputes (12 percent). There are also occasional instances of worshippers attempting to locate missing persons or lost objects, convicted criminals or their loved ones confessing their guilt and expressing their hope for a lighter sentence or a second chance, and even a parent trying to cope with a rambunctious child (see Table 2).

I should also note that the identity of the deities listed in these petitions varies according to the type of petition being filed, with the Lord of the Hordes and his chthonic minions being worshipped in instances of disputes and other legal problems among the living, as well as people being haunted by the dead (including the souls of wronged relatives and creditors). However, in instances when worshippers wish to transmit offerings to ancestors or save the souls of fetus ghosts, the deity of choice is the Bodhisattva Dizang.

Table 2 Petitions filed at the Dizang Abbey, March–September 2006

Rank	*Type*	*No.*	*%*
1	Offerings to ancestors	62	35
2	Disputes (financial, marital, etc.)	60	34
3	Hauntings	23	13
4	Lawsuits in progress	20	12
5	Missing persons	6	3
6	Lost items	3	1.5
7	Reduced sentence	2	1
8	Disobedient child	1	0.5
Total		177	100

7 According to Mr. Lai, this percentage is unusually high, and can be explained by the fact that our sample covered the Tomb Sweeping Festival and the Ghost Month, when people tend to be more concerned than usual with their ancestors' welfare. At the same time, however, we should remember that such petitions are also commonly used at other Taiwanese temples dedicated to underworld deities (see Chapter 7).

We also collected data on the geographic distribution of 299 worshippers who filed underworld petitions. Of these, over nine-tenths came from cities and counties in northern Taiwan in close proximity to the Dizang Abbey, with 195 worshippers (65 percent) residing in Taipei County, 57 (19 percent) in Taipei City, and 23 (8 percent) in Taoyuan County. This is hardly surprising, especially considering the fact that almost identical distributions occurred for worshippers who consulted the temple's spirit-medium (see below). The geographic distribution of worshippers residing in Taipei County was more striking, however, particularly when compared to data compiled by Ch'en Yu-ch'i about worshippers who commissioned the Dizang Abbey to light various lanterns of good fortune (*diandeng* 點燈) on behalf of themselves or their loved ones (Ch'en Yu-ch'i 2005). Only slightly more than 25 percent of the Taipei County worshippers who came to the Dizang Abbey to file petitions resided in Xinzhuang, as opposed to over 46 percent of the worshippers who had lanterns lit. In contrast, 20.5 percent of worshippers who filed petitions came from the city of Banqiao 板橋 (Pan-chiao), as opposed to 10.9 percent who had lanterns lit. For another city, Sanchong 三重 (San-chung), the figures are 14.9 percent and 10.2 percent respectively. This suggests that the rite of filing an underworld petition attracts worshippers from a wider geographic spectrum, most likely due to the fact that fewer temples provide such a service. Far more temples offer the option of having lanterns lit on their premises, meaning that people can do so at one closer to where they reside.

Gender was another variable that we included in our analysis. We were able to record such data for 396 individuals who filed underworld petitions, including 168 men (42.4 percent) and 228 women (57.6 percent).[8] These figures are almost identical to those for worshippers who offered certificates of gratitude during the period when we were conducting field research at the Dizang Abbey (42.6 percent; 57.4 percent), but contrast markedly with data on worshippers who consulted the spirit-medium (51.5 percent; 48.5 percent) or offered certificates of gratitude from 1996 to 2001 (58.9 percent; 41.1 percent).

In terms of actual content, many petitions dealing with financial disputes tend to reflect issues related to modern Taiwanese commercial practices, especially shady stock transactions and intellectual property rights. One of these petitions concerned accusations of plagiarizing software programs, while another centered on a clothing company accusing one of its rivals of selling counterfeit goods. In another instance, a Taiwanese storeowner claimed to have been wrongly accused by a Japanese company of selling its goods without having first obtained marketing rights. There was even a case

8 Some plaints are filed by individual on behalf of an organization, while in other cases couples or other small groups of worshippers join together to file a plaint.

of the chairman of the board of an overseas Taiwanese company in Los Angeles filing a plaint accusing some executives of misusing company funds. The chairman, a Christian, was reluctant to perform such a rite, but had been pressured into doing so by the other board members. Most of the above cases were already being litigated in court, with the party who had chosen to file the petition asking the gods either to effect a reconciliation before the case proceeded any further, or else to ensure a favorable verdict.

Other petitions describing financial issues concerned problems such as money-lending disputes, land disputes, landlord–tenant disputes, etc. There was also a petition by a mother whose son had borrowed money from one of Taiwan's many underground banks (*dixia qianzhuang* 地下錢莊), extralegal financial institutions often linked to gangsters that many Taiwanese turn to when pressed for cash. In this case, the woman's son and his friends had been unable to repay their loan, with the son being badly beaten. The woman then repaid her son's debt, but "representatives" of the bank then sought her out to repay the money that her son's friends had borrowed. As a result, she filed a petition asking that the Dizang Abbey's underworld deities protect her from further harassment, while also helping her son's friends deal with their debts as expeditiously as possible.

Family disputes tend to reflect the generation gap in modern Taiwan (see also the discussion of the temple's spirit-medium below). In one instance, an elderly woman filed a ritual plaint against her own daughter, accusing her of illegally withdrawing NT$2 million from her savings account. She had also filed a plaint a few months earlier, which had resulted in the daughter paying back one-third of the money. The goal of this ritual was for the gods to persuade her to return the rest. Another petition involved a mother and her adopted daughter (*yangnü* 養女)[9] who were engaged in a protracted inheritance dispute that was also being litigated in court, with the mother having applied to have the adopted daughter's assets frozen. In this case, the bitterness between the two women was so extreme that no reconciliation was sought; the mother simply wanted to win her lawsuit.

Other petitions concerned rebellious young people, such as two filed in close succession by a distraught father whose daughter had run off with her boyfriend. He hoped that the temple's underworld deities would help his daughter return home and punish the boyfriend, but Mr. Lai declined to write out the latter part of the plaint, ostensibly because the father was unable to provide the boy's name and address, but perhaps also because he did not want to become too directly involved in a complicated family affair. Another case involved a woman whose 34-year-old son had been living with a divorcee ten years his senior and even fathered a child with her. In this instance, the mother prayed to the gods to cause this couple to break

9 For more on adopted daughters in Taiwanese society, see Wolf and Huang 1980.

up (literally "break apart improper karmic affinities" or *chaisan nieyuan* 拆散孽緣).

In some instances, the petitions filed at the Dizang Abbey vividly portray families in turmoil during hard times. This was the case for a married couple who asked Mr. Lai to prepare a petition concerning the husband's younger brother and his wife. The younger brother had been sent to prison for an undisclosed crime, and had asked the older brother and his wife to help take care of the young couple's infant daughter. However, the younger woman and the couple filing the petition disagreed over how to raise the child, and the former accused the latter of child abuse. This had prompted the married couple to file a petition asking that the gods help bring about a reconciliation.

Nearly all the petitions involving marital disputes were filed by women against their current or ex-husbands, a practice that seems somewhat similar to the plaints filed by women described in Chapter 4, especially in terms of challenging traditional views of male authority and legitimating women's concerns. Most of these cases were of husbands taking a mistress, particularly after the birth of a child, which can be a stressful time for couples even in the best of circumstances. In some instances, resourceful wives had just discovered their husbands' activities by checking cell phone records or hiring private detectives, while in others the adultery had been long term, with the wife making a number of visits to the temple. Regardless of the circumstances of the affair, however, such petitions invariably expressed a wish for the errant husband to return home and be reconciled with his wife. One particularly moving text concluded with the wife wishing that her husband not sink deeper into the trap of adultery, and that his lover stop disrupting their marriage. She concluded by asking the gods to grant her the strength to save her family. The desire for reconciliation was far less common in instances when ex-husbands were harassing their wives and children, including physically abusing them. Such plaints were usually filed by the wife's mother, and asked the gods to punish the abusive husband and force him to leave everyone alone.

There were also a few plaints filed by quarreling friends. In one instance, a woman (Miss A) slapped one of her female friends who had been spreading rumors about her love life. The woman who had been slapped (Miss B) filed a report with the police, and, despite efforts at reconciliation, insisted on taking the case to court and asking for NT$200,000 in damages, prompting Miss A to implore Mr. Lai to write a petition asking the temple's gods to resolve this issue. However, Mr. Lai appeared reluctant to get involved in this case, first asking Miss A to perform a divination ritual to see if the gods approved of her action, and then suggesting that she go to court a file a countersuit accusing Miss B of slander. In the end, he stalled for time, saying that he could only write the petition once the courts had started to hear the case and Miss A could bring the relevant court documents to the temple to submit to the gods. A similar case involved a woman who had made three visits to the Dizang Abbey in order to ask for the gods to help resolve a dispute that had started when she and another woman had come to blows over the use of funds for a high school class reunion. Because the case was already being litigated, and she had brought proper documentation with her, Mr. Lai proved willing to write a petition on her behalf asking the gods to help her win her case in court.

A few petitions dealt with criminal cases, particularly instances of theft or assault. One elderly man whose prized motorcycle had been stolen asked the gods for help in recovering it before it could be disassembled and shipped across the Taiwan Straits to be sold in China. Another case involved a woman who was being constantly harassed and even beaten by a local bully who apparently had such clout that the police had proved unable to stop him, prompting her to ask the temple's deities to punish the bully before the situation deteriorated any further. There was also an instance of a woman who had been subpoenaed as a witness in a robbery trial where her friend was the defendant. She was clearly nervous about the predicament she found herself in, and pleaded with the gods to help her tell the truth without causing any additional trouble.

Some of the most heart-wrenching petitions feature men and women who confess their own or their loved ones' wrongdoing while also pleading with the gods to lessen any punishments. This was the case for a distraught mother whose son had been arrested for attempted murder and whose trial was due to begin very soon. She recognized that he was guilty as charged, but hoped that the gods would ensure a light sentence so that he would have the chance to reform and start over. Another petition was filed by a woman on behalf of her 80-year-old father, who had been convicted on charges of vote-buying and whose case was currently under appeal. She asked Mr. Lai to write a petition asking the gods to have him punished with a fine instead of imprisonment, to which Mr. Lai responded that, while he was willing to compose the text in question, the gods would not be able to protect a wrong-doer, meaning that the father would have to suffer the consequences for his misdeeds if the higher court upheld the guilty verdict. Mr. Lai gave a similar response to a 51-year-old employee of a construction company who had been arrested on charges of bribery but was currently out on bail. She hoped that the gods could persuade the men and women who were to judge her case to show leniency, but Mr. Lai warned her that the petition would be of no value if she were in fact guilty as charged.

Apart from disputes and criminal cases among the living, Mr. Lai also composes petitions to resolve conflicts between the living and the dead, especially those that worshippers feel result from being the subject of an underworld indictment. As I noted in the conclusion to Chapter 4, it is essential to distinguish between legitimate retribution by the aggrieved dead and illegitimate hauntings by the unruly dead or malevolent sprites. In the case of the Dizang Abbey's underworld petitions, if Mr. Lai feels that the suffering results from wrongdoing by the worshipper, he will recommend making offerings to the offended spirit in order to achieve reconciliation, and also supports the practice of arranging ghost marriages (*minghun* 冥婚) in cases of unmarried female ghosts (literally "lonely maidens" or *guniang* 孤娘; *ko-niu-a* 孤娘 in Southern Min) with legitimate grievances.[10] This was the case for a father who filed a petition on behalf of his son, who claimed to be haunted by the ghost of his girlfriend. Inasmuch as the girl had died from injuries suffered in an accident while riding on the son's motorcycle, Mr. Lai deemed the son to be partially responsible for her untimely death, which obligated him to marry her ghost. If the haunting spirit's actions are unjustified, however, Mr. Lai will compose a plaint asking the gods to expel the offending spirit. Many women also ask Mr. Lai to write plaints in order to placate the souls of fetus ghosts (*yingling* 嬰靈), including both those that have been aborted and those that have miscarried.[11] There are also cases of worshippers claiming that the wronged ghosts of their relatives wished to present their cases to the temple's deities, including one in which a man and his mother had dreamt of the man's elder brother claiming that his death at a construction site was not an accident but murder. This had confirmed the family's original suspicions about his untimely death, thereby prompting them to ask the Lord of the Hordes and the temple's other underworld deities to find the man's murderers and right the wrong that had been committed.

In observing the processes by which worshippers file underworld petitions at the Dizang Abbey, my assistant and I have been particularly struck by Mr. Lai's role in framing the language used to describe the dispute, as well as guiding worshippers to find solutions to their problems. During a number of interviews, Mr. Lai stated that he makes every effort to carefully observe worshippers and listen to their accounts in order to avoid the risk of taking sides or making hasty judgments about the merits of those cases that are presented to him. Mr. Lai is particularly wary about filing petitions on behalf of guilty parties, as he fears doing so will make things worse for all involved (the expression he used was "Helping [the Shang dynasty's last evil king] Zhou commit [acts of] cruelty" or *zhu Zhou weinui* 助紂為虐). Moreover, in cases where Mr. Lai is unsure about whether the worshipper's petition is justified, he will ask them to perform divination rites in the presence of the Dizang Abbey's deities to confirm that they concur with the plaintiff. In other instances, Mr. Lai will not hesitate to suggest that some worshippers take their cases to court or file a report with the police.

10 For more on cults to lonely maidens and related practices, see Huang 2008.

11 Some women who have had between three to five abortions by their thirties appear to have been prostitutes.

Mr. Lai also espouses traditional moral and social points of view. When confronted by a party embroiled in a dispute, he tends to encourage reconciliation whenever possible, especially in cases of personal or familial quarrels. Mr. Lai also tries to prevent divorces, except in cases of spousal abuse (the expression he used was "advising reconciliation, not separation" or *quanhe buquanli* 勸和不勸離). In addition, Mr. Lai does not allow children to file plaints against their parents, as this violates traditional filial ethics (*weifan wulun changli* 違反五倫常理); however, he will allow children to ask the gods to "remind" (*dianxing* 點醒; *tixing* 提醒) their parents if they feel the parents in question are making unfair arrangements for their inheritance. Mr. Lai also does not object to people indicting their relatives, or wives filing plaints against their husbands, but he once flatly refused to write a plaint on behalf of a woman whose lover had been cheating on her, on the grounds that they were not married.

Reconciliation is the primary goal of most petitions that Mr. Lai composes in cases of financial disputes. Such texts tend to stress the recovery of any lost or owed money, without requesting that the gods visit retribution on the guilty parties involved. Many of these petitions place great value on the need for compromise and the reduction of tension (*dashi huaxiao, xiaoshi huawu* 大事化小、小事化無). Thus, in only one example (a bitter land dispute that had languished in the courts for seven years) did the petition include a statement wishing that the guilty party suffer punishment. In cases of theft, the goal of most petitions is simply for the stolen object/money to be returned. In cases of violent crime, however, more emphasis is placed on punishment. Many of these latter petitions contain statements expressing traditional views of the ideology of justice, and especially the inevitability of karmic retribution, such as "Heaven is watching" (*laotian youyan* 老天有眼) or "The wicked will get their just deserts" (*e you e bao* 惡有惡報).

While considerable research remains to be done on Mr. Lai and the texts that he writes, I would hypothesize that one of his most important roles involves trying to decrease tensions and other negative feelings among individuals who are involved in disputes. Admittedly, this is made easier by the fact that only one party to the dispute consults Mr. Lai (in only a few cases do both disputants come to the temple in order to file a plaint, but almost never simultaneously). At the same time, however, it is clear that most people choose to file a petition only when they feel that efforts at reconciliation have failed, meaning that they often come to Mr. Lai with anger or resentment in their hearts. In the course of explaining their cases to Mr. Lai, they are given an opportunity to express their true feelings without fear of any adverse consequences. However, the fact that the consultation takes place in a temple to underworld deities serves to discourage highly dramatic outbursts, and the actual filing of a petition involves a key shift from emotional speech act to standardized written text, all of which may also serve to further reduce tensions (for more on this issue, see Chapter 4).

Spirit-medium

While the act of consulting with a spirit-medium differs from that of filing a petition in that the former is not a judicial ritual per se, some issues raised during these sessions have clear links to the ideology of justice, particularly those pertaining to legal affairs and other problems having to do with dispute resolution. After interviewing both Mr. Yang and the ritual master who works alongside him, Ts'ai Chin-chu 蔡金助, I was able to persuade them to lend my assistant and me the slips of paper they use to record the names, addresses, and requests of worshippers who come to their altar in the temple. Subsequently, we were able to record three months' worth of slips (for the first through third lunar months of 2006), a goldmine of information that provides an unprecedented opportunity to undertake a statistical analysis of a spirit-medium and his clientele. Unfortunately, however, these slips only provide a one-sentence summary of the issues being presented to the Lord of the Hordes, which inhibited a more detailed analysis of their contents.

We ended up collecting a total of 3,841 slips for worshippers who had consulted with Mr. Yang, but our statistical analysis only includes categories for which 10 or more cases occurred during the three-month period covered by our research (a total of 3,811 cases; see Table 3). It should come as no surprise that nearly 65 percent of these slips deal with issues of health, education, or career, as such concerns are preeminent at nearly all spirit-medium altars in Taiwan. However, nearly one-third of the worshippers who go to Mr. Yang's altar were concerned about judicial issues, including dispute resolution. Most family disputes involved conflicts between parents and their teenage children, particularly in terms of disobedience, poor grades, making

Table 3 Worshippers' requests made at the altar of the Dizang Abbey's spirit-medium, 1st–3rd lunar months, 2006

Rank	*Type*	*No.*	*%*
1	Health (individual)	1,508	39.3
2	Professional concerns	888	23.2
3	Family disputes	395	10.3
4	Marital disputes	285	7.4
5	Disputes (nature unknown)	180	4.7
6	Missing items	115	3.0
7	Housing disputes	97	2.5
8	Health (family)	95	2.4
9	Missing persons	78	2.0
10	Lawsuits in progress	67	1.7
11	Success in exams	40	1.0
12	Missing pets	37	0.9
13	Theft/robbery	26	0.7
Total		3,811	100

"bad friends", and even running away from home. Marital disputes featured wives complaining about their husbands' infidelity, as well as gambling or drinking problems. Housing disputes tended to involve quarrels between landlords and their tenants. Other worshippers were concerned with financial disputes (mainly having to do with money-lending), lawsuits, missing persons (including one Vietnamese bride), and the recovery of lost or stolen items and motor vehicles (especially trucks, motorcycles, and bicycles, which reflects the Dizang Abbey's largely blue-collar community of worshippers).

Because of the huge size of our sample, we were only able to calculate geographic distribution for worshippers who consulted Mr. Yang regarding various forms of disputes and judicial matters. As in the case of worshippers who filed petitions, over nine-tenths were from northern cities and counties surrounding the Dizang Abbey, including 820 (67 percent) from Taipei County, 215 (17 percent) from Taipei City, and 109 (9 percent) from Taoyuan County. In addition, the distribution of Taipei County worshippers appears somewhat closer to that contained in Ch'en Yu-ch'i's analysis of worshippers who had lanterns lit at the temple, with 263 worshippers (32 percent) residing in Xinzhuang, 111 (13.5 percent) residing in Banqiao, and 86 (10.5 percent) residing in Sanchong. The similarity between these data and those collected by Ch'en might be due to the fact that consulting a spirit-medium is a service provided by a larger number of temples than those that allow worshippers to file underworld petitions.

Certificates of gratitude

My fieldwork at the Dizang Abbey also included collecting certificates of gratitude. Some worshippers prepare these certificates after consulting the temple's scribe or spirit-medium; others do so after making offerings to the temple's deities without consulting one of its specialists.

The initial stage of my research at the Dizang Abbey focused on the analysis of certificates of gratitude posted at the temple between January 1996 and August 2001, including those preserved by the Dizang Abbey temple committee, those preserved by a local ward chief (*lizhang* 里長) named Chien Ch'uan-sheng 簡傳盛, and those that I had collected while doing fieldwork at the temple in 1998–1999.[12] We were able to collect a total of 451 certificates of gratitude that were posted at the Dizang Abbey during this six-year period, for which we formulated a seven-category typology (see below). While slightly over one-fifth of these texts deal with healing and general good fortune, which worshippers could pray for at any temple, nearly all the rest are related to issues that are largely unique to the Dizang Abbey,

12 Many thanks to Li Tsung-yi 李宗益, Lin Chun-te 林俊德, and Tseng Su-yueh 曾素月 for their help in collecting these documents.

Table 4 Certificates of gratitude, January 1996–August 2001

Rank	*Type*	*No.*	*%*
1	Stolen vehicles	204	45.2
2	Health/good fortune	105	23.3
3	Disputes	89	19.7
4	Lost items	29	6.4
5	Missing persons	12	2.7
6	Vague "matters"	9	2.0
7	Missing pets	3	0.7
Total		451	100

including vehicle theft (especially trucks, motorcycles, and bicycles), disputes, recovering lost items (including the modern traveler's bane, missing luggage), and locating loved ones (including daughters-in-law and even one Chinese bride) or missing pets (see Table 4). In addition, while worshippers who post certificates of gratitude do not indicate their addresses (meaning that we were unable to analyze geographic distribution), our data indicate that more men (275 or 58.9 percent) than women (192; 41.1 percent) engaged in this practice during that period of time.

Our analysis also included a second set of 102 certificates of gratitude posted at the Dizang Abbey from February to September 2006 (see Table 5). Perhaps the most fascinating aspect of this sample is that while the percentages for healing and disputes have remained nearly unchanged, there was a sizeable increase in the percentage of certificates posted following the retrieval of lost pets (both dogs and cats), which far outnumbered certificates for missing persons and also corresponded with a nearly identical decline for certificates posted following the recovery of lost or stolen vehicles. It is tempting to speculate that the increasing number of women worshippers posting certificates of gratitude (89 women = 57.4 percent, as opposed to 66 men = 42.6 percent), might be due to the fact that some female worshippers

Table 5 Certificates of gratitude, February–September 2006

Rank	*Type*	*No.*	*%*
1	Stolen vehicles	33	32.3
2	Health/good fortune	25	24.5
3	Disputes	20	19.6
4	Missing pets	13	12.7
5	Lost items	7	6.9
6	Missing persons	2	2.0
7	Vague "matters"	2	2.0
Total		102	100

today seem especially concerned with the well-being of their pets. One woman even posted a certificate thanking the gods for helping her pet dog recover from an operation.[13]

During the past decade, approximately one-quarter of the certificates of gratitude posted at the Dizang Abbey have dealt with issues of health and good fortune, and in many of these cases no judicial deities are invoked, only Buddhist ones. One particularly moving text from the summer of 1998 was posted by a wife whose husband had been hospitalized after falling from the eighth floor at a construction site. His leg was injured, gangrene had set in, and the doctors were ready to amputate. The text continues as follows: "I did not know what to do. For someone so young to lose his leg seemed so unfair. Then I thought of offering prayers to the Bodhisattva Dizang and the Bodhisattva Guanyin. Tears streaming down my face, I lit twelve sticks of incense . . . I could barely even speak. That night my husband dreamt of the Bodhisattva Dizang, who told him that he would be cured once the doctors had cut away the last of the gangrenous flesh. Now his leg is fine, and we have been touched by the Bodhisattva's numinous response." Other certificates in this category are about renting out factories or passing exams to become licensed as a beautician or a nutritionist, all of which were posted by working-class worshippers.

Although the act of posting a certificate of gratitude is not a judicial ritual in its own right, many of these documents express worshippers' concerns with judicial issues, particularly financial disputes (see Figure 11). In one instance, which occurred during the spring of 2001, a woman who was owed a sizeable sum of money made two visits to the temple to ask the Lord of the Hordes and other judicial deities to persuade the debtor to pay the money back in a timely manner (whether she had filed a plaint or consulted with the spirit-medium is unclear). Just one week after her second visit, the debtor called her and offered to repay 20 percent of the sum right away, and the rest in regular installments. Another certificate concerned a woman who had been able to recover NT$50,000 that she had been defrauded of, while a third was posted by a woman who had been owed months of back pay and bonuses by the insurance company she worked for. One common issue concerned compensation following car accidents, including fatal ones, disputes over which regularly drag out for months or even years before an agreement can be reached, with many drivers resorting to hiding from the victim's family or refusing to make payment outright. In some cases, disputes were being litigated in court, but since certificates of gratitude are supposed to be

13 Accounts describing the efficacy of the Dizang Abbey's underworld deities in helping retrieve lost pets have been posted on pet lover websites and blogs. For samples of such texts, see http://diary.yam.com/pets/article/1065546; http://www.supervr.net/catbbs/topic.cgi?forum=7&topic=2031; http://www.crazy4dog.com/board/board-detail.asp?id=26807.

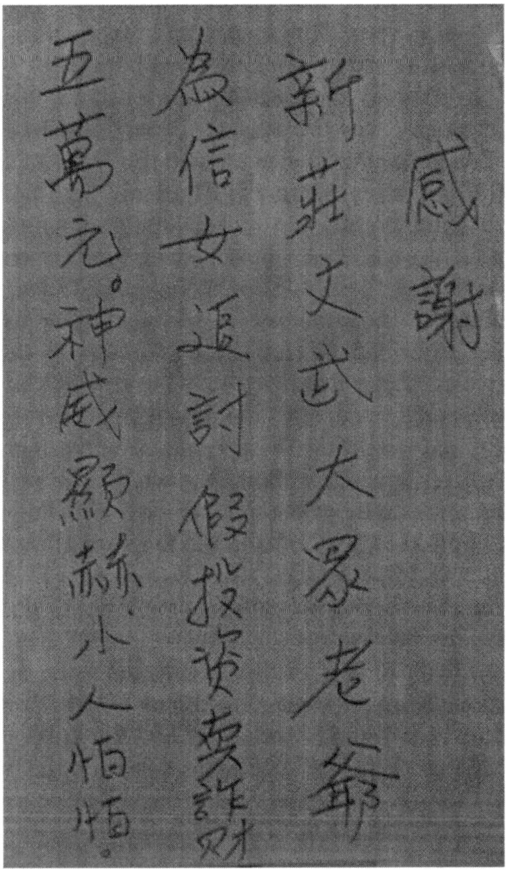

Figure 11 Certificate of gratitude posted at the Dizang Abbey thanking the temple's deities for their help in resolving a case of investment fraud; photo by Kang Shih-yu.

signed by the worshipper, most only vaguely referred to "winning one's court case" (*daying guansi* 打贏官司) without providing any details. A few were more specific, including one about a financial dispute and one about a land dispute.

The most prevalent concern among those who have posted certificates of gratitude has been the successful recovery of stolen vehicles. One certificate, composed by a taxi driver on August 5, 1999, recounted how he had been robbed on July 31 by two passengers (a man and woman), who had subsequently driven off with his vehicle. He went to the temple the very next day to ask the gods to help catch the robbers, and just two days later they were apprehended and his taxi returned. This particular story was also reported in the local press. Other certificates, nearly all of which were posted by working-class men and women from Xinzhuang and its environs, described the recovery of stolen motorcycles, trucks, and even bicycles.

The Lord of the Hordes is especially renowned for his power to find missing items (especially motor vehicles). Other Taiwanese deities widely worshipped for this particular ability include the Duke of the Red Banner (Hongqi gong 紅旗公), whose temple in Zhushan 竹山 (Nantou County) is surrounded by bulletin boards festooned with photographs of recovered motor vehicles such as cars, trucks, motorcycles, forklifts, etc.[14] Deities with similar abilities were also worshipped in late imperial China, with their cults usually being linked to those of underworld gods. One example involves a large iron deity enshrined in Hangzhou's Temple to the Eastern Peak colloquially known as "Elder Brother Iron" (Tie gege 鐵哥哥). According to one Qing-dynasty source, "people whose money had been stolen would pray to this iron [god], and would receive a response within ten days" (*Lüyuan conghua*, 14.375). Late imperial worshippers would also seek the assistance of underworld deities in cases of missing persons, including a filial son who made offerings to both the City God and the Emperor of the Eastern Peak in order to help locate his missing father (*Yan Yuan ji*, pp. 417–418).

The Lord of the Hordes and his chthonic minions are also offered certificates of gratitude for helping capture other types of criminals, especially thieves and hit-and-run drivers. A few certificates even treat instances of violent crime, especially one posted in the fall of 1995 by family members of a woman who had been brutally murdered and her corpse burned. Newspaper accounts of this particular case focus solely on the police work that went into solving this case, but in the eyes of the victim's family members the gods deserved a share of the credit as well.[15]

Police and prosecutors

The fact that the Dizang Abbey's deities are efficacious in terms of catching wanted criminals makes this sacred site especially appealing to law enforcement personnel, with police and prosecutors regularly performing rituals at the temple (for more on these practices, see Chapter 7). While most police and prosecutors who come to the temple tend to be from Xinzhuang and nearby areas (including Sanchong and Banqiao), there have also been cases of officials coming from as far away as Guishan (Kuei-shan 龜山) Township and the town of Yangmei 楊梅 (both are in Taoyuan County), in order to seek the assistance of the temple's deities in solving tough criminal cases.

14 For more on this deity, a spirit representing the ghosts of people who died during feuds, see Wang 2003: 188–189, 197–200.

15 See the November 8, 1995 issue of the *United Daily News*, p. 7.

One frequently recounted story tells how the police brought an arson suspect to the temple and asked him to count the number of statues of the Lord of the Hordes. He was only able to point out three (the actual total is four), and subsequently confessed his crime due to his terror of being punished by the deity. A top police official named Wang Chin-wang 王進旺 (who recently served as the Chief of the R.O.C. Coast Guard) also worshipped at the temple in the course of investigating the kidnap and brutal murder of Pai Hsiao-yen 白曉燕, the only daughter of the TV actress Pai Ping-ping 白冰冰's by three local gangsters in the spring of 1997. Pai Ping-ping also filed an underworld indictment at the Dizang Abbey on the seventh day after the young girl's death, and is reported to have said, "I am not afraid of being laughed at as superstitious, for this is something that I can do [for my daughter]!"[16] Members of the temple committee followed the case with intense interest, and crossed out photos of each man on a wanted poster circulated by the police as each one was captured or killed. The Dizang Abbey's reputation in fighting crime has become so widespread that a Taiwanese TV program on local culture dramatized the role of this temple's deities in cracking tough cases during an episode broadcast in June 2000 entitled "The Temple of the Criminal Police" (Xingjing Miao 刑警廟).

The temple keeper

The Dizang Abbey's role as a site for reconciliation of aggrieved parties can also be seen in the actions of its temple keeper (*miaogong* 廟公), Mr. Chou Cheng-fu 周正富. He is often the first member of the temple's staff to observe worshippers who are about to perform judicial rites, particularly those who bypass Mr. Lai or Mr. Yang, as well as those who come to the temple during the evening hours, when these two specialists have gone home. For example, one night three friends brought a fourth friend to the Dizang Abbey to force him to make an oath to repay their money as soon as possible. Sensing the tenseness of the situation, Chou intervened, pointing out: "Would you lend me NT$100,000? Of course not! You don't even know me. So why did you lend him money? Because he is your friend! If you trusted him that much, you must have been very good friends. For the sake of your friendship, why don't all of you take a step back (*ge tui yibu* 各退一步) [and try to find a solution]." The friends reconsidered; no oath was taken.

Concluding remarks

This chapter has shown that the Dizang Abbey and its specialists help worshippers deal with the various forms of disputes described in the

16 See the June 2, 1997 issue of the *United Daily News*, p. 7.

Introduction, including those that have entered the court system (especially commercial disputes, land disputes, and actual crimes) and those that the courts normally do not deal with (such as marital infidelity or disputes between parents and their children). We have seen instances of worshippers hoping to achieve reconciliation (particularly in cases of family and marital quarrels, as well as money-lending disputes among friends), yet also requests that the temple's gods punish guilty parties (usually in instances where a crime has been committed or in the course of a financial dispute among business associates). Two aspects of the data seem particularly striking: first, The act of a family member petitioning the temple's deities for assistance in resolving quarrels appears to constitute a form of pressure, be it on unfaithful husbands, disobedient children, etc. Such pressure is applied outside the court system, but may be no less effective. Second, not only do a sizeable portion of worshippers continue to rely on the court system despite going to the temple and presenting their cases to the gods, some are even encouraged to do so by the temple's specialists. In other words, the flourishing of the ideology of justice in Taiwanese society is now accompanied by a growing sense of confidence in the state's ability to help resolve certain types of disputes, particularly financial ones. This suggests that the practices described in this chapter are in no danger of disappearing, and may even gain in popularity as citizens acquire greater confidence in all facets of Taiwanese legal culture.

CONCLUSION

This book has attempted to shed new light on what the ideology of justice and judicial rituals reveal about the importance of religious beliefs and practices in Chinese legal culture. In terms of ideas about jurisprudence, the reverberation between religion and the law seems intimately linked to a deep concern with the pursuit of justice. Because this ideal was rarely realized in earthly courts, many men and women placed their faith in judicial deities like the City God and the Emperor of the Eastern Peak. Sacred sites to these and other chthonic bureaucrats were designed to inspire a sense of the inevitability of divine justice. One moving inscription carved in 1847 on a pair of wooden placards in Tainan's City God Temple vividly expresses these sentiments as follows:

> . . . I ask you, what have you done during your lifetime? Grasped at other peoples' wealth, ruined their lives, fornicated with their women, destroyed their morals . . . When you come here, all injustice will be requited. Reduce your lifespan! Destroy your possessions! Annihilate your descendants! Punish your licentiousness! Open your eyes, fear ye not? Of all those violent and vicious [souls who have come here], how many can escape [their fate]?
>
> (Lü 1992: 24)

Other temples contain abacuses used by the gods to calculate the misdeeds of the living, as well as placards bearing the words "So, you [too] have come [to be judged]!" (*Ni/er [ye] laile* 你/爾[也]來了) (Duara 1988: 12; Lü 1992: 23). The combination of fear and awe that these sacred sites inspired may be seen in the following description of Suzhou's temple to the Emperor of the Eastern Peak: "The statues of the gods were fierce and terrifying (*ningzheng* 獰猙), while ghostly beings entered and left [the temple]. Even people who went to the temple during the day would break out in a [cold] sweat" (*Xiqiao yeji*, 2.606). Similar sentiments were expressed by many of the worshippers I interviewed at the Dizang Abbey.

Despite the fact that some works of literature portray the underworld bureaucracy as being corrupt, the ideology of justice was clearly predicated on the notion that this system provided better justice than its earthly counterpart. As Valerie Hansen so aptly puts it: "Structured much like this-worldly courts, and populated by many of the same corrupt figures, the courts of the dead differed in one important way: they usually implemented justice" (Hansen 1995: 190). The accounts presented in this book provide numerous examples of popular trust in this ideal. The wrongly accused Sichuan soldier who had been tortured into confessing, the Putian man whose mother had been brutally murdered, the chaste widows who had resisted rape only to have their reputations besmirched, and many, many others ranging from gentry to peasants all placed their faith in judicial rituals and the chthonic bureaucracy they invoked. Macgowan provides this moving description of a man who filed an underworld indictment in Amoy's City God temple against a younger brother who had cheated him out of his inheritance: "[His farm and home] were irretrievably lost to him, but he had the satisfaction of having, as he believed, set in motion a power that would never rest or sleep until it had executed dire vengeance on the man who had wronged him" (Macgowan 1912: 134–135). One can also consider the players in the Song-dynasty story of Registrar Xia. When confronted by a wealthy elite's underlings, Liu Yuan Balang indignantly replied: "If there is such a court [in the underworld], it must have a place where wrongs can be righted" (Hansen 1995: 217). Other people who lived during the Song dynasty placed profound faith in the renowned Judge Bao, with a popular saying from the Northern Song capital of Kaifeng 開封 effectively embodying local faith in the chthonic bureaucracy: "Bribery will get you nowhere, for Old Bao (Judge Bao), the king of the underworld, is here" (Hayden 1978: 18). Such sentiments persist in China, as may be seen in an article published in the *San Francisco Chronicle* dated November 25, 1994 which vividly describes the popularity of a revived Judge Bao temple in Hefei 合肥 (Anhui). According to the article, over 250 people visit the temple each day, most of whom seek the god's aid in their dealings with corrupt officials: "With no one to turn to for recourse, dozens of Chinese come here [to the temple] each day to light incense and pray to Judge Bao, the Sung (Song) dynasty judge with a reputation for incorruptibility and the power to right almost any wrong."[1]

Another striking feature of the Chinese ideology of justice is that representations of moral death involve more legal features than in the West. As we saw in Chapter 1 (and subsequent chapters as well), ancient and early medieval Chinese representations of the underworld portrayed the dead as being subject to judicial inquisition in the courts of underworld deities conceived of as legal bureaucrats, with the guilty being forced to suffer tor-

1 I am extremely grateful to David K. Jordan for e-mailing me a copy of this article.

ments that resemble punitive measures of earthly legal practice. This varies significantly from contemporary conceptions of moral death in the Middle East and Europe, which, despite also emphasizing a wide range of gory torments, tended to place less emphasis on the bureaucratic nature of underworld procedures and punishments. The development of moral death with legal overtones in Chinese culture was the result of a wide range of factors, including not only the rise of centralized bureaucratic states with standardized legal systems, but also the growth of indigenous religious traditions like Taoism, which created a complex set of legalistic rituals for filing suits or countersuits in the courts of the chthonic kings. As a result, the Buddhist conquest of China did not so much displace indigenous beliefs and practices in the Chinese underworld as it provided new ways of representing the causes of postmortem torment (karmic retribution) and coping with its consequences (performing rituals believed to save the souls of the dead while also bypassing the chthonic bureaucracy).

As for legal practice, we have seen that judicial rituals have long coexisted with private mediation and the courts, all of which comprise the Chinese judicial continuum discussed in Chapter 2. This continuum encompasses not only the conduct of criminal and civil procedures, but also efforts aimed at resolving disputes, which can be mediated both in the courts and in temples. Data in Chapters 3, 7, and 8 demonstrate that the performance of oath-making rites involves a subsequent waiting period for the gods to pass judgment, during which mediators can work to reduce tensions and resolve the dispute in question. This is also the case for many indictment rituals described in Chapters 4, 7, and 8, with the added feature that the shift from emotive oral expressions of grievance to standardized written texts can help defuse emotions and allow dispute resolution mechanisms an additional opportunity to take hold.

Another important aspect of the judicial rituals described in this book is that many function as expressions of legitimacy, and the widespread popularity of oath-making rituals among people ranging in status from high-ranking officials to peasants can be partially explained by the fact that such rites serve as speech acts designed to add cultural sanction to one's claims. Similarly, indictment rituals filed against other members of the living can legitimate the causes of people involved in disputes. It seems particularly significant that late imperial officials used oaths and indictment rituals to enhance their legitimacy when dealing with natural disasters, human threats to their authority like bandits and rebels, and even unsanctioned local cults and malevolent spiritual forces. However, this should not cause us to overlook the fact that individuals and groups attempting to resist the state's hegemony could also file plaints against members of the officialdom, especially those they viewed as being corrupt. A similar pattern of dueling rites of legitimacy could also shape gender and family issues, with husbands indicting disobedient wives and chaste widows or other wronged women (and even female ghosts) filing underworld indictments as "weapons of the weak" that could enhance the legitimacy of their causes.

The issue of legitimacy has also shaped the development of one key facet of Chinese religious traditions, namely the belief that the judicial mechanisms of this world overlap with those of the underworld, which means that the wronged dead have the right to file plaints in chthonic courts against their persecutors, and even return to the world of the living to exact retribution if their suits are judged as being legitimate. One result of this belief is that many men and women suffering from illnesses assumed to be the result of a successful lawsuit filed by the dead have chosen to perform penitential rituals like trials of the insane or dressing up as a criminal (see Chapter 5). In contrast, people attempting to cope with the effects of illegitimate hauntings by the unruly dead or malevolent sprites have hired specialists to perform exorcistic rituals that involve the offending spirit being put on trial. All of these rites, be they penitential or exorcistic, exhibit clear overlap with actual judicial practice.

This book has also shown the ways in which judicial rituals shaped modern colonial and immigrant history in both Asia and the West. As we saw in Chapter 6, Chinese in colonies like Batavia, the Straits Settlements, and Hong Kong, as well as those who immigrated to countries like Australia and the United States, performed judicial rites like chicken-beheadings, as well as rites seemingly modified to suit Western tastes (or deceive Western overlords), such as shattering plates or blowing out matches and candles. Throughout the nineteenth and twentieth centuries, Western officials in charge of overseeing Chinese populations have continually had to ponder the degree to which they could accept the presence of polycultural legal practices. This in turn reflects a problem that has marked the history of Western colonial and immigrant history throughout the world, namely the question of whether the modern nation-state would prove willing to accept, regulate, or prohibit non-Western ideas of judicial authority. The struggle over multiculturalism in legal practice is far from over, as can be seen in the on-going debates over the presence of Sharia law among Muslim communities in Europe.

Judicial rituals continue to shape legitimation and dispute resolution in modern, high-tech Chinese societies like Taiwan, where people rely on such rites to resolve issues that are not readily addressed in the courtroom (particularly family tensions), as well as put pressure on rebellious children or unfaithful/abusive husbands. At the same time, however, numerous worshippers who choose to file underworld indictments in temples are also willing to take their cases to court (and in some instances are even encouraged to do so by temple specialists), which suggests the increasing viability of the legal system in the eyes of the Taiwanese people. We now appear to be witnessing a new phase of the development of the judicial continuum in modern Taiwan, one that is marked by a concurrent increase in the legitimacy of all of its aspects (mediation, the courts, and judicial rituals) that is also enhancing popular confidence in the ideology of justice.

This contrasts rather sharply with the fate of the ideology of justice and the judicial continuum in China today. On the one hand, China is experiencing a period of rapid religious revival. As Daniel L. Overmyer pointed out in his introduction to a special issue of *The China Quarterly*, "Religious beliefs and rituals are an important and growing reality in modern Chinese society, which cannot be fully understood without taking them into account" (Overmyer 2003b: 1; see also Overmyer 2003a).[2] Recent research has shed new light on the ways in which charismatic local elites have helped revive ritual economies that had been nearly extinguished during the Maoist era (Anagnost 1994; Chau 2005, 2006; Feuchtwang and Wang 2001; Katz 2006b; Yang 2000, 2004). Nevertheless, religious beliefs and practices have constantly faced the very real threat of state persecution during the modern era, particularly in instances when they were labeled "heterodox teachings" (*xiejiao* 邪教) or "superstitions" (*mixin* 迷信) (Bays 2004; Goossaert 2006; Ownby 2001; Smith 1998).[3] During the Republican era in particular, the state's definition of religion came to be predicated on notions of civic faith and secularized ceremonies that were meant to be primarily representational and symbolic (Harrison 2000; Nedostup 2007: 33, 37). In addition, one particularly striking aspect of state-sponsored campaigns to suppress communal religious traditions is that many targeted City God temples. This should hardly come as a surprise, as the data presented in this book reveal that such sacred sites were vital public spaces for the operation of local socioeconomic and cultural systems, including the administration of justice. As a result, once the state decided to impose its own ideals of civic order, as well as to assert hegemony over judicial practice, the logical next step was to vigorously challenge the cults of underworld deities that had so long defined the ideals and practices of justice. Such confrontations could be highly emotional, and occasionally prompted violent responses on the part of local communities, while in other instances temple patrons went to court to try and protect their interests. However, the long-term effects of war, revolution, and natural disasters ended up combining with the effects of government policies to contribute to the diminution of religion's essential position in the operation of the judicial continuum (Duara 1995: 85–113; Goossaert 2002a, 2006; Nedostup 2007, forthcoming).

2 See also the special issue entitled "Asian Ritual Systems: Syncretisms and Ruptures", edited by Pamela J. Stewart and Andrew Strathern and published in the *Journal of Ritual Studies* (Volume 19.1, June 2005). This special issue has also been published in book form (Stewart & Strathern 2006).

3 This is also the case for life-cycle rituals like marriages and funerals (Whyte 1988), and especially body practices like so-called "national arts" (*guoshu* 國術, including the martial arts) and *qigong* 氣功 techniques (Chen 2003; Ownby 2003; Palmer 2007).

The extent to which the Chinese authorities may be willing to tolerate the return of judicial rituals remains to be seen. While I have seen evidence of worshippers filing underworld indictments in Quanzhou's temples to the City God and the Emperor of the Eastern Peak, and have discovered additional evidence of similar rituals being revived in other parts of China (such as at the Judge Bao temple in Anhui described above), these practices have largely disappeared, meaning that the judicial continuum in China today remains fragmentary and inchoate. As I noted in the Introduction, the achievement of justice is an essential prerequisite for any harmonious society, while the effective functioning of a legal system requires some degree of entirety. In the case of Chinese legal culture, both ideas of justice and judicial practices have been inseparable from religion, with the ideology of justice providing a profound sense of hope for the achievement of justice and judicial rituals a means of achieving this goal. The anguished protests of parents whose children were crushed to death in so-called "tofu schools" during the horrific 2008 Sichuan earthquake, as well as the efforts by hundreds of people who feel that they have been wronged to participate in the venerable petitioning system known as *xinfang* 信訪 (literally "letters and visits"; this practice was suspended in Beijing as part of preparations for the 2008 Olympics) reveal that the longing for justice in China described in this book's Introduction remains as pressing as ever. Judicious policies towards this aspect of China's religious revival may go a long way towards fulfilling such aspirations.

BIBLIOGRAPHY

The Aeneid. Vergil (70–19 BCE). Trans. Robert Fagles. New York: Penguin Books, 2006.

Alford, William P. (1997) "Law, Law, What Law? Why Western Scholars of Chinese History and Society Have not Had More to Say about its Law." *Modern China*, 23.4:398–419.

——. ed. (2007) *Raising the Bar. The Emerging Legal Profession in East Asia*. Cambridge, MA: Harvard University Press.

Allee, Mark A. (1994a) *Law and Local Society in Late Imperial China. Northern Taiwan in the Nineteenth Century*. Stanford: Stanford University Press.

——. (1994b) "Code, Culture, and Custom: Foundations of Civil Case Verdicts in a Nineteenth-Century County Court." In Kathryn Bernhardt and Philip C.C. Huang, eds., *Civil Law in Qing and Republican China*. Stanford: Stanford University Press, pp. 122–141.

Anagnost, Ann S. (1994) "The Politics of Ritual Displacement." In Charles F. Keyes, Laurel Kendall, and Helen Hardacre, eds., *Asian Visions of Authority: Religions and the Modern States of East and Southeast Asia*. Honolulu: University of Hawaii Press, pp. 221–254.

Arkush, R. David and Dong Xiaoping 董曉萍. (1995) *Huabei minjian wenhua* 華北民間文化. Hebei: Hebei jiaoyu chubanshe.

Arnheim, Michael, ed. (1994) *Common Law*. New York: New York University Press.

Asad, Talal. (2003) *Formations of the Secular: Christianity, Islam, Modernity*. Stanford: Stanford University Press.

Aubin, Françoise. (1978) "Cheval céleste et bovin chtonien." In Rémy Dor and Michèle Nicolas, eds., *Quand le crible état dans la paille . . . Hommage à Pertev Naili Boratav*. Paris: G.-P. Maisonneuve et Larose, pp. 37–63.

Bailian pan ji 白蓮泮集. Cheng Deliang 程德良. Wanli 萬曆 era (1563–1620) edition preserved at the Center for Chinese Studies, Taipei.

Bao Leshi 包樂史 (Leonard Blussé) and Wu Fengbin 吳鳳斌. (2002) *Bacheng Gongguan dang'an yanjiu: 18 shijimo Badaweiya Tangren shehui* 吧城公館檔案研究, 18世紀末吧達維亞唐人社會. Xiamen: Xiamen daxue chubanshe.

Barth, G. (1964) *Bitter Strength: A History of Chinese in the United States, 1850–1870*. Cambridge, MA: Harvard University Press.

Bartlett, Robert. (1986) *Trial by Fire and Water. The Medieval Judicial Ordeal*. Oxford: Clarendon Press.

Bauman, Richard and Charles L. Briggs. (1990) "Poetics and Performance as Critical Perspectives on Language and Social Life." *American Review of Anthropology*, 19: 59–88.

Baxian zhi 巴縣志. (1939) In *Xinxiu fangzhi congkan* 新修方志叢刊, Number 6, *Sichuan fangzhi* 四川方志. Taipei: Xuesheng shuju, 1967.

Bays, Daniel H. (2004) "A Tradition of State Dominance." In Jason Kindopp and Carol Lee Hamrin, eds., *God and Caesar in China: Policy Implications of Church–State Tensions*. Washington, D.C.: Brookings Institution Press, pp. 25–39.

Beattie, Hilary. (1979) *Land and Lineage in China: A Study of T'ung-ch'eng County, Anhui*. Cambridge: Cambridge University Press.

Beckett, Greg. (2004) "Master of the Wood: Moral Authority and Political Imaginaries in Haiti." *PoLAR*, 27.2: 1–19.

Beiyou lu 北游錄. Tan Qian 談遷 (1594–1657). Beijing: Zhonghua shuju, 1960.

Benn, James A. (1998) "Where Text Meets Flesh: Burning the Body as an Apocryphal Practice in Chinese Buddhism." *History of Religions*, 37:295–322.

——. (2007) *Burning for the Buddha: Self-Immolation in Chinese Buddhism. Studies in East Asian Buddhism*, No. 19. Honolulu: University of Hawai'i Press.

Benton, Lauren. (2002) *Law and Colonial Cultures: Legal Regimes in World History, 1400–1900*. Cambridge and New York: Cambridge University Press.

Berger, Peter L. (1995) "The Gross National Product and the Gods." In S. Gordon Redding, ed., *International Cultural Differences (International Library of Management)*. Hanover, NH: Dartmouth Publishing Group, pp. 463–476.

Berman, Harold Joseph. (1983) *Law and Revolution: The Formation of the Western Legal Tradition*. Cambridge, MA: Harvard University Press.

Berncastle, Julius. (1850) *A Voyage to China, Including a Visit to the Bombay Presidency; the Mahratta Country; the Cave Temples of Western India, Singapore, the Straits of Malacca and Sunda and the Cape of Good Hope*. London: William Shoberl.

Bernhardt, Kathryn and Philip C.C. Huang, eds. (1994) *Civil Law in Qing and Republican China*. Stanford: Stanford University Press.

Bernstein, Alan. (1993) *The Formation of Hell: Death and Retribution in the Ancient and Early Christian Worlds.* Ithaca, NY: Cornell University Press.

——. (2006) "Heaven, Hell, and Purgatory: 1100–1500." Chapter for *The Cambridge History of Christianity*. Volume IV: *Christianity in Western Europe, c.1100-c.1500*, ed. Miri Rubin and Walter Simons. In press.

Bird, Isabella L. (1883) *The Golden Chersonese and the Way Thither*. New York: G. P. Putnam's Sons.

Bodde, Derk. 1981 (1963) "Basic Concepts of Chinese Law: The Genesis and Evolution of Legal Thought in Traditional China." In *idem*, *Essays on Chinese Civilization*. Edited and introduced by Charles Le Blanc and Dorothy Borei. Princeton, NJ: Princeton University Press, pp. 171–194; originally published in *Proceedings of the Americal Philosophical Society*, 107: 375–398.

Bodde, Derk, and Clarence Morris. (1967) *Law in Imperial China: Exemplified by 190 Ch'ing Dynasty Cases Translated from the* Hsing-an hui-lan. Cambridge, MA: Harvard University Press.

Bohannan, Paul. (1989) *Justice and Judgment among the Tiv*. Prospect Heights, IL: Waveland Press.

Bokenkamp, Stephen R. (1994) "Time after Time: Taoist Apocalyptic History and the Founding of the T'ang Dynasty." *Asia Major*, 3rd series, 7: 59–88.

—— ed. (1997) *Early Daoist Scriptures*. Berkeley: University of California Press.

——. (2007) *Ancestors and Anxiety. Daoism and the Birth of Rebirth in China*. Berkeley. University of California Press.

Boltz, Judith M. (1987) *A Survey of Taoist Literature: Tenth to Seventeenth Centuries*. Berkeley: Institute of East Asian Studies.

——. (1993) "Not by the Seal of Office Alone: New Weapons in the Battle with the Supernatural." In Patricia B. Ebrey and Peter N. Gregory, eds., *Religion and Society in T'ang and Sung China*. Honolulu: University of Hawai'i Press, pp. 241–305.

Bourdieu, Pierre. (1987) "The Force of Law: Toward a Sociology of the Juridical Field." *The Hastings Law Journal*, 38: 805–853.

Bourgon, Jérôme. (2002) "Uncivil Dialogue: Law and Custom Did not Merge into Civil Law under the Qing." *Late Imperial China*, 23.1: 50–90.

——. (2004) "Rights, Freedoms, and Customs in the Making of Chinese Civil Law, 1900–1936." In William C. Kirby, ed., *Realms of Freedom in Modern China*. Stanford: Stanford University Press, pp. 84–112.

Bowring, Sir John. (1865) "Chinese Characteristics." *Catholic World*, 2.7: 102–110.

Braddell, Roland St. John. (1915) *The Law of the Straits Settlements: A Commentary*. Singapore: Kelly and Walsh.

Brandon, S.G.F. (1967) *The Judgment of the Dead: The Idea of Life after Death in the Major Religions*. New York: Charles Scribner's Sons.

Brokaw, Cynthia. (1991) *The Ledgers of Merit and Demerit*. Princeton, NJ: Princeton University Press.

Brook, Timothy. (1993) *Praying for Power: Buddhism and the Formation of Gentry Society in Late-Ming China*. Cambridge, MA: Harvard University Press.

Brook, Timothy and B. Michael Frolic, eds. (1997) *Civil Society in China*. Armonk, NY: M.E. Sharpe.

Brook, Timothy, Jérôme Bourgon, and Gregory Blue. (2007) *Death by a Thousand Cuts*. Cambridge, MA: Harvard University Press.

Bruce, Steve. (1992) "Introduction." In Steve Bruce, ed., *Religion and Modernization: Sociologists and Historians Debate the Secularization Thesis*. Oxford and New York: Oxford University Press, pp. 1–7.

Buoye, Thomas. (2007) "Filial Felons: Leniency and Legal Reasoning in Qing China." In Robert E. Hegel and Katherine Carlitz, eds., *Writing and Law in Late Imperial China. Crime, Conflict, and Judgment*. Seattle: University of Washington Press, pp. 109–124.

Burkert, Walter. (1985) *Greek Religion*. Trans. by John Raffan. Cambridge, MA: Harvard University Press.

Buswell, Robert E., ed. (1990) *Chinese Buddhist Apocrypha*. Honolulu: University of Hawai'i Press.

Buxbaum, David C. (1971) "Some Aspects of Civil Procedure and Practice at the Trial Level in Tanshui and Hsinchu from 1789 to 1895." *The Journal of Asian Studies*, 30.2: 255–279.

Bynum, Caroline Walker and Paul Freedman, eds. (2000) *Last Things: Death and the Apocalypse in the Middle Ages*. Philadelphia: University of Pennsylvania Press.

Cai Qiguo 蔡啟國. (1986) "Zhongguo chuantong juchang zhi guiju yu jinji: Chuanju" 中國傳統劇場之規矩與禁忌: 川劇, *Minsu quyi* 民俗曲藝, 40: 45–60.

Cai Yongshun. (2006) *State and Laid-Off Workers in Reform China: The Silence and Collective Action of the Retrenched*. London: Routledge.

California State Senate Report of the Special Committee on Chinese Immigration. Sacramento, Superintendent of State Printing, 1878.

Campany, Robert Ford. (1995) "To Hell and Back: Death, Near-Death and Other Worldly Journeys in Early Medieval China." In *Death, Ecstasy, and Other Worldly Journeys*. Albany, NY: State University of New York Press, pp. 339–356.

——. (1996) *Strange Writing: Anomaly Accounts in Early Medieval China*. Albany: SUNY Press.

Cao Lin曹琳. (1996) *Jiangsu sheng Nantong shi Zhadong xiang Gongyuan cun Hanren de mianzai shenghui* 江蘇省南通市閘東鄉公園村漢人的免災勝會. In *Minsu quyi congshu* 民俗曲藝叢書, Volume 4. Taipei: Caituan faren Shi Hezheng minsu wenhua jijinhui.

Carlitz, Katherine. (2007) "Genre and Justice in Late Qing China: Wu Woyao's *Strange Case of Nine Murders* and its Antecedents." In Robert E. Hegel and Katherine Carlitz, eds., *Writing and Law in Late Imperial China. Crime, Conflict, and Judgment*. Seattle: University of Washington Press, pp. 234–257.

Casanova, José. (1994) *Public Religions in the Modern World*. Chicago: University of Chicago Press.

——. (2006) "Secularization Revisited: A Reply to Talal Asad." In David Scott and Charles Hirschkind, eds., *Powers of the Secular Modern: Talal Asad and His Interlocutors*. Stanford: Stanford University Press.

Cedzich, Ursula-Angelika. (1995) "The Cult of the Wu-t'ung/Wu-hsien 五通/五顯 in History and Fiction." In David Johnson, ed., *Ritual and Scripture in Chinese Popular Religion. Five Studies*. Berkeley: Publications of the Chinese Popular Culture Project, Number 3, pp. 137–218.

Chakrabarty, Dipesh. (2002) *Habitations of Modernity. Essays in the Wake of Subaltern Studies*. Chicago: University of Chicago Press.

Chan, Tak-hung Leo. (1998) *The Discourse on Foxes and Ghosts: Ji Yun and Eighteenth-Century Literati Storytelling*. Honolulu: University of Hawai'i Press.

Chang Hsun 張珣 and Jiang Tsann-terng 江燦騰, eds. (2001) *Dangdai Taiwan bentu zongjiao yanjiu daolun* 當代臺灣本土宗教研究導論. Taipei: SMC Publishing Inc.

Chang Hsun 張珣 and Jiang Tsann-terng 江燦騰, eds. (2003) *Taiwan bentu zongjiao yanjiu de xin shiye han xin siwei* 臺灣本土宗教研究的新視野和新思維. Taipei: SMC Publishing Inc.

Chang Wejen. (2000) "Foreword." In Karen Turner, James V. Feinerman, and R. Kent Guy, eds., *The Limits of the Rule of Law in China*. Seattle and London: University of Washington Press, pp. vii-xii.

Chanock, Martin. (1985) *Law, Custom, and Social Order: The Colonial Experience in Malawi and Zambia*. Cambridge and New York: Cambridge University Press.

Chaolin bitan 巢林筆談. Gong Wei 龔煒 (1704–1769). Beijing: Zhonghua shuju, 1981.

Chao Wei-pang. (1944) "Yang-Ko. The Rural Theatre in Ting-hsien, Hopei." *Folklore Studies*, III.1: 17–38.

Chau, Adam Yuet. (2005) "The Politics of Legitimation and the Revival of Popular Religion in Shaanbei, North-Central China." *Modern China*, 31.2: 236–278.

——. (2006) *Miraculous Response. Doing Popular Religion in Contemporary China*. Stanford: Stanford University Press.

Chen Bali 陳巴黎. (2000) "Beijing Dongyue miao qishiliu si gaishu" 北京東嶽廟七十六司概述. *Zhongguo Daojiao* 中國道教, 2: 47–52.

Chen Bofeng 陳柏峰. (2004) "Chansong, xinfang yu xin Zhongguo falü chuantong falü zhuanxing shiqi de chansong wenti" 纏訟、信訪與新中國法律傳統法律轉型時期的纏訟問題. *Zhongwai faxue* 中外法學, 16.2: 226–238.

Ch'en Ch'un-mu 陳春木. (1979) "Ta-pa-ni shijian 'Tso-chen' diqu zaonan caifang ji" 噍吧哖事件「左鎮」地區遭難採訪記. *Nanying wenxian* 南瀛文獻, 24: 95–113.

Chen Hsi-yuan 陳熙遠. (1999) "Confucianism Encounters Religion: The Formation of Religious Discourse and the Confucian Movement in Modern China." PhD dissertation, Harvard University.

Chen, Nancy N. (2003) "Healing Sects and Anti-Cult Campaigns." In Daniel L. Overmyer ed., *Religion in China Today*. The China Quarterly Special Issues, New Series, No. 3. Cambridge: Cambridge University Press, pp. 199–214.

Ch'en Teng-wu 陳登武. (2005) *Cong renjian shi dao diyu jie: Tangdai de fazhi, shehui yu guojia* 人間世到幽冥界, 唐代的法制、社會與國家. Taipei: Wunan tushu gufen youxian gongsi.

Chen Tsung-jen 陳宗仁. (1996) *Cong caodi dao jieshi: Shiba shiji Xinzhuang jie de yanjiu* 從草地到街市, 十八世紀新庄街的研究. Panchiao: Tao-hsiang chubanshe.

Ch'en Yu-ch'i 陳又琦. (2005) "Dushi miaoyu wenhua kongjian zhi xingdongzhe wanglu fenxi – Yi Xinzhuang Dizang An wei li" 都市廟宇文化空間之行動者網絡分析-以新莊地藏庵為例. M.A. thesis. National Taipei University.

Chen Yung-fa. (1986) *Making Revolution. The Communist Movement in Eastern and Central China*. Berkeley: University of California Press.

Ch'eng Ta-hsüeh 程大學. (1978) *Taiwan xianxian liezhuan (Di er ji): Yü Ch'ing-fang zhuan* 台灣先賢列傳(第二輯):余清芳傳. Nantou: Taiwan Provincial Documents Commission.

Chenivesse, Sandrine. (1998) "Fengdu: Cite de l'abondance, cite de la male mort." *Cahiers d'Extrême Asie*, 10: 287–339.

Chiba, Masaji. (1989) *Legal Pluralism: Toward a General Theory through Japanese Legal Culture*. Tokyo: Tokai University Press.

Chibei outan 池北偶談. Wang Shizhen 王士禛 (1634–1711). Beijing: Zhonghua shuju, 1982.

Chien Shuo-ch'eng 簡朔成. (2001) "Zongjiao yu sifa – Ming-Qing 'shenpan' ziliao ju'ou" 宗教與司法「明清「神判」史料舉隅. Term paper for graduate seminar "Religion and Society in Late Imperial China."

Chin Ko-lin. (1996) *Chinatown Gangs: Extortion, Enterprise, and Ethnicity*. New York: Oxford University Press.

Chinese Immigration: The Social, Moral, and Political Effect of Chinese Immigration. Testimony taken before a Committee of the Senate of the State of California, Appointed April 3rd, 1876. Sacramento: State Printing Office, 1876.

Chiu Chung-lin 邱仲麟. (1995) "Buxiao zhi xiao – Tang yilai gegu liaoqin xianxiang de shehuishi chutan" 不孝之孝「唐以來割股療親現象的社會史初探. *Xinshixue* 新史學, 6.1: 49–94.

Chiu, Martha Li. (1981) "Insanity in Imperial China: A Legal Case Study." In Arthur Kleinman and Lin Tsung-yi, eds., *Normal and Abnormal Behavior in Chinese Culture*. Dordrecht (Netherlands), London and Boston: D. Reidel Publishing Company, pp. 75–94.

Chiu Pengsheng 邱澎生 (2008) *Dang falü yushang jingji – Ming-Qing Zhongguo de shangye falü* 當法律遇上經濟 – 明清中國的商業法律. Taipei: Wunan tushu gufen youxian gongsi.

Chongzhen jiwenlu 崇禎記聞錄. Author and date of publication unknown. In *Taiwan wenxian congkan* 臺灣文獻叢刊. Number 272. Taipei: Bank of Taiwan, 1968.

Chu Chai. (1932) "Administration of Law among the Chinese in Chicago." *Journal of Criminal Law and Criminology (1931–1951)*, 22.6: 806–818.

Ch'ü T'ung-tsu. (1961) *Law and Society in Traditional China*. Paris: Moulon.

——. (1962) *Local Government in China under the Ch'ing*. Cambridge, MA: Harvard University Press.

Clart, Philip A. (1996) "The Ritual Context of Morality Books: A Case Study of a Taiwanese Spirit-Writing Cult." Ph.D. thesis, University of British Columbia.

——. (2003) "Chinese Tradition and Taiwanese Modernity: Morality Books as Social Commentary and Critique." In Philip A. Clart and Charles B. Jones, eds., *Religion in Modern Taiwan: Tradition and Innovation in a Changing Society*. Honolulu: University of Hawai'i Press, pp. 84–97.

Clart, Philip and Charles B. Jones, eds. (2003) *Religion in Modern Taiwan: Tradition and Innovation in a Changing Society*. Honolulu: University of Hawai'i Press.

Clegg, Stewart R. and S. Gordon Redding, eds. Assisted by Monica Cartner. (1990) *Capitalism in Contrasting Cultures*. Berlin and New York: W. de Gruyter.

Cohen, Alvin, ed. and trans. (1982) *Tales of Vengeful Souls. A Sixth Century Collection of Chinese Avenging Ghost Stories* (Translation of Yan Zhitui 顏之推 (531–591), *Yuanhun zhi* 冤魂志). Taipei, Paris, Hong Kong: Institut Ricci.

Cohen, Jerome A. (2008) "After Thirty Years of Law Reform, Is China Unique?" Lecture presented at East Asian Legal Studies, Harvard Law School, February 4.

Cohen, Paul A. (1997) *History in Three Keys. The Boxers as Event, Experience and Myth*. New York: Columbia University Press.

Cohn, Bernard S. (1996) *Colonialism and its Forms of Knowledge. The British in India*. Princeton, NJ: Princeton University Press.

Cohen, Esther. (1992) *The Crossroads of Justice: Law and Culture in Late Medieval France*. Leiden: E.J. Brill.

Colman, Rebecca V. (1974) "Reason and Unreason in Early Medieval Law." *Journal of Interdisciplinary History*, 4.4: 571–591.

Comaroff, Jean and John L. Comaroff, eds. (2006) *Law and Disorder in the Postcolony*. Chicago: University of Chicago Press.

Comaroff, John L. (1997) "Legality, Modernity, and Ethnicity in Colonial South Africa: An Excursion in the Historical Anthropology of Law." In R. Rawlings, ed., *Law, Society and Economy: Centenary Essays for the London School of Economics and Political Science 1895–1995*. Oxford: Clarendon Press.

——. (2001) "Law, Culture, and Colonialism: A Foreword." *Law and Social Inquiry*, 26(2): 305–314.

——. (2004) "Criminal Justice, Cultural Justice: The Limits of Liberalism and the Pragmatics of Difference in the New South Africa." *American Ethnologist*, 31.2: 188–204.

Comaroff, John L. and Jean Comaroff. (1986) "Christianity and Colonialism in South Africa." *American Ethnologist*, 13.1: 1–22.

Comaroff, John L. and Simon A. Roberts. (1981) *Rules and Processes: The Cultural Logic of Dispute in an African Context*. Chicago: University of Chicago Press.

Conner, Alison W. (2000) "True Confessions? Chinese Confessions Then and Now." In Karen Turner, James V. Feinerman, and R. Kent Guy, eds., *The Limits of the Rule of Law in China*. Seattle and London: University of Washington Press, pp. 132–162.

Dalley, Stephanie. (1989) *Myths from Mesopotamia: Creation, the Flood, Gilgamesh, and Others*. Oxford: Oxford University Press.

Darnton, Robert. (1984) *The Great Cat Massacre: And Other Episodes in French Cultural History*. New York: Basic Books.

Davies, Wendy and Paul Fouracre, eds. (1986) *The Settlement of Disputes in Early Medieval Europe*. Cambridge and New York: Cambridge University Press.

Davis, Edward L. (1985) "Arms and the Tao, 1: Hero Cult and Empire in Traditional China." In *Sōdai no shakai to shūkyō* 宋代の社會と宗教. Tokyo: Kyūko sho'in, pp. 1–56.

——. (2001) *Society and the Supernatural in Song China*. Honolulu: University of Hawai'i Press.

Dean, Kenneth. (1998a) *Lord of the Three in One. The Spread of a Cult in Southeast China*. Princeton, NJ: Princeton University Press.

——. (1998b) "Transformations of the *she* (Altars of the Soil) in Fujian." *Cahiers d'Extrême Asie*, 10: 19–75.

DeBernardi, Jean. (2004) *Rites of Belonging: Memory, Modernity, and Identity in a Malaysian Chinese Community*. Stanford: Stanford University Press.

Diamant, Neil J., Stanley B. Lubman, and Kevin J. O'Brien, eds. (2005) *Engaging the Law in China. State, Society, and Possibilities for Justice*. Stanford: Stanford University Press.

Dianshizhai huabao 點石齋畫報. 1882–1898. Guangzhou: Guangdong renmin chubanshe, 1983.

Dicker, Laverne Mau. (1979) *The Chinese in San Francisco: A Pictorial History*. New York: Dover Publications.

Dirks, Nicholas B. (2001) *Castes of Mind. Colonialism and the Making of Modern India*. Princeton, NJ: Princeton University Press.

Dobbelaere, Karel. 2002 *Secularization: An Analysis at Three Levels*. Brussels: P.I.E.-Peter Lang.

Dobson, W.A.C.H. (1968) "Some Legal Instruments in Ancient China: The Ming and the Meng." In Chow Tse-tung, ed., *Wen-lin: Studies in the Chinese Humanities*. Madison: University of Wisconsin Press, pp. 269–282.

Dongying shilue 東瀛識略. Ding Shaoyi 丁紹儀 (Qing). In *Taiwan wenxian congkan* 臺灣文獻叢刊. Number 2. Taipei: Bank of Taiwan, 1957.

Doo Leigh-wai. (1973) "Dispute Settlement in Chinese-American Communities", *Harvard Law School. Studies in East Asian Law: China*, 21: 627–655.

Doolittle, The Rev. Justus. (1986) *Social Life of the Chinese*. 2 Volumes. Singapore, Graham Brash (Pte.) Ltd. reprint of 1865–1876 edition.

Dott, Brian R. (2004) *Identity Reflections: Pilgrimages to Mount Tai in Late Imperial China*. Cambridge, MA: Harvard University Press.

Du Wenzhong 杜文忠. (1999) "Zhong-Xi shenpan bijiao yanjiu" 中西神判比較研究. *Guizhou shifan daxue xuebao (Shehui kexue ban)* 貴州師范大學學報(社會科學版), 4: 28–30.

——. (2002) "Shenpan qiyuan kaolue" 神判起源考略. *Sixiang zhanxian* 思想戰線, 6: 112–115.

——. (2004) "Shenpan yu zaoqi fa de lishi yanjin" 神判與早期法的歷史演進. *Minzu yanjiu* 民族研究, 3: 47–53.

Duara, Prasenjit. (1988) *Culture, Power, and the State: Rural North China, 1900–1942*. Stanford: Stanford University Press.

——. (1995) *Rescuing History from the Nation. Questioning Narratives of Modern China*. Chicago: University of Chicago Press.

DuBois, Thomas. (2006) "In a Court of Puppets, Who Pulls the Strings? Assessing the Independence of the Manzhouguo Judiciary." Paper presented at the nineteenth IAHA Conference. Manila, November 22–24.

Dudbridge, Glen. (1995) *Religious Experience and Lay Society in T'ang China. A Reading of Tai Fu's Kuang-i chi*. Cambridge: Cambridge University Press.

——. 2004 (1978). *The Legend of Miaoshan*. Oxford: Oxford University Press.

Dutton, Michael R. (1992) *Policing and Punishment in China. From Patriarchy to "the People"*. Cambridge and New York: Cambridge University Press.

Eberhard, Wolfram. (1967) *Guilt and Sin in Traditional China*. Berkeley: University of California Press.

Edlin, Douglas E., ed. (2007) *Common Law Theory*. Cambridge and New York: Cambridge University Press.

Electra. Euripides (ca. 480 BCE–406 BCE). Trans. Emily Vermule. Chicago: University of Chicago Press, 1959.

Endacott, George B. 2005. *A Biographical Sketch-Book of Early Hong Kong*. Hong Kong: Hong Kong University Press.

Engel, David M. (1978) *Code and Custom in a Thai Provincial Court: The Interaction of Formal and Informal Systems of Justice*. Tucson: University of Arizona Press.

Epstein, Maram. (2007) "Characterizing the Filial Son." In Robert E. Hegel and Katherine Carlitz, eds., *Writing and Law in Late Imperial China. Crime, Conflict, and Judgment*. Seattle: University of Washington Press, pp. 27–43.

Ergene, Bogac. (2004) "Pursuing Justice in an Islamic Context." *PoLAR*, 27.1: 51–71.

Erke pai'an jingqi 二刻拍案驚奇. Ling Mengchu 凌濛初 (1580–1644). Shanghai: Shanghai guji chubanshe, 1988.

Erxin 耳新. Zheng Zhongkui 鄭仲夔. *Congshu jicheng* 叢書集成 edition. Volume 2946. Shanghai: Shangwu yinshuguan, 1925.

Fang Ling 方玲. (2001) "La tradition sacrée de la médecine chinoise ancienne: Étude sur le *Livre des exorcismes* du Sun Simiao (581–682)." Ph.D. thesis, École Pratique des Hautes Études.

Faure, David. (1986) *The Structure of Chinese Rural Society*. Hong Kong: Oxford University Press.

——. (1990) "What Made Foshan 佛山 a Town? The Evolution of Rural-Urban Identities in Ming-Qing China." *Late Imperial China*, 11.2: 1–32.

——. (2007) *Emperor and Ancestor. State and Lineage in South China*. Stanford: Stanford University Press.

Ferrari, Silvio. (2002) "Canon Law as a Religious Legal System." In Andrew Huxley, ed., *Religion, Law, and Tradition: Comparative Studies in Religious Law*. London: RoutledgeCurzon, pp. 49–60.

Feuchtwang, Stephan and Wang Mingming. (2001) *Grassroots Charisma. Four Local Leaders in China*. London: Routledge.

Fish, Stanley. (1980) *Is There a Text in this Class? The Authority of Interpretive Communities*. Cambridge, MA: Harvard University Press.

Fleming, Robin. (1998) *Domesday Book and the Law: Society and Legal Custom in Early Medieval England*. Cambridge and New York: Cambridge University Press.

Foucault, Michel. 1971 (1961) *Madness and Civilization*. London: Tavistock.

Freedman, Maurice. (1950) "Colonial Law and Chinese Society." *Journal of the Royal Anthropological Institute of Great Britain and Ireland*, 80: 97–125.

Friedman, Lawrence. (1975) *The Legal System: A Social Perspective*. New York: Russell Sage.

Fu-hui ch'üan-shu 福惠全書. (1699) Huang Liu-hung 黃六鴻 (1633–1693). Trans. and ed. by Djang Chu. Tucson, Arizona: The University of Arizona Press, 1984.

Furth, Charlotte. (2007) "Introduction." In Charlotte Furth, Judith T. Zeitlin, and Ping-chen Hsiung, eds., *Thinking with Cases: Specialist Knowledge in Chinese Cultural History*. Honolulu: University of Hawai'i Press, pp. 1–27.

Gager, John G. (1992) *Curse Tablets and Binding Spells from the Ancient World*. New York and Oxford: Oxford University Press.

Geary, Patrick J. (1994) *Living with the Dead in the Middle Ages*. Ithaca, NY: Cornell University Press.

Geertz, Clifford. (1983) "Local Knowledge: Fact and Law in Comparative Perspective." In *idem*, *Local Knowledge: Further Essays in Interpretive Anthropology*. New York: Basic Books, pp. 167–234.

Gengsi bian 庚巳編. Lu Can 陸粲 (1494–1551). Beijing: Zhonghua shuju, 1985.

Georgieva, Valentina. (2000) "Buddhist Nuns in China: From the Six Dynasties to the Tang." Ph.D. thesis, University of Leiden.

Girard, Rene. (1979) *Violence and the Sacred*. Trans. by Patrick Gregory. Baltimore and London: The Johns Hopkins University Press.

Gjertson, Daniel E. (1989) *Miraculous Retribution. A Study and Translation of T'ang Lin's* Ming-pao chi. Berkeley: Berkeley Buddhist Studies Series.

Goh Bee Chen. (2002) *Law without Lawyers, Justice without Courts. On Traditional Chinese Mediation*. Aldershot, Hampshire: Ashgate.

Goodman, Bryna. (1995) *Native Place, City, and Nation. Regional Networks and Identities in Shanghai, 1853–1937*. Berkeley: University of California Press.

Goodrich, Anne Swan. (1964) *The Peking Temple of the Eastern Peak: The Tung-yüeh Miao in Peking and its Lore*. Nagoya: Monumenta Serica.

——. (1981) *Chinese Hells: The Peking Temple of Eighteen Hells and Chinese Conceptions of Hell*. St. Augustin: Monumenta Serica.

Goody, Jack. (1987) *The Interface between the Written and the Oral*. Cambridge, MA: Cambridge University Press.

Goossaert, Vincent. (2001) "La gestion des temples chinois au xixe siècle: droit coutumier ou laissez-faire?" *Extrême Orient, Extrême Occident*, 23: 11–24.

——, ed. (2002a) "Anticléricalisme en Chine." *Extrême Orient, Extrême-Occident*, 24.

——. (2002b) "Starved of Resources. Clerical Hunger and Enclosures in Nineteenth-Century China." *Harvard Journal of Asiatic Studies*, 62.1: 77–133.

——. (2005) *L'Interdit du boeuf en Chine. Agriculture, éthique et sacrifice*. Paris: Collège de France, Institut des Hautes Études Chinoises.

——. (2006) "1898: The Beginning of the End for Chinese Religion?" *The Journal of Asian Studies*, 65.2: 307–336.

——. (2008) "The Impossible Repression of Female Public Piety: Late Imperial Bans on Women in Chinese Temples." *Nan Nü: Men, Women and Gender in Early Imperial China*, Volume 10. In press.

Graff, David A. (2000) "Dou Jiande's Dilemma: Logistics, Strategy, and State Formation in Seventh-Century China." In Hans van de Ven, ed., *Warfare in Chinese History*. Leiden: E.J. Brill, 77–105.

Grimes, Ronald L. (1985) "Victor Turner's Social Drama and T.S. Eliot's Ritual Drama." *Anthropologica*, N.S., 27.1–2: 79–100.

——. (1990) "Victor Turner's Definition, Theory, and Sense of Ritual." In Kathleen M. Ashley, ed., *Victor Turner and the Construction of Cultural Criticism*. Bloomington: Indiana University Press, pp. 141–146.

de Groot, Jan J.M. (1892–1910) *The Religious System of China*. 6 Volumes. Leiden: E.J. Brill.

Guangdong xinyu 廣東新語. Qu Dajun 屈大均 (1630–1696). Beijing: Zhonghua shuju, 1985.

Guha, Ranajit. (1997) *Dominance without Hegemony. History and Power in Colonial India*. Cambridge, MA: Harvard University Press.

Guo Qitao. (2003) *Exorcism and Money: The Symbolic World of the Five-Fury Spirits in Late Imperial China*. China Research Monograph 55. Berkeley: Institute of East Asian Studies.

Guthrie, W.K.C. (1962) *The Greeks and their Gods*. London: Methuen & Co. Ltd.

Haakonssen, Knud. (1995) *Natural Law and Moral Philosophy: From Grotius to the Scottish Enlightenment*. New York: Cambridge University Press.

Han Xiutao 韓秀桃. (2000) "*Jiaomin bangwen* suojian Mingchu jiceng lilaoren lisong zhidu"《教民榜文》所見明初基層里老人理訟制度. *Faxue yanjiu* 法學研究, 3: 137–147.

Hansen, Valerie. (1990) *Changing Gods in Medieval China, 1127–1276*. Princeton: Princeton University Press.

——. (1995) *Negotiating Daily Life in Traditional China: How Ordinary People Used Contracts, 600–1400*. New Haven: Yale University Press.

——. (1996) "The Law of the Spirits." In Donald S. Lopez, ed., *Religions of China in Practice*. Princeton, NJ: Princeton University Press, pp. 284–292.

Hao Tiechuan 郝鐵川. (1997) *Zhongguo faxi yanjiu* 中國法系研究. Shanghai: Fudan daxue chubanshe.

Harper, Donald. (1994) "Resurrection in Warring States Popular Religion." *Taoist Resources*, 5.2: 13–28.

Harrell, C. Stevan. (1974) "When a Ghost Becomes a God." In Arthur P. Wolf, ed., *Religion and Ritual in Chinese Society*. Stanford: Stanford University Press, pp. 193–206.

Harrison, Henrietta. (2000) *The Making of the Republican Citizen: Political Ceremonies and Symbols in China, 1911–1929*. Oxford: Oxford University Press.

Harrison, Jane Ellen. 1991. *Prolegomena to the Study of Greek Religion*. Princeton: Princeton University Press.

Hasian, Marouf Arif. (2002) *Colonial Legacies in Postcolonial Contexts: A Critical Rhetorical Examination of Legal Histories*. Oxford and New York: Peter Lang.

Hayden, George A. (1978) *Crime and Punishment in Medieval Chinese Drama: Three Judge Bao Plays*. Cambridge, MA: Harvard University Press.

Hegel, Robert E. (2007a) "Introduction: Writing and the Law." In Robert E. Hegel and Katherine Carlitz, eds., *Writing and Law in Late Imperial China. Crime, Conflict, and Judgment*. Seattle: University of Washington Press, pp. 3–23.

——. (2007b) "The Art of Persuasian in Literature and Law." In Robert E. Hegel and Katherine Carlitz, eds., *Writing and Law in Late Imperial China. Crime, Conflict, and Judgment*. Seattle: University of Washington Press, pp. 81–106.

Hendrischke, Barbara, trans. (2006) *The Scripture on Great Peace: The Taiping jing and the Beginnings of Daoism*. Berkeley: University of California Press.

Henninger, Joseph. (1987a) "Sacrifice." Trans. by Matthew J. O'Connell. In *The Encyclopedia of Religion*. New York: Macmillan Publishing Company. Volume 12, pp. 544–557.

——. (1987b) "Scapegoat." Trans. by Matthew J. O'Connell. In *The Encyclopedia of Religion*. New York: Macmillan Publishing Company. Volume 13, pp. 92–95.

Himmelfarb, Martha. (1983) *Tours of Hell: An Apocalyptic Form in Jewish and Christian Literature*. Philadelphia: University of Pennsylvania Press.

Ho, Virgil Kit-yiu. (2000) "Butchering Fish and Executing Criminals: Public Executions and the Meanings of Violence in Late Imperial and Modern China." In Göran Aijmer and Jos Abbink, eds., *Meanings of Violence: A Cross Cultural Perspective*. Oxford: Berg, pp. 141–160.

Hoebel, E. Adamson. (1954) *The Law of Primitive Man: A Study in Comparative Legal Dynamics*. Cambridge, MA: Harvard University Press.

Hooker, M.B., ed. and comp. (1967) *A Source Book of Adat, Chinese Law and The History of Common Law in the Malayan Peninsula*. Singapore: Faculty of Law, University of Singapore.

——. (1975) *Legal Pluralism: An Introduction to Colonial and Neo-colonial Laws*. Oxford: Clarendon Press.

——. (2002) *Law and the Chinese in Southeast Asia*. Singapore: Institute of Southeast Asian Studies.

Hope, Nicholas C., Dennis Tao Yang, and Mu Yang Li, eds. (2003) *How Far Across the River? Chinese Policy Reform at the Millennium*. Stanford: Stanford University Press.

Hornung, Erik. (1999) *The Ancient Egyptian Books of the Afterlife*. Translated from the German by David Lorton. Ithaca, NY: Cornell University Press.

Houguan xian xiangtu zhi 侯官縣鄉土志. (1906) In *Zhongguo fangzhi congshu, Huanan difang, Fujian sheng* 中國方志叢書, 華南地方, 福建省. Number 227; 2 volumes. Taipei: Chengwen chubanshe, 1974.

Hsieh Kang. 謝康. (1972) *Maiyin zhidu yu Taiwan changji wenti* 賣淫制度與臺灣娼妓問題. Taipei: Ta-feng.

Hsu Chia-ming 許嘉明. (1978) "Zhan jitou kao" 斬雞頭考, *Zonghe yuekan* 綜合月刊, 110: pp. 137–143.

Hsu Li-ling 許麗玲. (2003) "Jibing yu e'yun de zhuanyi: Taiwan beibu hongtou fashi Dabuyun yishi fenxi" 疾病與厄運的轉移, 台灣北部紅頭法師大補運儀式分析. In Lin Mei-rong 林美容, ed., *Xinyang, yishu, yu shehui: Disanjie guoji Hanxue huiyi lunwenji* 信仰、儀式與社會, 第三屆國際漢學會議論文集. Nankang: Institute of Ethnology, Academia Sinica, pp. 339–365.

Hu Pu'an 胡樸安. 1990 (1923) *Zhonghua quanguo fengsu zhi* 中華全國風俗誌. Beijing: Zhongzhou guji chubanshe.

Huang Ching-chia 黄靜嘉. (2002) *Chunfan louxia wantao ji: Riben due Taiwan de zhimin tongzhi ji qi yingxiang* 春帆樓下晚濤急: 日本對台灣的殖民統治及其影響. Taipei: Shangwu yinshuguan.

Huang Chun-chieh and Erik Zürcher, eds. (1995) *Time and Space in Chinese Culture*. Leiden and New York: E.J. Brill.

Huang, Philip C.C. (1996) *Civil Justice in China*. Stanford: Stanford University Press.

——. (2001) *Code, Custom, and Legal Practice in China. The Qing and Republic Compared*. Stanford: Stanford University Press.

——. (2005) "Divorce Law Practices and the Origins, Myths, and Realities of Judicial Mediation in China." *Modern China*, 31.2: 151–203.

——. (2006) "Civil Adjudication in China: Past and Present." *Modern China*, 32.2: 135–180.

Huang Pingying 黃萍瑛. (2008) *Taiwan minjian xinyang "guniang" de fengsi – Yige Taiwan shehuishi de kaocha.* 台灣民間信仰「孤娘」的奉祀 – 一個台灣社會史的考察 Pan-chiao: Tao-hsiang chubanshe.

Huangshi richao 黃氏日抄. Huang Zhen黃震 (1213–1280). In *Wenyuange Siku quanshu* 文淵閣四庫全書. Taipei: Shangwu yinshuguan, 1983. Volumes 707–708.

Huang Te-shih 黃得時. (1943) "Shinsō Gai no rekishi to bunka" 新莊街の歷史と文化. *Minzoku Taiwan* 民俗台灣, 3.6: 44–46.

Huang Wenbo 黃文博. (1994) *Nanying minsu zhi* 南瀛民俗誌. 2 volumes. Hsin-ying: Tainan xianli wenhua zhongxin.

——. (1995) *Nanying lishi yu fengtu* 南瀛歷史與風土. Taipei: Changmin wenhua chubanshe.

Huang Yu-hsing 黃有興. (1992) *Penghu de minjian xinyang* 澎湖的民間信仰. Taipei: Taiyuan chubanshe.

Huang Yuansheng 黃源盛. (1999) "Minguo chunian jindai xingshi susong de shengcheng yu kaizhan" 民國初年近代刑事訴訟的生成與開展, *Zhengda faxue pinglun* 政大法學評論, 61: 35–86.

——. (2001) "Cong chuantong lüli dao jindai xingfa: Qingmo Minchu jindai fadian de biancuan yu Okada Asatarō" 從傳統律例到近代刑法: 清末民初近代刑法典的編纂與岡田朝太郎. *Yuedan faxue* 月旦法學, 75: 73–86.

Huang Zhanyue 黃展岳. (1986) "Shenpanfa yu xiezhi juesong" 神判法與獬豸決訟. In *Gudai lizhi fengsu mantan* 古代禮制風俗漫談. Volume 2. Beijing: Zhonghua shuju, pp. 13–18.

Huizui bian 薈蕞編. Yu Yue 俞樾 (1821–1906). In *Biji xiaoshuo daguan* 筆記小說大觀. Second Series, Number 4. Taipei: Xinxing shuju, 1988.

Hummel, Arthur H., ed. (1943) *Eminent Chinese of the Ch'ing Period, 1644–1912*. Washington, DC: U.S. Government Printing Office.

Hung Ts'an-nan 洪燦南. (1976) "Xinzhuang zhen de yange" 新莊鎮的沿革. *Taibei wenxian* 台北文獻 38: 64–73.

Huntington, Rania. (2003) *Alien Kind: Foxes and Late Imperial Chinese Narrative*. Cambridge, MA: Harvard University Press.

——. (2005) "Ghosts Seeking Substitutes: Female Suicide and Repetition." *Late Imperial China*, 26.1: 1–40.

——. (2007) "Memory, Mourning, and Genre in the Works of Yu Yue." *Harvard Journal of Asiatic Studies*, 67.2: 253–293.

Husken, Ute, ed. (2007) *When Rituals Go Wrong: Mistakes, Failure, and the Dynamics of Ritual*. Leiden: Koninklijke Brill NV.

Huxley, Andrew, ed. (2002) *Religion, Law, and Tradition: Comparative Studies in Religious Law*. London: RoutledgeCurzon.

Hymes, Robert. (2002) *Way and Byway. Taoism, Local Religion, and Models of Divinity in Sung and Modern China*. Berkeley: University of California Press.

Idema, Wilt L. (1990) "The Founding of the Han Dynasty in Early Drama: The

Autocratic Suppression of Popular Debunking." In W.L. Idema and Eric Zürcher, eds. *Thought and Law in Qin and Han China. Studies Dedicated to Anthony Hulsewe on the Occasion of his Eightieth Birthday*. Leiden: E.J. Brill, pp. 183–207.

——, trans. and ed. (2008) *Personal Salvation and Filial Piety. Two Precious Scroll Narratives of Guanyin and Her Acolytes*. Kuroda Institute Classics in East Asian Buddhism. Honolulu: University of Hawai'i Press.

Idema, Wilt L. and Erik Zürcher, eds. (1990) *Thought and Law in Qin and Han China: Studies Dedicated to Anthony Hulsewé on the Occasion of his Eightieth Birthday*. Leiden and New York: E.J. Brill.

Ingalls, Robert P. (1988) *Urban Vigilantes in the New South: Tampa, 1882–1936*. Knoxville: University of Tennessee Press.

Itō Seiji 伊藤清司. (1986) "Tiehuo shenpan xipu zaji" 鐵火神判系譜雜記. Trans. by Yang Defang 楊德芳. *Guizhou minzu yanjiu* 貴州民族研究, 1:137–143.

Ja'affar, Fadhzila Binte. (2007) "Space and Memory in the Reconstruction of Religious Myth: A Study on the Community Surrounding Kampung Hulu Mosque." Unpublished manuscript.

Jain, M.P. (1994) "Custom as a Source of Law in India." In Alison Dundes Renteln and Alan Dundes, eds., *Folk Law: Essays in the Theory and Practice of* Lex Non Scripta. 2 volumes. Madison: The University of Wisconsin Press, pp. 49–82.

Ji Zong'an 紀宗安 and Yan Lijin 顏麗金. (2004) "Shixi Baguo Huaren gongtang de mengshen shenpan" 試析吧國華人公堂的盟神審判. *Dongnanya yanjiu* 東南亞研究, 3: 66–71.

Jiandeng xinhua 剪燈新話. Qu You 瞿佑 (1341–1427). In *Zheng Zhenduo shijie wenku* 鄭振鐸世界文庫, Volumes 5 and 6. Shijiazhuang: Hebei renmin chubanshe, 1991.

Jianyang xian xuzhi 簡陽縣續志. (1927) Lin Zhimao 林志茂, et. al., ed. and comp. In *Xinxiu fangzhi congkan* 新修方志叢刊, Series 5. *Sichuan fangzhi* 四川方志, Volume 5. Taipei: Taiwan xuesheng shuju, 1967.

Jiangnan tongzhi 江南通志. (1736) Huang Zhijuan 黃之雋 (1668–1748), et. al., ed. and comp. In *Wenyuange Siku quanshu* 文淵閣四庫全書. Taipei: Shangwu yinshuguan, 1983. Volumes 507–512.

Jiang Yonglin and Wu Yanhong. (2007) "Satisfying Both Sentiment and Law: Fairness-Centered Judicial Reasoning as Seen in Late Ming Casebooks." In Charlotte Furth, Judith T. Zeitlin, and Ping-chen Hsiung, eds., *Thinking with Cases: Specialist Knowledge in Chinese Cultural History*. Honolulu: University of Hawai'i Press, pp. 31–61.

Johnson, David. (1989) "Actions Speak Louder than Words: The Cultural Significance of Chinese Ritual Opera." In *idem*, ed., *Ritual Opera, Operatic Ritual: "Mu-lien Rescues his Mother" in Chinese Popular Culture*. Berkeley: Publications of the Chinese Popular Culture Project, Number 1, pp. 1–45.

Jordan, David K. (1985) "Sworn Brothers: A Study in Chinese Ritual Kinship." In Hsieh Jih-chang and Chuang Ying-chang, eds., *The Chinese Family and its Ritual Behavior*. Nankang: Institute of Ethnology, Academia Sinica, pp. 232–262.

Jordan, David K. and Daniel L. Overmyer. (1986) *The Flying Phoenix. Aspects of Chinese Sectarianism in Taiwan*. Princeton: Princeton University Press.

Jung Shawwu 容邵武. (2007a) "'We are not Talking of Law Here': Law and Local Culture at District Mediation Committee in Taiwan." Paper presented at the Law, Culture and Society Workshop, National Tsing-hua University, Taiwan, May 27.

——. (2007b) "Wenhua, falü yu celue: Xiangzhen tiaojie guocheng de yanjiu" 文化、法律與策略, 鄉鎮調解過程的研究. *Taiwan shehui xuekan* 臺灣社會學刊, 38: 57–104.

Just, Peter. (1992) "History, Power, Ideology, and Culture: Current Directions in the Anthropology of Law." *Law & Society Review*, 26.2: 373–412.

——. (2001) *Dou Donggo Justice: Conflict and Morality in an Indonesian Society*. Lanham: Rowman & Littlefield Publishers.

Kadri, Sadakat. (2006) *The Trial. A History, from Socrates to O.J. Simpson*. New York: Random House.

Kaltenmark, Max. (1979) "The Ideology of the *T'ai-p'ing ching*." In Holmes Welch and Anna Seidel, eds., *Facets of Taoism*. New Haven and London: Yale University Press, pp. 19–45.

Kang Xiaofei. (2006) *The Cult of the Fox: Power, Gender, and Popular Religion in Late Imperial and Modern China*. New York: Columbia University Press.

Karasawa Yasuhiko. (2007a) "Between Oral and Written Cultures: Buddhist Monks in Qing Legal Plaints." In Robert E. Hegel and Katherine Carlitz, eds., *Writing and Law in Late Imperial China. Crime, Conflict, and Judgment*. Seattle: University of Washington Press, pp. 64–80.

——. (2007b) "From Oral Testimony to Written Records in Qing Legal Cases." In Charlotte Furth, Judith T. Zeitlin, and Ping-chen Hsiung, eds., *Thinking with Cases: Specialist Knowledge in Chinese Cultural History*. Honolulu: University of Hawai'i Press, pp. 101–122.

Kataoka Iwao 片岡巖. 1981 (1921) *Taiwan fengsu zhi* 臺灣風俗誌. Trans. by Ch'en Chin-t'ien 陳金田 and Feng Tso-min 馮作民. Taipei: Ta-li Publishing Company.

Katz, Paul R. (1995a) *Demon Hordes and Burning Boats: The Cult of Marshal Wen in Late Imperial Chekiang*. Albany: SUNY Press.

——. (1995b) "The Pacification of Plagues: A Chinese Rite of Affliction." *Journal of Ritual Studies*, 9.1: pp. 55–100.

——. (1997) *Taiwan de wangye xinyang* 台灣的王爺信仰. Taipei: Shangding wenhua chubanshe.

——. (1998) "Xinzhuang Dizang An de dazhong ye chongbai" 新莊地藏庵的大眾爺崇拜. *Journal of Humanities East/West*, 16:123–159.

——. (1999a) "Temple Cults and the Creation of Hsin-chuang Local Society." In T'ang Hsi-yung, ed., *Papers from the Seventh Conference on Chinese Maritime History*. Nankang: Sun Yat-sen Institute of Social Sciences, pp.735–798.

——. (1999b) *Images of the Immortal. The Cult of Lü Dongbin at the Palace of Eternal Joy*. Honolulu: University of Hawai'i Press.

——. (2000) "Hanren shehui de shenpan yishi chutan – Cong zhan jitou shuoqi" 漢人社會的神判儀式初探 – 從斬雞頭說起. *Bulletin of the Institute of Ethnology, Academia Sinica*, 88:173–202.

——. (2001) "Divine Justice: Chicken-Beheading Rituals in Japanese Occupation Taiwan and their Historical Antecedents." Published in *Proceedings of the International Conference on Society, Ethnicity, and Cultural Performance*, edited by Wang Ch'iu-kuei 王秋桂, Chuang Ying-chang莊英章 and Chen Chung-min 陳中民. Taipei: Center for Chinese Studies, pp. 111–160.

——. (2003a) "Local Elites and Sacred Sites in Hsin-chuang – The Growth of the Ti-tsang An during the Japanese Occupation." In Lin Mei-rong 林美容, ed., *Xinyang, yishi, yu shehui: Disanjie guoji Hanxue huiyi lunwenji* 信仰、儀式與社會,

第三屆國際漢學會議論文集. Nankang: Institute of Ethnology, Academia Sinica, pp. 179–227.
——. (2003b) "Religion and the State in Postwar Taiwan." In Daniel L. Overmyer, ed., *Religion in China Today*. The China Quarterly Special Issues, New Series, No. 3. Cambridge: Cambridge University Press, pp. 89–106.
——. (2004a) "Daoism and Local Cults – A Case Study of the Cult of Marshal Wen." In Kwang-ching Liu and Richard Shek, eds., *Heterodoxy in Late Imperial China*. Honolulu: University of Hawai'i Press, pp. 172–208.
——. (2004b) "Divine Justice in Late Imperial China: A Preliminary Study of Indictments, Oaths, and Ordeals." In John Lagerwey, ed., *Religion and Chinese Society*. Hong Kong: The Chinese University Press, pp. 869–902.
——. (2004c) "Fowl Play – Chicken-Beheading Rituals and Dispute Resolution in Taiwan." In David K. Jordan, Andrew D. Morris, and Marc L. Moskowitz, eds., *The Minor Arts of Daily Life: Popular Culture in Taiwan*. Honolulu: University of Hawai'i Press, pp. 35–49.
——. (2005) *When Valleys Turned Blood Red: The Ta-pa-ni Incident in Colonial Taiwan*. Honolulu: University of Hawai'i Press.
——. (2006a) "Banner Worship and Human Sacrifice in Late Imperial and Modern China." Presented at "Chinese Culture, Past and Present: An International Conference in Commemoration of Frederick W. Mote." Chung-li, Taiwan, November 19–21. Originally presented at the International Conference "As China Meets the World: China's Changing Position in the International Community, 1840 – 2000." Vienna, Austria, May 17–18, 2004.
——. (2006b) "Festivals and the Recreation of Identity in South China: A Case Study of Processions and Expulsion Rites in Pucheng, Zhejiang." In Pamela J. Stewart and Andrew Strathern, eds., *Asian Ritual Systems: Syncretisms and Ruptures*. Durham, NC: Carolina Academic Press, pp. 153–182.
——. (2007a) "Orthopraxy and Heteropraxy Beyond the State: Standardizing Ritual in Chinese Society." *Modern China*, 33.1: 72–90.
——. (2007b) "Indictment Rituals and the Judicial Continuum in Late Imperial China." In Robert E. Hegel and Katherine Carlitz, eds., *Writing and Law in Late Imperial China. Crime, Conflict, and Judgment*. Seattle: University of Washington Press, pp. 161–185.
——. (2008) "Trial by Power: On the Judicial Roles of Taoist Martial Deities." Paper presented at the Association of Asian Studies Annual Meeting. Atlanta, April 3–6.
Katz, Paul R. and Murray A. Rubinstein. (2003) *Religion and the Formation of Taiwanese Identities*. New York: Palgrave Macmillan.
Keightley, David N. (1978) "The Religious Commitment: Shang Theology and the Genesis of Chinese Political Culture." *History of Religions*, 17: 211–225.
Kieschnick, John. (1997) *The Eminent Monk: Buddhist Ideals in Medieval Chinese Hagiography*. Honolulu: University of Hawai'i Press, 1997.
Kim, Marie Seong-Hak. (2007) "Law and Custom under the Chosŏn Dynasty and Colonial Korea: A Comparative Perspective." *The Journal of Asian Studies*, 66.4: 1067–1097.
King, Charles. (1998) "The Living and the Dead: Ancient Roman Conceptions of the Afterlife." Ph.D. thesis, University of Chicago.
Kinkley, Jeffrey C. (2000) *Chinese Justice, the Fiction. Law and Literature in Modern China*. Stanford: Stanford University Press.

Kleeman, Terry F. (1994) *A God's Own Tale. The Book of Transformations of Wenchang, the Divine Lord of Zitong*. Albany: SUNY Press.

——. (2005) "Traditional Chinese Jurisprudence and the Supernatural: Can Ghosts Give Evidence?" Unpublished manuscript.

Kleinman, Arthur. M.D. (1980) *Patients and Healers in the Context of Culture*. Berkeley: University of California Press.

——. (1986) *Social Origins of Distress and Disease*. New Haven and London: Yale University Press.

Klinger, Elmar. (1987) "Vows and Oaths." Trans. by Russell M. Stockman. In *The Encyclopedia of Religion*. New York: Macmillan Publishing Company. Volume 15, pp. 301–305.

Ko, Dorothy. (1994) *Teachers of the Inner Chambers: Women and Culture in Seventeenth-Century China*. Stanford: Stanford University Press.

Kohler, Kaufmann. (1923) *Heaven and Hell in Comparative Religion*. New York: The Macmillan Company.

Kohn, Livia. (1998) "Counting Good Deeds and Days of Life: The Quantification of Fate in Medieval China." *Asiatische Studieren*, 52: 833–870.

Kollewijn, R.D. (1994) "Conflicts of Western and non-Western Law." In Alison Dundes Renteln and Alan Dundes, eds., *Folk Law: Essays in the Theory and Practice of* Lex Non Scripta. 2 volumes. Madison: The University of Wisconsin Press, pp. 775–793.

Kotenev, A.M. (1925) *Shanghai: Its Mixed Court and Council*. Shanghai: North China Daily News & Herald.

Kratz, Corinne A. (1989) "Genres of Power: A Comparative Analysis of Okiek Blessings, Curses and Oaths." *Man* (N.S.), 24: 299–317.

Kubo Noritada 窪德忠. (1972) "Taiwan no jōkōshin shinkō" 臺灣の城隍神信仰. In *Tōhō gakuhō sōritsu nijūgō kinen. Tōhōgaku ronshū* 東方學會創立二十五週年記念·東方學論集. Tokyo: Tōhō gakuhō, pp. 311–326.

——. (1975) "Taiwan chū, hokubu ni okeru jōkōshin shinkō" 臺灣中, 北部における城隍神信仰. In *Suzuki Shun Sensei koki kinen tōyōshi ronsō* 鈴木俊先生古稀記念東洋史論叢. Tokyo: Yamakawa shuppansha, pp. 165–180.

Kuhn, Philip A. (1991) *Soulstealers. The Chinese Sorcery Scare of 1768*. Cambridge, MA: Harvard University Press.

Kuo Li-ying. (1994) *Confession et contrition dans le bouddhisme chinois du ve au xe siècle*. Paris: École Française d'Extrême Orient.

Lagerwey, John. (1987) *Taoist Ritual in Chinese Society and History*. New York: Macmillan Publishing Company.

——. (1994) "Notes on the Symbolic Life of a Hakka Village." *Proceedings of the International Conference on Popular Beliefs and Chinese Culture*. Taipei: Center for Chinese Studies, pp. 733–761.

——. (1998) "Dingguang gufo: Oral and Written Sources in the Study of a Saint." *Cahiers d'Extrême Asie*, 10: 77–129.

Lai Chi-tim 黎志添. (2002) "The *Demon Statutes of Nüqing* and the Problem of the Bureaucratization of the Netherworld in Early Heavenly Master Daoism." *T'oung Pao*, 88: 251–281.

Lammers, John C. (1988) "The Accommodation of Chinese Immigrants in Early California Courts." *Sociological Perspectives*, 31.4: 446–465.

Lariviere, Richard W. (1981) "Ordeals in Europe and India." *Journal of the American Oriental Society*, 101.3: 347–349.

Lazarus-Black, Mindie and Susan F. Hirsch, eds. (1994) *Contested States: Law, Hegemony, and Resistance*. New York: Routledge.

Lea, Henry Charles. 1974 *The Duel and the Oath*. Philadelphia: University of Pennsylvania Press.

Le Goff, Jacques. (1984) *The Birth of Purgatory*. Chicago: The University of Chicago Press.

Lee Fong-Mao 李豐楙, et. al. (1998) *Donggang yingwang – Donggang Donglong Gong dingchou nian zhengke ping'an jidian* 東港迎王 – 東港東隆宮丁丑年正科平安祭典. Taipei: Taiwan xuesheng shuju.

Leung, Conita S. C. (1997) "From Colony to Special Administrative Region." In Tan Poh-ling, ed., *Asian Legal Systems: Law, Society and Pluralism in East Asia*. Sydney: Butterworths, pp. 67–79.

Lewis, Mark Edward. (1990) *Sanctioned Violence in Early China*. Albany, NY: SUNY Press.

——. (1999) *Writing and Authority in Early China*. Albany, NY: SUNY Press.

Li Huiyun 李慧筠. (2003) "Xianggang jingcha de Guandi chongbai" 香港警察的關帝崇拜. *Taiwan zongjiao yanjiu tongxun* 臺灣宗教研究通訊, 5: 223–236.

Li Yih-yuan 李亦園. (1983) "Zhan jitou" 斬雞頭. In *Shitu, shenhua, yu qita* 師徒、神話及其他. Taipei: Cheng-chung.

——. (1995) "Notions of Time, Space and Harmony in Chinese Popular Culture." In Huang Chun-chieh and Erik Zürcher, eds., *Time and Space in Chinese Culture*. Leiden and New York: E.J. Brill, pp. 383–402.

Lian Shaoming 連劭名. (1996) "Jianxing nianbanian (341) 'songren' jiechujian kaoshu" 建興廿八年(341)「松人」解除簡考述. *Shijie zongjiao yaniu* 世界宗教研究, 3: 116–119.

Liang Zhiping 梁治平. (1996) *Qingdai xiguanfa: Shehui yu guojia* 清代習慣法: 社會與國家. Beijing: Zhongguo zhengfa daxue chubanshe.

Liaozhai zhiyi: huijiao, huizhu, huiping 聊齋誌異:會校,會評,會註. Pu Songling 蒲松齡 (1640–1715). Zhang Youhe 張友鶴, ed. Shanghai: Guji chubanshe, 1978.

Lim, Irene. (1999) *Secret Societies in Singapore*. Singapore: Singapore History Museum, National Heritage Board.

Lin Duan 林端. (2000) "'Guojia zhidingfa' yu 'minjian xiguan': Taiwan 'jisi gongye' de lishi shehuixue fenxi"「國家制定法」與「民間習慣」, 台灣「祭祀公業」的歷史社會學分析. *Fazhishi yanjiu* 法制史研究, 1: 117–151.

——. (2003) *Wei Bo lun Zhongguo chuantong falü: Wei Bo bijiao shehuixue de pipan* 韋伯論中國傳統法律: 韋伯比較社會學的批判. Taipei: Sanmin shuju.

Lin Ching-chih. (2007) "Canguing Children in Processions of Chinese Popular Religion: Religious Practices as Means of Constructing Family Solidarity". Unpublished manuscript.

Lin Fu-shih 林富士. (1995) *Guhun yu guixiong de shijie – Bei Taiwan de ligui xinyang* 孤魂與鬼雄的世界 – 北台灣的厲鬼信仰. Panchiao: Taipei County Government.

——. (2005) "Yizhe huo bingren: Jitong zai Taiwan shehuizhong de jiaose yu xingxiang" 醫者或病人, 童乩在臺灣社會中的角色與形象. *Bulletin of the Institute of History & Philology*, Academia Sinica, 76.3: 511–568

Lin Shuimei 林水梅 and Xie Jizhong 謝濟中. (1997) "Liancheng Xian Chengguan de

Chenghuang miaohui" 連城縣城關的城隍廟會. In Yang Yanjie 楊彥杰, ed., *Minxi de chengxiang miaohui yu cunluo wenhua* 閩西的城鄉廟會與村落文化. Traditional Hakka Society Series, Volume 4. Hong Kong: International Hakka Studies Association, Overseas Chinese Archives, École Française d'Extrême Orient, pp. 18–33.

Lin Yongzhong 林用中 and Zhang Songshou 章松壽. (1936) *Lao Dongyue: miaohui diaocha baogao* 老東嶽, 廟會調查報告. Hangzhou: Zhejiang yinshuaju.

Ling Shuyuan 凌淑菀. (2003) "Taiwan Chenghuang xinyang de jianli yu fazhan (1683–1945)" 臺灣城隍信仰的建立與發展 (1683–1945). M.A. thesis, National Chung Cheng University.

Little, Lester K. (1993) *Benedictine Maledictions*. Ithaca, NY: Cornell University Press.

Liu Bingrong 劉秉榮. (1993) *Junfa yu mixin* 軍閥與迷信. Beijing: Huawen chubanshe.

Liu Chih-wan 劉枝萬. (1983) *Taiwan minjian xinyang lunji* 台灣民間信仰論集. Taipei: Lien-ching.

Liu Dake 劉大可. (2003) "Lun chuantong Kejia cunluo de fenzheng chuli chengxu – Minxi Wubei cunluo de tianye diaocha yanjiu" 論傳統客家村落的紛爭處理程序 – 閩西武北村落的田野調查研究. *Minzu yanjiu* 民族研究, 6: 54–63.

Liu Ducai 劉篤才. (1994) "Zhongguo gudai de shi, meng yu chengwenfa de guanxi" 中國古代的誓、盟與成文法的關系. *Liaoning daxue xuebao (Zhexue shehui kexue bao)* 遼寧大學學報 (哲學社會科學版), 6: 96–98.

Liu Hsia-ru 劉夏如. (2002) "Fa, jindai, minzu zhuyi – 1920 niandai Taiwan jisi gongye gaifei lunzheng" 法 . 近代 . 民族主義 – 1920年代台灣祭祀公業改廢論爭. *Taiwan fengwu* 台灣風物, 52.2: 17–69.

Liu Jingfeng 劉勁峰. (2000) *Gannan zongzu shehui yu Daojiao wenhua yanjiu* 贛南宗族社會與道教文化研究. Traditional Hakka Society Series. Volume 8. Hong Kong: International Hakka Studies Association, Overseas Chinese Archives, École Française d'Extrême Orient.

Liu Yongping. (1998) *Origins of Chinese Law*. Hong Kong: Oxford University Press.

Liu Zhongyu 劉仲宇. (2002) *Daojiao fashu* 道教法術. Shanghai: Shanghai wenhua chubanshe.

Lo Shih-chieh 羅士傑. (2002) "Luelun Qing Tongzhi nianjian Taiwan Dai Chaochun an yu Tiandihui de guanxi" 略論清同治年間台灣戴潮春案與天地會之關係. *Minsu quyi* 民俗曲藝, 138: 279–303.

Loewe, Michael. 2002 (1967) *Records of Han Administration*. London: RoutledgeCurzon.

Lu Jin 魯金. (2007) *Xianggang miaoqu* 香港廟趣. Hong Kong: Ciwenhuatang.

Lu Yan 魯言 (Liang Tao 梁濤). (1979) *Xianggang zhanggu* 香港掌故. Hong Kong: Guangjiaojing chubanshe.

Luckmann, Thomas. (1967) *The Invisible Religion: The Problem of Religion in Modern Society*. New York: Macmillan.

Lunheng 論衡. Wang Chong 王充 (27–97?). Trans. and annotated by Alfred Forke. 2nd edn. New York: Paragon, 1962.

Lügong shizhenglu 呂公實政錄. Lü Kun 呂坤 (1536–1618). Tainan: Zhuangyan, 1995.

Lü Lizheng 呂理政. (1992) *Chuantong xinyang yu xiandai shehui* 傳統信仰與現代社會. Panchiao: Tao-hsiang chubanshe.

Lü Xiaobo 閭小波 and Xu Min 許敏. (2003) "Sun Zhongshan yu Minguo xuanshi zhidu zhi jianli" 孫中山與民國宣誓制度之建立, *Jiangsu shehui kexue* 江蘇社會科學, 3: 160–164.

Lü Yangzheng 呂養正. (2002) "Qingdai Miaoguan zhidu dui Miaozu shenpan quanwexing hecheng zhi yingxiang" 清代苗官制度對苗族神判權威性合成之影響. *Jishou daxue xuebao (Shehui kexueban)* 吉首大學學報 (社會科學版), 2: 85–88.

Lüyuan conghua 履園叢話. Qian Yong 錢泳 (1759–1844). Beijing: Zhonghua shuju, 1983.

Ma Shutian 馬書田. (1998) *Zhongguo mingjie zhushen* 中國冥界諸神. Beijing: Tuanjie chubanshe.

Ma Yau-woon. (1975) "The Textual Tradition of Ming *kung-an* 公案Fiction: A Study of the *Lung-t'u kung-an* 龍圖公案." *Harvard Journal of Asiatic Studies*, 35: 190–220.

Macaskie, C. F. C. (1921) "The Law and Legislation of the State of North Borneo." *Journal of Comparative Legislation and International Law*, 3rd Series, Volume 3, No. 3: 200–222.

Macauley, Melissa. (1994) "Civil and Uncivil Disputes in Southeast Coastal China." In Kathryn Bernhardt and Philip C.C. Huang, eds., *Civil Law in Qing and Republican China*. Stanford: Stanford University Press, pp. 85–121.

——. (1998) *Social Power and Legal Culture: Litigation Masters in Late Imperial China*. Stanford: Stanford University Press.

MacCormack, Geoffrey. (1991) "Suicide in Traditional Chinese Law." *Chinese Culture: A Quarterly Review*, 32.2: 33–47.

——. (1995) "Was the Ordeal Known in Ancient China?" *Revue Internationale des Droits de l'Antiquité*. Third Series, Volume 42, pp. 71–93.

——. (1996) *The Spirit of Traditional Chinese Law*. Athens, GA: University of Georgia Press.

Macgowan, D.J. (1886–1887) "Chinese Guilds or Chambers of Commerce and Trades Unions." *Journal of the North China Branch of the Royal Asiatic Society*, 21: 133–192.

Macgowan, Rev. J. (1910) *Chinese Folklore Tales*. London: Macmillan and Company.

——. (1912) *Men and Manners of Modern China*. London: T. Fisher Unwin.

Madsen, Richard. (2007) *Democracy's Dharma. Religious Renaissance and Political Development in Taiwan*. Berkeley: University of California Press.

Maine, Sir Henry Sumner. (1917) *Ancient Law*. London and Toronto: J.M. Dent & Sons.

Malinowski, Bronislaw. (1926) *Crime and Custom in Savage Society*. London: Kegan Paul, Trench, Trubner & Co.

Mann, Susan. (1997) *Precious Records: Women in China's Long Eighteenth Century*. Stanford: Stanford University Press.

Mao Dun 茅盾. (2001) "Fuqin de sannian zhi bing" 父親的三年之病, *Wangshi zixü* 往事自敘. In *Maodun sanwenji* 茅盾散文集, *juan* 3. *Maodun quanji* 茅盾全集, *juan* 18. Beijing: Renmin wenxue chubanshe, 1984–2001.

Martin, Virginia. (2004) "Kazakh Oath-Taking in Colonial Courtrooms: Legal Culture and Russian Empire-Building." *Kritika: Explorations in Russian and Eurasian History*, 5.3: 483–514.

Masaaki, Tsuchiya. (2002) "Confession of Sins and Awareness of Self in the *Taiping jing*." In Livia Kohn and Harold D. Roth, eds., *Daoist Identity, History, Lineage, and Ritual*. Honolulu: University of Hawai'i Press, pp. 39–57.

Maspero, Henri. 1981 *Taoism and Chinese Religion*. Trans. by Frank Kierman. Amherst: The University of Massachusetts Press.

Masuda Fukutaro 増田福太郎. 1996 *Minzoku shinkyō o chūshin toshite – Tōa hōchitsujo josetsu* 民族信仰を中心として–東亞法制序說. Taipei: Southern Materials Center reprint.

Matsumoto Koichi 松本浩一. (2006) *Sōdai no Dōkyō to minkan shūkyō* 宋代の道教と民間信仰. Tokyo: Kyūko sho'in.

Maurer, Bill. (2004) "The Cultural Power of Law? Conjunctive Readings." *Law & Society Review*, 38.4: 843–850.

McLeod, A. (1947) *Pigtails and Gold Dust*. Caxton, ID: Caldwell.

Mengliang lu 夢梁錄. Wu Zimu 吳自牧 (Southern Song). In *Dongjing menghualu wai sizhong* 東京夢華錄外四種. Shanghai: Shanghai gudian wenxue chubanshe, 1956.

Merry, Sally Engle. (1992) "Anthropology, Law, and Transnational Processes." *Annual Review of Anthropology*, 21: 357–379.

Mertz, Elizabeth. (1994) "Legal Language: Pragmatics, Poetics, and Social Power." *Annual Review of Anthropology*, 23: 435–455.

Meulenbeld, Mark. (2008) "Images of Deified Demons in Vernacular Fiction and Daoist Ritual." Paper presented at the Association of Asian Studies Annual Meeting, Atlanta, April 3–6.

Ming shilu 明實錄. Taipei: Institute of History & Philology. Academia Sinica, 1966.

Mollier, Christine. (1997) "La méthode de l'Empereur du Nord du Mont Fengdu: Une tradition exorciste du taoisme médiéval." *T'oung Pao*, 83: 329–385.

——. (2008) *Buddhism and Taoism Face to Face: Scripture, Ritual, and Iconographic Exchange in Medieval China*. Honolulu: University of Hawai'i Press.

Mommsen, W.J. (1992) "Introduction." In W.J. Mommsen and J.A. de Moor, eds., *European Expansion and Law: The Encounter of European and Indigenous Law in 19th- and 20th-Century Africa and Asia*. Oxford and New York: Berg, pp. 1–14.

Moore, Sally Falk, ed. (2005) *Law and Anthropology: A Reader*. Oxford: Blackwell Publishing.

Moskowitz, Marc L. (2001) *The Haunting Fetus: Abortion, Sexuality, and the Spirit World in Taiwan*. Honolulu: University of Hawai'i Press.

Mo Tzu: Basic Writings. (1963) Trans. by Burton Watson. New York: Columbia University Press.

Mozina, David. (2008) "Images of Identity: Martial Deities and Lineage Identity in Contemporary Hunan." Paper presented at the Association of Asian Studies Annual Meeting, Atlanta, April 3–6.

Mukōyama Hirō 向山寛夫. 1999 (1987) *Riben tongzhi xia de Taiwan minzu yundong* 日本統治下的台灣民族運動. Yang Hung-ju 楊鴻儒, ed. and trans. Taipei: Fulushou xingye gufen youxian gongsi.

Munn, Christopher. (2001) *Anglo-China. Chinese People and British Rule in Hong Kong 1841–1880*. Richmond: Curzon.

Nader, Laura, ed. (1969) *Law in Culture and Society*. Chicago: Aldine.

——. (1990) *Harmony Ideology: Justice and Control in a Zapotec Mountain Village*. Stanford: Stanford University Press.

Nanying zazu 南瀛雜俎. Tainan County Government, ed. and comp. Tainan: Lunghung Yin-shua-ch'ang, 1982.

Nedostup, Rebecca. (2007) "Civic Faith and Hybrid Rituals in Nationalist China." In Denis Washburn and A. Kevin Reinhart, eds., *Converting Cultures: Religion, Ideology, and Transformations of Modernity*. Leiden & Boston: E.J. Brill, pp. 27–56.

——. (forthcoming) *Superstitious Regimes: Religion and the Politics of Chinese Modernity*. Cambridge, MA: Harvard Univerity Press.

Ng, Vivian W. (1990) *Madness in Late Imperial China. From Illness to Deviance*. London and Norman: University of Oklahoma Press.

Nickerson, Peter. (1996a) "Taoism, Death, and Bureaucracy in Early Medieval China." Ph.D. thesis, University of California, Berkeley.

——. (1996b) "Abridged Codes of Master Lu for the Taoist Community." In Donald S. Lopez, ed., *Religions of China in Practice*. Princeton: Princeton, NJ University Press, pp. 347–359.

——. (1997) "The Great Petition for Sepulchral Plaints." In Stephen R. Bokenkamp, ed., *Early Daoist Scriptures*. Berkeley: University of California Press, pp. 230–274.

——. (2002) "'Opening the Way': Exorcism, Travel, and Soteriology in Early Daoist Mortuary Practice and its Antecedents." In Livia Kohn and Harold D. Roth, eds., *Daoist Identity. History, Lineage, and Ritual*. Honolulu: University of Hawai'i Press, pp. 58–77.

——. (2007) *Taoism, Bureaucracy and Popular Religion in Early Medieval China*. Cambridge, MA: Harvard University Press (revised version of 1996 Ph.D. thesis).

——. (2008) "Demons and Spirits." In Fabrizio Pregadio, ed., *The Encyclopedia of Taoism*. 2 volumes. London and New York: Routledge, Volume 1, pp. 63–67.

Niida Noboru 仁井田陞. (1950) "The International and Commercial Guilds of Peking and Religion and Fellowcountrymanship as Elements of their Coherence." *Folklore Studies*, 9: 179–206.

——. (1964) *Chūgoku hōseishi kenkyū: hō to kanshū, hō to dōtoku* 中國法制史研究, 法と慣習,法と道德. Tokyo: Tokyo daigaku.

Nilsson, Martin P. (1925) *A History of Greek Religion*. Trans. by F. J. Fielden. Oxford: The Clarendon Press.

Norton-Kyshe, James William. (1898) *The History of the Laws and Courts of Hong Kong*. 2 volumes. London: T. Fisher Unwin; Hong Kong: Noronha and Company.

O'Brien, H.A. (1891) "An Old Minute by Sir Stamford Raffles." *Journal of the Straits Branch of the Royal Asiatic Society*, 24: 1–12.

O'Brien, Kevin and Lianjiang Li. (2006) *Rightful Resistance in Rural China*. New York: Cambridge University Press.

Ocko, Jonathan. (2007) "Interpretive Communities: Legal Meaning in Qing Law." In Robert E. Hegel and Katherine Carlitz, eds., *Writing and Law in Late Imperial China. Crime, Conflict, and Judgment*. Seattle: University of Washington Press, pp. 261–283.

Ong, Walter. (1982) *Orality and Literacy: The Technologizing of the Word*. London and New York: Methuen.

Overmyer, Daniel L. (1989–1990) "Attitudes Toward Popular Religion in the Ritual Texts of the Chinese State: *The Collected Statutes of the Great Ming*." *Cahiers d'Extrême Asie*, 5:191–221.

——. ed. (2003a) *Religion in China Today*. The China Quarterly Special Issues, New Series, No. 3. Cambridge: Cambridge University Press.

——. (2003b) "Introduction." In *idem*, ed., *Religion in China Today*. The China Quarterly Special Issues, New Series, No. 3. Cambridge: Cambridge University Press, pp. 1–10.

Ownby, David. (1996) *Brotherhoods and Secret Societies in Early and Mid-Qing China*. Stanford: Stanford University Press.

——. (2001) "Imperial Fantasies: The Chinese Communists and Peasant Rebellions." *Comparative Studies in Society and History*, 43.1: 65–91.

——. (2003) "A History for Falun Gong: Popular Religion and the Chinese State Since the End of the Ming Dynasty." *Nova Religio*, 6.2: 223–243.

Palmer, David A. (2007) *Qigong Fever. Body, Science, and Utopia in China*. New York: Columbia University Press.

Peerenboom, Randall. (2002) "Law and Religion in Early China." In Andrew Huxley, ed., *Religion, Law, and Tradition: Comparative Studies in Religious Law*. London: RoutledgeCurzon, pp. 84–107.

Peng Zeyi 澎澤益. (1984) *Zhongguo jindai shougongyeshi ziliao* 中國近代手工業史資料. Beijing: Zhonghua shuju.

Perry, Elizabeth J. (2008) "Chinese Conceptions of 'Rights': From Mencius to Mao – and Now." *Perspectives on Politics*, 6.1: 37–50.

Perry, Elizabeth J. and Merle Goldman, eds. (2007) *Grassroots Politics in China*. Cambridge, MA: Harvard University Press.

Peterson, Derek R. (2006) "Morality Plays: Marriage, Church Courts, and Colonial Agency in Central Tanganyika, ca. 1876–1928." *The American Historical Review*, 111.4: 983–1010.

Pomerantz-Zhang, Linda. (1992) *Wu Tingfang (1842–1922): Reform and Modernization in Modern Chinese History*. Hong Kong: Hong Kong University Press.

Pomeranz, Kenneth. (1997) "Power, Gender, and Pluralism in the Cult of the Goddess of Taishan." In Theodore Huters, R. Bin Wong, and Pauline Yu, eds., *Culture and State in Chinese History. Conventions, Accommodations, and Critiques*. Stanford: Stanford University Press, pp. 182–204.

Poo Mu-chou 蒲慕洲. (1998) *In Search of Personal Welfare: A View of Ancient Chinese Religion*. Albany, NY: SUNY Press.

Poon Shuk-wah 潘淑華. (2008) "Modernity, and Urban Space: The City God Temple in Republican Guangzhou." *Modern China*, 34.2: 247–275.

Porter, Roy. (1987) *A Social History of Madness: Stories of the Insane*. London: Weidenfeld & Nicolson.

——. (2002) *Madness: A Brief History*. Oxford: Oxford University Press.

Potter, Pitman B. (2001) *The Chinese Legal System: Globalization and Local Legal Culture*. London: Routledge.

Poulter, Sebastian M. (1986) *English Law and Ethnic Minority Customs*. London: Butterworths.

Purcell, Victor W.W.S. (1967) *The Chinese in Malaya*. London and New York: Oxford University Press.

Putian xianzhi 莆田縣志. (2000) Zhang Qin 張琴 and Shi Youji 石有紀, ed. and comp. Shanghai: Shanghai shudian chubanshe.

Qian Mu 錢穆. (1998) "Zhongguoren zhi falü guannian" 中國人之法律觀念. In *idem*, *Zhengxue ziyan* 政學私言, *Qian Binsi xiansheng quanji* 錢賓四先生全集. Taipei: Lien-ching, Volume 40, pp. 225–249.

Qiang Shigong 強世功, ed. (2001) *Tiaojie, fazhi yu xiandaixing: Zhongguo tiaojie zhidu yanjiu* 調解 法制與現代性: 中國調解制度研究. Beijing: Zhongguo fazhi chubanshe.

Qinding Gujin tushu jicheng 欽定古今圖書集成. (1725) Chen Menglei 陳夢雷 (d. 1741), et. al., ed. and comp. 100 volumes. Taipei: Wenxing chubanshe, 1964.

Qinding pingding Taiwan jilue 欽定平定臺灣紀略. In *Taiwan wenxian congkan* 臺灣文獻叢刊. Number 102. Taipei: Bank of Taiwan, 1961.

Qingchao wenxian tongkao 清朝文獻通考. (1644–1785). 2 volumes. Shanghai: Shangwu yinshuguan, 1936.

Qingdai biji xiaoshuo leibian 清代筆記小說類編. Hefei: Huangshan shushe, 1994.

Qingjia lu 清嘉錄. Gu Lu 顧祿 (Qing). Wang Mai 王邁, ed. Nanjing: Jiangsu guji chubanshe, 1999.

Qiu Jie 邱捷. (2003) "Qingmo Guangzhou jumin de jimiao yishi 清末廣州居民的集廟議事." *Jinda shi yanjiu* 近代史研究, 2: 187–203.

——. (2005) "WanQing Guangdong de "gongju" – Shishen kongzhi xiangcun shehui de quanli jigou" 晚清廣東的"公局" – 士紳控制鄉村基層社會的權力機構. *Zhongshan daxue xuebao (Shexue kexueban)* 中山大學學報(社會科學版), 4: 45–51.

Quan Tangwen 全唐文. Dong Gao 董誥 (1740–1818), ed. and comp. Beijing: Zhonghua shuju, 1983.

Redding, S. Gordon. (1990) *The Spirit of Chinese Capitalism*. Berlin and New York: W. de Gruyter.

Reed, Bradly W. (2000) *Talons and Teeth: County Clerks and Runners in the Qing Dynasty*. Stanford: Stanford University Press.

Renteln, Alison Dundes. (1994) "Culture and Culpability: A Study of Contrasts." In Alison Dundes Renteln and Alan Dundes, eds., *Folk Law: Essays in the Theory and Practice of* Lex Non Scripta. 2 volumes. Madison: The University of Wisconsin Press, pp. 863–879.

Renteln, Alison Dundes and Alan Dundes. (1994) "Introduction." In *idem*, eds., *Folk Law: Essays in the Theory and Practice of* Lex Non Scripta. 2 volumes. Madison: The University of Wisconsin Press, pp. xiii-xvi.

Report of the Joint Special Committee to Investigate Chinese Immigration. Washington, DC: Government Printing Office, 1877.

Roberts, John M. (1965) "Oaths, Autonomic Ordeals, and Power." *American Anthropologist*, New Series, 67.66: 186–212.

Robinson, Olivia F. (2007) *Penal Practice and Penal Policy in Ancient Rome*. New York and London: Routledge.

Robbins, Joel. (2004) *Becoming Sinners: Christianity and Moral Torment in a Papua New Guinea Society*. Berkeley: University of California Press.

Ronquillo, Remigio B. (1934) "The Administration of Law among the Chinese in Chicago." *Journal of Criminal Law and Criminology (1931–1951)*, 25.2: 205–224.

Ropp, Paul R. (2001) "Passionate Women: Female Suicide in Late Imperial China." *Nan Nü*, 3.1: 3–21.

Rosen, George. (1968) *Madness in Society. Chapters in the Historical Sociology of Mental Illness*. Chicago: The University of Chicago Press.

Rosen, Lawrence. (1989) *The Anthropology of Justice: Law as Culture in Islamic Society*. Cambridge and New York: Cambridge University Press.

Rowe, William T. (1989) *Hankow: Conflict and Community in a Chinese City, 1796–1895*. Stanford: Stanford University Press.

——. (1990) "The Public Sphere in Modern China." *Modern China*, 16.3: 309–329.

——. (1993) "The Problem of 'Civil Society' in Late Imperial China." *Modern China*, 19.2: 139–157.

——. (2007) *Crimson Rain: Seven Centuries of Violence in a Chinese County*. Stanford: Stanford University Press.

Rüpke, Jörg. (1992) "You Shall Not Kill. Hierarchies of Norms in Ancient Rome." *Numen* 39.1: 58–79.

Sabbatucci, Dario. (1987) "Ordeal." In *The Encyclopedia of Religion*. New York: Macmillan Publishing Company. Volume 11, pp. 92–97.

Sawada Mizuho 澤田瑞穗. (1968) *Jigoku hen: Chūgoku no meikai setsu* 地獄變: 中國の冥界說. Kyoto: Hozokan.

Sayer, Geoffrey Robley. (1980) *Hong Kong, 1841–1862: Birth, Adolescence, and Coming of Age*. Hong Kong: Hong Kong University Press.

Schafer, Sarah. (2007) "China: Rich and Lawless." *Newsweek*, February 19, pp. 22–24.

Schipper, Kristofer M. (1985) "Vernacular and Classical Ritual in Taoism." *The Journal of Asian Studies*, 45.1: 21–57.

Scogin, Hugh. (1990) "Between Heaven and Man: Contract and the State in Han Dynasty China." *Southern California Law Review*, 63: 1326–1440.

Scott, James C. (1985) *Weapons of the Weak: Everyday Forms of Peasant Resistance*. New Haven: Yale University Press.

——. (1990) *Domination and the Arts of Resistance: Hidden Transcripts*. New Haven and London: Yale University Press.

Seaman, Gary. (1978) *Temple Organization in a Chinese Village*. Taipei: Chinese Association for Folklore, Orient Cultural Service.

Segal, Alan F. (2004) *Life after Death: A History of the Afterlife in Western Religion*. New York, Doubleday.

Seidel, Anna. (1987) "Traces of Han Religion in Funerary Texts Found in Tombs." In Akizuki Kanei 秋月觀暎, ed., *Dōkyō to shūkyō bunka* 道教と宗教文化. Tokyo: Hirakawa, pp. 21–57.

Serruys, Henry. (1958) "A Note on Arrows and Oaths among the Mongols." *Journal of the American Oriental Society*, 78.4: 279–294.

Seward, George F. (1881) *Chinese Immigration in its Social and Economical Aspects*. New York: Charles Scribner's Sons.

Shahar, Meir. (1998) *Crazy Ji. Chinese Religion and Popular Literature*. Cambridge, MA: Harvard University Press.

Shahar, Meir and Robert P. Weller, eds. (1996) *Unruly Gods: Divinity and Society in China*. Honolulu: University of Hawai'i Press.

Shan E Tu 善惡圖. *Guben xiaoshuo jicheng* 古本小說集成. Series II, volumes 140–141. Beijing: Zhonghua shuju, 1990.

Shanghai xianzhi 上海縣志. (1871) Ed. and comp. by Yu Yue 俞樾 (1821–1906). In *Zhongguo fangzhi congshu, Huazhong difang, Jiangsu sheng* 中國方志叢書, 華中地方, 江蘇省. Number 169. Taipei: Chengwen chubanshe, 1975.

Shenbao 申報. (1872–1949) Shanghai: Shenbaoguan.

Shen Mei-jen 沈美真. (1990) *Taiwan beihai changji yu changji zhengce* 臺灣被害娼妓與娼妓政策. Taipei: Avanguard Publishing Company.

Shepherd, John R. (1993) *Statecraft and Political Economy on the Taiwan Frontier, 1600–1800*. Stanford: Stanford University Press.

Shiga Shūzō 滋賀秀三. (1984) *Shindai Chūgoku no hō to saiban* 清代中國の法と裁判. Tokyo: Sōbunsha.

Shirakawa Shizuka 白川靜. (1983) *Zhongguo gudai wenhua* 中國古代文化. Trans. by Kaji Nobumeki 加地伸行 and Fan Yuejiao 范月嬌. Taipei: Wenjin chubanshe.

Shishi baoguan Wushen quannian huabao 時事報館戊申全年畫報. (1909) 8 Volumes. In *Qingmo Minchu baokan tuhua jicheng* 清末民初報刊圖畫集成, Volumes 10–17. Beijing: Quanguo tushuguan wencian suowei fuzhi zhongxin, 2003.

Shoemaker, Karl Blaine. (2001) "The Problem of Pain in Punishment: A Historical Perspective." In Austin Sarat, ed., *Pain, Death, and the Law*. Ann Arbor: University of Michigan Press, pp. 15–42.

Shuichuang chunyi 水窗春囈. Ouyang Zhaoxiong 歐陽兆熊 (ca. 1840s-1850s). Beijing: Zhonghua shuju, 1984.

Skar, Lowell. (1996–1997) "Administering Thunder: A Thirteenth-Century Memorial Deliberating the Thunder Rites." *Cahiers d'Extrême Asie*, 9: 159–202.

——. (2000) "Ritual Movements, Deity Cults, and the Transformation of Daoism in Song and Yuan Times." In Livia Kohn, ed. *Daoism Handbook*. Leiden: E.J. Brill, pp. 413–463.

Skrynnikova, T.D. (1992/1993) "Sülde – The Basic Idea of the Chinggis-Khan Cult." *Acta Orientalia Academiae Scientiarum Hungaricae*, 46.1: 51–59.

Smith, Jane Idleman and Yvonne Yazbeck Haddad. (1981) *The Islamic Understanding of Death and Resurrection*. Albany: SUNY Press.

Smith, Richard J. (1998) "The Teachings of Ritual and the Rectification of Customs: Echoes of Tradition in the Political Culture of Modern China." In Hao Yen-ping 郝延平 and Wei Hsiu-mei 魏秀梅, eds., *Jindai Zhongguo zhi chuantong yu tuibian: Liu Kwang-ching yuanshi qishiwu sui zhushou lunwenji* 近世中國之傳統與蛻變: 劉廣京院士七十五歲祝壽論文集. Nankang. Institute of Modern History, Academia Sinica. Volume 2, pp. 1173–1216.

Sommer, Matthew H. (1996) "The Uses of Chastity: Sex, Law, and the Property of Widows in Qing China." *Late Imperial China*, 17.2: 77–130.

——. (2000) *Sex, Law, and Society in Late Imperial China*. Stanford: Stanford University Press.

The Songs of the South: An Ancient Chinese Anthology of Poems by Qu Yuan and Other Poets. Translated, annotated and introduced by David Hawkes. Harmondsworth and New York: Penguin, 1985.

Spence, Jonathan. (1978) *The Death of Woman Wang*. New York: The Viking Press.

St. André, James. (2007). "Reading Court Cases from the Song and the Ming: Fact and Fiction, Law and Literature." In Robert E. Hegel and Katherine Carlitz, eds., *Writing and Law in Late Imperial China. Crime, Conflict, and Judgment*. Seattle: University of Washington Press, pp. 189–214.

Stark, Rodney. (1999) "Secularization, R.I.P. (Rest in peace)." *Sociology of Religion*, 60.3: 249–273.

Starr, June and Jane F. Collier, eds. (1989) *History and Power in the Study of Law: New Directions in Legal Anthropology*. Ithaca: Cornell University Press.

Stein, Rolf A. 1990 *The World in Miniature. Container Gardens and Dwellings in Far Eastern Religious Thought*. Trans. by Phyllis Brooks. Stanford: Stanford University Press.

Stewart, Pamela J. and Andrew Strathern, eds. (2006) *Asian Ritual Systems: Syncretisms and Ruptures*. Durham, NC: Carolina Academic Press.

Stilwell, Gary A. (2005) *Afterlife: Post-Mortem Judgments in Ancient Egypt and Ancient Greece*. Lincoln, NE. iUniverse, Inc.

The Story of the Stone (*Honglou meng* 紅樓夢 = *The Dream of the Red Chamber*). Cao

Xueqin 曹雪芹 (ca. 1717–1763). Translated by David Hawkes. 5 volumes. Harmondsworth: Penguin, 1973–1986.

Strickmann, Michel. (2002) *Chinese Magical Medicine*. Edited by Bernard Faure. Stanford: Stanford University Press.

Su Li 蘇力. (2000) *Songfa xia xiang: Zhongguo jiceng sifa zhidu yanjiu* 送法下鄉, 中國基層司法制度研究. Beijing: Zhongguo zhengfa daxue chubanshe.

Sun Huei-min 孫慧敏. (2006) "Qingmo Zhongguo dui lüshi zhidu de renshi yu yinjie" 清末中國對律師制度的認識與引介. *Bulletin of the Institute of Modern History*, Academia Sinica, 52: 165–210.

Sung Kuang-yu 宋光宇. (1982) "*Diyu youji* suo xianshi de dangqian shehui wenti" 地獄游記所顯示的當前社會問題. In *Minjian xinyang yu shehui yantaohui lunwenji* 民間信仰與社會研討會論文集. Taichung: Taiwan shengzhengfu.

——. (1995) "Xiahai Chenghuang jidian yu Taibei Dadaocheng shangye fazhan de guanxi" 霞海城隍祭典與台北大稻埕商業發展的關係. In *idem.*, *Zongjiao yu shehui* 宗教與社會. Taipei: Tung-ta Publishing Company, pp. 103–163.

Sutton, Donald S. (2003a) "Violence and Ethnicity on a Qing Colonial Frontier: Customary Statuary Law in the Eighteenth-Century Miao Pale." *Modern Asian Studies*, 37.1: 41–80.

——. (2003b) "Ethnic Revolt in the Qing Empire: The Miao Uprising of 1795–1796 Reexamined." *Asia Major*, 3rd series, Vol. 17.1 (2003; published 2005): 105–151.

——. (2004) "Prefect Feng and the Yangzhou Drought of 1490: A Ming Social Crisis and the Rewards of Sincerity." *Minsu quyi* 民俗曲藝, 143: 13–48.

Szonyi, Michael. (1997) "The Illusion of Standardizing the Gods: The Cult of the Five Emperors in Late Imperial China." *The Journal of Asian Studies*, 56.1: 113–135.

——. (2000) "Local Cult, *Lijia*, and Lineage: Religious and Social Organization in the Fuzhou Region in the Ming and Qing." *Journal of Chinese Religions*, 28: 93–125.

——. (2002) *Practicing Kinship: Lineage and Descent in Late Imperial China*. Stanford: Stanford University Press.

Tai Hsüan-chih. (1985) *The Red Spears, 1916–1949*. Trans. by Ronald Suleski. Ann Arbor: Center for Chinese Studies.

Taiquan xiangli 泰泉鄉禮. Huang Zuo 黃佐 (1490–1566). In *Wenyuange Siku quanshu* 文淵閣四庫全書. Taipei: Shangwu yinshuguan, 1983. Volume 142.

Taiwan geming shi 台灣革命史. Hanren 漢人 (Huang Yuzhai 黃玉齋). Shanghai: Qindong shuju, 1925.

Taiwan Sōtokufu keisatsu enkakushi 臺灣總督府警察沿革誌. Taipei: Taiwan sōtokufu keimuku, 1938.

Taiwan tongzhi 臺灣通志. Late Qing. 2 volumes. In *Taiwan wenxian congkan* 臺灣文獻叢刊. Number 64. Taipei: Bank of Taiwan, 1961.

Tai Wen-feng 戴文鋒. (1997) "Taiwan minjian xinyang Youying Gong kaoshi" 台灣民間信仰有應公考實. *Taiwan fengwu* 台灣風物, 46.4:53–109.

Takahashi Bunji 高橋文治. (1991) "Sai Fukun o megutte – Gendai no byō To densetsu to bungaku" 崔府君をぐって – 元代の廟と傳說と文化. In *Tanaka Kenji hakase shōju kinen Chūgoku koten gikyoku ronshū* 田中嫌二博士頌壽紀念中國古典戲曲論集. Tokyo: Kyūko shōyin, pp. 35–81.

Tan Poh-Ling. (1997a) "Introduction." In *idem*, ed., *Asian Legal Systems: Law, Society and Pluralism in East Asia*. Sydney: Butterworths, pp. 1–13.

——. (1997b) "Malaysia." In *idem*, ed., *Asian Legal Systems: Law, Society and Pluralism in East Asia*, pp. 263–313.

Tanaka Issei 田仲一成. (1968) *Shindai chihogeki shiryō shū: Kachū, Kanan hen* 清代地方劇資料集 華中、華南篇. Tokyo: Tōyō bunka kenkyūjō.

Tatsuo Obata 小畑龍雄. (1952) "Meidai gōson no kyōka to saiban" 明代郷村の教化と裁判 *Tōyōshi kenkyū* 東洋史研究, XI.5–6: 23–43.

Tay, Alice Erh-Soon. (1997) "People's Republic of China." In Tan Poh-Ling, ed., *Asian Legal Systems: Law, Society and Pluralism in East Asia*. Sydney: Butterworths, pp. 14–67.

Taylor, Romeyn. (1990) "Official and Popular Religion and the Political Organization of Chinese Society in the Ming." In Liu Kwang-ching, ed., *Orthodoxy in Late Imperial China*. Berkeley: University of California Press, pp. 126–157.

Teiser, Stephen F. (1988) "'Having Once Died and Come Back to Life': Representations of Hell in Medieval China." *Harvard Journal of Asiatic Studies*, 48.1:433–464.

——. (1993) "The Growth of Purgatory." In Patricia B. Ebrey and Peter N. Gregory, eds., *Religion and Society in T'ang and Sung China*. Honolulu: University of Hawai'i Press, pp. 115–145.

——. (1994) *The Scripture on the Ten Kings and the Making of Purgatory in Medieval Chinese Buddhism*. Honolulu: Kuroda Institute.

Tentler, Thomas N. (1977) *Sin and Confession on the Eve of the Reformation*. Princeton, NJ: Princeton University Press.

Ter Haar, Barend. (1990) "The Genesis and Spread of Temple Cults in Fukien." In E.B. Vermeer, ed., *Development and Decline of Fukien Province in the 17th and 18th Centuries*. Leiden: E.J. Brill, pp. 349–396.

——. (1992) *The White Lotus Teachings in Chinese Religious History*. Leiden: E.J. Brill.

——. (1995) "Local Society and the Organization of Cults in Early Modern China: A Preliminary Study." *Studies in Central and East Asian Religions*, 8: 1–43.

——. (1998) *Ritual and Mythology of the Chinese Triads: Creating an Identity*. Leiden: E.J. Brill.

——. (2000) "Rethinking 'Violence' in Chinese Culture." In Göran Aijmer and Jos Abbink, eds., *Meanings of Violence: a Cross Cultural Perspective.* Oxford: Berg, pp. 123–140.

——. (2006a) *Telling Stories: Witchcraft and Scapegoating in Chinese History*. Leiden: E.J. Brill.

——. (2006b) "The Teachings of the Dragon Flower as a Continuation of Song-Yuan Activist Lay-Buddhism." Paper presented at The Fourth Fu Jen University International Sinological Symposium, "Research on Religions in China: *Status quo* and Perspectives." Fu Jen University, Taiwan. November 24–25.

Theiss, Janet M. (2004) *Disgraceful Matters: The Politics of Chastity in Eighteenth-Century China*. Berkeley and Los Angeles: University of California Press.

——. (2007) "Explaining the Shrew: Narratives of Spousal Violence and the Critique of Masculinity in Eighteenth-Century Criminal Cases." In Robert E. Hegel and Katherine Carlitz, eds., *Writing and Law in Late Imperial China. Crime, Conflict, and Judgment*. Seattle: University of Washington Press, pp. 44–63.

Thompson, Laurence G. (1975) "Yu Ying Kung: The Cult of Bereaved Spirits in Taiwan." In *idem*, ed., *Studia Asiatica. Essays in Felicitation of the Seventy-Fifth Anniversary of Professor Ch'en Shou-yi*. San Francisco

Tian Zhaoyuan 田兆元. (2000) *Mengshi shi* 盟誓史. Nanning: Guangxi minzu chubanshe.

Tie, Warwick. (1999) *Legal Pluralism: Toward a Multicultural Conception of Law*. Aldershot: Ashgate/Dartmouth.

Trumbower, Jeffrey A. (2001) *Rescue for the Dead: The Posthumous Salvaton of Non-Christians in Early Christianity*. Oxford: Oxford University Press.

Ts'ai Chin-t'ang 蔡錦堂. (2004) "Masuda Fukutaro de simiao yu shensheguan" 增田福太郎的寺廟與神社觀. *Guangwu tongshi xuebao* 光武通識學報, 1: 191–209.

Tsai Jung-fang. (1993) *Hong Kong in Chinese History: Community and Social Unrest in the British Colony, 1842–1913*. New York: Columbia University Press.

Tsai, Kathryn Ann, trans. (1994) *Lives of the Nuns: Biographies of Chinese Buddhist Nuns from the Fourth to Sixth Centuries: A Translation of the* Pi-chiu-ni chuan *compiled by Shih Pao-chang*. Honolulu: University of Hawai'i Press.

Tschannen, O. (1992) *Les théories de la secularisation*. Geneva: Librairie Droz.

Tsu, Timothy. (1998) "Between Superstition and Morality – Japanese Views of Taiwanese Religion in the Colonial Period, 1895–1945." *ZINBUN*, 33:31–56.

Turner, Alice K. (1993) *The History of Hell*. New York: Harcourt Brace.

Turner, Victor. (1968) *The Drums of Affliction*. Oxford: Clarendon Press.

——. (1985) *On the Edge of the Bush*. Tucson: University of Arizona Press.

United States Senate Report of the Special Joint Committee to Investigate Chinese Immigration, Report 869. Washington, Government Printing Office, 1877.

Unschuld, Paul. (1985) *Medicine in China: A History of Ideas*. Berkeley: University of California Press.

Vanderlinden, Jacques. (2002) "Religious Laws as Systems of Law – A Comparatist's View." In Andrew Huxley, ed., *Religion, Law, and Tradition: Comparative Studies in Religious Law*. London: RoutledgeCurzon, pp. 165–182.

Van den Bergh, G.C.J.J. (1994) "The Concept of Folk Law in Historical Context: A Brief Outline." In Alison Dundes Renteln and Alan Dundes, eds., *Folk Law: Essays in the Theory and Practice of* Lex Non Scripta. 2 volumes. Madison: The University of Wisconsin Press, pp. 5–31.

Van der Loon, Piet. (1977) "Les Origines rituelles du Théâtre chinois." *Journal Asiatique*, 165: 141–168.

——. (1979) "A Taoist Collection of the Fourteenth Century." In *Studia Sina-Mongolica: Festschrift fur Herbert Franke*. Wiesbaden: Franz Steiner Verlag, pp. 401–405.

Van Hoecke, Mark and Mark Warrington. (1998) "Legal Cultures and Legal Paradigms: Towards a New Model for Comparative Law." *International and Comparative Law Quarterly*, 47: 495–536.

Van Vollenhoven, C. (1994) "Aspects of the Controversy on Customary Law in India." In Alison Dundes Renteln and Alan Dundes, eds., *Folk Law: Essays in the Theory and Practice of* Lex Non Scripta. 2 volumes. Madison: The University of Wisconsin Press, pp. 251–262.

Vaughan, Jonas Daniel. (1971) *The Manners and Customs of the Chinese of the Straits Settlements*. Kuala Lumpur: Oxford University Press.

Veith, Ilza. (1963) "The Supernatural in Far Eastern Concepts of Mental Disease." *Bulletin of the History of Medicine*, 37:139–155.

Vergil. *The Aeneid*. Trans. by Robert Fagles. New York: Penguin Books, 2006.

Von Falkenhausen, Lothar. (1994) "Sources of Taoism: Reflections on Archaeological Indicators of Religious Change in Eastern Zhou China." *Taoist Resources*, 5.2: 1–12.

Von Glahn, Richard. (2004) *The Sinister Way. The Divine and the Demonic in Chinese Religious Culture*. Berkeley: University of California Press.

Waley, Arthur. (1960) *Ballads and Stories from Tun-huang. An Anthology*. New York: The Macmillan Company.

Waley-Cohen, Joanna. (1993) "Politics and the Supernatural in Mid-Qing Legal Culture." *Modern China*, 19.3: 330–353.

Wallis, Roy and Steve Bruce. (1992) "Secularization: The Orthodox Model." In Steve Bruce, ed., *Religion and Modernization: Sociologists and Historians Debate the Secularization Thesis*. Oxford and New York: Oxford University Press, pp. 8–22.

Waltner, Ann. (1990) "From Casebook to Fiction: *Kung-an* 公案 in Late Imperial China." *Journal of the American Oriental Society*, 110.2:281–289.

Wan, Margaret Baptist. (2000) "'Green Peony' as New Popular Fiction: The Birth of the Martial Romance in Early Nineteenth-Century China." Ph.D. thesis, Harvard University.

Wang Chih-yu 王志宇. (2003) "Taiwan de wusi guhun xinyang xinlun – Yi Zhushan diqu cimiao wei zhongxin de tantao" 台灣的無祀孤魂信仰新論 – 以竹山地區祠廟為中心的探討. *Fengjia renwen shehui xuebao* 逢甲人文社會學報, 6: 183–210.

Wang Di. (2000) "The Idle and the Busy: Teahouses and Public Life in Early Twentieth-Century Chengdu." *Journal of Urban History* 26.4: 411–437.

——. (2006) "Struggling for Livelihood: Social Conflict through the Teahouse in Republican Chengdu." *European Journal of East Asian Studies* 5.2: 247–273.

Wang Gengnian 汪庚年. (1910) *Faxue huibian – Xongshi susongfa* 法學彙編 – 刑事訴訟法. Beijing: Faxue huibianjishe.

Wang Guomo 王國謨. (1996) "Fasheng zai 1927 nian de jijian shi" 發生在1927年的幾件事, *Zhenping wenshi ziliao, di 9 ji* 鎮平文史資料第9輯. Zhenping: Zhenpingxian zhengxie, pp. 93–110.

Wang Mingming. (1995) "Place, Administration, and Territorial Cults in Late Imperial China: A Case Study from South Fujian." *Late Imperial China*, 16.1: 33–78.

Wang Mingming 王銘銘 and Wang Sifu 王斯福 (Stephan Feucthwang), eds. (1997) *Xiangtu shehui de zhixu, gongzheng yu quanwei* 鄉土社會的秩序、公正與權威. Beijing: Zhongguo Zhengfa daxue chubanshe.

Wang Tay-sheng. (2000) *Legal Reform in Taiwan under Japanese Colonial Rule, 1895–1945: The Reception of Western Law*. Seattle and London: University of Washington Press.

Wang-Toutain, Françoise. (1998) *Le Bodhisattva Ksitigarbha en Chine du Ve au XIIIe siècle*. Paris: École Française d'Extrême Orient.

Wang Zheng 王政. (2002) "Liu Zongyuan *Jidao wen, Piya wen* yu gu zhi piji" 柳宗元《祭纛文》、《痞牙文》與古之痞祭. *Huaibei meishiyuan xuebao (Zhexue shehuikexueban)*, 淮北煤師院學報(哲學社會科學版). 23.5: 52–53.

Wang Ziquan 王紫詮. (1969) *Yingruan zazhi* 瀛壖雜志. In *Zhonghua wenshi congshu* 中華文史叢書. Volume 97. Taipei: Huawen shuju.

Ward, J.S.M. and W.G. Stirling. (1925) *The Hung Society or the Society of Heaven and Earth*. London: Baskerville Press.

Watson, James L. (1985) "Standardizing the Gods: The Promotion of T'ien-hou ('Empress of Heaven') along the South China Coast, 960–1960." In David G. Johnson, Andrew J. Nathan, and Evelyn S. Rawski, eds., *Popular Culture in Late Imperial China*. Berkeley: University of California Press, pp. 292–324.

——. (1988) "Introduction: The Structure of Chinese Funerary Rites." In James L. Watson and Evelyn S. Rawski, eds., *Death Ritual in Late Imperial and Modern China*. Berkeley: University of California Press, pp. 3–19.

——. (1993) "Rites or Beliefs? The Construction of a Unified Culture in Late Imperial China." In Lowell Dittmer and Samuel S. Kim, eds., *China's Quest for National Identity*. Ithaca, NY: Cornell University Press, pp. 80–103.

Weber, Max. (1951) *The Religion of China*. New York: The Free Press.

Welch, Ian. (2006) "The Chinese and the Courts in Australia." Unpublished manuscript.

Weller, Robert P. (1994) *Resistance, Chaos and Control in China: Taiping Rebels, Taiwanese Ghosts and Tiananmen*. Seattle: University of Washington Press.

——. (1999) *Alternate Civilities. Democracy and Culture in China and Taiwan*. Boulder, CO: Westview Press.

Wenduanji 文端集. Zhang Ying 張英. In *Wenyuange Siku quanshu* 文淵閣四庫全書. Taipei: Shangwu yinshuguan, 1983. Volume 1319.

Werle, Helga. (1973) "Swatow (Chaozhou) Horizontal Stick Puppets." *Journal of the Hong Kong Branch of the Royal Asiatic Society*, 13: 73–84.

West, Stephen H. (2003) "Text and Ideology: Ming Editors and Northern Drama." In Paul Jakov Smith and Richard von Glahn, eds., *The Song-Yuan-Ming Transition in Chinese History*. Cambridge, MA: Harvard University Press, pp. 329–373.

Westermarck, Edward. (1926) *Ritual and Belief in Morocco*. London: Macmillan.

Wheeler, Kenneth George. (1998) "Shen Jiaben (1840–1913): Toward a Reformation of Chinese Criminal Justice." Ph.D. thesis, Yale University.

Whyte, Martin K. (1988) "Death in the People's Republic of China." In James L. Watson and Evelyn S. Rawski, eds., *Death Ritual in Late Imperial and Modern China*. Berkeley: University of California Press, pp. 289–316.

Will, Pierre-Étienne. (2007) "Developing Forensic Knowledge through Cases in the Qing Dynasty." In Charlotte Furth, Judith T. Zeitlin, and Ping-chen Hsiung, eds., *Thinking with Cases: Specialist Knowledge in Chinese Cultural History*. Honolulu: University of Hawai'i Press, pp. 62–100.

Willen, Richard S. (1983) "Rationalization of Anglo-Legal Culture: The Testimonial Oath." *The British Journal of Sociology*, 34.1: 109–128.

Williams, C.A.S. (1941) *Outlines of Chinese Symbolism and Art Motives*. Shanghai: Kelley & Walsh.

Williams, Yoko. (2003) *Tsumi (罪) – Offense and Retribution in Early Japan*. New York: RoutledgeCurzon.

Wilson, Bryan R. (1992) "Reflections on a Many Sided Controversy." In Steve Bruce, ed., *Religion and Modernization: Sociologists and Historians Debate the Secularization Thesis*. Oxford and New York: Oxford University Press, pp. 195–210.

Wolf, Arthur P. (1974) "Gods, Ghosts, and Ancestors." In *idem*, ed., *Religion and Ritual in Chinese Society*. Stanford: Stanford University Press, pp. 131–182.

Wolf, Arthur P., and Huang Chieh-shan. (1980) *Marriage and Adoption in China*. Stanford: Stanford University Press.

Wong, R. Bin, Theodore Huters, and Pauline Yu. (1997) "Introduction." In Theodore Huters, R. Bin Wong, and Pauline Yu, eds., *Culture and State in Chinese History. Conventions, Accommodations, and Critiques*. Stanford: Stanford University Press, pp. 1–26.

Woon, Walter. (1997) "Singapore." In Tan Poh-Ling, ed., *Asian Legal Systems: Law, Society and Pluralism in East Asia*. Sydney: Butterworths, pp. 314–355.

Wu Cheng-han. (1988) "The Temple Fairs in Late Imperial China." Ph.D. thesis, Princeton University.

Wu Hao-jen 吳豪人. (2003) "Fanyong zhi e – 'fa' xuezhe Masuda Fukutaro yu ta de shidai" 凡庸之惡 –「法」學者增田福太郎與他的時代. Commemorative Conference on Masuda Fukutaro and Taiwan Studies. Institute of Ethnology, Academia Sinica, December 5.

Wu Jen-shu 巫仁恕. (2000) "Jieqing, xinyang, yu kangzheng – Ming-Qing chenghuang xinyang yu chengshi qunzhong de jiti kangyi xingwei" 節慶,信仰,與抗爭 – 明清城隍信仰與城市群眾的集體抗議行為. *Bulletin of the Institute of Modern History*, Academia Sinica, 34: 145–210.

Wu Jialun 伍加倫 and Jiang Yuxiang 江玉祥, eds. (1990) *Gudai xinan sichou zhi luyanjiu* 古代西南絲綢之路研究. Chengdu: Sichuan daxue chubanshe.

Wu, Yenna. (1995) *The Chinese Virago: A Literary Theme*. Cambridge, MA: Harvard University Press.

Wu Ying-t'ao 吳瀛濤. (1987) *Taiwan minsu* 臺灣民俗. Taipei: Chung-wen.

Wu Zhen 吳真. (1995) "Suichang miaosi kaoxi – Zhejiang xinan shanqu xinyang minsu diaocha zhi er" 遂昌廟祀考析 – 浙江西南山區信仰民俗調查之二. In *Zhongguo minjian wenhua* 中國民間文化. Shanghai: Xuelin chubanshe. Volume 18, pp. 8–32.

Wunder, John R. (1986) "Chinese in Trouble: Criminal Law and Race on the Trans-Mississippi West Frontier." *The Western Historical Quarterly*, 17.1: 25–41.

——. (1990) "Territory of New Mexico v. Yee Shun (1882): A Turning Point in Chinese Legal Relationships in the Trans-Mississippi West." *New Mexico Historical Review*, 65.3: 305–318.

Xiamen zhi 廈門志. Zhou Kai 周凱 (Qing). In *Taiwan wenxian congkan* 臺灣文獻叢刊. Number 95. Taipei: Bank of Taiwan, 1961.

Xiang Qifen 向啟芬. (2003) "Ji zai Chuanxi minsuzhong de gongyong ji xinghcneg chutan" 雞在川西民俗中的功用及形成初探. *Xinan minzu daxue xuebao (Renwen shekeban)* 西南民族大學學報 (人文社科版), 9: 65–69.

Xia Zhiqian 夏之乾. (1990) *Shenpan* 神判. Shanghai: Sanlian shudian.

——. (1993) *Shenyi caipan* 神意裁判. Beijing: Tuanjie chubanshe.

Xihu youlanzhi 西湖遊覽志. Tian Rucheng 田汝成 (1503–1557). In *Congshu jicheng xubian* 叢書集成續編, Volume 63. Shanghai: Shanghai shudian, 1994.

Xinzheng lu 信徵錄. Ed. and comp. by Xu Qing 徐慶 (Qing). In *Biji xiaoshuo daguan* 筆記小說大觀. Series 39, Volume 7.

Xinzhu xianzhi chugao 新竹縣志初稿. (1893) Zheng Pengyun 鄭鵬雲 and Zeng Fengchen曾逢辰. In *Taiwan wenxian congkan* 臺灣文獻叢刊. Number 61. Taipei: Bank of Taiwan, 1959.

Xiqiao yeji 西樵野紀. Hou Dian 侯甸 (Ming). In *Siku quanshu cunmu congshu* 四庫全書存目叢書, volume 246. Tainan: Zhuangyan chubanshe (based on Wanli 萬曆 edition in the Beijing Library), 1995.

Xu Chunlei 徐春雷. (1994) "Tongxiang shenge gaishu" 桐鄉神歌概述. In *Zhongguo minjian wenhua* 中國民間文化. Shanghai: Xuelin chubanshe, 1994. Volume 14, pp. 189–208.

Xu Xiaoguang 徐曉光 and Wu Dahua 吳大華. (2000) "Shenpan yu falü qiwu wenhua" 神判與法律器物文化. *Guizhou Minzu xueyuan xuebao (Zhexue shehui kexueban)* 貴州民族學院學報 (哲學社會科學版), 1: 15–19.

Xu Xiaowang 徐曉望. (1993) *Fujian minjian xinyang yuanliu* 福建民間信仰源流. Fuzhou: Fujian jiaoyu chubanshe.

Xu Zhizhu tan 續隻塵譚. Hu Chengpu 胡承譜 (Qing). In *Congshu jicheng, chubian* 叢書集成, 初編. Volume 2968. Shanghai: Shangwu yinshu guan, 1936.

Xu Zizhi tongjian changbian 續資治通鑑長編. Li Tao 李燾 (1115–1184). Beijing: Zhonghua shuju, 2004.

Xu Zhongming 徐忠明. (1995) "*Huo diyu* yu wanQing zhouxian sifa yanjiu" 《活地獄》與晚清州縣司法研究, *Bijiao yanjiao* 比較法研究, 3: 240–250.

Yan Yuan ji 顏元集. Yan Yuan 顏元 (1635–1704). Beijing: Zhonghua shuju.

Yang, C.K. (1961) *Religion in Chinese Society*. Berkeley: University of California Press.

Yang Lien-sheng 楊聯陞. (1989) "Daxiang weishi xiaokao" 打像為誓小考. In Center for Medieval Chinese History, Beijing University, ed., *Jinian Chen Yinke xiansheng danchen bainian xueshu lunwenji* 紀念陳寅恪先生誕辰百年學術論文集. Beijing: Beijing daxue chubanshe, pp. 281–283.

Yang, Mayfair Mei-hui. (2000) "Putting Global Capitalism in its Place. Economic Hybridity, Bataille, and Ritual Expenditure." *Current Anthropology*, 41.4: 477–510.

——. (2004) "Spatial Struggles: Postcolonial Complex, State Disenchantment, and Popular Reappropriation of Space in Rural Southeast China." *The Journal of Asian Studies*, 63.3: 719–755.

Yang Yanjie 楊彥杰. (1996) *Minxi kejia zongzu shehui yanjiu* 閩西客家宗族社會研究. Traditional Hakka Society Series. Volume 2. Hong Kong: International Hakka Studies Association, Overseas Chinese Archives, École Française d'Extrême Orient.

——. (1998) "Fuzhou Chenghuangmiao yu Min-Tai Chenghuang xinyang" 福州城隍廟與閩台城隍信仰. *Dongnan xueshu*, 東南學術, 5: 78–84.

——. (2002) "Zhuotian de zongzu, jingji, yu miaohui" 濯田的宗族、經濟與廟會. In *idem*, ed., *Changting xian de zongzu, jingji, yu minsu* 長汀縣的宗族、經濟與民俗. Traditional Hakka Society Series. Volumes 15–16. Hong Kong: International Hakka Studies Association, Overseas Chinese Archives, École Française d'Extrême Orient.

Yao Hanqiu 姚漢秋. (1981) "Cong Minnan fengsu tan Taiwan de yifeng yisu"從閩南風俗談台灣的移風移俗. *Taiwan wenxian* 台灣文獻, 32.2:99–122.

Ye Dabing 葉大兵. (1991) "Wen Yuanshuai xinyang yu Dongyue miaohui" 溫元帥信仰與東嶽廟會. *Minsu quyi* 民俗曲藝, 72/73:102–128.

——. (1992) "Wenzhou Dongyue miaohui poxi" 溫州東嶽廟會剖析. In *Zhongguo minjian wenhua* 中國民間文化. Shanghai: Xuelin chubanshe. Volume 5, pp. 235–251.

Ye Xiaoqing. (2003) *The* Dianshizhai *Pictorial: Shanghai Urban Life, 1884–1898*. Ann Arbor: Center for Chinese Studies, The University of Michigan.

Yijian zhi 夷堅志. 1157–1202. Hong Mai 洪邁 (1123–1201). 4 volumes. Beijing: Zhonghua shuju, 1981.

Yin Chang-yi 尹章義. (1989) *Taiwan kaifashi yanjiu* 台灣開發史研究. Taipei: Lianjing chubanshe.

Yongxian zhai biji 庸閒齋筆記. Chen Qiyuan 陳其元 (1811–1881). Taipei: Guangwen shuju, 1982.

Yongzheng chao Hanwen zhupi zouzhe ziliao huibian 雍正朝漢文朱批奏摺資料彙編. 40 volumes. Shanghai: Jiangsu guji chubanshe, 1989–1991.

Yoshioka Yoshitoto 吉岡義豐. (1970) *Dōkyō to Bukkyō* 道教と佛教. Volume 2. Tokyo: Toshima Shobō.

You Ziyong 游自勇. (2007) "Tulufan xinchu 'Mingsong wenshu' yu zhonggu qianqi de mingjie guannian" 吐魯番新出《冥訟文書》與中古前期的冥界觀念. *Zhonghua wenshi luncong* 中華文史論叢, 4: 31–63.

Youd, Daniel M. (2007) "Beyond *Bao*: Moral Ambiguity and the Law in Late Imperial Chinese Narrative Literature." In Robert E. Hegel and Katherine Carlitz, eds., *Writing and Law in Late Imperial China. Crime, Conflict, and Judgment*. Seattle: University of Washington Press, pp. 215–233.

Youtai xianguan biji 右台仙館筆記. 1888. Yu Yue 俞樾 (1821–1906). Taipei: Guangwen shuju, 1967.

Yu, Anthony C. (2005) *State and Religion in China. Historical and Textual Perspectives*. Chicago and La Salle: Open Court.

Yu Shengwu 余繩武 and Liu Cunkuan 劉存寬, eds. (1994) *Shijiu shiji de Xianggang* 十九世紀的香港. Hong Kong: Qilin shuye.

Yü Ying-shih. (1987) "O Soul, Come Back!' A Study in the Changing Conceptions of the Soul and Afterlife in Pre-Buddhist China." *Harvard Journal of Asiatic Studies*, 47.2 (Dec. 1987): 363–395.

Yuan Aiguo 袁愛國. (1995) "Ji Yun yu Taishan" 紀昀與泰山. *Tai'an shizhuanxuebao* 泰安師專學報, 4: 402–407.

Yuewei caotang biji 閱微草堂筆記. Ji Yun 紀昀 (1724–1805). Taipei: Da Zhongguo tushu gongsi, 1992.

Yun-lin, Liu-chia deng kangri shijian guanxi dangan 雲林、六甲等抗日事件關係檔案. Nantou: Taiwan Provincial Documents Commission, 1978.

Yushi mingyan 喻世明言. Feng Menglong 馮夢龍 (1574–1646), ed. and comp. Beijing: Renmin wenxue chubanshe.

Zaidman, Louise Bruit and Pauline Schmitt Pantel. 1992 (1989) *Religion in the Ancient Greek City*. Cambridge: Cambridge University Press.

Zeitlin, Judith T. (1993) *Historian of the Strange: Pu Songling and the Chinese Classical Tale*. Stanford: Stanford University Press.

Zeng Cai 曾材. (1998) "Huiyi Ningdu chenghuang miao" 回憶寧都城隍廟. In Luo Yong 羅勇 and Lin Xiaoping 林曉平, eds., *Gannan miaohui yu minsu* 贛南廟會與民俗. Traditional Hakka Society Series. Volume 7. Hong Kong: International Hakka Studies Association, Overseas Chinese Archives, École Française d'Extrême Orient, pp. 230–240.

Zeng Zhi 曾志. (1999) *Yige geming de xingcunzhe: Zeng Zhi huiyi shilu* – 個革命的倖存者, 曾志回憶實錄. Guangzhou: Guangdong renmin chubanshe, 1999.

Zhang Guanzi 張冠梓. (2000) *Lun fa de chengzhang – Lai zi Zhongguo nanfang shandi falu minzuzhi de quanshi* 論法的成長 – 來自中國南方山地法律民族誌的詮釋. Beijing: Shehui kexue wenxian chubanshe.

Zhang Hongxiang 張鴻祥. (1997) "Tingzhou chengqu de miaohui daguan" 汀州城區的廟會大觀. In Yang Yanjie 楊彥杰, ed., *Minxi de chengxiang miaohui yu cunluo wenhua* 閩西的城鄉廟會與村落文化. Traditional Hakka Society Series. Volume 4. Hong Kong: International Hakka Studies Association, Overseas Chinese Archives, École Française d'Extrême Orient, pp. 80–113.

Zhang Hongze 張澤洪. (1995) "Chenghuangshen ji qi xinyang" 城隍神及其信仰. *Shijie zongjiao yanjiu* 世界宗教研究, 1: 109–116.

Zhanghua xianzhi 彰化縣志, Zhou Xi 周璽 (Qing). In *Taiwan wenxian congkan* 臺灣文獻叢刊. Number 156. Taipei: Bank of Taiwan, 1962.

Zhang Xunliao 張勳燎 and Bai Shan 白彬. (2005) "QianLiang Jianxing nianbanian 'songren' mudujie fuguiwen yanjiu" 前涼建興廿八年「松人」木牘解復鬼文研究. *Taiwan zongjiao yanjiu* 臺灣宗教研究, 3.2: 104–123.

Zhao Fulin 晁福林. (1995) "Chunqiu shiqi de 'zu' ji qi shehui yingxiang" 春秋時期的'詛'及其影響. *Shixue yuekan* 史學月刊, 5: 22–25, 53.

Zhao Fuxing 趙復興. (2006) *Gu'an diqu minsu jilu* 固安地區民俗輯錄. *Huabei nongcun minjian wenhua yanjiu congshu* 華北農村民間文化研究叢書. Ou Danian 歐大年 (Daniel L. Overmyer) and Fan Lizhu 范麗珠, eds. Tianjin: Tianjin guji chubanshe.

Zhao Shiyu 趙世瑜. (1998) "Guojia zhengsi yu minjian xinyang de hudong – Yi Ming-Qing jingshi de "ding" yu Dongyuemiao wei ge'an" 國家正祀與民間信仰的互動 – 以明清京師的「頂」與東嶽廟為個案. *Beijing Shifan daxue xuebao (Shehui kexueban)* 北京師范大學學報(社會科學版), 6: 18–26.

Zheng Minwen 鄭敏文. (1991) *Shenpan lun* 神判論. Guizhou renmin chubanshe.

Zheng Tuyou 鄭土有 and Liu Qiaolin 劉巧林. (2005) *Chenghuang xinyang de renleixue kaocha* 城隍信仰的人類學考察. Shanghai: Shanghai cishu chubanshe.

Zheng Tuyou 鄭土有 and Wang Xiansen 王賢森. (1994) *Zhongguo chenghuang xinyang* 中國城隍信仰. Shanghai: Sanlian shudian.

Zheng Zhenman 鄭振滿. (1997) "Shenmiao jidian yu shequ kongjian zhixu" 神廟祭典與社區空間秩序. In Wang Mingming 王銘銘 and Wang Sifu 王斯福 (Stephan Feucthwang), eds., *Xiangtu shehui de zhixu, gongzheng yu quanwei* 鄉土社會的秩序、公正與權威. Beijing: Zhongguo Zhengfa daxue chubanshe, pp. 171–204.

Zhiru. (2007) *The Making of a Savior: Bodhisattva Dizang in Medieval China*. Kuroda Institute Classics in East Asian Buddhism. Honolulu: University of Hawai'i Press.

Zhongguo minjian zhushen 中國民間諸神. Lü Zongli 呂宗力 and Luan Baoqun 欒保群, eds. Taipei: Xuesheng shuju, 1991 (originally published by Hebei renmin chubanshe in 1986).

Zhongsu ji 忠肅集. Yu Qian 于謙 (1398–1457). In *Wenyuange Siku quanshu* 文淵閣四庫全書. Taipei: Shangwu yinshuguan, 1983. Volume 1244.

Zhou Guangyuan. (1995) "Beneath the Law: Chinese Local Legal Culture during the Qing." Ph.D. thesis, UCLA.

Zhu Jianming 朱建明. (2000) "Shanghai Chenghuang miao de Sanxun hui jisi" 上海城隍廟的三巡會祭祀. *Minsu quyi* 民俗曲藝, 125: 119–132.

Zhu Zhongxi 祝中熹. (2001) "Cong shenpan dao renpan – Mantan xiezhi yu fa" 從神判到人判 – 漫談獬豸與法. *Sichou zhi lu* 絲綢之路, S1: 76–79.

Zibuyu 子不語; *Xu Zibuyu* 續子不語. Yuan Mei 袁枚 (1716–1797). In *Yuan Mei quanji* 袁枚全集. Wang Zhiying 王志英, ed. 8 volumes. Shanghai: Jiangsu guji chubanshe, 1993.

Zürcher, Erik. (1959) *The Buddhist Conquest of China*. Leiden: E.J. Brill.

——. (1980) "Buddhist Influence on Early Taoism." *T'oung Pao*, 66.1/3: 84–147.

INDEX

adultery 22, 58, 83, 101–102, 152, 167. *See also* divorce, marital disputes
afterlife 20, 24, 26–27, 42. *See also* underworld judicial system
Alford, William P. 14
Allee, Mark 51–52
Amoy 55, 75, 100, 180
Analects 135
ancestors 36–37, 41, 44–45, 63–64, 74, 95, 97, 151, 156, 160, 164. *See also* forebears
Anstey, Thomas Chisholm 128–131, 135, 140
Asad, Talal 10–11

banner worship 63, 66–68. *See also* human sacrifice
bao (*baoying*). See retribution
Beckett, Greg 17
Benton, Laura 116
Berman, Harold Joseph 11–12, 79
Bernstein, Alan 20, 24
Bible (and Chinese oaths) 135, 137, 139
Bodde, Derk 11, 13
Bodhisattva Dizang 5, 19, 86, 142, 160, 174
Bodhisattva Guanyin. *See* Guanyin
Boltz, Judith 38
Bourgon, Jérôme 4, 9
Bowring, Sir John 128
Brook, Timothy 4
Buddhism 21, 24–25, 27, 28, 35, 37, 40–45, 70–71, 107, 114, 174, 181

Caldwell, Daniel R. 127–128, 141
Casanova, José 11
Cay, Robert Dundas 127
certificates of gratitude 23, 162, 165, 172–176
Chang Wejen 14
Chaolin bitan 98
chaste widows. *See* widows
Chau, Adam 16 (note 26) 90
Chen Shuibian 148
Chen Ting-nan 158
Ch'en Teng-wu 44
chengfu. *See* inherited burden
Chou Cheng-fu 177
Chou Yu-k'ou 153
Christianity 24, 26–27, 45, 61, 120, 134, 140
City God (Chenghuang shen) 5, 38, 59, 79, 95, 106, 107–108, 123, 142, 176, 193; and female ghosts 101–103; and judicial rituals, 9–10, 58–59, 70, 72, 73, 76–77, 79, 85–86, 88–89, 96–98, 100–101, 106–107, 109–110, 143–145, 148, 153, 155–156,; and officials 54–56, 58, 71, 90–91, 98–99; and resistance 66, 70
City God temples (Chenghuang miao) 22, 54–55, 59, 66, 70–71, 79, 84–89, 91, 95–99, 101–102, 106, 108, 111, 130, 144, 155, 183; Amoy City God temple 75–76, 180; Fengshan City God temple 149; Hangzhou City God temple 88; Hualien City God temple 152; Jiayi City God temple 135; Jilong City God temple 153; Quanzhou City God temple 184; Tainan City God temple 158, 179; Taizhong City God temple 143, 147, 150; Xiahai chenghuang miao 145; Xinzhu City God temple 19,

52, 110–113, 146, 149–150, 152–154, 156; Zhenping City God temple 99
civil society 1, 6, 23. *See also* public sphere
cogeneration 25
Cohen, Jerome A. 3
colonialism 121, 123
Comaroff, John 117, 123
confession 20, 22, 114–115, 144. *See also* penance
contingent curses 62, 64, 74, 151
courts (of law) 1, 2, 12, 22, 49, 50–52, 59, 85, 132–133, 135, 137, 139–140, 143, 155, 159, 167, 170, 178, 179, 181, 183; and judicial rituals 54–55, 58, 80–81, 151; colonial courts 22, 116, 118, 121, 123, 125–126, 129. *See also* judicial continuum, officials, Shanghai Mixed Court, underworld judicial system
curse tablets 82
customary law 6, 60, 118, 129

Daofa huiyuan 39, 75, 98
Daoism. *See* Taoism
Davis, Edward 18, 38
Dazhongye. *See* Lord of the Hordes
Dean, Kenneth 18
depression 100. *See also* mental illness
Dianshizhai huabao 57, 86, 87, 108
disease 8, 22, 35–36, 62, 70, 71, 90, 94–97, 100, 105, 107, 108, 110, 113, 182. *See also* mental illness, retribution
divorce 91, 103, 131, 151, 166, 170. *See also* adultery, marital disputes
diyu. *See* Earthly Prison
Diyu youji. See *Journey to Purgatory*
Dizang Abbey (Dizang An) 19, 145, Chapter 8
Dizangwang pusa. *See* Bodhisattva Dizang
Dongyue dadi. *See* Emperor of the Eastern Peak
drinking mediation tea 47
Duke of the Red Banner 176

Earl of the Soil 28
Earth God 53, 78, 88, 90, 95, 98–99, 161. *See also* Earl of the Soil, Lord of the Soil, Officer of the Soil
Earthly Prison (*diyu*) 32, 34, 40, 45–46, 107. *See also* underworld judicial system
elites 7, 15, 16 (note 26), 47, 48, 51, 58, 59, 69, 71, 161–162, 183; and colonial officials 118, 119, 125, 138; and judicial rituals 53–54, 65 (+Figure 2), 70, 72–73, 87–88, 90, 180. *See also* mediation
Emperor of the Eastern Peak 19, 32, 38, 58, 110, 123, 142, 176, 179, 184; and female ghosts 100–103; and judicial rituals 5, 53, 83–84, 85, 88 (note 9) 95–96, 106–108, 156, 157; and officials 56. *See also* Mount Tai
exorcism 21, 34, 37–38, 69, 75, 100, 103–104, 107, 162, 182

family disputes 22, 32, 36, 104, 164, 166, 171, 181, 182
Faure, David 18
female ghosts (*nügui*) 22, 83, 101–103, 169, 182. *See also* ghost marriage, widows
Fengdu 34, 103. *See also* underworld judicial system
fetus ghosts 163, 164, 169
filial piety 31 (notes 10 and 11), 41, 45, 53, 70, 101, 109, 170, 176
financial disputes 5, 23, 79, 119, 130, 150–151, 160, 163–166, 170, 172, 174, 175, 178
Five Emperors 84
forebears 30–31, 35–37, 42, 45, 102. *See also* ancestors
fox spirits 20, 99, 106, 152
Freedman, Maurice 120
Fuzhou 53, 55, 66, 84

ghost marriage 169
Girard, René 78
Goossaert, Vincent 19, 109
Guangong (Guandi; Guan Yu) 16, 55, 66, 154, 161
Guanyin 16, 65, 119, 174

Hangzhou 57, 79, 88, 89, 97, 107–108, 176
Hansen, Valerie 39, 180
harmony 8, 14, 47, 50, 52–53, 104, 141, 184
Harper, Donald 29, 43
hauntings 22, 24, 83, 99, 104, 113, 156, 162, 164; illegitimate 97–98, 104, 113, 168, 182; legitimate 35, 96, 113, 169. *See also* ideology of justice, retribution, underworld judicial system

Heaven and Earth Associations 66. *See also* secret societies, Triads
Hegel, Robert 93
hell. *See* purgatory
Hillier, Charles B. 126, 138–139
Hmong 138
Hong Mai 85, 94. *See also* Yijian zhi
Huang, Philip C.C. 9, 48,
human sacrifice 68–69. *See also* banner worship

ideology of justice 3–7, 9, 20, 23, 47, 50, 57, 105, 114–115, 158, 162, 170, 171, 178–180, 183–184. *See also* karma, legitimacy, moral death, postmortem punishment, retribution, underworld judicial system
immanent justice 6
inherited burden 30, 35, 45
innocence, *See also* legitimacy

Jade Emperor 4
Ji Yun, 56. *See also* Yuewei caotang biji
Jones, Paul Anthony 134
Jordan, David K. 63 (note 3)
Journey to Purgatory 157
Judge Bao 95, 124, 152, 159, 180, 184
judicial continuum 2, 7–8, 13, 21, 84, 159, 181–184; Chapter 2
Just, Peter 15, 16, 17, 18

Kang Xiaofei 99
kaozhao (investigation and summoning rituals) 38, 98
karma (karmic retribution) 30, 35, 40, 45, 105, 111, 167, 170, 181. *See also* ideology of justice, moral death, retribution, underworld judicial system
King Yama (Yanluo wang) 41, 89
Kratz, Corinne A. 17
Kuhn, Philip 49, 86

Lai Ming-hsien 23, 162–170, 177
legal anthropology 14, 17–18
legitimacy 1, 10, 37, 54, 60, 66, 81, 84, 96, 136, 144, 146, 151–152; and judicial rituals 15–17, 20, 23, 61, 62, 72, 93, 100, 101, 103–104, 113–114, 115, 147, 152, 181–182; and officials 55, 98–99, 124, 125, 129; and politicians 154, 159; and resistance 54, 69. *See also* ideology of justice, innocence, legitimation
legitimation 7, 15–16, 45, 47, 59, 61, 63, 70–71, 81, 105, 149, 182. *See also* legitimacy
leifa. *See* thunder rituals
Lewis, Mark Edward 63
li 禮; (ritual; ritual propriety) 7, 27
Liaozhai zhiyi 58
lijia system 10, 53
Li Yih-yuan 8, 145
Lin Ching-chih 108
Lin Shuangwen rebellion 68, 75
litigation masters 51, 59
Liu Yongping 72
Lord Brougham (Henry Brougham) 131
Lord Hardwicke (Philip Yorke Hardwicke) 119–120, 121
Lord of the Hordes 19, 23, 151, 160, 162, 164, 169, 171, 174, 176–177
Lord of the Soil (Shegong) 98. *See also* Earth God, Officer of the Soil
luantang. *See* phoenix halls, spirit-writing
Lüshan Taoism 99
Lüyuan conghua 58, 102

MacCormack, Geoffrey 12
Macgowan, John 75–76, 144, 180
Mandate of Heaven 9
Mao Dun 108–109
marital disputes 12, 50, 111, 151–152, 164, 167, 171–172, 178. *See also* adultery, divorce
Marshal Wen (Wen Qiong) 56, 83–84, 97–98
Marshal Zhao (Zhao Gongming) 67
martial deities 38, 64, 67
Masuda Fukutaro 117–118, 143–145
Maxwell, Benson 122
Mazu 147, 161
mediation 2, 6, 7, 10, 13, 15, 17, 21, 47–50, 51–52, 54, 59–60, 78, 80, 93, 130, 156, 181, 183. *See also* elites, judicial continuum
mental illness 105–107, 140, 154. *See also* depression, disease, retribution
Miao (ethnic group) 58, 78, 90
Miaoshan 71
money-lending disputes 79, 119, 151, 166, 172, 178. *See also* financial disputes
moral death 24, 29–30, 33, 37–38, 45–46, 180–181. *See also* ideology of justice, karma, purgatory, retribution, underworld judicial system

morality books 97, 156–157
Mount Tai 31, 34, 40–41, 45. *See also* Emperor of the Eastern Peak
Mozi 44, 77

Nader, Laura 15, 16
natural law 6
neutral death (neutral underworld) 24, 28, 29, 42
Nickerson, Peter 18, 34, 42
Niida Noboru 64, 73
Norris, William 121, 129, 141
Norton-Kyshe, James William 123, 129

Officer of the Soil (Sheguan) 99. *See also* Earth God, Lord of the Soil
officials 6, 21, 22, 44, 50, 102, 104, 132, 181, 182; and corruption 2, 58, 70, 101, 104, 180; and judicial rituals 54–59, 71, 90–91, 98–99, 136–137, 145, 176–177, 181; colonial officials 80, 118–120, 123–125, 129–130, 182; judicial officials 4, 22, 38, 77, 130, 136, 151, 176–177. *See also* courts of law, police, prosecutors
Omichund v. Barker 119, 121, 125
ordeal 6, 11–12, 18, 21, 63, 79–80
Overmyer, Daniel L. 9 (note 4), 183
Ownby, David 66

Pai Hsiao-yen 177
Pai Ping-ping 177
Pavilions for Explicating Clarity 48, 100
Peerenboom, Randall 13, 14
penance (penitential rituals) 5, 8, 17, 22, 27, 43, 104–114, 182. *See also* confession
perjury 2, 61, 62, 74, 78, 80, 120, 123, 126, 128, 133, 138
Perry, Elizabeth 2, 9
petitions (*cheng*) 12, 51, 91–93
phoenix halls 156
Pixley, Frank M. 137
plague expulsion festivals 8, 114, 153–154
police (and judicial rituals) 2, 16, 22, 23, 59, 117, 122, 136–137, 143, 145, 154–155, 176–177. *See also* officials, prosecutors
politicians (and judicial rituals) 2, 23, 145–148, 159
polycultural judicial practices 117, 118, 122, 182
Poo Mu-chou 28, 29
porous death 24, 104
postmortem punishment (punitive underworld) 4, 24, 26–27, 32–34, 41–46, 160, 181. *See also* moral death, retribution, underworld judicial system
Pottinger, Henry 124, 131
private punishments (*sixing*) 49. *See also* vigilante justice,
prosecutors (and judicial rituals) 2, 23, 117, 135, 143, 154–155, 176–177. *See also* courts, officials, police
prostitutes (and judicial rituals) 23, 109, 149
public sphere/space 6, 9, 107, 183. *See also* civil society, third realm
purgatory 3, 45; in Western religions 26, 45–46
Putian 53, 55, 109, 180

Qilu deng 59
Quanzhou 55, 184

Raffles, Thomas Stamford 121, 141
Ramkissenseat v. Barker 119, 120
rape 22, 70, 83, 89, 100–102, 138, 180
retribution 4–5, 20, 22, 25, 27, 30, 44, 57, 58, 69, 84, 89, 128, 168, 170; in the underworld 5, 25, 33–35, 40, 45, 59, 181; in this lifetime 4, 62, 80, 98, 100–102, 104, 105–107, 111, 150, 182. *See also* disease, hauntings, ideology of justice, karma, moral death, postmortem punishment, underworld judicial system
reverberation 9, 11, 24, 25, 27, 45, 46, 59, 179
rites of affliction 17–18, 32
Rosen, Lawrence 7, 16
Royal Lords 110, 154, 161

Scripture of Great Peace 33–34
sectarian religions 42, 71
secularization 10–11, 14, 183
Seidel, Anna 32
sepulchral plaints 19, 34–37, 42, 93, 102
Shan E Tu 89, 95
Shanghai 73
Shanghai Mixed Court 129–130
shanshu. *See* morality books
Sharia 140–141, 182

Shenbao 73, 109
songshi. *See* litigation masters
Soong, James 146, 147–148
speech acts 15, 17, 61, 62, 72, 84, 146, 170, 181
spirit codes 21, 39
spirit-mediums 107, 165–166, 171–172, 174. *See also* Yang Wen-li
Strickmann, Michel 18
substitutes (*tishen*) 31, 99–100, 107, 146,
suffrages 26, 37, 41, 45–46
suicide 70, 102–103, 156
Sutton, Donald 69, 71
Suzhou 56, 88, 91, 103, 179
Szonyi, Michael 18, 53

Ta-pa-ni Incident 18, 68
Tainan 19, 151, 156–158, 179,
Taiping jing. See *Scripture of Great Peace*
Taishan. *See* Mount Tai
Taizhou 65, 97
Taoism 21, 24, 29, 30, 97, 114; and Buddhism 37, 41, 42–43, 45, 181; and judicial rituals 28, 35–38, 75, 95–96, 99–100, 103, 109, 111, 155, 163; and underworld judicial system 27–28, 33–35, 38–39, 41, 42, 44–45, 103, 181. *See also* exorcism, *kaozhao*
Teiser, Stephen F. 41
Ter Haar, Barend 19, 50, 66, 69, 161
Territory of New Mexico v. Yee Shun 135–136
theft 49, 83; and judicial rituals 72–73, 76–77, 86, 119, 127, 130, 133–134, 150, 168, 170, 171, 172–173, 175–176; and retribution 56, 85–86, 98, 150, 154
third realm. *See also* public sphere
thunder rituals 38, 75, 98
Tiandi Hui. *See* Heaven and Earth Associations
tomb ordinances 19, 29–33, 35, 36, 40, 156
torment (in the underworld) 24–28, 32, 33, 41, 42, 44, 45–46, 56–57, 59, 101, 157, 181
torture (judicial) 26, 52, 55, 57, 85, 107, 115, 126, 129, 158, 180
Tudi gong. *See* Earth God
Turner, Victor 17–18, 32

underworld. *See* neutral underworld, moral death, purgatory, torment, underworld judicial system, underworld petitions
underworld judicial system 5, 25, 27, 32–33, 35, 38, 39–40, 42, 44, 45, 53, 56–58, 59, 61, 86, 88, 89, 94, 96, 100, 104, 126, 158, 164, 176, 179–182. *See also* Earthly Prison, Fengdu, hauntings, ideology of justice, karma, moral death, Mount Tai, postmortem punishment, retribution
underworld petitions 162–170

vigilante justice 49–50, 62–63. *See also* private punishments
Von Glahn, Richard 31 (note 10)

Wang Chong 34, 77
wangye. *See* Royal Lords
Welch, Ian 132
Wen Qiong. *See* Marshal Wen
Wenzhou 83–84, 100
widows (and judicial rituals) 48–49, 70, 98–102, 104, 143–144, 150, 180, 181. *See also* female ghosts
Wutong 106

Xia Zhiqian 78, 79
Xiahai chenghuang miao. *See* City God temples
Xiamen. *See* Amoy
xiangyue (community compact) system 10, 48, 53
xiezhi (mythical one-horned creature) 11, 77
xinfang (petitioning system) 184
Xinzheng lu 87–88, 106
Xinzhu (Hsin-chu). *See* Xinzhu City God temple
Xinzhuang (Hsin-chuang). *See* Dizang Abbey. *See also* Chapter 8
Xu Zibuyu 56

Yang Wen-li 165–166, 171–172, 177
Yang Yanjie 18
Yanluo wang. *See* King Yama
Yasuhiko Karasawa 17, 92
Yen Ch'ing-piao 147, 153
Yijian zhi 85, 87, 94
yingling. *See* fetus ghosts
Yuan Mei 56, 97. *See also* Xu Zibuyu, Zibuyu
Yuewei caotang biji 56, 88, 95

Zhao Gongming. *See* Marshal Zhao
Zheng Zhenman 53
Zhu Yuanzhang 48, 66
Zibuyu 56, 88, 95, 97–98, 101, 107
Zuozhuan 63, 64, 72